HOW THERAPISTS CHANGE

Personal and Professional Reflections

Edited by
Marvin R. Goldfried

American Psychological Association
Washington, DC

Published by
American Psychological Association
750 First Street, NE
Washington, DC 20002

Copies may be ordered from
APA Order Department
P.O. Box 92984
Washington, DC 20090-2984

In the U.K., Europe, Africa, and the Middle
 East, copies may be ordered from
American Psychological Association
3 Henrietta Street
Covent Garden, London
WC2E 8LU England

Typeset in Goudy by World Composition Services, Inc., Sterling, VA

Printer: Sheridan Books, Ann Arbor, MI
Dust jacket designer: Watermark Design Office, Alexandria, VA
Technical/Production Editor: Amy J. Clarke

The opinions and statements published are the responsibility of the authors, and such opinions and statements do not necessarily represent the policies of the American Psychological Association.

Library of Congress Cataloging-in-Publication Data
How therapists change : personal and professional reflections / edited by Marvin R.
  Goldfried.
    p. cm.
  Includes bibliographical references and index.
  ISBN 1-55798-727-0 (casebound : acid-free paper)
  1. Eclectic psychotherapy. 2. Eclectic psychotherapy—Miscellanea. I. Goldfried,
Marvin R.
  RC489.E24 H693 2001
  616.89′14—dc21   00-042140

British Library Cataloguing-in-Publication Data
A CIP record is available from the British Library.

Printed in the United States of America
First Edition

CONTENTS

CONTRIBUTORS

Lorna Smith Benjamin, PhD, Department of Psychology, University of Utah, Salt Lake City

Larry E. Beutler, PhD, Department of Education, Graduate School of Education, University of California, Santa Barbara

Arthur C. Bohart, PhD, Department of Psychology, California State University, Dominguez Hills

Morris N. Eagle, PhD, Derner Institute of Advanced Psychological Studies, Adelphi University, Garden City, NY

Herbert Fensterheim, PhD, Department of Psychiatry, Weill School of Medicine, Cornell University, Ithaca, NY

Iris E. Fodor, PhD, Department of Applied Psychology, New York University, New York

Marvin R. Goldfried, PhD, Psychology Department, State University of New York at Stony Brook

Alan J. Goldstein, PhD, Department of Psychology, University of North Carolina at Chapel Hill

Leslie S. Greenberg, PhD, Department of Psychology, York University, North York, Ontario, Canada

Lynne Jacobs, PhD, private practice, Los Angeles, CA

Arnold A. Lazarus, PhD, Graduate School of Applied & Professional Psychology, Rutgers University, and Center for Multimodal Psychological Services, Princeton, NJ

Michael J. Mahoney, PhD, Department of Psychology, University of North Texas, Denton

John M. Rhoads, MD, Department of Psychiatry and Behavioral Sciences, Duke University Medical Center, Durham, NC

George Stricker, PhD, Derner Institute of Advanced Psychological Studies, Adelphi University, Garden City, NY

Paul L. Wachtel, PhD, Department of Psychology, City College, City University of New York

Barry E. Wolfe, PhD, American School of Professional Psychology, Virginia Campus, Arlington

PREFACE

The title of this book is somewhat unusual as is the content. When we think about psychotherapists and change, we typically think about how they help others to change. One rarely has the opportunity to observe changes among therapists themselves. Yet within recent years, an increasing number of therapists have changed in the way they work clinically. Except for those "true believers" who never depart from what they originally learned, most therapists move away or modify their original way of practicing and broaden their therapeutic methods and their view of the change process.

The premise for this book is based on an observation made by the well-known psychiatrist Harry Stack Sullivan, who once commented that people were more human than otherwise. Although Sullivan was talking about his patients, he might just as well have been referring to his colleagues. We have in common with our patients certain needs, aspirations, foibles, and frustrations. Moreover, we are all dutiful citizens of human nature in that we obey all its laws—including those that involve how people change. There has been a good deal written about how patients change; this volume is a personal look at how therapists change.

The book consists of the personal and professional reflections of a sampling of prominent therapists who have expanded their professional horizons and clinical interventions. Some are known for their psychodynamic orientation, others as cognitive–behavior therapists, and still others as experiential therapists. All have been seasoned by both their clinical and life experiences, and this volume provides the venue in which most of them describe their professional evolution for the first time.

The book begins with an introduction that provides the context for these professional memoirs, describing the growing development of the movement within psychotherapy responsible for lowering the theoretical barriers that have long existed among different schools of thought and the societal forces that gave this movement its impetus. The description of these forces underscores the reality that movements such as these are the result of changes within individuals. The idea that people—including therapists—are more human than otherwise naturally leads to the personal and professional reflections of the contributors, which comprise the essence of this volume. The contributors were asked to narrate their growth experiences, illustrating the change process with anecdotes and illustrations. Although this book is primarily about how these therapists changed in their professional work, personal life experiences often served to shape these changes.

The contributors were given guidelines for presenting their reflections, making it easier for the reader to compare the evolution of changes described by each and the influences that contributed to these changes. They were asked to begin by describing the lessons they originally learned when they began functioning as therapists, such as how they worked clinically and how they viewed the process of change. Next, they describe the strengths of their original orientation and its limitations. Their personal and professional accounts of what influenced them to change include the contributors' clinical experiences over the years, their life experiences and crises, the literature they read or encountered in ongoing continuing educational experiences, and the influences of colleagues and other professionals. Each contributor then describes how he or she currently views the therapeutic change process.

In the final section of the volume, I discuss the common themes that are reflected in these therapists' memoirs, drawing parallels to what we know about how therapy patients undergo change. Therapists are just as human as their clients. The themes and parallels include the need for an understanding and supportive interpersonal context, the growing awareness of ineffective ways of functioning, the recognition of what may be a better way of functioning, the willingness to take the risk to do things differently, and the use of these ongoing corrective experiences to revise the current way of functioning.

This volume was written with several audiences in mind. It is likely that these reflections will appeal to therapists who believe—or are just beginning to recognize—that they cannot function effectively without moving outside of the theoretical model within which they have originally been trained. A book such as this can, I hope, provide the insight and support of respected therapists who have gone through comparable experiences. Moreover, it is hoped that this book will be of help to graduate students who are just learning to become therapists. As these beginning therapists are involved in a change process, personal narratives can be a particularly important source of inspiration and guidance. In short, these reflections speak to all therapists—those beginning clinicians struggling to form their identity as therapists, those already on the path, and those whose clinical work has been seasoned by professionals and personal life experiences.

However, the appeal of this book is likely to go beyond the specified professional audience. I hope that people who have experienced change during the course of personal psychotherapy—as well as those who have changed by other means—will find the experiences described in this volume to be personally meaningful.

This book is clearly the product of many people. I am deeply indebted to each of the contributors for their fascinating and candid accounts of how they have evolved personally and professionally over the years. I would also like to thank Margaret Schlegel for her enthusiastic support of the idea for this volume, Linda McCarter for her invaluable creative assistance in the development of this idea, and Amy Clarke for her involvement in its actual implementation. Finally, warm appreciation goes to those individuals who have contributed to my own personal and professional growth: my wife and two sons, my colleagues and friends, my students, and—certainly not the least—my clients.

I

THE CONTEXT OF CHANGE

1

INTRODUCTION:
THE EVOLUTION OF THERAPISTS

MARVIN R. GOLDFRIED

It is hard for me to recall exactly when I began to experience the limitations of my cognitive–behavioral orientation. I suspect it was a gradual process that brought about this change. However, I do recall one pivotal event that occurred in the mid-1970s, when I was demonstrating the course of therapy for a group of graduate students behind a one-way mirror. The point of the demonstration was to illustrate how cognitive–behavior therapy may be used to increase self-assertiveness in an otherwise unassertive woman. Although I had carefully selected a client for whom assertiveness training would be relatively straightforward, I found myself confronted with an unexpected and repeated dilemma during the course of therapy: Should I do what my best clinical sense told me to do, or should I respond the way a cognitive–behavior therapist was supposed to respond? For example, during one session, I found myself thinking the following:

> This client really needs to get in better touch with her feelings, and that's what we need to be working on at this time. Not only that, but

she needs feedback on how she's being unassertive in dealing with me right now. But I can't do that. That would no longer be practicing cognitive–behavior therapy. For me to make that shift would only confuse the students. However, if I were really working with this woman clinically, that's what I would do. Why do I have this strange feeling that it would be "cheating" if I did something that wasn't behavior therapy?

With some trepidation, I decided I would finally reveal my dilemma to the students. When I went back to speak to them after the session, I confessed that I was not practicing the way I usually did, as I wanted to show them what "pure" behavior therapy looked like. They were very supportive and assured me that they would much prefer to watch me conduct therapy in the way I believed to be most effective. I vividly recall this experience as one in which I had "come out" from behind the one-way mirror.

Clearly, practicing therapists do not typically have the opportunity to demonstrate therapy behind a one-way screen, so this experience might be somewhat unique. Still, it is not at all atypical for practicing clinicians to encounter instances in which they find their theoretical approach to be lacking, where they then decide to borrow methods from other orientations. And perhaps in more philosophical moments, it is also likely that they might consider the possibility that the complexity of human functioning and the therapeutic change process cannot be captured adequately by their particular school of thought. Indeed, Wachtel (1985), who has been a key figure in the psychotherapy integration movement, once suggested, "if your theoretical perspective has remained constant throughout your career, it's a good sign that you've been looking at too narrow a range of data" (p. 16).

Because my graduate education took place in the late 1950s, my original approach was psychodynamic, the predominant orientation at the time. I also was schooled in experimental psychology and learning theory, however, which prepared me for becoming involved with behavior therapy when I joined the Psychology Department at the State University of New York at Stony Brook in the mid-1960s. When behavior therapy began to take into account the importance of cognitive factors in understanding and changing human behavior in the 1970s, it opened the way for broadening my conceptual horizon. Around that time, Stony Brook had an accreditation visit from the American Psychological Association, which resulted in the clinical faculty agreeing to expand the scope of the graduate psychotherapy course—which I was teaching—so as to include some exposure to orientations other than behavior therapy. I went back to many of the psychoanalytic books I had read in graduate school and was surprised to find that with some translations in theoretical language, there were not only some interesting similarities between psychoanalytic and behavior therapy but also the potential for the two approaches to be complementary. Informal, late-night discussions with colleagues at meetings of the Association for the Advancement of Behavior Therapy (AABT) got me to recognize that I was not the only one beginning to consider the potential usefulness of other orientations. Interestingly enough, these colleagues often consisted of well-known people who were contributing actively to the behavior therapy literature, although they had been officially silent on the issue of rapprochement with the other orientations. In short, it was part of what was called the "therapeutic underground" (Wachtel, 1977).

In 1975, the AABT meeting was held in San Francisco. Following my active participation at the meeting, I went down to spend a week at the Esalen Institute south of San Francisco to learn more about gestalt therapy and other experiential approaches that were popular at the time. I traveled with a two-sided suitcase: one side for my AABT clothing and the other, much smaller side for Esalen; back in the 1970s, clothing was optional at Esalen.

It was also around this time that Davison and I were preparing our manuscript for *Clinical Behavior Therapy* (Goldfried & Davison, 1976), in which we began to be open about our professional self-exploration. In the introduction to the book, we suggested that

> in the attempt to expand knowledge and to improve the quality of our clinical services, it is time for behavior therapists to stop regarding themselves as an outgroup and instead to enter into serious and hopefully mutually fruitful dialogues with their nonbehavioral colleagues. Just as we firmly believe that there is much that behavior therapy can say to clinicians of other orientations, we reject the assumption that the slate should be wiped clean and that therapeutic innovation should be— and even can be—completely novel. (p. 15)

As one might expect, not all our behavioral colleagues were sympathetic to our position. Indeed, one colleague who read the manuscript commented by writing "Whores!" next to this paragraph. Psychotherapy integration was not all that popular an idea at the time.

THE MOVEMENT TOWARD PSYCHOTHERAPY INTEGRATION

Throughout much of the first 100 years that psychotherapy has been in existence, therapists have tended to work clinically within a specified theoretical orientation. Moreover, the differing theoretical and philosophical underpinnings, the differing language systems, the different intervention procedures, and the differing social and professional networks have kept us compartmentalized. Although pursuing the same goal, we each proceeded in our own way, taking little serious regard—and, indeed, stereotyping— the others. Psychoanalytic therapists were viewed by others as distant, woolly headed, and overly speculative; behavior therapists were perceived as manipulative, cold, and calculating; and experiential therapists were seen as anti-intellectual, "touchy–feely," and nonthinking. The views held about therapists from other orientations helped each group to maintain its own identity and led it to believe that it had the inside track on truth. However, just as personal schemas can limit the functioning of our clients, so have our theoretical schemas traditionally kept us, their therapists, from benefiting from the contributions of our colleagues and being as clinically effective as we might be.

Since the 1980s, an increasing number of therapists have begun to move beyond their original theoretical orientations. Like their clients who enter treatment to change the cognitive, affective, and behavioral patterns that are no longer successful in helping them cope with their current life situation, many therapists have come to recognize that their orientation of origin might not always work for them clinically and that contributions from other orientations might enhance their clinical effectiveness.

Just as there is an evolution in the professional lives of therapists, so has the field of psychotherapy evolved over the years. Starting with the classical psychoanalytic paradigm, there was a gradual—and then more rapid—proliferation of various theoretical orientations. For reasons that will be noted below, however, the field has now become less encapsulated by theoretical orientations, and this movement toward psychotherapy integration has created a climate in which therapists feel less bound by their theory of origin. Hence, the appreciation of how any given therapist has evolved can best be understood within the broader context of the movement toward psychotherapy integration.

Although the psychotherapy integration movement has been in existence only since the 1980s, its roots go back a half century before then (Goldfried & Newman, 1992). In one of the earliest attempts at psychotherapy integration, Thomas French stood before the audience of the 1932 meeting of the American Psychiatric Association to make the connection between psychoanalysis and Pavlovian conditioning. His provocative presentation was published in the following year (French, 1933) with the mixed reviews he received from those in the audience at the time. Some were supportive, and others were quite negative. One particularly outraged observer reported

> I was tempted to call for a bell-boy and ask him to page John B. Watson, Ivan Pavlov, and Sigmund Freud, while Dr. French was reading his paper. I think Pavlov would have exploded; and what would have happened to Watson is scandalous to contemplate, since the whole of his behavioristic school is founded on the conditioned reflex. . . . Freud . . . would be scandalized by such a rapprochement made by one of his pupils, reading a paper of this kind. (French, 1933, p. 1201)

Clearly, an essential tension exists within scientific and professional fields, in that the desire for change and advancement exists alongside the need to maintain the status quo.

Scattered writings over the next two to three decades dealt with the issue of moving conceptually and procedurally beyond one's particular therapeutic orientation, but it was not until the 1960s that the field witnessed a dramatic increase in articles, chapters, and books dealing with the rapprochement across the therapies. The number of written contributions to psychotherapy integration continued to increase for the next 20 years, but professional involvement in this issue remained a latent theme within the field. It was only in the 1980s that it finally emerged into a clearly defined area of interest—indeed, a therapeutic movement.

What contributed to this progression? Although one can never know for certain, it has been suggested that a variety of interrelated forces may have been at work (Norcross & Newman, 1992). One important factor has involved the proliferation of different therapeutic schools, causing confusion, fragmentation, and the sense that we did not know what we were doing. Along with this "hyperinflation of brand-name therapies," there was the realization that none of these different approaches applied in all clinical instances. External socioeconomic factors also came into play, bringing pressures for accountability from the federal government and third-party payers. Such attacks from outside the system may have evoked the attitude once put into words by Benjamin Franklin: "We must all hang together, or assuredly we shall hang separately."

For a variety of reasons, there was an increased focus on short-term interventions, and these constraints led to a greater willingness to make use of any clinical procedures that might work, regardless of their theoretical origin. More opportunity existed for observing and trying out different approaches to therapy, either through cross-fertilization within clinical settings that dealt with specific problems (e.g., anxiety disorders) or through the greater accessibility of workshops and therapy manuals. As more outcome studies revealed that for some clinical problems, no one approach was more effective than another, there was a growing acknowledgement that no one orientation had the corner on truth. With this difficulty in finding a consistent superiority of any given school of therapy, more attention was paid to the possibility that there might exist common change principles across different approaches. Finally, a particularly significant impetus to the psychotherapy integration movement was the formation of a professional network— the Society for the Exploration of Psychotherapy Integration (SEPI)[1]— which is dedicated to promoting an open dialogue across the orientations.

---

[1] For information about SEPI, contact George Stricker, Derner Institute, Adelphi University, Garden City, NY 11530, stricker@adelphi.edu.

Most therapists have traditionally been socialized to affiliate with a given theoretical orientation, be it psychodynamic, behavioral, or experiential in nature. Therapeutic orientations help us make sense out of complex clinical phenomena, provide us with a network of colleagues, and influence us in deciding which conferences to attend and which journals to read. Unfortunately, they also limit our perspective. This last issue led me in 1979 to visit with a psychodynamic colleague—Hans Strupp—to discuss this issue at length. Based on the fact that Strupp recently had been attending the behavior therapy meetings and also had written about the limitations of psychodynamic therapy, I had reason to believe he would be interested in this topic. As a result of this meeting, we agreed that the field was in need of a more comprehensive professional reference group, one that was dedicated to open and constructive dialogue both across the different therapeutic orientations and between clinicians and researchers. From what we had read and whom we knew in the field, we compiled a list of professionals who we believed might be interested in a rapprochement among the therapies and sent them a letter asking them to become part of an informal network. We offered that such a list would enable people to more readily identify others sharing this general viewpoint and could be used to exchange reprints on topics of mutual interest and for purposes of generating symposia, workshops, or conferences. We received many favorable replies, but then again, we were not asking for much—simply to add one's name to a list. As Strupp said to me during that 1979 visit, "not much is going to happen unless you breathe some life into this list."

At this point, I moved to New York City, which provided me with the fortunate opportunity to have regular contact with Paul Wachtel, a psychodynamic therapist who was interested in the interface between psychoanalysis and behavior therapy (Wachtel, 1977). More than 35 years after French delivered his presentation at the meetings of the American Psychiatric Association, Wachtel and I regularly met for lunch—and then later, for dinner—to discuss these issues. Through these dinner meetings, we recognized that we needed to do something with the mailing list that had been compiled. On the basis of our professional correspondence and networking, we added additional names to the list and sent out a questionnaire in late 1982. We received completed questionnaires from close to 200 people who expressed an interest in rapprochement and gave suggestions on how to proceed.

One of the key questions we asked was whether we should form an organization. Of those who responded, 72% indicated that it should be done, with 28% indicating no or having reservations. What was particularly remarkable was not just the number of people who endorsed the formation of an organization, but the enthusiasm with which they offered it. People did not simply respond with a yes answer; they responded with *Yes!* Many of them offered their willingness to put in time and effort to get the organization up and running.

What about those who voted against the formation of an organization? From the reasons they provided, their objection did not seem to be against an organization per se, but rather a concern that it might turn into still another therapeutic school. There was also a concern that a formal organization would not be the best way to facilitate the kind of informal interaction that was needed.

Both Wachtel and I were becoming somewhat overwhelmed by the task we had before us and therefore decided to enlist the help of a small group of other people who we knew were receptive to the general topic of therapeutic rapprochement. During the summer of 1983, we met with Lee Birk, Jeanne Phillips, George Stricker, and Barry Wolfe to discuss the results of the questionnaire. We appointed ourselves as an organizing committee and decided to go forward with the formation of an organization. Although some respondents had reported reservations about forming an organization, it became clear that little, if anything, would happen if the decision were made to not form one. Moreover, it was decided that even though it was a "formal" organization, it would be dedicated to the facilitation of "informal contacts" among its members. At this meeting, SEPI was born.

The list of professionals out of which SEPI was formed represented a diverse array of professionals. Some members had a clearly identified theoretical orientation but acknowledged that things could be learned from other approaches. Others had an interest in searching for elements that all approaches had in common. Still others were primarily concerned with developing theoretically integrated models of change. Some members were beginning to drift from their original orientation and were searching for clearer clinical guidelines that could capture what they had been doing intuitively. In addition, some members had no formal organization of their own— they always had been eclectic—and this network provided them with a professional home. Despite this diversity, they all shared an openness to any contribution, regardless of its school of origin, that could help them to improve their clinical effectiveness.

WHAT IS PSYCHOTHERAPY INTEGRATION?

Within the field of psychotherapy, the term *integration* has grown in popularity. A clear indication of this growth is the promotional use of the term that publishers often include in trying to extol the merits of a new book. Apparently, it is a good thing to describe a book as being "integrative," even if the term is used loosely.

Because psychotherapy integration does not refer to a particular school, even though some people erroneously view it that way, it can be difficult to define. It is not simply about the attempt to create a grand theory of change. It is not solely about the effort to specify the principles of change that are common to all approaches. And it is not about the eclectic use of techniques that have their origins in different orientations. In fact, it is about all of these things. It is about finding ways to keep practicing clinicians from limiting themselves by consistently adhering to a single theoretical approach that may not always work. In short, it is about keeping oneself from being limited by the attitude reflected in the cartoon below.

Within the general umbrella term of psychotherapy integration, one may find three general areas of focus: technical eclecticism, theoretical integration, and common factors (Norcross & Goldfried, 1992). *Technical eclecticism* emphasizes procedures for selecting clinical techniques or methods that have originated from different schools of thought. Stemming from the

philosophy that it is clinically wise to do what works, the techniques advocated may be based on what research has shown to be empirically effective, or on a conceptual–theoretical framework about the change process that can allow for such diversity. Thus, a behavior therapist may make use of the gestalt two-chair technique to have patients articulate their unrealistic thoughts in one chair and reevaluate them from the other, whereas a gestalt therapist may make suggestions to a patient for between-session homework. In short, the notion of technical eclecticism is based on the philosophy that clinical procedures are not "owned" by a given school of thought.

The second area of interest by those involved in psychotherapy integration consists of attempts to synthesize or combine the theories underlying the different approaches to therapy, somewhat sardonically called "theory smushing" by the late Perry London (1986). *Theoretical integration* does not necessarily imply that everything theoretical from psychodynamic therapy is combined with everything from behavior therapy, but rather that certain concepts from one system may be fruitfully combined with another system. Thus, a behavior therapist can think of the importance of the therapeutic relationship as a setting in which to help facilitate a patient's assertive skills.

In searching for *common factors*, the goal is to arrive at a set of principles of change that reflect what goes on in psychodynamic, behavioral, and experiential interventions (Goldfried & Padawer, 1982). These principles may be viewed as being at a level of conceptual abstraction somewhere between theory and technique. Not as general as theory or as specific as technique, common principles of change may consist of clients' expectations that therapy can be helpful; the presence of an optimal therapeutic relationship; the facilitation of an increased awareness by clients about various aspects of their lives; the encouragement of new, corrective experiences; and the processing of these new experiences to further facilitate increased awareness. Although different techniques may be used to implement these principles and different theories may be evoked to explain why they are important, the principles themselves are likely to resonate with therapists of different orientations.

Take, for example, the principle of encouraging new, corrective experiences. Some years ago, the psychoanalyst Otto Fenichel (1941) observed that in dealing with a patient's fears, experiential encounters with the fear situation is the treatment of choice:

> When a person is afraid but experiences a situation in which what was feared occurs without any harm resulting, he will not immediately trust the outcome of his new experience; however, the second time he will have a little less fear, the third time less. (p. 83)

This clinical observation was discovered and empirically confirmed years later by behavior therapists in the use of "exposure techniques" for fear reduction. The explanation by behavior therapists of why this works can take the following form: "Extinction of avoidance behavior is achieved by repeated exposure to subjectively threatening stimuli under conditions designed to ensure that neither the avoidance responses nor the anticipated adverse consequences occur" (Bandura, 1969, p. 414). Except for the theoretical jargon, Bandura and Fenichel seem to be speaking the same language.

Although I have described technical eclecticism, theoretical integration, and common factors as different areas of interest within psychotherapy integration, it should not be taken to mean that they are mutually exclusive or even unrelated. Indeed, it is quite easy to integrate these approaches to integration. By starting with common principles of change, we are able to focus at a level where different schools of thought appear to converge and agree, providing us with a useful starting point. Coming from different theoretical origins, this convergence may tell us that we have robust phenomena because they have managed to emerge despite the potential biases or distortions resulting from different theoretical schemas. It follows that such common principles are potentially fruitful arenas in which to look further, both clinically and empirically. As we do look more closely, we can uncover the parameters associated with each principle (e.g., the specific aspects of their life patients should become aware of) and different ways in which the principle may be implemented (e.g., therapist interpretation or between-session record keeping?).

The consideration of these parameters brings us to technical eclecticism, which involves the selection of specific techniques to use in various circumstances. Having information about what works under what conditions, it is possible to engage in inductive, bottom-up theory construction. Although the techniques that prove to be effective may have been based on certain theory-specific constructs (e.g., focusing on the therapist–patient relationship is important for dealing with unresolved conflicts), the availability of an eclectic array of effective techniques ultimately may necessitate the construction of a new theoretical understanding that can better account for why they work (e.g., focusing on the therapist–patient relationship to provide an example of how the patient deals with others). Until then, many therapists feel comfortable incorporating contributions from other orientations and continuing to retain their original theoretical identity— what Messer (1992) called *assimilative* integration.

THE PROFESSIONAL EVOLUTION OF THERAPISTS

I have presented a brief overview of the psychotherapy integration movement as a way of providing a backdrop for better understanding the professional evolution of individual therapists. In studying the growth and development of psychotherapists, Skovholt and Rønnestad (1995) found that precisely such a supportive professional context was essential to the therapist's change process:

> It is important to have an environment supportive of one's search, an environment where the person is connected to other professional searchers. Such an environment is not dogmatic or rigid but is supportive of professional development and increased competence. Such an environment values high standards of performance and a searching process as opposed to the process of total acceptance of a preordained set of ideological principles. Such an environment supports an exploratory, investigative approach. Such an environment values diversity and has an opening up stance versus a simplification of the complex world, i.e., in working with a client case, such an environment will encourage looking for as many associations on a case as possible versus reinforcing only a narrow, prescribed theory or method. (pp. 106–107)

This description of the characteristics of a supportive context is consistent with my personal experiences and those of my colleagues attending SEPI conferences. Unlike traditional, adversarial dialogues among therapists of different orientations, where the goal is to prove how one's colleague is wrongheaded, interactions at SEPI meetings are more collaborative in nature. Therapists attending these conferences actually listen to each other and often leave having learned something new about how to work clinically.

In questioning therapists about the specific sources of influence in their professional development, Skovholt and Rønnestad originally had anticipated that informants would comment about the impact of theory and research. Instead, therapists placed far greater emphasis on the impact that *people* made in changing how they worked clinically. Most influential were their clients. This finding is not surprising, but it presents a bit of a paradox in light of the fact that the therapeutic situation was designed to bring about change in clients, not their therapists. Still, I always have felt that our clients are a rich source of corrective feedback for us. Given the fact that clients do not read the professional literature, they are less influenced by what is professionally "in" at the time and do not always change in the ways the textbooks say they should.

In their research on how therapists change, Skovholt and Rønnestad found that next in order of professional influence in the work context were professional elders, followed by colleagues, and then serving as a teacher for others. They also found that a major source of influence came from personal life experience, such as marriage, divorce, parenting, and life crises. If part of our role as therapists is to help others travel through life, it clearly helps if we ourselves have walked the walk. In general, they report that by the time therapists reach the "professional individuation" stage of development, where there is a blending of their professional and personal selves, the major influences in their professional functioning have become less external and more internal: "There are few external mentors by this time, although internal mentors and constant interaction with others may guide the individual. Within an ethical and competent context, the individual freely chooses the framework and form of professional functioning" (Skovholt & Rønnestad, 1995, p. 105). My own research on how master therapists work clinically within the naturalistic setting found this to be the case (Goldfried, Raue, & Castonguay, 1998).

With regard to the nature of the change, Orlinsky et al. (1999) conducted an international collaborative study of the development of psychotherapists and reported that 79% of the therapists questioned felt that their clinical work had markedly improved since they received their training. One noteworthy area of growth was respondents' feeling that they had deepened their understanding of the therapeutic process, perhaps because they have been able to blend their professional and personal selves.

These themes in the professional development of therapists, although stated in general terms, do not occur in the abstract. They are based on the professional and personal experiences in the lives of therapists. It is the goal of this book to illustrate those experiences with the reflections of a select group of psychoanalytic, behavioral, and experiential therapists.

A GUIDE TO WHAT FOLLOWS

The chapters in this volume contain the professional reflections of a group of prominent therapists who have expanded their theoretical horizons and interventions. Some are known for their psychodynamic orientation, others as behavior therapists, and still others as experiential therapists. All have been seasoned by their clinical and personal experiences; this volume provides the venue in which most of them will describe their professional evolution for the first time. In their reflections, the contributors narrate and illustrate their change process, addressing the following five key aspects of their evolution:

1. *Lessons originally learned.* To begin, the contributors were asked to provide an account of the lessons they originally learned about how to be an effective therapist. In addition to describing how they initially worked clinically, they also were asked to comment on how they viewed the therapeutic change process as understood from within their original orientation.

2. *Strengths of original orientation.* Having described the lessons originally learned, the contributors commented on aspects of their original orientation that have continued to work well

for them, underscoring what they believe to be the particular strengths of their original way of practicing.

3. *Limitations of original orientation.* The contributors then were asked to characterize the limitations of the way they originally conducted therapy, indicating the particular problems or issues that were not readily handled from within this way of viewing change or by the methods they had at their disposal.

4. *How change occurred.* Contributors were asked to describe what had caused them to change over the years, including such factors as direct clinical experiences, personal life experiences, things they have read, and the influence of colleagues and other professionals. They also were asked to indicate how they actually went about expanding their orientation, once they realized that they needed to do so.

5. *Current approach.* Finally, they were asked to describe how they currently worked clinically and how they now viewed the process of change.

By having contributors frame their reflections within the guidelines described above, it was possible to detect thematic issues, both within and across the three therapeutic orientations. It also was possible to see how the limitations of any given approach have been complemented by the strengths of another. This thematic overview is presented in the final chapter. But for now, let us turn to the personal reflections that bring to life these therapists' professional journeys.

REFERENCES

Bandura, A. (1969). *Principles of behavior modification.* New York: Holt, Rinehart, & Winston.

Fenichel, O. (1941). *Problems of psychoanalytic technique.* Albany, NY: Psychoanalytic Quarterly.

French, T. M. (1933). Interrelations between psychoanalysis and the experimental work of Pavlov. *American Journal of Psychiatry, 89,* 1165–1203.

Goldfried, M. R., & Davison, G. C. (1976). *Clinical behavior therapy.* New York: Holt, Rinehart, & Winston.

Goldfried, M. R., & Newman, C. F. (1992). A history of psychotherapy integration. In J. C. Norcross & M. R. Goldfried (Eds.), *Handbook of psychotherapy integration* (pp. 46–93). New York: Basic Books.

Goldfried, M. R., & Padawer, W. (1982). Current status and future directions in psychotherapy. In M. R. Goldfried (Ed.), *Converging themes in psychotherapy: Trends in psychodynamic, humanistic, and behavioral practice* (pp. 3–49). New York: Springer.

Goldfried, M. R., Raue, P. J., & Castonguay, L. G. (1998). The therapeutic focus in significant sessions of master therapists: A comparison of cognitive–behavioral and psychodynamic–interpersonal interventions. *Journal of Consulting and Clinical Psychology, 66*, 803–810.

London, P. (1986). *The modes and morals of psychotherapy* (2nd ed.). Washington, DC: Hemisphere.

Messer, S. B. (1992). A critical examination of belief structures in integrative and eclectic psychotherapy. In J. C. Norcross, M. R. Goldfried, et al. (Eds.), *Handbook of psychotherapy integration* (pp. 130–165). New York: Basic Books.

Norcross, J. C., & Goldfried, M. R. (Eds.). (1992). *Handbook of psychotherapy integration*. New York: Basic Books.

Norcross, J. C., & Newman, C. F. (1992). Psychotherapy integration: Setting the context. In J. C. Norcross & M. R. Goldfried (Eds.), *Handbook of psychotherapy integration* (pp. 3–45). New York: Basic Books.

Orlinsky, D., Ambühl, H., Rønnestad, M. H., Davis, J., Gerin, P., Davis, M., Willutzki, U., Botermans, J., Dazord, A., Cierpka, M., et al. (1999). Development of psychotherapists: Concepts, questions, and methods of a collaborative international study. *Psychotherapy Research, 9*, 127–153.

Skovholt, T. M., & Rønnestad, M. H. (1995). *The evolving professional self: Stages and themes in therapist and counselor development*. Chichester, UK: Wiley.

Wachtel, P. L. (1977). *Psychoanalysis and behavior therapy: Toward an integration*. New York: Basic Books.

Wachtel, P. L. (1985). Need for theory. *International Newsletter of Paradigmatic Psychology, 1*, 15–17.

II

PROFESSIONAL MEMOIRS OF PSYCHODYNAMIC THERAPISTS

2

A DEVELOPMENTAL HISTORY OF A BELIEVER IN HISTORY

LORNA SMITH BENJAMIN

It seems likely that one of the more important messages from this book will be that much that is learned during training is useful, but individual therapists must and will modify their original learning to create a unique therapeutic orientation. The most difficult challenge in this project was writing this chapter, which is supposed to be so much about me: Despite early learning to the effect that it is not acceptable either to discuss one's personal business or to pry into that of others, I nevertheless forge ahead.

These days, therapy is supposed to focus sharply on symptom change. Psychodynamic approaches, with their penchant for discussing the past, are thought to be less effective. Nonetheless, I join those who believe that conditions during growth greatly affect outcome, so it makes sense to study the developmental histories of both patients and therapists.

I understand the purpose of this book and would like to facilitate it. Hearing how it was and how it turned out conceivably can help developing therapists stay centered and feel less lost as they struggle with consolidating their own personal identity. But right away, I must say that during my training and afterwards, there was no one with whom I felt I could identify.

You see, I was trained in the 1950s and early 1960s. In my clinical training, I was unwelcome in ways that would never happen in contemporary culture, thanks to those (customarily said with disdain) "wimmin's libbers"—Freidan, Steinem, and others. Here is an example of the dreadful related experiences that remain in my mind: A distinguished seminar leader once proclaimed that "a man who goes to see a woman therapist must choose between being a patient and being a man."

Once, I disagreed with a senior professor who scolded a patient for "castrating" her husband because she had insisting on driving the car when he was drunk. I thought her judgment was good and that perhaps his insistence on driving when drunk could be a therapeutic focus, too. Maybe the couple's dependency–control–blame–withdraw interaction pattern should have been the focus rather than just her alleged aggressiveness. My suggestion was ignored during the seminar, and the professor asked me to stay afterwards. In private, he sternly informed me: "You are getting in the way. The fellows don't like it." Needless to say, that was the last time I attended that seminar. I also wondered when it was that he had discussed this with "the fellows." I must have missed something during the seminar.

Another time, when I was on backup call for the emergency room, I learned that a couple had arrived during the night in the midst of a fight. At the morning review of the call, the service chief and I heard from the resident about the problem and its disposition. The husband had come in brandishing a knife and was apparently trying to kill his wife. The wife, who was extremely agitated, was hospitalized for evaluation for treatment with lithium. The husband was sent home. I objected to the failure to assess the husband and once again was dismissed.

I could tell many more such stories, some of them more invasive personally, but this much is enough to explain at least in part why I could not find anyone with whom to "identify."[1] For whatever the reasons, over time I learned to say the following to myself: "Never mind if nobody provides personal support and shows you how. Just stay very open and put it all together by yourself. You can do it."

LESSONS ORIGINALLY LEARNED

Originally, I was taught well within two wonderful models: client-centered therapy and psychoanalysis. When Carl Rogers was at the University of Wisconsin, I took several seminars from him and was his supervisee

---

[1] Later on, much later on, I became the beneficiary of wonderful support and advocacy. For that, I am deeply grateful. Special thanks for unwavering encouragement and significant help go to Allen Frances, Ted Millon, and Bob Carson.

for 6 months. I treasured and continue to hold dear the basic importance of truly hearing what the patient[2] is saying and letting him or her know. I still adhere to the idea that the baseline position for a good therapist is one of empathy, understanding, and nonjudgment—all traits that were described first and best by Rogers (1951).

In my 4 years of postdoctoral training at the University of Wisconsin Department of Psychiatry, I was supervised mostly by psychiatrists and psychologists trained in psychoanalysis. From basic psychoanalytic theory, I learned that early experience has a lot to do with adult personality and with what needs to be addressed in psychotherapy. From the theory's emphasis on interpretation, I learned the importance of having a model from which to make decisions. From the idea of a "blank screen," I learned that it can be really important to know when to keep silent. From the teaching about defenses, I learned that people distort and that they distort for good reasons. From the discussions of dream analysis and free association, I learned about the power and relevance of the unconscious. From the practice of teaching by letting would-be therapists struggle without much more input than commentary on supervisory notes, I learned that the norm is that each person has to figure how to put all the pieces together for himself or herself.

Like almost every trainee until the advent of rational–emotive therapy and cognitive–behavior therapy, I was uncomfortable with the vagueness of it all. I quickly learned that it was a sign of rigidity (probably obsessive–compulsive disorder) to expect clearer teaching and a better understanding of how therapy was supposed to work. I figured out that to learn dynamically oriented therapy, one was supposed to hang around people who claimed to know and try to do what one imagined they did. Therapy was a highly private matter, so observing a senior clinician doing therapy was out of the question. The next best thing was to stay close and hang on every word of the master. But then, as I stated above, hanging around and identifying with someone were not about to happen for me.

Later, when I was a part-time staff person, I was permitted to attend seminars conducted by Carl Whitaker. There I really learned about the astounding power of families. I learned how important it is to think about and work with them and their perspectives. I started to follow the family literature because there is serious wisdom there, along with a palpable dose of "cowboyism." Carl himself modeled an irreverence that I struggled to understand. I was fascinated by some of the things he would do. For example,

---

[2]Rogers, of course, used the term *client* instead of *patient*. He did this to emphasize that he did not feel in control of or superior to the client. The distinction assumes that anybody who uses the word *patient* functions within the medical model as practiced in the fifties and as understood by Rogers. I personally do not like the word *client* either because of its business connotations. So I use the word *patient*, despite its shortcomings. I can attend to my attitude about patients in ways that are more meaningful than whether they are called patients or clients.

one time he reported that a young man had telephoned the preceding week to announce that he was suicidal and "couldn't take it anymore." Whitaker said, "That's too bad. Call me when you feel better" and hung up. He explained that he was in no mood to "play games." I struggled hard to figure out how he could know when to react that way and when to take such a call seriously. Whitaker's supporters said he simply had a marvelous intuition; his detractors said that he might be a good clinician, but when the residents imitated him, it was too often disastrous. From Whitaker, whom I did admire, I learned that no matter how good one is as a clinician, it is important to be able to explain what one does and why. It also is essential that one follow up to assess the impact of the therapeutic encounter.

From Milton Miller, a devotee of Binswanger, I learned the value of the existential and experiential approaches. He would reduce complex ideas to vivid, if not altogether clear, imagery that I value to this day. For example, here is his explanation of why patients did what they did: "You know what you know." That one really works. Miller would diagnose "out-of-gas syndrome" (when you run out of gas, you will know it; a common problem these days) or say, "this person walks though the snows of life without leaving footprints." I love that kind of simple wisdom, and for that reason, I give myself permission to free associate about patients in therapy and tell them about it. Patients almost always are moved in a good way by such a connection.

At first—and to this day—I assumed the basic empathic position proposed by Rogers, which includes frequent expressions of understanding as distinct from the quietness of the psychoanalyst. I always have assumed that developmental history is a vital part of the adult personality. I continue to use much of the psychoanalytic wisdom, including the fact (if not the nature) of unconscious conflict, defenses, the effectiveness (if not the interpretations) of dream analysis and the tracking of free associations, and the relevance of self-understanding.

At first and for many years thereafter, I did not feel that I understood what was really meant by "working through"—the heart of change, according to psychoanalysis. I kept the faith, however, and I did see patients "work through" issues. After a while, many (not all) people truly changed. They "got better" in both their opinion and mine. As I look back over the years and reflect on the outcomes for those who keep in touch and for those who are in the public eye, I see that many of them are doing extremely well. I just love that.

In summary, at first I did what I had been taught, but I did not feel that I really understood why I should do whatever I did when I did it. Rather, I was directed mostly by "intuition." I would use bits and pieces of technique when it felt right. Perhaps the process is analogous to learning a language by hearing it a lot, without formal studies of grammar.

I was not content with this state of affairs and was particularly challenged when I became a supervisor. I vowed not to repeat evasive answers that I had heard, such as "when you have enough experience, you will understand. You will know what to do." Rather, I would try to think it through and find some reason for what seemed right. I began to notice that my intuition apparently was being directed by a combination of learning theory and psychoanalysis. That is, I was really aware of the "Greenspoon effect," named after the researcher who found that the content of a conversation could be directed by the interest of the listener. This phenomenon suggests that the topics to be discussed would be those in which the therapist was interested. I knew that the therapy relationship was at least as important as "insight." So the Greenspoon effect invokes principles of operant conditioning but sees the therapy relationship as a "reinforcer."

To try to figure out what really goes on, I began to take notes in transcript form. I wanted to think about what happened after sessions, and I wanted to have a record uncontaminated by my thoughts and interpretations of what happened—raw data, so to speak. I wanted to be able to look back at difficult sessions and track what happened the next time. Making transcripts is a habit that has continued for almost three decades now. The fruits of that effort are finally becoming tangible. Making literal transcripts, including what I say and what the patient says, has taught me some important lessons, including the following:

- Think about what you say. Writing down your own words is sharply confrontational.
- Do not forget your training as a scientist (the need for data and for consistent, testable ways to interpret it).
- Be patient with the learning process; it is slow. It is like a pendulum on a moving track: Although there is backtracking, the overall movement is in a better direction.

STRENGTHS OF ORIGINAL ORIENTATION

As mentioned above, I still value and need active empathy, place a heavy burden on understanding the connections between the developmental history and the presenting problems, and always remain aware of unconscious, unwelcome wishes and defenses against them. I still find many of the marvelous "techniques" (dream analysis and free association) from psychoanalysis to be useful. The latter-day derivatives of psychoanalysis are handy, too. For example, it is good to think of the patient in terms of conflicting parts: One part is the left behind child who needs to be discovered, nurtured, and grown, and the other is the child who adjusted by adopting the habits and values that seemed to be wanted by important others. I do not think I name the parts the way others do. I do not, for example, find the Gestalt psychology views of Adult and Child to be compatible with my method of case analysis. But the idea that there are parts with different constellations of associated behaviors and wishes is powerful. Examples of other contemporary derivatives of psychoanalysis that I like include role-playing conflict using the two-chair technique and attending to (but not pointing out) nonverbal cues during the session.

I still take families seriously. I often invite them in to help with the identified patient (IP). I do not usually attempt to work with the family system, however. My favorite intervention for individual therapy cases that are blocked is to have a brief series of tape-recorded sessions with the family that can be reviewed in individual therapy afterward. Listening to the tape in subsequent individual sessions often can help the IP understand that his or her wishes simply are never going to be realized. He or she needs to accept that and get on with managing his or her own life free of old hopes and hurts. Lots of other things can happen, but facilitation of differentiation (i.e., psychological separation from the internalized representations of these important people) is the central purpose for this intervention. If the family is responsive during these few sessions and wants to switch to working as a family unit, I sometimes do. But more often, families are defensive and more interested in "shaping up" the IP. I do not mind that assignment, if it is defined in a way that facilitates the interests of the IP. The patient, after all, is deeply tied to his or her family. My job is to alter that tie so that it works better, not to get rid of it. Moreover, I know that if the family does not understand and support the individual therapy, its prognosis is truly poor.

LIMITATIONS OF ORIGINAL ORIENTATION

Nothing in my training prepared me for what happened with my second "case." He was a pleasant-looking young man, tall and strong. The third-year resident who did his intake gave him a diagnosis of paranoid schizophrenia. Although the patient actively hallucinated and was socially isolated, he had a job and seemed well enough to participate in a supportive therapy. Our first session followed an expectable format, and we agreed to meet once a week. When I opened my office door to invite him in for our second session, he was standing right there. He stepped in the office, closed the door and grabbed me in a giant bear hug. He just held me tightly. I began to say things like, "We don't do this in therapy." I also thought about asking "What are you thinking" or "What are you feeling," but somehow did not want to know the answer. So I mostly just stood there, occasionally mumbling something or other. Finally, I said, "Time's up." He let go, confirmed his next appointment, said goodbye, and left.

The next time, I was a bit more wary on opening the door. He came in peacefully and sat down in a chair, ready for an interview. We discussed the previous session and agreed that the grabbing and holding would not happen again. If it did, that would be the end of this therapy. He, too, had been unhappy with the session and told me about a plan he had developed that would allow him to divert those impulses successfully. His method worked, and we went on to meet once a week for about 2 years. He did well (he kept his job, adjusted acceptably well to his social isolation, and never engaged in self-destructive or antisocial behaviors) and eventually moved to another city to be closer to family. Chlorpromazine, Stelazine, and Haldol were not yet the "treatment of choice" for such cases, and as it turns out, major tranquilizers were not needed. His wish to maintain our relationship was enough.

The fact that I had no concepts or "techniques" to see such a situation coming or to deal with it bothered me. Training should be helpful for such expectable events. I did use and do remember one relevant remark Milton Miller made in a grand rounds case conference: "You rarely need more to protect yourself other than knowing how to talk to patients. I would much rather have my ability to talk than any conceivable method of physical coercion." Unfortunately, the lesson in knowing how to talk did not follow this appealing observation. Again, the details of the skill were left up to the clinician's intuition. In my current book (Benjamin, in press), I explicitly address such dilemmas both conceptually and concretely in terms of what to do in what order and for what reasons.

For many years, the therapy I conducted was not as efficiently focused as it might have been. Listening, facilitating expression of affect, talking about the past, and helping the patient see connections among the pieces of his or her life all are good activities. But I know now that those interventions are not always "good" or even appropriate. It is important to know what to do when, and why.

In addition, the severely disturbed folks I like to work with need a lot more structure than classical dynamic therapy offers. "My" folks, the "untreatables," need tireless, patient, well-organized intuitive wisdom uniquely focused on them. They also need major help with trust. Warmth and empathy, which are indeed good attitudes, are not enough for people who have failed to response to treatment as usual (e.g., medications or cognitive–behavioral or Klerman–Weissman's interpersonal therapy). Empathy must be accompanied by high competence, graceful honesty, and therapist palpability—personal disclosure about matters relevant to the treatment. Of course, classical training, among other things, forbids personal disclosure.

Another problem for me was overinvolvement and burnout. I did not know how to set limits on myself in terms of what I could and could not do. For example, I would agree to telephone conversations and meetings at odd hours—something I know that I would not do now. Even in my regular hours, I sometimes was overloaded and less attentive than the patients deserved. I still believe that therapists ought to be as careful about their state of alertness as, for example, airline pilots. It is important to keep the caseload sane, to be well rested, and, of course, to keep one's proper emotional balance in relation to patients and their struggles.

The main values that were communicated during my training seemed to include the following:

- Be empathic, warm, and loving.
- Never control and never self-disclose.
- Be tolerant, accepting, and relatively inactive.
- Let the patient be with himself or herself in a safe, warm, and nonjudgmental setting, and he or she will be free to grow.

I still like those values as aspects of an ideal position, but I have learned that many times, those attitudes and their associated behaviors do not suffice.

As suggested above, little in my training prepared me for working with severely disturbed patients. I knew how to be part of a team subduing an out-of-control patient in a confined space. I knew how to commit. I knew how to anticipate violent acting out and some specific legal things to do if it occurred. But these techniques all had to do with containment, not cure. The idea seemed to be that one did those forceful things (or got somebody else to do them) if absolutely necessary. Otherwise, one assumed the "classical" position of warmth and tolerance. Of course, some people simply cannot make use of the warm, permissive therapeutic climate.

I wanted to do more. I wanted to affect patients' lack of motivation to change and help them alter their irrational devotion to patterns that obviously did not serve them well. I wanted to know much more about how to listen and talk to people to help them grow. Somehow, many of them did change and grow, but I was restless in the knowledge that I did not clearly know how and why. I thought I knew how to do what most good therapists do, but I did not know how to optimize this talking therapy. There were too many times in which therapy felt like treading water. Yes, I knew about being patient. But when was being patient not appropriate?

The original rationale for therapist passivity was that the unconscious would take the therapy where it needed to be. Analysts explained that a blank slate needed to be free of contamination by therapist behaviors so that patient projections would be clearly identifiable. Rogerian therapy emphasized warm reflection because it was thought that unfettered acknowledgment is all that a person really needs for self-discovery. From both of those classical perspectives, therapist intrusion into the therapy process reflects immature impatience and an inability to bind the urge to control.

I have since decided that without a lot of therapist intervention, the regressive forces are more likely to take the therapy where they want it to be—and that is not good. I find no evidence that it is appropriate to blame patients who fail to progress in a warm, permissive environment. As a matter of fact, I think that widespread practice of such laissez-faire therapist attitudes probably have had a lot to do with the appearance of unduly lengthy and remarkably ineffective therapies (not mine or yours, of course). This unhappy situation set the scene for the arrival of modern brief treatments that "target" symptoms and problems. Partly in reaction to interminable and not so effective classical therapies, therapists now must make a clear diagnosis of the problem and a specific, quick-acting treatment that has demonstrated efficacy with that specific problem. No More Nonsense: Now we must know exactly what is wrong and exactly what to do about it, and quickly.

Of course the burgeoning population of untreatables (i.e., patients with personality disorders) belies the simple and hopeful claim that disorders like depression or anxiety or problem behaviors can be dispensed with in a relatively brief trial of an empirically validated therapy. The "failures" are the folks who interest me most. I love to work with seriously troubled people who are driving everyone else crazy and have been unresponsive to many previous treatments. The reason is that they usually are quite talented, and if they are still looking for treatment, they must have a strong drive for health somewhere. Moreover, by the time I get them, all fantasies about magic bullets (whether by chemistry or charisma) have long since been crushed by reality. They are ready for serious work.

I am not interested in admiring or being admired. I don't want to give or receive "warm fuzzies." I want to help relieve suffering. I want to see change in the patient's personal life. I want to see the patient rediscover delight and to thrive. I want patients to become fully engaged in their lives to the best of their abilities. The best reward for me is to see people who were once remarkable for causing trouble, for being almost nonexistent, or for other unhappy reasons, learn to fly. This no-nonsense attitude frightens some people away. The clarity and the data-based nature of my approach rapidly make the choices clear. To their credit, most who decline to proceed say they are "just not ready to deal with it."

HOW CHANGE OCCURRED

Direct Clinical Practice

Direct clinical practice has been the greatest and most rewarding teacher. For me, the "data" that emerged working with many people over the years eventually consolidated in ways I never envisioned. Clinical experience provides the raw data for therapist understanding. I believe that familiarity with the structural analysis of social behavior model (SASB; Benjamin, 1974) greatly enhanced my ability to notice patterns and connections among relationships in patient narratives and their ways of relating with me. Without the vision the SASB model provides, I do not think I would have ended up with such a clear idea of how to "put it together."

The challenge of teaching therapy also was helpful to my development. I always welcome and try hard to give meaningful answers to students' questions. They have a right to ask and to receive a decent answer. Often I work out answers with students. One of my most frequent responses to questions is to say what I would recommend for the situation at hand, followed by "Let me see, why do I think that is the right thing to do?" As I struggle to articulate general principles over many such examples, those principles begin to emerge.

Personal Life Experiences

What a person says in answer to the question of how personal life experiences have led to change is at high risk for the self-serving tendencies I hinted at in the introduction. But in this section I try to say at least some of what is relevant, more or less in chronological order:

Studying music for many years as a youngster and through adolescence taught me the rewards of self-discipline, hard work, patience, and persistence. No doubt my willingness to do that was enhanced by my liking for a nursery tale my mother often read to me, *The Little Engine That Could*. In any case, studying music made clear the many rewards of working long and hard. It is obvious that when learning to master a complex task, one simply does not get results in a short period of time.

This lesson is not to be taken for granted by beginning therapists. Expertise does not come in the first months or even years. For example, not long ago at a health club that served customers at a nearby hotel, I noticed a few members of a visiting professional basketball team playing an informal game. The fantastic moves were observed carefully by some local adolescent males. When the pros left, one of the young locals went out on the floor, taking extravagant and fancy shots in apparent imitation of the experts. He missed every one by a country mile. Eventually he tired and left the floor. He seemed to have no idea that he had to learn first to make simple shots and then progressively master more difficult versions. Apparently he had to have spectacular results right away, or he would give up. The idea of being able to master a therapy approach in a 1-day workshop or short course of training, in my opinion, reflects a similar perspective.

Maybe my persistence in learning to do complicated things also is related to the fact that for a long time in my early childhood, all the kids in the neighborhood were male. I also had two older brothers. Boys are tough on each other; girls who hang out with them have to be tough, too. I knew, for example, that either I would learn to master challenges or I would be left out. I did not like to be left out. So I became good at athletics; that takes time and a lot of practice. I also learned never to say "I can't" and never, never to whine.

When I was in the eighth grade, my parents fulfilled my wildest fantasy by buying me a western quarter horse, brought back to upstate New York from "out west." It turned out that she had been severely abused and was quite aggressive. She fended off everyone in sight, especially men. People reasoned that it must have been men who abused her—but she reserved the right to kick, bite, and throw off anyone without warning, including me. So there was my fantasy, biting and kicking and bucking. I either had to deal with it or lose a dream.

I dealt with it. More than that, we became good friends, the horse and I. From that experience, I learned more about not being easily scared and, once again, to take things slowly and with great patience. I also learned about the impossibility of controlling another creature. The most you can do is persuade and negotiate your mutual interests as you move with the other. Only under the most desperate conditions would one move against another.

Eventually my uncles arranged to take her to stud, and she delivered. By then, however, I was well into other interests of adolescence. My Hero did not have a horse, and he was far more interested in football than just about anything else. Although I did train the young horse to saddle, we never developed the intimacy I had with the mother. But those two had trouble differentiating: For years, the grown horse nursed from her mother. I suppose it had to do with their social isolation. Mothers who have nobody appropriate to relate to sometimes maintain inappropriate relationships with their offspring, and offspring can develop inappropriate expectations of their mother. That bizarre scene was an object lesson that later, along with everything else the horse taught me about working with people with personality disorders, became relevant to therapy.

The most important and most positive learning for me came from being a mother. My children continue to teach me more than I could possibly say about what is wonderful in life and how to go about realizing it. I am incomparably blessed to have had them . . . and grandchildren have started the process all over again! Having a sense of how good it can be is part of being a therapist too.

Another important personal factor in my development as a therapist comes under the heading of spirituality. Everyone has it in some form or other, and engaging a patient's spirituality can help the therapy process move in a better direction. A therapist's spirituality also is a powerful factor. It is present, whether acknowledged or not. I think that spiritual energy needs to be recognized within one's own mind and heart during therapy. I am not talking about discussing any particular religion or doctrine. The particular form that spirituality takes is personal and private. So I am content to ask patients to use their preferred form of spirituality and truly enjoy hearing how they do that, if they care to share. If they ask about mine, I disclose that it is present and real to me but that its particular form is not an appropriate part of the therapy process.

I further add comments here about SASB, which has been central to my therapy learning and practice. It seeks to define an infinite array of interpersonal positions in terms of just three underlying dimensions. The idea of organizing behavior in that way had many roots that are not relevant here. But at a personal level, it had everything to do with my awe of the periodic table of the elements. I was, as one would say today, "blown away" by the thought that absolutely everything physical can be described in terms of the dimensions of atomic number and weight. The classification even predicted the existence of elements that were not known but ultimately were discovered. That table, combined with subsequent developments, has made monumental contributions to understanding of the physical world. Why was I so impressed by the chemical table? Well, I do think it is impressive. But I guess that I should also provide the fact that my father was a research chemist, and I adored my father.

Many people have observed that it would be nice to be able to organize behavior in a single table according to a few underlying dimensions. My version of an organizer for social interactions aims to describe all interpersonal and intrapsychic interactions in terms of focus, love–hate, and enmeshment–differentiation. So far, it has performed pretty well.

Things I Have Read

Any therapist-in-training who aspires to be more than a technician does well to read and reread broadly. The following are some of the books that had the most influence on me; I also include a brief description of why they were influential:

- Freud (see Jones, 1959)—for showing, through compelling case examples, the impact of childhood learning on the adult psyche.
- Reik (1949)—for teaching how to track the unconscious by attending to the associative process and to dreams.
- Fromm-Reichmann (see Bullard, 1959)—for teaching how to maintain deep empathy and a nonjudgmental approach in the face of substantial provocation.

- Sullivan (1953)—for teaching about the importance of interpersonal process and giving permission to look at the role of peers and other extrafamilial social forces.
- Bowlby (1969)—for showing unequivocally that attachment is primary. It does not depend on being fed or comforted or getting M&Ms.
- Heidegger (1960)—for stating so clearly that one can only understand and truly "be present" by fully appreciating the impact of history and by mindfully anticipating the future.

The Influence of Colleagues and Other Professionals

The influence of colleagues and other professionals is not always easy to recognize. That is, it rarely comes from a workshop, meeting, lecture, or paper covering topics with which one is familiar. Rather, the impact of colleagues is more subtle and personal. One hears an offhand remark, files it away in memory for use when appropriate, and, after a while, forgets where it came from. Therapy learning in general, like language learning, "seeps in" over time. Thousands of repetitions of the same theme occur in a variety of contexts over the years. I value this subtle and constant barrage of learning and cultivate it as much as I can. My current favorite source for such learning is students. Their questions and challenges make it clear to me how I need to modify what I have recommended, where I need to elaborate, where I have been unclear, and so on. In the earlier years, my learning came mainly from my teachers—people like Norman Greenfield, Milton Miller, Joseph Kepecs, and Carl Whitaker. They provided many remarks, examples, and thoughts that I continually find to be useful in therapy.

MY CURRENT APPROACH

An initial description of my clinical approach appears in Benjamin (1996a). The first draft of a book describing the details of the therapy with so-called untreatable patients is nearing completion (Benjamin, in press). I call my approach *interpersonal reconstructive therapy* (IRT); in brief, an explicit case formulation method directly links the presenting problems to early learning. The maladaptive patterns characteristic of personality disorder and their comorbid symptomatology (e.g., anxiety or depression) are specifically related to attachment to early important figures (mother, father, big brother, uncle who lived in the house, and so on). The testable hypothesis is that the problem patterns in adulthood conform to rules and values learned in childhood. The patterns are sustained in adulthood not because they work but because they are nourished by unconscious wishes to be affirmed by early figures associated with those particular patterns.

I summarize these ideas with the following phrase from the title of one of my articles: "Every psychopathology is a 'gift of love' " (Benjamin, 1993). For example, if the parent was perceived as hateful and feeling that the patient was always "in the way," the patient is likely to hate him- or herself and become suicidal at times, "reasoning" that current loved ones would be much better off without him or her. The self-attack and self-removal are gifts of love to past figures and the current ones. The unconscious hope goes something like this: "If she (e.g., one's mother) thought I was so bad and felt that I was just in the way, I provide testimony of my love for her if I agree with her. I give her what she seemed to want, and I show her she was right. Perhaps then she will approve of and love me."

Links between these early attachments and current problems are startlingly direct when seen through the SASB lens. Most of them are described by one or more of three copy processes (Benjamin, 1995, 1996a, 1996b): Be like him or her; act as though he or she is still here and in charge; treat yourself as he or she did. The fact of the links is usually easy to establish. The reasons for them are more difficult to support with easily observable data. The therapy is nonetheless organized by the assumption that the copying represents a gift of love. Over time, the data in support of that assumption usually emerge. If they do not, the idea is abandoned.

Occasionally, copy links are seen through opposites (precisely defined in the SASB model). For example, consider a patient rigidly devoted to letting children decide everything for themselves (SASB coded: "emancipate"). The patient had a father who was overcontrolling (SASB coded: "control"). Because control and emancipate are opposites on the SASB model, the copy process of patient to father is identification in reverse.

Once a case formulation is created in terms of copy processes and gifts of love, the therapist knows what is driving the problem patterns. That understanding tells where to focus therapy efforts. If trashing the marriage, sabotaging professional success, suicidality, and child abuse are testimonials to an earlier caregiving figure, then the presently imagined relationship with that early figure must be transformed. This is a functional analysis of the disorder that defines purpose in terms of imagined relationships with internalized representations of important early figures. The therapy learning also is based on a rather concrete (i.e., SASB-coded) version of attachment theory.

The therapeutic transformation of the relationship with the underlying internalized representations (called "important persons and their internalized representations") draws on all known therapy techniques and schools of therapy. There are five more or less hierarchically arranged therapy steps:

1. Collaborate.
2. Learn about patterns—where they are from and what they are for.
3. Block maladaptive patterns.
4. Enable the will to change.
5. Learn new patterns.

For the most part, the latter steps depend on maintenance of the earlier ones. Collaboration (Step 1) must be intact for any progress to be made. Awareness of the problem (Step 2) is necessary and needs to be viewed collaboratively. Maladaptive patterns (Step 3) cannot be enabled or there will not be good learning. The will to change (Step 4) must prevail over the wish to remain loyal to the earlier ways. Finally, no new patterns (Step 5) can be sustained if the will to change is not intact. New learning depends on all four preceding steps. Attempts to do behavioral treatments without sorting through the first four phases either will be unstable or will fail altogether. If one effectively attends to all levels all the time, the untreatables become treatable.

My new book explicitly relates known techniques (e.g., interpretation, empathy, confrontation, role plays, changes in self-talk, and use of dreams and free association) to those five steps. The techniques are grouped into two major domains or tracks: (a) the self-discovery, self-revealed, experiential track and (b) the self-management, or "pull your socks up," track. Dream analysis is an example of a self-discovery activity; stress inoculation is an example of a self-management activity. Both types of activity are much required when working with the severely disordered folks who have not responded to other treatments, whether the treatments were biological or psychosocial.

Every intervention is chosen and evaluated in light of the case formulation and the five steps. Exchanges usually include careful attention to the basic ABCs (affect, behavior, and cognition). The challenge is to focus maximally on the patient's relationship with the underlying organizing attachments. That effort makes it more likely that the treatment will succeed and proceed as rapidly as possible. There is no claim that this treatment is brief. It is accelerated but not brief. I believe that it is effective for the long term.

My forthcoming book provides many flowcharts outlining options when untreatables present the nightmarish dilemmas so characteristic of personality disorder (e.g., "Well, I see all that, but my feelings don't change. This is not helping, and the only way out is to kill myself.") The flowcharts basically guide the therapist through options that end up with one of two outcomes: (a) The working relationship is restored, and the process of working through (also explicitly defined) is resumed or (b) the therapy switches to pure symptom management, which consists of standard HMO-type approaches using medications or behavioral targeting. Most patients view the threat to stop talking about patterns and relationships with important others as "punishment" because the therapy relationship (because it is not short term) is valuable to them. The threat of switching to symptom management almost always gets patients back to the work of challenging their familiar and often beloved maladaptive habits.

I believe that both insight and relationship, the two factors often argued to be change agents in the literature, are relevant to the process of change. In IRT, patients need to understand the exact nature of their problem patterns: where the patterns came from and what they are for. That insight alone does not effect change; however, it usually contributes significantly to Step 4, the will to change. If patients see how and why they do what they do, they are in a better position to choose to change.

The therapy relationship is vital, too, but it must be of the right sort, or else it will simply enable the problem patterns. A warm, friendly, and approving therapist may make a self-centered exploiter comfortable, but the work will do almost nothing to help him or her change in relation to loved ones or associates. The therapy relationship constantly must build collaboration in the fight against old loyalties and the problem patterns, and it should facilitate friendly (not confrontational) differentiation (psychological but not necessarily physical separation) from the driving figures. The therapy relationship must be strong and truly helpful; it must provide severely disordered patients with enough basic security that they dare to try something new. It must truly celebrate their growing strength and ultimate autonomy. It must ask nothing of the patient other than to pay the bill and work hard to become strong and free. In addition, it almost never encourages alienation from or confrontation with family or other loved ones. As in the case of any other learned task (whether becoming a musician, a scientist, or an athlete), the model provided by the relationship with the "coach" can become internalized and serve as one of many guides to future desired and more functional, happier behaviors.

CONCLUSION

I did what I am guessing other authors in this book also did. I have changed as a therapist by putting together bits and pieces of helpful elements of training and learning by experience. It took me a long time. I confess that I am now trying hard to change that situation: I want to tell my students how to learn faster. I want them to only have to work a few years, rather than a few decades, at becoming experts. Why should they have to "reinvent the wheel?" Objective evidence in recent years suggests that beginning students, with intensive supervision and clear didactics, can learn to use

IRT to deal successfully with extremely difficult cases who have long and scary previous records of untreatability.

Although I have done it for almost 3 decades, I have never before been so clear and so highly organized in my teaching of therapy ideas and skills. If my current students choose to think of IRT as one of their "bits and pieces" and to end up with something that looks quite different, that will be fine with me. But perhaps they will find that IRT continues to work well. Perhaps they will continually see copy processes and associated gifts of love. Will they continue to feel that IRT—the five learning steps and two tracks of self-discovery and self-management—provide a valuable framework for making treatment decisions? I look forward with great interest to seeing what happens. Their data will be valuable.

REFERENCES

Benjamin, L. S. (1974). Structural analysis of social behavior. *Psychological Review, 81*, 392–425.

Benjamin, L. S. (1993). Every psychopathology is a gift of love. *Psychotherapy Research, 3*, 1–24.

Benjamin, L. S. (1995). Good defenses make good neighbors. In H. Conte & R. Plutchik (Eds.), *Ego defenses: theory and measurement* (pp. 53–78). New York: Wiley Interscience.

Benjamin, L. S. (1996a). *Interpersonal diagnosis and treatment of personality disorder* (2nd ed.). New York: Guilford Press.

Benjamin, L. S. (1996b). An interpersonal theory of personality disorders. In J. F. Clarkin (Ed.), *Major theories of personality disorder* (pp. 141–220). New York: Guilford Press.

Benjamin, L. S. (in press). *Treating the untreatables: Reconstructive learning therapy for nonresponders*. New York: Guilford Press.

Bowlby, J. (1969). *Attachment and loss: Vol. I. Attachment*. London: Tavistock Institute of Human Relations.

Bullard, D. M. (Ed.). (1959). *Psychoanalysis and psychotherapy: Selected papers of Frieda Fromm-Reichmann*. Chicago: University of Chicago Press.

Heidegger, M. (1960). *Sein und zeit* [Being and time]. Tübingen, Germany: Max Niemeyer Verlag.

Jones, E. (Ed.). (1959). *Sigmund Freud: Collected papers* (Vols. 1–5). New York: Basic Books.

Reik, T. (1949). *Listening with the third ear*. New York: Farrar, Straus.

Rogers, C. R. (1951). *Client-centered therapy*. Boston: Houghton Mifflin.

Sullivan, H. S. (1953). *The interpersonal theory of psychiatry*. New York: Norton.

3

REFLECTIONS OF A
PSYCHOANALYTIC THERAPIST

MORRIS N. EAGLE

I want to begin with some introductory comments and provide some background of the experiences, people, and factors that influenced me—where, so to speak, I started. I also want to try to describe a basic position I have in regard to doing therapy, my personal sense of where I locate myself in this whole therapy enterprise.

First, the introductory comments: Although I have been providing psychodynamic psychotherapy for more than 40 years, I always have done it on a part-time basis. I cannot imagine, unless my livelihood entirely depended on it, doing psychotherapy on a full-time basis. I do not think that I could or would be an effective therapist under those circumstances. I often wonder how therapists who handle 40 or more patient hours per week can be effective. I know that I could not be.

One of the reasons that I cannot imagine doing psychotherapy full-time is that I am vitally interested in doing other things, including teaching, conducting and supervising research, and writing about research and theory. The psychoanalytic community has a tendency to view someone like me, who is interested in research and theory and writes about them, as not a "real" clinician, that appellation and status apparently reserved for those who are not interested in those areas and are proud of that lack of interest. This state of affairs used to bother me a great deal; it no longer does, at least not to the same extent.

My identity as a psychologist, who does psychotherapy among other things, was strongly forged by the wonderful educational experiences I had, both at the City College of New York (CCNY), where I did my undergraduate and some graduate work, and at New York University, where I did my doctoral training. I came to City College during the glory days of the psychology department. Its faculty included Gardner Murphy, Joseph Barmack, Max Hertzman, Lawrence Plotkin, Daniel Lehrman, Alexander Mintz, and Martin Scheerer. After receiving my undergraduate degree, I was accepted into CCNY's extraordinary master's program in clinical psychology organized by Joseph Barmack, following his experience as a research candidate at the New York Psychoanalytic Institute. Among the faculty offering lectures and courses were Ernst Kris, David Beres, Ruth Munroe, Bela Mittleman, Roy Schafer, Kurt Goldstein, Katherine Wolf, Ulrich Sonneman, Karen Machover, and Lois Murphy. The program was heavily psychoanalytic and was, quite simply, the most stimulating and exciting educational experience I have ever had.

LESSONS ORIGINALLY LEARNED

The most important personal experiences that led to my becoming a psychotherapist had to do with the role I played in dealing with my mother's "nervous spells." I learned early on how to calm my mother when she was experiencing, what is now clear to me, her anxiety attacks. I believe that I continue to be good at this with friends, in other intimate relationships, and with patients. Some friends have referred to this quality as my "therapeutic personality." I do not believe that this sort of thing has much to do with theory—although taking some theoretical stance, such as the traditional psychoanalytic belief that an analyst could be a "blank screen"—will tend to "kill" this quality. Nor do I believe that it is entirely a matter of training and experience, although both may build on and help develop this quality. However, as is the case with taking an unrealistic theoretical stance, certain kinds of training may dilute "natural" therapeutic characteristics of one's personality. I have increasingly come to believe—and here is one way in which I have changed as a therapist—that the personal characteristics of the therapist, as well as the match between patient and therapist, are the most important factors in determining therapeutic outcome. Of course, this is an empirical question. I would love to see more research in this area.

STRENGTHS OF ORIGINAL ORIENTATION

I have always found a major strength of a traditional psychoanalytic or psychodynamic orientation to be its focus on the pervasiveness of inner conflict. This has helped me to avoid taking sides in the patient's conflicts and to be sensitive to a side of the conflict that the patient does not emphasize or externalizes and generally does not seem to be aware of. Attending to the patient's inner conflicts also has been extremely helpful in doing supervision. I recall supervising a graduate student at a university clinic whose female patient, an undergraduate student, came to the clinic because of the distress she was experiencing in connection with a conflict with her parents over her desire to move into her own apartment. The graduate student therapist obviously identified with her patient, sided with her "against" her parents, and encouraged the patient's desire to move. The therapist did not pay sufficient attention to the possibility that the patient had her own anxieties and conflicts about separation and had externalized her conflict: Her parents represented the unexpressed side, and she presented the conflict entirely as an interpersonal one (i.e., between her and her parents) rather than as, at least in part, an intrapersonal one. Indeed, when the patient's parents relented somewhat and it seemed more possible for the patient to move into her own apartment without evoking their wrath and causing a major family crisis, she became acutely aware of her own anxiety and ambivalence about separation. However, she quit therapy. I suspect that one important reason for quitting was that the therapist had understandably become too identified in the patient's mind with only one side of the patient's conflict.

The caution about taking sides in the patient's conflicts is related to what I believe is a central value in psychoanalysis, namely, the achievement of autonomy in the sense of an increase in the patient's capacity to choose his or her way of life rather than feel compelled or driven in a particular direction. The therapist's task is not to advocate or direct the patient toward a particular way of life but to reduce the impediments to a more autonomous choice. I am aware that this is an ideal that can only be approached, but it is a value that is highly compatible with my own value system.

Another strength of a psychoanalytic orientation is its appreciation of the depth and complexity of mental life. People have conflicts and mixed motives and often are driven by what seems to them to be irrational passions. We rationalize some of our motives and often hide from ourselves certain desires, wishes, and fantasies. This view does more justice to the nature of human nature than views that omit these aspects of mental life.

Finally, another strength of a psychoanalytic orientation is its emphasis on the importance of self-reflection. Although, as I discuss later in this chapter, insight and awareness may not always be therapeutically effective or even therapeutically necessary, I believe, in general, that Socrates was right in maintaining that the unexamined life is a diminished one and that the examined life is more meaningful. This, too, is part of my value system that is highly compatible with a psychoanalytic orientation.

LIMITATIONS OF ORIGINAL ORIENTATION

Although I believe that a psychoanalytic orientation has many strengths, as will be seen, I have a good deal to say about its limitations. This is so partly because it often is easier to describe the limitations of one's own approach—one knows them from the inside. Also, I am far more comfortable with the role of critic than of true believer. I would also note my belief that one general source of limitations for psychoanalysis is the tendency for psychoanalytic views to be too much governed by fads and fashions and presumably authoritative pronouncements and assertions, which are then taken as demonstrated truths. For example, it now appears to be the received wisdom in the psychoanalytic community that analysis of the transference is at the heart of psychoanalytic treatment and that extratransference interpretations are not especially useful. However, whatever limited research is available on this topic does not support the claim that transference interpretations are especially associated with positive therapeutic outcome. My own clinical experience supports my belief that certain therapeutic interactions, or "corrective emotional experiences," should not be made explicit—indeed, that making them explicit may detract from their significance or reduce their positive impact. I no longer believe that even as a psychoanalytically oriented therapist, I need to interpret and make all transference reactions and patient–therapist interactions explicit. Certain reactions and interactions—particularly if they entail a corrective emotional experience—can be left alone to have their "silent" benevolent effects.

One set of limitations of the traditional psychoanalytic orientation that has come to be widely recognized by many contemporary analysts has to do with the idea that the analyst should attempt to be a blank screen (i.e., to be as neutral and as personally unrevealing as possible). The patient then would project onto that screen his or her wishes, conflicts, fantasies, and so forth. The blank-screen role led, in many instances, to the analyst's coldness, excessive silence, and artificial stodginess.

One of the phenomena that fascinate me is the degree to which some experiences one thinks of as deeply personal—for example, one's intuitions and insights—turn out to be "in the air," part of the *zeitgeist*, and shared by many other people. For example, many contemporary analysts now share my "gut" rejection of the blank-screen role of the analyst and of the stodginess and stiltedness that often accompanied that role. Indeed, as I have argued elsewhere (Eagle, 1987), I believe that many young analysts had the same gut reactions that I did but felt that their reactions were illicit and prevented them from being "real" analysts. General theoretical changes and modifications in the conception of psychoanalytic treatment and of therapeutic action that began to appear in the literature gave their intuitions and gut reactions a new legitimacy. I am referring to such concepts as the "real" relationship; Kohut's (1977, 1984) emphasis on the importance of empathic understanding and of the empathic stance; and Gill's (1982, 1994) insistence that the analyst could not really be a blank screen (i.e., could not help but emit cues) and that the patient's transference reactions always were, in part, a response to the cues emitted by the analyst.

I recall experiencing the limitations of the blank-screen conception in at least two ways. One, when I was a graduate student and looking for an analyst, the prevailing opinion, at least among Freudian analysts, was that all well-trained analysts (of course, "well trained" meant being trained in a Freudian orientation) were interchangeable. I never really accepted that idea, and it certainly did not conform to my experience when I chose my analyst. Two, as a beginning therapist, I felt constrained and experienced even greater awkwardness than I normally would feel by the thought that I needed to approach the ideal of the blank-screen role. I should add that the blank screen can serve as a cover for hiding one's discomfort and for not relating to the patient in a meaningful way. I certainly recall having such experiences. Fortunately, one of the core changes in contemporary psychoanalysis is the rejection of the conception of the entirely neutral analyst as a blank screen. It is now recognized that the analyst, whether he or she likes it or not, is constantly emitting cues to which the patient reacts—just as the patient is constantly emitting cues to which the therapist reacts. This seems like a perfectly commonsense and relatively simple observation. Yet it was a long time in coming, at least among noninterpersonal theory analysts, and despite its simplicity, the idea has important implications for how one does therapy and how one understands it.

The blank-screen view became untenable when it became apparent that I could not help but emit cues—just as anyone involved in any interpersonal interaction cannot help but emit cues. As Gill (1994) pointed out, silence and uttering nothing or little but "ums" can be quite powerful cues. If analysts or therapists are not interchangeable and if they cannot help but emit personal cues that influence the general emotional atmosphere and other aspects of the therapeutic interaction, it would seem to follow that the personal qualities of the analyst will strongly affect the kind and effectiveness of therapy. I strongly believe that this is the case.

I would add as another limitation of a psychoanalytic orientation— although it is not inherent to that orientation—a strong tendency within the psychoanalytic community to dismiss research as irrelevant or trivial and to express total disinterest in it. Indeed, such disinterest is taken by some to be a mark of a real clinician. As noted earlier, by noting the limited evidential value of clinical anecdotes, by noting the need for systematic and controlled outcome studies, by being interested in research (including research outside of but relevant to psychoanalysis, such as attachment research), and by taking a critical stance toward psychoanalytic theory, I have compromised my credentials as a real clinician in the eyes of some practitioners.

Although personal intuitions and convictions do and should play a significant role in how I and many other therapists function, as I wrote elsewhere (Eagle, 1999), there is a tendency in the current psychoanalytic literature to suggest that the analyst's own associations and affective reactions (now all viewed as aspects of the "totalistically" defined countertransference) can serve as virtually an unerring guide to the patient's unconscious mental contents. The preoccupation with the concept of projective identification—which often is left vague and undefined and seems to have almost as many meanings as the number of people who use the term—is one expression of this tendency. This tendency toward mystification is unfortunate and minimizes the role of evidence plus ordinary cognitive inference in arriving at clinical formulations and interventions. Personal experiences and intuitions regarding what is effective may be mistaken and are not an adequate substitute for well-controlled and systematic outcome studies (or preferably, integrated process and outcome studies).

A final limitation of a psychoanalytic orientation that I want to describe, again, may not be intrinsic to it but nevertheless may represent an abuse to which that orientation is susceptible. I will illustrate an unfortunate tendency among some analysts by sharing with the reader a disturbing experience I had in connection with presenting a case to a group that consisted mainly of analysts. The experience helped clarify for me a number of issues, including the nature of a certain stereotypical psychoanalytic stance that I abhor, and reinforced my conviction that that sort of stance should be avoided.

The patient I presented, O. E., was a woman who became severely agoraphobic following the birth of her child and the plan to move to a new city where her husband had taken a job. O. E. became agoraphobic following a number of panic attacks during unsuccessful attempts to drive to the new city to see the house her husband had rented for them. In anticipation of moving to the new house, they had given up their apartment, so O. E., her husband, and their baby had to move in with O. E.'s parents. O. E.'s mother was on home dialysis, and for many years—including the time that O. E. and her husband lived in their own apartment—O. E. changed the filters. O. E. informed me of this fact but did not say much more about it, including how she felt about carrying out this task. Hence, I was surprised when O. E.

announced during one session that she had informed her mother that she no longer wanted to be involved in the latter's dialysis.

Her mother, O. E. informed me, seemed to react with equanimity. However, a day or two later, mother went off on a trip to visit her sister in Detroit and had to return precipitously because she had "forgotten" to take an adequate number of filters. On telling me this story, O. E. suddenly exclaimed, with great emotion: "Oh, my God. No wonder I had to move back home. This way I can take care of both my mother and Erik [her baby]."

During that session and subsequent sessions, O. E. recalled and talked about other, more subtle "messages" from her mother throughout her up-bringing that she needed O. E. to take care of her if she, the mother, were to survive. From this point on, O. E. made rapid progress and within a few months became virtually free of agoraphobic symptoms.

I had occasional contact with O. E. for more than 15 years. The last contact was occasioned by a telephone call in which she said she was fine but wanted to see me and tell me about her mother's death. As she put it, she wanted a "witness" and felt that I could uniquely understand the signifi-cance of how her mother died. O. E.'s mother became ill, was hospitalized, went into a profound coma, and needed to be on life support "if she was not to die." She had made out a living will indicating that she did not want to be kept alive that way. However, O. E.'s older sister felt unable to take the necessary steps, and it fell to O. E. to make the decision to "kill" her mother. Bravely and courageously, she made that decision. After recounting this, she said: "Only you would understand what it took for me to do this." It was clear from the context that she was referring to her struggle to lead her own life without feeling that by doing so she was killing her mother. Finally, she had to "kill" her mother. She was quietly proud that she could do what was necessary—indeed, carry out her mother's wishes despite the profound complexity of the situation—"without falling apart" and "without paralyzing guilt." I found my last meeting with O. E. extremely moving. Without, I hope, sounding overly sentimental, this whole episode—as much else of O. E.'s life—impressed me as a testimony to some people's capacity for growth and for struggle to lead a meaningful and satisfying life.

After presenting the above and other material about O. E., during the discussion period, a well-known analyst made the following comment in connection with O. E.'s role in her mother's death: "So, she finally got her wish, she killed her mother." I was horrified by the heartlessness and mindless reductionism conveyed by the remark and made my reaction clear by the tone, if not the content, of my reply. Another well-known analyst then chimed in with some extended remarks regarding an analytic patient of his with a flying phobia (he did not attempt to make clear the connection to agoraphobia). The gist of his remarks, to the extent that I could follow them, was that although separation–individuation issues were relevant, his patients' "real" underlying unconscious wish was to kill the pilot—which, of course, he pointed out, was expressed in the transference as a wish to kill the analyst. I had no idea what all this stuff about killing the pilot and the analyst had to do with agoraphobia and with my presentation of O. E. I suppose the connecting associations had something to do with O. E. "killing" her mother and the previous analyst's comment.

As I noted earlier, this sort of experience strengthens my distaste for a certain kind of one-upmanship that I associate with the worst features of the psychoanalytic community. A premium is placed on coming up with arcane and clever meanings that the other fellow overlooked or did not think of and that purportedly represent the heart of the matter. I also observe this behavior too frequently among graduate students at our case conferences. I try to discourage such behavior, being careful not to be too deflating. I am especially concerned that the attitude may find expression in clinical work with patients—where the therapist engages in second-guessing the patient. There is perhaps a thin line between, on the one hand, offering a fresh perspective or interpreting a dynamic or mental content or process (i.e., a wish or defense) to which the patient did not have access and, on the other hand, engaging in second-guessing or making arcane interpretations that do not remotely connect with the patient's accessible experiences. One of the ways in which I have changed as a therapist is that I have even less faith (I never had much) in the therapeutic value of "deep" interpretations that are remote from the patients' current conscious experience. I am deeply suspicious regarding the theoretical validity and therapeutic value of overly complex and highly esoteric formulations and interpretations (e.g., those in which the concept of projective identification is prominent; Eagle, 1999).

My description of O. E.'s central dynamics were not especially complex, did not require any specialized esoteric concepts, and were not far removed from her conscious experiences. I have come to believe more and more that interpretations and other interventions that are "experience near" and theoretical formulations that are limited to ordinary cognitive and affective processes about which we know a good deal are likely to be most therapeutically useful and conceptually valid.

It is entirely possible that O. E. did harbor death wishes toward her mother. Even if this were the case, however, it does not follow that such wishes constitute the "deep" meaning of O. E.'s symptoms or, indeed, that they play any special role in the development and maintenance of those symptoms. What about the fact that this issue was not fully explored in the course of treatment? My response to this question gives me an opportunity to articulate my evolving attitude toward the question of unexplored issues in treatment.

Let us assume that O. E. had unconscious death wishes toward her mother, which remained unexplored during the treatment. This does not strike me as especially important. In my view, in every treatment certain issues remain relatively unexplored. The title of Freud's (1937/1964) essay, "Analysis Terminable and Interminable," suggests that this is the case and that the idea of a complete analysis is a myth. What is important is that certain central issues are sufficiently dealt with so that distress and crippling symptoms are ameliorated and the quality and level of satisfaction of the patient's life are enhanced. In O. E.'s case, this certainly occurred. Furthermore, she dealt with her mother's death in an admirable and courageous way. All this suggests—although it certainly does not prove—that the treatment did deal with central issues in O. E.'s life. I am not especially concerned that it did not deal explicitly with all the conflicts and concerns that were present in O. E.'s life. Indeed, with some patients it is wise to leave certain issues implicit.

HOW CHANGE OCCURRED

Five factors have most heavily influenced me and the way I do therapy. They are, roughly in order of importance,

1. my own development
2. particularly memorable experiences with particular patients
3. books and articles that presented a point of view that felt personally cogent and meaningful and that in some way helped me understand the memorable experiences with patients
4. research findings showing that a particular factor, technique, or intervention was either especially helpful or especially ineffective, or research findings that shed light on the nature of a particular clinical syndrome (i.e., the factors that are involved in it)
5. debates in the literature on a particular issue that helped me clarify my own position on that issue.

In what follows I try to present material that illustrates the role of some of the above factors.

One consistent experience I have had with patients is, paradoxically, a kind of inconsistency. That is, despite the talk about common factors in the psychotherapy literature and about overarching goals—such as insight and making the unconscious conscious—in the psychoanalytic literature, my personal experience was that what worked often varied with different patients. For example, with O. E., insight into her unconscious pathogenic belief that "if she separated from mother, mother would die" seemed to play a pivotal role in her recovery, whereas for another, an enactment and testing of a pathological defiance/punishment-and-pain pattern, both within and outside the treatment, rather than insight, seemed more important in the amelioration of her symptoms.

I learned that with certain patients (in my experience, not especially psychologically minded patients), a small dose of insight can be extremely helpful. It often transforms a seemingly incomprehensible and bewildering set of experiences into something meaningful and purposive and, in doing so, relieves anxiety. I also learned, again with certain patients, that such insight is unlikely to be self-generated and requires the therapist's interpretations. In contrast, other patients' insights do not especially require interpretations because they are more capable of achieving them on their own. Something I relearned rather than learned is that interpretations need to be geared so that they can be used and assimilated by the patient. A brilliant and correct interpretation may be gratifying to the therapist but is of little therapeutic value if it cannot be used profitably by the patient.

An experience that I have had repeatedly is that good things are more likely to happen and the therapeutic sessions are more likely to come alive when I am effectively present—by which I mean such things as interested, engaged, feeling responsive, spontaneous, and energized. I recall one session with a patient that came at the end of a long day. My patient, I felt, was droning on about how well she was doing. I felt tired and somewhat bored and that the account of her improvement seemed compliant (i.e., things she thought I wanted to hear) rather than authentic (she earlier had described this pattern as the way she is with men). I said to the patient that I thought that she was saying things that she thought I wanted to hear. At that point, she burst into tears and described the following: She saw my head turn slightly to the right (I have a clock to the right and behind where my patients sit), thought I was distracted and not interested, and tried to think of things that would interest me. She cried, she said, because she was always doing this with men. She also expressed relief that I had identified what was going on. I commented that I had looked off to the right and noted that the clock was there—a fact that she did not mention. We also discussed her reaction to her sense that I was uninterested—namely, trying to come up with material that she thought would interest me rather than ask me what was going on.

Following the above exchange, the session came alive. I no longer felt tired or bored but involved and effectively present. And my patient went on to talk about her relationships with men in a genuine and meaningful way. I want to note that my self-disclosure was minimal. I did not disclose to my patient that I was bored or that I looked at the clock to see how much time was left in the session—although I did, in effect, acknowledge that I was looking at the clock by remarking that the clock was on the right. I cannot prove any of this, of course, but I felt intuitively that any further self-disclosure would not have been useful or productive and would likely have been hurtful to the patient. I certainly can say that I would have felt uncomfortable doing so. I believe that the real issue is the degree to which the therapist is effectively present rather than the degree of self-disclosure. As Strachey (1934) suggested, what may be important about transference interpretations is that they refer to here-and-now reactions and, therefore, may be associated with a greater emotional immediacy. Transference interpretations, however, also can be presented in a flat, over-intellectualized, and lifeless way, particularly if the therapist views him- or herself as a blank screen and does not deal with his or her role in the patient's transference reactions. Hence, the critical variable is likely to be not simply the content of the interpretations—transference versus nontransference—but also the degree to which they convey the therapist's affective presence. I can sum up much of the above by saying that along with many other analysts, I focus more on the therapeutic interaction between the patient and me and do not subscribe as exclusively to the primary goal of making the unconscious conscious.

Next, I describe an experience with a patient, E. S., that had a significant impact on my approach to doing therapy. Some years ago I worked with a woman who developed an intense erotic transference toward me. After a period of time, this gave way to an equally intense anger and rage. Every interpretation I made she reacted to with ridicule and anger. At one point, she said: "I don't want any more of your damn interpretations. I just want you to listen to me." I happened to be reading Kohut on the importance of empathic understanding, the reaction of rage that may follow failures of such understanding, and the importance of the therapist acknowledging his or her failure. His observations resonated with my patient's comment and with my overall experience with her. For the next few months I refrained from any interpretations and tried to limit my interventions to attempting to understand what she was experiencing. Her anger and rage diminished markedly and seemed to evaporate.

One seemingly trivial incident stands out in my memory as a significant marker in that process. At one point during the session, my patient became tearful and reached for a tissue, only to find the tissue box empty. She reacted with anger and said, "Why don't you have a sign on your door: 'Dr. Eagle, no crying here.' " I reacted by saying, "I'm sorry there are no tissues. Had I been more thoughtful, I would have noticed that"—and made no further attempts to interpret her anger. My patient then commented on her "overreaction" and proceeded to relate her reaction to earlier events in her life. This became a pattern. As long as I limited my intervention to attempts to understand her experience and to acknowledge my empathic failures, she provided the interpretations regarding dynamics and early events in her life. After a period in which this pattern repeated itself many times, my interpretative interventions felt more like a back and forth, joint, cooperative endeavor rather than my offering interpretations and her receiving or rejecting them.

What went on here, and what lessons are to be learned? Or, at least, what lessons did I learn? One of the dynamics between us that became clear as time went on is that when I had made earlier interpretations—say, linking my patient's reactions to me and her reactions to her father—she experienced me as trying to get "off the hook." That is, from her point of view, I was saying something like "It's not me you're reacting to—it's your father. Therefore, I had nothing to do with it—I'm not at fault." This would drive her into a rage. Experiencing her parents trying to get off the hook by not acknowledging their behavior was a familiar and repetitive pattern for my patient. It always would drive her into a rage. In a wonderful paradox, in making interpretations characterized by pointing to similarities in her reactions to me and her reactions to her father, without acknowledging my contribution to these reactions, I was, in my patient's experience, behaving like her parents—namely, trying to get off the hook. She would then react with her usual rage.

It's not that my interpretations were necessarily inaccurate or wrong. They were, indeed, generally accurate—my patient was reacting to me the way she reacted to her father. The problem was that I did not acknowledge my contribution to the whole repetitive pattern. Only when I could and did acknowledge my behavior could my patient—on her own and without prompting from me—experience and examine the links between her reactions to me and to her father. The entire interactional pattern I have described serves as a good example of what can happen when the therapist is unaware of or unable to acknowledge his or her possible contributions to the patient's transference reactions.

In a certain sense, I have seen in myself and in others how traditional interpretations, in which the patients' reactions to the therapists are too easily linked to reactions to parental figures, indeed can serve as a way of getting the therapist off the hook. As I suggested earlier, this point is implicit in Gill's (1982, 1994) insistence that the patient's transference reactions are not simply a "distortion" but frequently are based on plausible construals of cues emitted by the therapist. That is, when one does not acknowledge one's behavior, the implication may be that the patient's reaction is woven out of whole cloth. In contrast, when one acknowledges the cues one has emitted, including one's empathic failures and their possible contributions to the patient's reactions, one validates the patient's experience. This phenomenon does not mean that one cannot explore possible distortions or what seem like overly intense reactions to the therapist's behavior. Rather the patient may be more likely to explore these issues when the therapist acknowledges the possible contributions of his or her own behavior.

The unfolding of events with E. S. further clarified one aspect of what is wrong with the dichotomy between interpretation and insight on the one hand and relationship factors on the other: the overly tight coupling of insight with interpretation. That is, I learned that insight is not necessarily the result of interpretation but may just as likely follow on empathic listening and understanding or a corrective emotional experience. In E. S.'s case, her exploration and understanding of any connections between her response to me and her response to her father were not generated or facilitated by my interpretations to that effect; indeed, as we have seen, they seemed to be hindered by such interpretations. Rather, her insights into these connections followed on and seemed to be facilitated by a period of desisting from making interpretations and instead just listening, trying to understand her experiences, and trying to understand and acknowledge the role of my behavior in her reactions.

MY CURRENT APPROACH

Comparing my early way of practicing with my current way brings to mind the awkwardness I felt when I first began doing therapy. I felt that I was role-playing and that the person I was when I was doing therapy was radically different from the person I was when I was not doing therapy. I would say that the washing away of that marked discrepancy between person as therapist and just person and the accompanying reduction in my awkward-ness—replaced by a greater sense of ease and naturalness—are the most important ways in which I have changed as a therapist. In short, early on I was anything but authentic and genuine as a therapist. I think I have become more so with the years.

I have used videos in teaching psychotherapy, and I am struck by the extraordinary absence of authenticity and genuineness in some of the therapists in the more recent videos. Characteristics such as authenticity, genuineness, and warmth are personal qualities that cannot simply be learned from courses and workshops and certainly cannot be role-played. Indeed, the nature of those characteristics is such that if one tries self-consciously and in an excessively practiced way to role-play authenticity and genuine-ness, one is no longer being authentic and genuine. These are organic qualities of a person that cannot be changed as one does a suit of clothes. The best one can hope for is that as part of one's personal growth, one becomes a more authentic and genuine person and therapist.

It is my strong belief that one's personal qualities are likely to be the most important factor in therapeutic effectiveness. If this notion is true, one could not legitimately talk simply about this or that set of techniques or therapeutic approaches. Instead, it would always be a matter of a particular person, with a particular set of personal qualities, carrying out this or that therapeutic approach. Hence, in thinking about how I have changed as a therapist and how therapists generally change, my emphasis would be on personal changes and growth rather than the adoption or relinquishment of a specific set of techniques (although, as will be seen, I qualify that somewhat later on). And the personal changes that seem most important are the ones I noted earlier—the greater ease and naturalness I feel as a therapist and the concomitant greater congruence I experience between who I am as a therapist and who I am when I am not doing therapy. I like to believe that this represents an increasing kind of authenticity.

Much of what I am saying adds up to the following belief and claim: Given the kind of therapy I do, how much I change as a therapist and how effective I am depend not only on the knowledge I acquire regarding what is effective (e.g., exposure is important in the treatment of agoraphobia) but also on my ability to maintain and convey a strong and positive affective presence and remain vitally involved in my interaction with my patients. The latter, in turn, depends on my ability to grow as a person and to maintain and enhance such personal qualities as enthusiasm, interest, and faith in the possibilities of growth and change. One may get by without those qualities. But to an undesirable extent, one simply gets by or to use Winnicott's words, "marks time." At some level, patients, like other people in everyday interactions, know the difference between the therapist going through the motions and being vitally involved. In short, I suggest that the way therapists change is not unlike the way other people change in their work. They learn more and become more skilled and more confident. In addition to knowledge and skill, however, when things go well, they maintain an interest and enthusiasm and an openness to new experiences, all of which are aspects of their growth as a person.

This recognition of the importance of the therapist's personal qualities brings the psychoanalytic point of view closer, in certain respects, to a Rogerian perspective, in which it is explicitly recognized that the therapist's characteristics, such as congruence, genuineness, and warmth, are a major factor in the treatment. Although the personal qualities of the therapist are critical elements, it seems that one also should take seriously specific reliable findings relevant to particular syndromes and clinical constellations. For example, from what I know of the clinical and research literature on agoraphobia, any treatment approach to it is not likely to be effective if it does not include, at some point and in some form, exposure to the feared situations. I do not believe that there is any evidence indicating the effectiveness of limiting treatment to interpretation of the symbolic meaning of the symptom, an approach that characterized early psychoanalytic treatment and may continue to characterize the treatment of some contemporary analysts. I believe that any therapist, whatever his or her theoretical orientation, has an obligation to be aware of clinical and research findings relevant to the set of problems he or she is treating. This seems to be a natural and meaningful way to achieve an integrative approach to treatment, rather than trying to integrate different theories.

From a more personal point of view, I find commonalities between different theoretical approaches exciting and meaningful, particularly when I can link them to clinical experiences. The recognition of such commonalities not only has influenced my work (e.g., like a cognitive therapist, I would have little hesitation identifying and conveying to a patient his or her implicit irrational belief system) but also has influenced my clinical identity. As noted earlier, I think of myself as a psychologist whose predominant orientation is psychodynamic or psychoanalytic but who would not hesitate to make use of techniques and interventions from other approaches, as long as I feel that I know what I am doing, as long as the use of such interventions does not feel awkward and unnatural, and as long as such use does not compromise or interfere with the possibility of a genuine and honest relationship with my patient or with the overall spirit and direction of our work.

CONCLUSION

In coming to the end of this chapter, I want to recapitulate and add perhaps one or two thoughts on the ways I believe I have changed most as a therapist and the factors that have most influenced me. As I stated earlier, the most obvious change I observe is that I have become more comfortable, natural, and authentic as a therapist, a change that comes with personal development, experience, and age, although the latter two do not guarantee it. I have become more modest—and, I believe, realistic—on the question of therapeutic goals in a number of ways. Despite the frequently voiced psychoanalytic position that symptom amelioration and relief are superficial goals (in contrast to, e.g., so-called structural change), I have come to value the importance of the former, particularly when they make a significant positive impact on the patient's life. In my experience, the disappearance of a patient's symptom makes a great difference in his or her life and facilitates other satisfactions and achievements, including the capacity for long-term, intimate relationships. The amelioration of O. E.'s agoraphobia certainly made an extraordinary difference in her life.

I recall reading Freud's comment to the effect that even in successful treatment patients reach the best compromises that they are able to achieve, given their personality structure. This sounds, perhaps, a bit pessimistic, but I do not think it is; it is realistic and a point of view that ultimately is of benefit to the patient. Therapists are always subject to the risks of arrogance and therapeutic zeal, which may be expressed in imposing on the patient theoretically driven goals, such as "structural change" or a resolution of the so-called "transference neurosis"—goals that may have little to do with the patient's experiences, purposes in seeking treatment, or capabilities. Apocalyptic and unrealistic goals, such as personality transformation and rebirth, do the patient a disservice because, among other things, they trivialize more realistic and more modest accomplishments, which, albeit modest, make an important difference in a person's life. Waiting for an epiphany or a dramatic transformation can itself be a neurotic expression, a kind of "what am I going to be and do when I grow up" or "then I will start living"— a halting of life until the hoped for magical transformation occurs. My impression is that many patients—and many people, in general—already devalue or find it difficult to derive satisfaction from small, everyday events in life. Setting unrealistic goals can exacerbate that tendency—a sort of iatrogenic phenomenon—and can justify seemingly endlessly lengthy treatment, with the patient waiting for the magical transformation.

I recall giving a talk to a group of about 50 analysts some years ago; at the time I had assigned a class that I was teaching some of Guntrip's (e.g., 1968) writings in which he talks about rebirth in treatment. I asked the audience whether they, in their own treatment, or any of their patients had experienced what could legitimately be called rebirth. Not one person raised his or her hand. Perhaps some people were reluctant to acknowledge such a personal experience publicly. My guess, however, is that no one in the audience actually had direct or indirect experience of rebirth. My sense is that many people walk around with the impression that the other has had these apocalyptic experiences—after all, they are written about in the literature—but their analysis or therapy failed to accomplish the transformation.

A final comment having to do with the issue of psychotherapy integration: As I think about how I have changed as a therapist and about the factors that have influenced me, I feel a much greater sense of kinship with therapists from a variety of different theoretical approaches. It may be naïve, but I believe that if one listens to patients, observes what is helpful to them, and tries to keep abreast of the relevant research, one cannot help but become more integrationist in one's thinking and in the way one does therapy. I do not believe there is a single approach that works for all patients. With one patient, what was most effective was just listening and acknowledging my failures; with another, what seemed efficacious was an enactment and testing of core maladaptive schemas both within and outside the treatment; and with a third, the combination of exposure, her use of me as a transitional object, and a dramatic insight into an unconscious pathogenic belief—generated not by an interpretation, but by a life experience—seemed to be the important elements. Finally, for still another patient, interpretations regarding the functions served by his symptom and the meaning of its waxing and waning proved most helpful.

I should add that with some of my patients, I have felt that little change has occurred (either on their part or mine) and that no intervention or approach has been especially helpful. In such cases, one has the responsibility, I believe, to refer the patient elsewhere, possibly to someone whose theoretical approach is entirely different from one's own. This practice implies a sense of collegiality and connection with therapists of different theoretical persuasions, a particular kind of integrationism, rather than a more parochial identity. In any case, if one is not totally wedded to one's own theory or theoretical approach, listens to patients, and observes what works and does not work with each of them, one inevitably becomes more of an integrationist therapist.

REFERENCES

Eagle, M. (1987). Theoretical and clinical shifts in psychoanalysis. *American Journal of Orthopsychiatry*, *57*, 175–185.

Eagle, M. (1999, April 14–18). *A critical evaluation of current conceptions of transference and countertransference*. Paper presented at the meeting of the Division of Psychoanalysis of the American Psychological Association, New York. [Also cited in Eagle, M. (2000). A critical evaluation of current conceptions of transference and countertransference. *Psychoanalytic Psychology*, *17*(1), 24–37.]

Freud, S. (1964). Analysis terminable and interminable. In J. Strachey (Ed.), *The standard edition of the complete psychological works of Sigmund Freud* (pp. 209–253). London: Hogarth Press. (Original work published 1937)

Gill, M. M. (1982). *Analysis of transference: Vol. 1. Theory and technique*. New York: International Universities Press.

Gill, M. M. (1994). *Psychoanalysis in transition: A personal view*. Hillsdale, NJ: Analytic Press.

Guntrip, H. (1968). *Schizoid phenomena, object relations and the self*. New York: International Universities Press.

Kohut, H. (1977). *Restoration of the self*. New York: International Universities Press.

Kohut, H. (1984). *How does analysis cure?* Chicago: University of Chicago Press.

Strachey, J. (1934). The nature of the therapeutic action of psychoanalysis. *International Journal of Psychoanalysis*, *15*, 127–159.

4

A THERAPIST'S JOURNEY

JOHN M. RHOADS

When I entered the field of psychiatry as a first-year resident at Temple University Hospital in the fall of 1944, there was little to offer in the way of therapy of any kind. There were no drugs, other than barbiturates, that had any significant effect on patients. Electroconvulsive therapy was the only effective treatment for psychoses, other than medical treatments for some physical diseases. Psychotherapy was just beginning to become recognized as an effective treatment for some of the neuroses. Psychoanalysis was the gold standard, and shortened versions of it were beginning to be used to treat those who could not afford 5 hours a week for 2 to 5 years, which, of course, was most of the population who might be helped by such treatment.

During World War II, Grinker and Spiegel (1944a, 1944b) devised the narcosynthesis technique to treat posttraumatic stress disorders among American troops in the North African campaign. To alleviate the symptoms, this therapy used a low level of barbiturate anesthesia to control overwhelming anxiety along with abreaction and interpretation based on psychoanalytic understanding. Another therapy to come out during World War II was group psychotherapy: Some was based on counseling, and some was based on what amounted to a modified group analysis. Some nonanalysts, who

55

had a good understanding of human nature, used a mixture of empathy, counseling, emotional release, and rational thinking and were effective psychotherapists. This was the situation I entered, thinking that I could switch to some other field in a year or so if more progress was not forthcoming. As a result of my experiences in a rotating internship, where I saw many medical and surgical patients whose primary or secondary problems were psychological, I had been impressed with the number of people who needed effective psychiatric therapy.

LESSONS ORIGINALLY LEARNED

A major reason for choosing Temple for a residency was that my chief there was O. Spurgeon English, who with an internist, Edward Weiss, coauthored a best-selling text (Weiss & English, 1943) on a psychiatric approach to medical and surgical patients whose psychological problems significantly affected their state of health. Because I was the first resident in psychiatry, I had the opportunity to work closely with both English and Weiss as well as two other faculty members with analytic training: Eleanor Steele and Herbert Freed. The educational emphasis was heavily psychoanalytic, with the exception of Freed, who was also a neurologist and with whom I shared interests in organic and psychotic disorders. I saw many patients on the wards; using my newly acquired psychoanalytic knowledge of the mechanisms of defense, I was able to help some of them cope better with their illnesses. I had less luck with the psychiatric outpatients. In retrospect, most of those patients had more chronic and more solidified illnesses. Because there was less time pressure in which to work with those patients, I was attempting to use a more standard psychoanalytic approach. What they wanted and needed was symptom relief. All too often, we were working at cross-purposes.

The U.S. Army called in early 1946, and after basic officer's training and the Army's "3-month-wonder" psychiatry school, I ended up assigned to a mental health clinic at Fort Ord, California. There, raw recruits underwent a 13-week cycle of intensive infantry training in how to become a foot soldier. It was a good experience because it taught me to look at the big picture—specifically, to see what training stresses led to breakdowns and how to help company officers deal with the affected recruits for them to become effective soldiers. Additionally, I had to deal with sick soldiers on a short-term basis, the goal being to help those who could cope with being in the army and to sort out those who could not before they became chronically incapacitated. Psychotherapy consisted of trying to elicit specific fears and problems and then counseling the soldiers in how to deal with them. I was impressed with the training of recruits and how, in 13 weeks, they learned to become soldiers. In retrospect, the military had long since learned basic principles of behavioral conditioning and group motivation.

STRENGTHS OF ORIGINAL ORIENTATION

When I began my supervised casework, I did so with great expectations and was not disappointed. The cases went well and made real progress. The supervision was helpful, and I was able to adapt what I learned by doing brief psychotherapy. Essentially this amounted to doing a structured evaluation to discern critical conflicts, areas of immaturity, and ego assets and deficits and to formulate a treatment plan based on an estimate of what could be accomplished given the limitations of time and finances. At this time, I was on the Temple psychiatry faculty and active in the outpatient clinic. Our staff were nearly all psychoanalysts or were in training; the treatment of patients followed analytic principles and, like the unconscious, was often timeless. The waiting list in the outpatient clinic was nearly endless.

When summer came and we were not involved with teaching duties, A. Victor Hansen (the clinic director) and I devised a plan to continue to use the faculty and simultaneously shorten the waiting list. We divided the waiting list among the staff and assigned patients with the proviso that there would be a limit of six visits. Patients who wanted more therapy could reapply. There were anguished cries from some of the staff that six visits was "ridiculous" and that "evaluation alone took that long." But we proceeded anyway. A social worker conducted a follow-up interview to evaluate what had happened. Interestingly, many patients believed they had benefited, about two-thirds of the total, as I recall. Of interest was the fact that with a few exceptions, the therapists who did not do well with the time-limited therapy were the child analysts and those interested in working with long-term psychotics. We concluded that psychoanalytically oriented therapy could be effective on a brief basis. In justice to the therapists who did not do well, we believed that their orientation to their usual patients did not fit the time-limited treatment situation. This experience further interested me in pondering ways to carry out effective brief psychotherapy because it was also clear from my beginning private practice that there was a need for effective and affordable short-term treatment. At the time, I thought only in terms of finding improved ways to apply psychoanalytic principles.

LIMITATIONS OF ORIGINAL ORIENTATION

I entered formal psychoanalytic education through the GI Bill and enrolled in the Philadelphia Psychoanalytic Institute for classwork and, later, for supervision of casework. I was accustomed to scientific thinking—to questioning and to testing. Unfortunately, orthodoxy was paramount, and much of the classwork consisted of memorizing dogma. It was a period when a number of psychoanalytic institutes suffered splits, allegedly over theoretical principles but to a considerable extent because of personality conflicts. The Philadelphia Institute suffered an angry division. That our elders could not manage their differences better was disappointing. We students dealt with it by joking that institutes were like Judaism: There were orthodox and reformed branches, with some trying to bridge the extremes and be conservative. At the time, my view was that Freudian psychoanalysis was the best way to understand human psychology and neurotic illnesses. Although mental processes and defenses operated in psychotic illness, just as in neurotics and "normals," they did not explain the basic pathology of those sicknesses.

The 1950s were a period when the *New Yorker* was filled with cartoons of analysts and their patients, psychoanalysis was booming, and there was as yet no effective medication for psychiatric illnesses. Few people seeking help could afford psychoanalysis or protracted therapy. Most of us starting out were well aware of this problem, so when the psychoanalytic society sponsored a lecture by a distinguished analyst on the subject of brief therapy, we found it amusing to hear that "brief" meant "only" 100 plus hours. It is interesting that Aaron Beck, who later developed cognitive therapy, was a classmate of mine in the institute.

HOW CHANGE OCCURRED

In the early 1950s my department chairman, Spurgeon English, gave a series of lectures at the Temple University Divinity School. Impressed, the dean asked him to teach graduate-level courses in pastoral counseling for master's degree and doctor of theology candidates. Because English had sufficient commitments already, it naturally devolved upon the most junior member of the department to take on this challenge.

I was greeted with half a dozen or so students of various denominations and faiths, all of whom were involved in active congregational work. Because lectures were the traditional method of instruction, I lectured. But after a few classes, I noticed that the students seemed apathetic and lacked a "feel" for the various disorders I so brilliantly described. Freud came to the rescue: I recalled his use of literature to illustrate his concepts (Freud, 1900/1938). The next subject for consideration was alcoholism; because some of the students were, by denominational requirement, teetotalers, I realized I needed to do something better than talk. I assigned *Lost Weekend* by Charles Jackson (1944), along with Alcoholics Anonymous literature. The result exceeded expectations. For the rest of that semester and during the following year, I used various novels in lieu of live subjects and lectures. The class members analyzed the various characters and their dilemmas and discussed how they might deal with such people in their respective congregational settings. Among some of the novels I used were *The Monk and the Hangman's Daughter* by Ambrose Bierce, *Sons and Lovers* by D. H. Lawrence, *Madame Bovary* by G. Flaubert, Shakespeare's *King Lear,* and *Bonjour Tristesse* by Françoise Sagan. Later, the class presented cases they had under way in their congregations, and it was gratifying to see how well they had picked up an understanding of pathology and principles of brief therapy and were able to apply them. When I moved to Duke University and took charge of the residency program, I offered an optional course for the residents in a study of psychopathology as illustrated in literature, with the aim of enhancing an understanding of unconscious motivation. I clearly was departing from the way things were usually done.

In my first years in private practice, I had the opportunity to work closely with Samuel B. Hadden, one of the pioneers in group therapy (Hadden, 1944). He was an intuitive psychotherapist who combined psycho-dynamic principles with education and counseling in his group therapy sessions. I was impressed with how rapidly some patients responded as well as with the economic advantages of group therapy. I had conducted some groups while still at Temple but never had the time available after my move to Duke. To expand the horizons of the psychiatric residents, however, I made sure that their curriculum included an exposure to group therapy, both in theory and clinical practice.

Another learning experience came with a psychosocial teaching experiment in the Temple University Hospital medical outpatient clinic. William Steiger, from the department of medicine, and A. Victor Hansen and I, from the department of psychiatry (Steiger, Hansen, & Rhoads, 1956) designed the medical aspects of the experiment, and Gertrude O'Connell, a social worker, organized those aspects of the project. Junior medical students were assigned to do a complete medical, psychiatric, and social work-up for a patient with a chronic illness, to make home visits, and to follow the patients for 2 years, if possible. In most instances patients had both medical and psychiatric disorders, and the chronic medical problems had led to secondary social problems. The need not only for medical treatment but also for brief psychotherapy of some type, counseling, and social interventions was clear, especially because everyone in this group was poor and unable to afford private therapy. Perhaps the most effective intervention for this group was social service aid. I already had a great appreciation for the value of social service from my experiences as an intern and resident at the Philadelphia General Hospital. The need for effective short-term intervention increasingly was impressed on me, but at this stage I was still trying to fit a psychoanalytic approach to the problem. It was not until the late 1960s that Ben Feather and I became aware of other approaches to brief therapy and began to experiment with them and incorporate them into our therapy.

In the early 1950s, chlorpromazine was introduced for the treatment of psychotic states. This discovery revolutionized psychiatry because it provided an effective medication for conditions that heretofore had been largely untreatable. This discovery led to further research and the introduction of specific drugs for the treatment of depression and mania as well as schizophrenia and related disorders. Although the psychoanalytic understanding of mental mechanisms still held true for psychoses, their treatment became largely biological, more hopeful in outlook, and more short term.

In 1956, I had the opportunity to move to Duke University. George Ham, chairman of the Department of Psychiatry at the University of North Carolina at Chapel Hill (UNC), with the support of E. W. Busse, his counterpart at Duke University, attempted to establish a psychoanalytic program in North Carolina. This effort succeeded, and a Psychoanalytic Institute was approved by the American Psychoanalytic Association in 1965. Meanwhile, I had become a training and supervising analyst and was director of residency training in the Department of Psychiatry. I considered it essential for the education of psychiatrists that they be exposed to various orientations, so the Duke program was always an eclectic one that included education in psychodynamic, biological, and group therapies. Behavioral approaches would be added later on.

The year 1958 marked the publication of Joseph Wolpe's classic work on a learning approach to therapy, *Psychotherapy by Reciprocal Inhibition*. The 1960s witnessed an explosion of a variety of methods of behavior therapy, led by the group at the Maudsley Hospital in London and other experimenters and researchers in London and in the United States. Best of all, many of these therapies could be proven effective by standard research methods.

In the late 1960s, I supervised Ben W. Feather for one of his cases in the psychoanalytic institute. Feather was a physician who had begun a program in psychology during his psychiatric residency, and at the time of my supervision, he had just received his PhD in experimental psychology. Because his case was progressing well, we had some extra time to discuss other mutual interests. We had been impressed by Wolpe's reports, but we were dubious. We both were interested in finding more effective and economical psychotherapies, however, and agreed that we should try his method to see if the reservations we had about it would prove to be unfounded. We decided that whichever of us first saw a suitable case would evaluate it from a psychodynamic standpoint, then refer the case to the other for behavioral treatment, and the former would follow the case to evaluate the outcome.

Soon after that decision, I was referred a woman who suffered from an incapacitating cockroach phobia. Not only was she disabled, but her compulsive efforts to avoid cockroaches had disrupted the life of the entire family. The illness had begun when she found herself unexpectedly pregnant in her early 40s, after having been assured she was unable to conceive. A curious feature of the illness was the fact that she had not seen the feared insect for nearly a year but had experienced no diminution of her frenzied washing and cleaning. Complicating factors were the family's limited income and the considerable distance she had to travel to therapy sessions. She was referred to Feather for desensitization therapy. There seemed little to be gained by desensitizing her to an insect she never encountered, so making use of the psychodynamic aspects of her disorder, which seemed to be her fear of being physically close enough to her husband to risk another unwanted pregnancy, we decided to desensitize her to her husband and to her sexual avoidance. Ben carried out this program using Wolpe's method of systematic desensitization with excellent results.

We continued to alternate cases and had continuing good outcomes (Feather & Rhoads, 1972a, 1972b). The fact that no symptom substitution took place was a bit of a surprise because that was a commonly held dogma among psychoanalysts. My earlier experience with that phenomenon had occurred some years before, when I hypnotized a young woman suffering from hysterical blindness and suggested that the blindness would go away, which it did. Unfortunately, she returned the following day with hysterical deafness. So much for symptom removal! Another belief among many analysts was that unless one dealt with the transference, a positive outcome would represent a "transference cure"—getting better merely to please the therapist—and would not be lasting. My experience at the Temple University clinic had not borne out the latter idea.

Another surprise was how rapidly positive results were obtained! We wondered what took so long when Wolpe reported that some of his cases took as many as 40 or so sessions. The puzzle was clarified when a colleague, Wilfred Abse, who had known Wolpe at the University of Virginia, informed us that Wolpe was an excellent psychotherapist and treated some cases extensively to prepare them to begin behavior therapy.

After further experience we arrived at the concept that desensitization worked well in some instances simply by using the procedure to alleviate disturbing symptoms. These symptoms often originated with or were related to some disturbing event in the past. Although the person had matured, he or she was left with the continuation of a "ghost symptom" that took on a life of its own, even though the underlying dynamic that had led to it had been resolved. In other instances, as in the case of the patient with the cockroach phobia, it had been necessary to understand how the forces that led to the illness were continuing in her current life and needed to be dealt with in the desensitization process.

In the process of working with desensitization procedures, we began to encounter the phenomena of resistance and transference (Rhoads & Feather, 1972). As happened with Freud, we found them interfering with the orderly process of therapy, even to the extent of interrupting the treatment. Looking back at these failures, we realized that we were being too rigid in our pursuance of the method and that perhaps we should practice what we were advocating, namely to integrate therapy by interpreting resistances and transference resistances or to make use of positive transference or positive rapport to facilitate movement.

Needless to say some of my psychoanalytic colleagues were surprised and upset by my rapprochement with behavior therapies. One first-year resident in psychiatry even told my wife that it was impossible to mix dynamic and behavioral treatments, that it "just isn't kosher." He later became a close friend and believer in integration. Despite doubts, I was elected director of the UNC–Duke psychoanalytic program.

Meanwhile, a whirlwind of progress was being made both in behavior therapy itself and in the integration of dynamic and behavioral treatments. Work in London by Gelder and Marks and others at the Maudsley Hospital and by Meyer at Middlesex Hospital was particularly influential for us. In the United States we were especially impressed by the work of Birk, the Wachtels, Goldfried, Lazarus, Cautela, and Agras and began adopting some of their techniques. During this period Feather left Duke to become chairman of the Department of Psychiatry at Brown University, and to our dismay our collaboration came to an end because of the press of his new responsibilities.

Through the efforts of an enthusiastic and dedicated group of psychologists and psychiatrists, in particular Lee Birk, Marvin Goldfried, Jeanne Phillips, George Stricker, Paul Wachtel, and Barry Wolfe, the steps were taken to found the Society for the Exploration of Psychotherapy Integration (SEPI), an interdisciplinary organization aiming to "encourage communication and serve as a reference group of individuals interested in approaches to psychotherapy not necessarily associated with a single theoretical orientation" (SEPI, 1990–1991). Its first annual conference was held at Annapolis, Maryland, in 1985 and afforded me the wonderful opportunity to meet colleagues interested in developing effective, efficient, short-term psychotherapies that use an integrative approach. In addition to those mentioned above—as well as Wolpe, whom I had met privately—I was privileged to form collaborative relationships with Hal Arkowitz, Herbert Fensterheim, Mary FitzPatrick, Douglas Powell, and, at Duke, with Francis Keefe, who had been a student of Lee Birk. I gradually incorporated the ideas and techniques of all these therapists into my own practice.

From Fensterheim, I learned and adapted to my practice his approach to hyperventilation and breathing retraining. When we met at SEPI meetings, we often discussed our respective efforts to combine psychoanalytic concepts with behavioral principles. Mary FitzPatrick, who had been a student of Fensterheim, and I collaborated on several presentations at meetings of cases involving combined interventions. Douglas Powell, from the Student Health Service at Harvard, and I similarly collaborated on presentations of cases at meetings. I was impressed by how effectively he was able to deal with students by using an integrated approach to counseling. In Boston, Lee Birk created an integrated psychoanalytic and behavioral group therapy. Francis Keefe, a pupil of his, later moved to Duke, where he and I taught a course in behavior therapy for a number of years to psychiatric residents. He became a specialist in treatment of chronic pain problems, using educational and behavioral methods to help patients learn coping techniques to deal with chronic pain.

MY CURRENT APPROACH

By the time of my retirement, my practice varied from formal psycho-analysis to various forms of behavior therapy to combinations of the two. The methods could be merged in a number of ways (Rhoads, 1984). Treatment for a given patient could begin by either a psychodynamic or behavioral method, whichever seemed most appropriate for that person and was most acceptable to him or her. I found a behavioral method to be the best means of dealing with certain specific symptoms, habits, or inhibitions, particularly for ghost symptoms (which once served a useful psychological purpose but no longer did, the ego having matured in the meantime), some phobias, compulsions, and symptoms or symptom complexes that were dangerous or disabling to the patient. Often after the patient achieved a measure of control over the symptoms, he or she began spontaneously to allude to their origins, or to their dynamic underpinnings past and present. Then a switch could be made to a dynamic therapy.

I also used behavior therapy to supplement ongoing dynamic therapy, as in the case of ego deficits, and where the acquisition of new adaptations, such as assertiveness or social skills, was indicated. Behavior therapy could be chosen on the basis not of the symptomatology but of the core dynamic conflict. Analytic interpretations or explanations could be given to cope with resistances arising in the course of behavior therapy, especially in instances where transference appeared to be a potential negative influence.

I found a psychoanalytic or modified psychodynamic approach to be more effective in treating characterologic and narcissistic disorders and complex neurotic problems.

The advent of new drugs added still another dimension to psychotherapy. The use of tricyclic antidepressants to treat depressions enabled those patients to become accessible to psychotherapy, particularly cognitive–behavior therapy. The discovery that these same drugs could effectively block the unpredictable occurrence of panic attacks made it possible to deal more effectively with the underlying psychological problems that existed. Serotonin-specific reuptake inhibitors and related drugs for the therapy of severe obsessive–compulsive disorder have made possible the behavioral and dynamic treatment of some previously resistant cases. Similarly, the ability of antipsychotic drugs to control the manifestations of some psychoses enabled previously hopeless cases to become amenable to counseling and supportive therapy. As with the use of behavior therapy to control symptoms, the ability of drugs to do so allowed many people to benefit from various types of psychotherapy.

CONCLUSION

What factors enter into the evolution of a psychotherapist? In my own instance, I believe that a lifelong interest in literature and history and a curiosity regarding the motivations of literary figures and historical personages were predisposing factors. A sound scientific education as an undergraduate of Virginia Tech added a need to see logical procedures and confirmable results. My experiences as a medical and surgical intern taught me that many cases are complicated by psychological or social problems and may even render the best treatments ineffective. Entering psychiatry when I did, it was all too apparent that change and progress were desperately needed. Fortunately, much change has taken place.

Both during my residency and on entering private practice, the need for effective short-term psychotherapy became evident. Psychoanalysis provided a good basis for understanding motivation and how the mind works to protect itself—and all too often, to defeat itself in the process. It especially provided an understanding of the concepts of transference and resistance—unsuccessful treatment arising from the failure to deal with them. The advent of ego psychology furnished better comprehension of the function of the whole person. Few people needing therapy, however, could afford the long process of analysis, even if not prevented by considerations such as the time investment and job and family mobility. Influences that pointed to the feasibility of effective rapid learning were my experiences in the army, in teaching, in public clinics, and with hospitalized patients.

The advent of behavior therapy opened up a whole new world, both in the application of behavioral methods and in various combinations with psychodynamic principles. Somewhere along the way, it belatedly dawned on me that behavior therapy was not completely new and that I had even been involved in it. Recollection of my experience as a psychiatrist in the army at Ford Ord, where in 13 weeks raw recruits were trained to become infantry soldiers, made me realize that such training could be thought of as a form of behavior therapy. Similarly, observing the amazing training of sheep dogs on a trip to New Zealand, and even my training of our poodle, should have alerted me to the effectiveness of reward–nonreward education.

Retirement came in 1989—mandatorily, as my university was still tied to the age-70 rule (since changed). During the ensuing years I did some consulting and a number of temporary stints at mental health clinics and hospitals. I found psychiatry becoming limited to short-term episodes, often limited, for practical purposes, to drug therapies, with little opportunity for long-term follow-up. The burdensome paperwork has further decreased the amount of time available for patients. Even with these limitations, I found that psychotherapy can be effective.

It is saddening that so many HMOs have adopted the attitude that limiting psychiatric and psychologic treatment is for the good of the economy, when so much evidence shows that it saves money in the long run both in terms of greater productivity and quality of life. Recently a psychiatrist recounted to me that one of these organizations refused hospitalization of one of his patients who had attempted suicide, on the grounds that it was self-inflicted! At one time I consulted for Blue Cross, but the director at the time and I could never convince the board that prevention is less costly than cure. Let us hope that our politicians can see their way clear to ignoring lobbyists and legislating for mental health parity.

REFERENCES

Feather, B. W., & Rhoads, J. M. (1972a). Psychodynamic behavior therapy: I. Theory and rationale. *Archives of General Psychiatry, 26*, 496–502.

Feather, B. W., & Rhoads, J. M. (1972b). Psychodynamic behavior therapy: II. Clinical aspects. *Archives of General Psychiatry, 26*, 503–511.

Freud, S. (1938). The interpretation of dreams. In A. A. Brill (Ed.), *The basic writings of Sigmund Freud* (pp. 307–311). New York: Modern Library. (Original work published 1900)

Grinker, R. R., & Spiegel, J. P. (1944a). Brief psychotherapy in war neuroses. *Psychosomatic Medicine, 6*, 123–131.

Grinker, R. R., & Spiegel, J. P. (1944b). Narcosynthesis: Psychotherapeutic method for acute war neurosis. *Air Surgeon's Bulletin, 1*, 1–5.

Hadden, S. B. (1944). Group psychotherapy: A superior method of treating Langer numbers of neurotic patients. *American Journal of Psychiatry, 101*, 68–72.

Jackson, C. (1944). *Lost weekend.* New York: Rinehart.

Rhoads, J. M. (1984). Relationships between psychodynamic and behavior therapies. In H. Arkowitz & S. B. Messer (Eds.), *Psychoanalytic therapy and behavior therapy* (pp. 195–211). New York: Plenum Press.

Rhoads, J. M., & Feather, B. W. (1972). Transference and resistance observed in behaviour therapy. *British Journal of Medical Psychology, 45*, 99–103.

Society for the Exploration of Psychotherapy Integration. (1990–1991). Introduction. In *SEPI Directory.* Garden City, NY: Author.

Steiger, W. A., Hansen, A. V., & Rhoads, J. M. (1956). Experiences in the teaching of comprehensive medicine. *Journal of Medical Education, 31*, 241–248.

Weiss, E., & English, O. S. (1943). *Psychosomatic medicine.* Philadelphia: Saunders.

Wolpe, J. (1958). *Psychotherapy by reciprocal inhibition.* Stanford, CA: Stanford University Press.

5

HOW I LEARNED TO ABANDON CERTAINTY AND EMBRACE CHANGE

GEORGE STRICKER

My basic clinical education was psychodynamic.[1] My clinical training, both doctoral and postdoctoral, was psychodynamic. My supervision, both doctoral and postdoctoral, was psychodynamic. My personal treatment was psychodynamic. I have taught, supervised, and administered in a doctoral program for more than 35 years, and it is psychodynamic. I have been on the faculty and taught in a postdoctoral psychodynamic training program. I have supervised doctoral and postdoctoral students who are psychodynamic. I have published in psychodynamic journals and presented at psychodynamic meetings. I have been on the editorial board of a psychodynamic journal. I have been on the board of directors of Division 39 (Psychoanalysis) of the American Psychological Association. Yet I consider that psychotherapy

---

[1] *Psychoanalysis* is a heterogeneous term that embraces a variety of theoretical positions and approaches to interventions. The term *psychodynamic* is more generic and refers to the aspects of psychoanalysis that may be seen as held in common by the spectrum of psychoanalytic approaches. Wherever appropriate, the term *psychodynamic* is used throughout this chapter.

integration is my primary theoretical orientation. How did this happen to come about?

This chapter provides an unusual opportunity to reflect about professional development, particularly about aspects of development that led to my change in orientation toward the practice of psychotherapy. We contributors to this volume have been given an outline to follow for the sake of uniformity, and it delineates a comprehensive approach to professional development and experience. I will be glad to comply with the outline. Particularly in light of the psychodynamic orientation mentioned above, however, it is difficult to conceptualize professional change as being independent of personal change or to see personal change as beginning with professional education or centering on professional experience. Unlike Aristotle, who believed that our character is shaped by our works, I am inclined toward the belief that our works are shaped by our character, although there probably is a reciprocal relationship between the two. Therefore, before addressing the questions suggested by the outline, I offer a brief sketch about my preprofessional experiences that may have set the stage for my professional development.

EARLY DEVELOPMENT

Among my earliest memories are two that involve a time when my family had just moved to a new area and I, younger than 5 years old at the time, wandered around exploring the area and got lost. The affect in both cases was one of engagement in the wandering rather than fear, and there was no anticipation of any punishment because I felt certain that my return would be greeted with happiness. There also was no hint that the journey would end anywhere other than back home. The metaphor of a secure base that allows for exploration with faith that there will be a happy ending, even if the steps along the way are unpredictable, is a good framework for understanding my path to psychotherapy integration. The ways in which this operated should become clear as I trace this path in later sections.

Two activities made up the bulk of my growing-up years. First, I was a voracious and indiscriminate reader, who seemed to want to learn as much as possible about as much as possible. The goal of knowing everything was present for as long as the fantasy could be sustained, but the more I learned, the more clear it became that the fantasy never could be realized. Second, all my hours outside school and home were spent playing one type of team sport or another, and I often was the captain of the team, even though I was not the best player. Although much to my disappointment, I never could describe myself as a star athlete, I usually was a competent athlete who was comfortable with many sports and at most levels of competition.

The themes here are a love of learning, often for its own sake, coupled with social, competitive, and leadership objectives. They intersected when I discovered that I often could make up for physical shortcomings by intellectual achievements without abandoning the ball field that was so attractive to me. The same characteristics also operated throughout my professional career and had some influence on my move toward psychotherapy integration.

Finally, I had the good fortune to do my undergraduate studies at the University of Chicago. I began at a very young age (15), but the program was one that attracted younger people, so I did not feel as socially out of place as I was, because there was such a large group of equally young students with whom to huddle. At the time, Chicago did not have undergraduate majors. Every student was responsible for the same core curriculum, and that curriculum embraced most of the highlights of Western culture. We did not read textbooks; everything was primary sources, and the major intellectual value was on an inquiring, questioning attitude. It was here that I first read Freud, Erikson, and many other psychological thinkers, but they were introduced for their contributions to the history of ideas rather than to psychology per se. My love of learning was satisfied in a way that was unprecedented for me because it became disciplined for the first time. My athletic interests helped me make a social adjustment; it was, indeed, an incomparable period of time. I could indulge all my wishes without any responsibility beyond those things that I loved to do.

But this had to come to an end, and having no major also meant having no clear career direction. My education was in the shadow of the Korean War, so my choice, on graduation, was to go to graduate school or to be drafted and go into military service. The choice between these options was much easier than the choice as to which field the graduate school should be in. At various times, I had entertained thoughts of law school, doctoral studies in history, and even accounting (during an unusually practical but short-lived stage). The need to choose, however, coincided with an interest in psychology, and that is how careers often are chosen. I wish that an option such as the Peace Corps had been available because I would have enjoyed the experience and benefited from some time to think seriously about the rest of my life; but it was not, and I never have regretted the choice I made, as uninformed as it was.

LESSONS ORIGINALLY LEARNED

I entered the University of Rochester's doctoral program in clinical psychology in 1956. It was a scientist–practitioner program, which appealed to my wish to learn and to engage in the world, but there was little choice in 1956 but to enter a scientist–practitioner program. Similarly, there was little choice but to enter a program with a psychodynamic orientation. Behaviorism was not yet an important influence on clinical training, and Rogers, although a decided influence (particularly at the University of Chicago), had not entered the mainstream of clinical training.

The first clinical experience I had was a particularly formative one. As a first-year student at a local Veterans Administration hospital, I undertook the diagnostic testing of one of the patients. He was a pleasant young man who entered the room in an ebullient fashion, engaged with me readily, and, after responding to several Thematic Apperception Test cards, began to cry inconsolably. Having had little background in psychopathology, and this being the first patient I had ever seen, I did not recognize him as being bipolar. Instead, I wondered what I had done to upset him, how inept I was, and whether I had chosen an appropriate career. The only way to come to terms with these concerns was to learn all that I could, so that I would never make such a mistake again. The deficit clearly was in confidence and in knowledge (I did not have a great deal of either when it came to clinical work), but I could bolster both by developing an intellectual mastery of what I was doing. Or so I thought.

This, then, was the first lesson: Learn everything, so you never will be caught short and run the risk of hurting the people you were trying to assist. The second lesson was more specific: Everything that was done (or left undone) in a psychotherapy hour had a meaning. The teacher of this lesson was Howard Friedman, a remarkable and charismatic chief of psychology at the Syracuse Veterans Administration hospital. I remember presenting a case to Howard and having him ask me why I did something that I had done. I told him that it was an intuitive response, and he told me that mine was a lazy answer. Further examination did make the source of my "intuition" more clear, and the lesson was indelibly learned: Everything could be understood if only I worked hard enough and knew enough to achieve that understanding. Another lesson that was implicit but less clear at the time was that much of learning is influenced by people—supervisors, therapists, patients, and colleagues—not just by books.

Underlying all of those lessons was a psychodynamic framework. What there was to be learned and how interactions and interventions were to be understood were through a psychodynamic lens. At the time, the version of psychodynamics that was prominent was classical and Freudian, with some tempering by ego psychology. Everything I learned about how to be an effective therapist thus was equivalent to lessons in how to be an effective psychodynamic therapist. It was important for the therapist to be quiet until he or she had something to say, and what was said was generated by a psychodynamic understanding of the process of the treatment. Patients who wanted more from me were "resisting," and well-chosen interventions would pierce the resistance and lead to engagement in psychotherapy as I knew and practiced it. Not all of my patients read the same books as I did, and their resistance was so great that they left treatment, but the ones who remained were able to comply with my model and benefit from it. There were enough of them, particularly in our university clinic, that I felt secure in my approach, and feeling secure was important to someone who wanted to know everything and felt he knew nothing.

The process of therapeutic change was achieved, so I learned, through self-understanding. The goal was to make the unconscious conscious, and when people became aware of their motives, they would change their behavior. If they didn't, then the awareness must have been only intellectual, and the solution was to achieve greater and deeper awareness. Again, enough people were able to make significant changes within this model that I didn't dare to stop to think about those who did not. There were cases in which the patient was at fault for not complying with the rules of the game, and others in which I was at fault because I could not discover the intervention that would have turned the treatment around. (I was certain that Howard, and other acute supervisors, would have known what to do.) The model and the theory were never wrong, however, because considering that possibility would have undermined my sense of knowing what I was doing, and it was important to feel that I knew what I was doing, partly for characterological reasons and partly because of the awesome responsibility of working with people's lives.

STRENGTHS OF ORIGINAL ORIENTATION

Aspects of my original orientation work well to this day and continue to influence my work. Leaving aside the specifics of the theory, the metapsychology that provided such a stimulating arena for pedantic debate, there are several pillars of psychodynamic belief, and I still find them useful. One pillar is the central role of the unconscious. Behavior is motivated (perhaps this is an even more fundamental pillar), and we often are not aware of the motivation. The unconscious is not simply a repository of out-of-awareness cognitions that can be readily recalled but includes many that are beyond recollection without considerable introspective work, whether or not assisted by psychotherapy. In addition, these unconscious forces (motives and cognitions) often seek expression, so that the unconscious is a dynamic rather than a passive force. The expression often is in the form of symptomatology, which brings our patients to us, but it more often is in what Freud referred to as the "psychopathology of everyday life," so that every human expression is capable of being understood in ways more complex than are obvious on the surface. Thus, the unconscious is not necessarily to be feared, nor is it the sole province of the pathological, but it is an aspect of all of our lives. I learned this lesson early but have had it reinforced through personal experiences within and external to psychotherapy. It still provides the framework for my attempt to understand my patients.

A second pillar of psychodynamic work is historical determinism. Understanding contemporary behavior requires some understanding of past behavior. Everything has a history, and it is useful to know that history. The standard intervention—"When else have you felt this way?"—goes to the heart of this question about history. Again, I continue to believe in the importance of a thorough historical understanding if I am truly to understand any behavior, but I am not as clear that every behavior has to be thoroughly understood.

The final pillar of psychodynamic thought, one that I did not understand as clearly then as I do now, is the importance of the therapeutic relationship. This is phrased in terms of the therapeutic alliance and the central role of transference and countertransference (there are many different understandings of these concepts within psychodynamic theory) to the relationship. I continue to value the centrality placed on these aspects of the therapeutic process—perhaps even more now than before—and certainly understand them better. The key difference in my understanding probably can be traced to a greater willingness to accept my role in the process, without doing so in a guilt-ridden way, rather than to assume that the theory was central and that any failure in the treatment was a failure in my understanding (or implementation) of the theory. The latter approach had been comforting, because perfection always was possible, if only I knew enough.

LIMITATIONS OF ORIGINAL ORIENTATION

The primary limitation of the psychodynamic orientation, at least as I approached it, was not in the understanding it provided but in the role of understanding in the process. Perhaps because of this emphasis, a corollary limitation was not in what the psychodynamic orientation did, but in what it failed to do. There were too many patients who were not changing in ways that they and I would have liked, and it was not their resistance (fault). For that matter, it was not my fault insofar as the practice of psychodynamic psychotherapy goes; I was good at it. Rather, the problem was that the approach was not suitable for accomplishing behavior change in a wide variety of patients. My fault lay in my persistence in doing what did not work because to consider anything else would throw me back to a state where I no longer felt as though I knew what I was doing, and that would not have been acceptable.

I remember an older woman whom I assessed at Sheppard Pratt Hospital. She had been hospitalized because of increasing dementia-like behaviors (today she would be diagnosed as having Alzheimer's disease, but the term was not used as loosely then). As part of the test battery, I administered a Bender–Gestalt,[2] and predictably, she had a great deal of difficulty with it. She then looked at me and said, "You seem like such a nice boy. Tell me, from this you can make a living?" This was a diagnostic rather than therapeutic incident, but the question of the appropriateness of what I was doing for the needs of the patient was one that struck home. Yes, I was making a living, but was I doing the service that could be done for the people who placed their confidence in me?

Psychodynamic psychotherapy is good as a process for understanding human behavior, and understanding human behavior often is helpful for reaching a variety of goals that a patient may bring to the session. However, patients legitimately may have other goals than self-understanding, and the nitty-gritty of behavior change is not approached best, or most efficiently, through intense self-exploration. Even in situations where it may be the treatment of choice, the choice often is that of the therapist rather than of the patient, and the impasse that results is not simply resistance because the patient has no a priori reason to adopt the approach of the therapist. The more I tried to adopt the frame of reference of the patient and seek the goals defined by the patient, the more I found psychodynamic approaches to fall short. True, there were patients who had goals and styles fitting for psychodynamic work, and it was a pleasure to work with them, but psychotherapy should not be about the pleasure of the therapist. Increasingly, I found that I was understanding the patient through the familiar psychodynamic lens but that my interventions were ones that I would not happily discuss with colleagues or supervisors.

The best way of summarizing a central criticism of psychodynamic psychotherapy, at least as I viewed it, is that the patient is not to blame for the failure of the treatment. How often have psychotherapists described patients as unsuitable for treatment or simply as being "bad" patients? This is a remarkable example of blaming the victim, as though the patient is at fault for our inability to be helpful. If a patient comes to us therapists with a problem and we cannot work with it, either the treatment we have to offer is insufficient to the task or we are not competent in offering that treatment. In either case, it is inappropriate to ask the patient to change

---

[2] A diagnostic test that asks the patient to copy a series of designs.

ABANDONING CERTAINTY AND EMBRACING CHANGE   73

before we offer treatment because he or she has come to us for our help in accomplishing change.

HOW CHANGE OCCURRED

My process of change can be described as two interwoven processes, each of which probably was essential to my ability to change. The first process was professional and intellectual, and the second was personal. As noted above, I was feeling increasing dissatisfaction with my clinical work because of the number of patients who were not making the progress both the patient and I wished for them, despite my attempts to be a good psychodynamic psychotherapist. It was not because they were not good psychodynamic patients; they were not psychodynamic patients at all, and had no need or wish to be. Rather, the source of the difficulty was my Procrustean insistence that they all fit the model that I was comfortable with.

I found, to my dismay, that when the patients would not change, I began to deviate from what I had learned. There was nobody at that time with whom I felt I could talk because I was ashamed of what I was doing. My supervisors would have been aghast (I thought), and my colleagues, who probably were struggling with the same issues, were no more open than I was. In retrospect, we all were working out personal styles but doing so in a secret fashion, embarrassed by deviation from the true path. This is the therapeutic underground that is populated by people who have some sense of effective approaches but no willingness to go public with their unorthodox views.

Fortunately, I had a good friend who was not a psychodynamic psychotherapist. Mike Merbaum was rare in being a behavioral therapist at Adelphi University, and he and I collaborated on many professional projects while competing at everything from gin rummy to basketball. When we discussed cases, we were free to disagree widely, because we did have different orientations. Neither of us would give the other the satisfaction of letting on that we were listening, but we did. Without telling anyone (certainly not Mike), I began to experiment with some behavioral techniques, and I had interesting experiences with them. With some, such as systematic desensitization, I knew the literature and the wisdom of the approach, but it struck me as superficial and stupid, and so I never had any success with it. With other, more cognitive interventions, however, I understood their bases, was sympathetic with them, and, sure enough, had some success with them.

I gained several important lessons in these experiences. First, nothing works if the therapist does not believe in it. The ability to have faith and transmit hope is critical to change and is a common factor that underlies all change (Frank, 1973). Second, a remarkable number of interventions work if the therapist does believe in them. Third, the basis for this effectiveness therefore must be rooted in something other than the techniques themselves, such as the therapeutic alliance. I also found out something that struck me as peculiar at the time. My technique was becoming increasingly eclectic, but my understanding of the patient remained solidly based in a psychodynamic approach. It was not until more than a decade later that Stan Messer (1992) gave this the name "assimilative integration" and led me to recognize that what I was doing all along was not unique to me or a necessary source of shame.

The use of the literature to validate a personal process of change had begun to occur many years earlier. The first step in this direction was Paul Wachtel's (1977) watershed contribution, a demonstration that it was possible to be a good psychodynamic therapist and still profit from the incorporation of other approaches. The next important contribution to my change was a journal article by Marv Goldfried (1980) that made the theoretical basis for integration more clear—rapprochement did not mean abandoning the theory of origin, nor was it as simple as a difference in language for the same concepts, but it could be achieved at a strategic level. I then became active in the newly developed Society for the Exploration of Psychotherapy Integration (SEPI), an organization that provided a home for people who were struggling with the same issues that had bedeviled me for so long. Presentations at SEPI meetings were helpful and affirming, but regular exchange with people who had the same dark secret I had was even more important. Finally, along with Jerry Gold, I edited a volume (Stricker & Gold, 1993) that gave me the opportunity to review a wide variety of contributions to the growing area of psychotherapy integration, each of which was stimulating and challenging, even if quite different. This helped me recognize that I was involved not in a search for a new religion but in a process that would provide a continuing sense of growth and change, at the expense of no certainty other than the wisdom of engaging in the search.

At the same time as this intellectual search was occurring, I found that my practice was changing. I experienced myself as far more active than I had been trained to be. (My patients, nonetheless, still commented that I wouldn't tell them what to do, so there was no point asking, but they didn't know how much more I was talking than I had previously. I'm sure the amount was more than my patients recognized and less than I thought.) My changed approach did not lead to any noticeable decrement in the progress that the patients were making; on the contrary, they seemed responsive and appreciative of being able to speak to a real person rather than to someone who was hiding behind a professional role (or so I perceived my previous self). In addition, although clearly a secondary benefit, I was more comfortable as I became less artificial and mannered in the way I conducted myself. There were still patients with whom I was relatively quiet and reflective, but there were others with whom I engaged fully and frequently. The difference was not in any specific behavior as much as it was in the heterogeneity of my therapeutic interventions, which now seemed more geared to the needs of each person rather than to the needs of a theory. (At this stage, it was critical to be sure that I was being guided by the needs of each patient and not simply by my own needs, a principle that remains important to me.)

At one time, I would have seen what I was doing as acting out and satisfying my own needs at the expense of the therapeutic process. I sometimes still wonder whether that is what I am doing; the danger is that the excuse of flexibility can mask an undisciplined and indiscriminate spontaneity that may not further the therapeutic process. As long as I can maintain what I have learned to call an "observing" ego, however, and reflect on what I am doing and why I am doing it (the old lesson that everything in the session has a reason still holds for me), I think the danger of acting out is reduced. The easier exchanges are not gossip between friends, but a joint search conducted by two people with a similar goal. The use of a variety of interventions allows more opportunity for change and growth in the patient than the more limited repertoire I previously displayed. The important underlying factor is a continuing need for me to try to understand what is going on, even if the patient does not; I still find a psychodynamic framework most useful for accomplishing this goal. The challenge is to try to understand why interventions that are not consistent with that framework seem to be so effective and what that says about the need for the theoretical framework to expand.

A personal experience also had a profound effect on my commitment to the value of a panoply of possible approaches. I have described this incident in a bit more detail elsewhere (Stricker, 1995). After the 1994 SEPI conference, which was held in Buenos Aires, Argentina, a small group of colleagues went to Iguazu Falls, a magnificent waterfall north of Buenos Aires. The hope of enjoying this experience conflicted with a discomfort with heights that I have experienced throughout my adult life, an anxiety that had not been altered by extensive approaches to understanding. I presented this conflict to Marv Goldfried, who accompanied me on that trip, and he promptly taught me a series of breathing and imaginal exercises that enabled me to cope with the heights and enjoy the falls thoroughly. Others in the group became caught up in my dilemma and responded with additional suggestions and a great deal of support, and I also see that as quite relevant to my therapeutic success. At this point 5 years later, I still do not relish the opportunity to peer down from heights, but I can do it far more easily than I used to. I have learned to use the exercises when I feel the old anxiety, and they still work, so the cure, such as it was, has proven to last over time without any obvious symptom substitution or relapse. Here was a real-life problem that had been resistant to insight but was solved rapidly and successfully with a simple solution. How could I continue to deny my patients that same benefit?

One more issue was critical to the process of change: the personal value that theory had for me. It always has been important for me to feel that I knew what I was doing, and psychodynamic theory gave me assurance that there was meaning to everything and that I had a way of understanding that meaning. To some extent, I have not lost that conviction. However, a corollary of that principle for me had been that theory and technique were inextricably connected, so psychodynamic understanding necessitated psychodynamic techniques. There was something comforting in that conviction because I knew not only what was going on but what to do about it. Unfortunately, the patients did not know and did not respond as well as I was led to expect that they would. At that point, I felt as though I had four choices: (a) ignore what seemed so obvious by branding the patients I had lost as resistant, (b) restrict my practice so that I only saw patients who were responsive to and wished to pursue the approach that I preferred, (c) reject the psychodynamic approach because it was not a panacea, or (d) expand the range of techniques that I used so that I could be more responsive to the patients who sought my services.

The first choice, the ostrich technique, was not possible for me; I already had seen too much and could not ignore it. The second choice was not possible practically, and it probably is not possible for most practitioners, especially in the age of managed care. Furthermore, it would not have been a satisfying choice even if it had been feasible because I prefer a wider range of activities than that would have allowed. The third choice struck me as akin to throwing out the baby with the bathwater; there was too much that I found of value in psychodynamic theory for me to abandon it unless there were no alternatives. The fourth option, the one I chose, required a decisive recognition, one that usually is not taught directly. It involved the disentangling of theory and technique and the recognition that each intervention is a theory–technique unit, with the relationship between the two not necessarily one of identity. This allowed a movement toward assimilative integration for me, and it is a change that I have found useful and, I think, one that my patients have found helpful.

As long as I could retain a sense that I knew something about what was going on in the session, I became less wedded to a rigid application of a single set of interventions. The idea of the need to maintain a strict therapeutic frame, deviation from which would lead to predictable and deleterious effects on the treatment (e.g., Langs, 1973, 1976), no longer was tenable. I still believe that Langs is one of the most helpful writers when it comes to understanding what is occurring in the session, but he is not nearly as helpful when it comes to recommendations about what then to do. When I freed myself to supplement my understanding with a wider variety of techniques, each of which was personally comfortable and not out of line with the understanding I had of therapeutic process, I had less certainty in each individual act but much confidence in the cluster of interventions that I was using. I always have felt that the ability to tolerate ambiguity may be the single most important trait for a prospective psychotherapist to have, and abandoning a single coherent approach for a less clearly defined one provides a stringent test of that tolerance.

MY CURRENT APPROACH

My current approach to psychotherapy is best described as an assimilative, psychodynamic approach (Stricker & Gold, 1996). This approach is predicated on a three-tier conception of personality structure and change (Gold & Stricker, 1993; Stricker & Gold, 1988). In this system, the first tier involves overt behavior; the second cognition, affect, perception, and sensation; and the third unconscious mental processes and their attendant motives, conflicts, images, and representations. Much of the work is based on formulations within the psychodynamic model characterized by the third tier, but interventions are widely drawn and directed at all three tiers. A significant influence on this approach comes from cyclical psychodynamics, as described by Wachtel (1977; Gold & Wachtel, 1993) and by Ryle (1990) in his cognitive–analytic therapy.

The major departure from more traditional psychodynamic thought is in the use of a multidimensional and circular model rather than a unidimensional model. Rather than insight leading directly to change and therefore directing interventions toward promoting insight, this model views change as resulting from several potential factors, including insight, and insight is seen as resulting from several potential factors, including change. Thus, interventions originate at any of the tiers and aim to produce change directly. As a result, an active intervention not only can lead directly to behavior change but also can lead indirectly to an effect on the third, dynamic tier. Resistance and defense can be handled through interpretation where appropriate but also may be approached through an active change in one of the first two tiers, which then will cast new light on the issue and may lead to a relaxation of the defense. This, in turn, can facilitate further behavioral or cognitive change, and so the circular process moves on in a synergistic fashion. Note that behavioral interventions may not be effective in some situations until some psychodynamic interventions have set the stage and prepared the patient to experiment with change in an area that has some symbolic meaning, which may not be readily apparent until the depth work is undertaken.

A description of how I currently work is easy and has been reported in several of the articles previously referenced as well as summarized briefly above (e.g., Stricker & Gold, 1996). It is far more difficult to address the question concerning the process of change. Initially, I was content with a goal of making the unconscious conscious, with the conviction that this would promote self-understanding, which, inexorably, would lead to behavioral change. Sometimes such a model works, but it has become abundantly clear that it is neither necessary nor sufficient. However, what can this formulation be replaced with?

Research repeatedly shows that psychotherapy is effective (e.g., Luborsky, Singer, & Luborsky, 1975; Smith, Glass, & Miller, 1980) but that there are no clear and repeatable differences among the various approaches to psychotherapy. This poses a clear challenge to any simple statement of mutative factors because other orientations, absent those factors (such as insight) seem to get similar results. Three considerations now guide my view of change and supplement insight as a central mechanism because I now believe that insight is helpful but not critical. (At times, I also believe that insight may be magic, but this view is neither helpful nor satisfactory.) First, change is not unidirectional; any change, whether it is at the behavioral, cognitive, or dynamic tier, can lead to changes at other tiers. Second, change is synergistic: Change of any sort can facilitate other changes. Finally, we as psychotherapists do not give sufficient attention to the world around the patient. The one-person psychology of early psychodynamic formulations has given way to a newer emphasis on a two-person psychology, but neither approach attends to the world in which the person lives. I have become more attuned to the necessity of considering the role of the patient's friends, family, and associates in maintaining and enabling the problems that bring the person to treatment; if we do not consider those factors, many changes that occur in the room will not generalize beyond it. This understanding has led to a new focus on the time and activities outside the consulting room, which includes the value of homework and the necessary consideration, either imaginally or through role playing, of the reaction of others, both real and imagined, to any change that the patient is contemplating.

As a result of these changes in my way of working and thinking, I have grown to a point at which I can do better work, but I understand that work less well than I did previously. As long as my patients do better, that is tolerable, but I do wish for a time when I could have the certainty of old coupled with the efficacy of the newer approach. Perhaps that is an impossible dream, and for now, I am content with the process as I currently experience it.

CONCLUSION

It has been a long, strange trip, and the moral of the story is that the trip is not over and never should be. Learning, much like psychotherapy, is a process rather than a product, and when learning stops, it also has failed. Understanding this premise implies a recognition that perfection and certainty are impossible and that we therapists must do the best we can and be content to be "good enough."

In reading this chapter over so that I could decide how to conclude, I was struck by the absence of any reference to the science of psychology. I regret that, both because it is a telling omission and because it probably reflects the state of the art. There are some important contributions of science, and I indirectly referred to them when I talked of the value of learning what there was to know. However, the most important role of science in psychotherapy, I have come to believe, is for the psychotherapist to have the attitude of a scientist, to function as a local clinical scientist (Stricker & Trierweiler, 1995; Trierweiler & Stricker, 1998), and to carry the same attitudes of curiosity, inquisitiveness, dedication, and self-reflection into the consulting room that the scientist displays in the laboratory. As long as that attitude can be maintained, learning will continue, and as long as learning continues, both the practice of psychotherapy and the welfare of the patient will be enhanced.

REFERENCES

Frank, J. D. (1973). *Persuasion and healing* (2nd ed.). Baltimore: Johns Hopkins University Press.

Gold, J. R., & Stricker, G. (1993). Psychotherapy integration with personality disorders. In G. Stricker & J. R. Gold (Eds.), *Comprehensive handbook of psychotherapy integration* (pp. 323–336). New York: Plenum Press.

Gold, J. R., & Wachtel, P. L. (1993). Cyclical psychodynamics. In G. Stricker & J. R. Gold (Eds.), *Comprehensive handbook of psychotherapy integration* (pp. 59–72). New York: Plenum Press.

Goldfried, M. R. (1980). Toward the delineation of therapeutic change principles. *American Psychologist, 35,* 991–999.

Langs, R. (1973). *The technique of psychoanalytic psychotherapy* (Vol. 1). New York: Aronson.

Langs, R. (1976). *The therapeutic interaction: Vol. II. A critical overview and synthesis.* New York: Aronson.

Luborsky, L., Singer, B., & Luborsky, L. (1975). Comparative studies of psychotherapies: Is it true that "Everyone has won and all must have prizes"? *Archives of General Psychiatry, 32,* 995–1008.

Messer, S. B. (1992). A critical examination of belief structures in interpretive and eclectic psychotherapy. In J. C. Norcross & M. R. Goldfried (Eds.), *Handbook of psychotherapy integration* (pp. 130–165). New York: Basic Books.

Ryle, A. (1990). *Cognitive–analytic therapy: Active participation in change.* Chichester, England: Wiley.

Smith, M. L., Glass, G. V., & Miller, T. I. (1980). *The benefits of psychotherapy.* Baltimore: Johns Hopkins University Press.

Stricker, G. (1995). Comment: Confessions of a reformed psychodynamicist. *Journal of Psychotherapy Integration, 5,* 266–267.

Stricker, G., & Gold, J. (1988). A psychodynamic approach to the personality disorders. *Journal of Personality Disorders, 2,* 350–359.

Stricker, G., & Gold, J. (Eds.). (1993). *Comprehensive handbook of psychotherapy integration.* New York: Plenum Press.

Stricker, G., & Gold, J. R. (1996). Psychotherapy integration: An assimilative, psychodynamic approach. *Clinical Psychology: Science and Practice, 3,* 47–58.

Stricker, G., & Trierweiler, S. J. (1995). The local clinical scientist: A bridge between science and practice. *American Psychologist, 50,* 995–1002.

Trierweiler, S. J., & Stricker, G. (1998). *The scientific practice of professional psychology.* New York: Plenum Press.

Wachtel, P. L. (1977). *Psychoanalysis and behavior therapy: Toward an integration.* New York: Basic Books.

6

AN (INEVITABLY) SELF-DECEIVING REFLECTION ON SELF-DECEPTION

PAUL L. WACHTEL

At some point in my education as a psychologist, I learned that memories are never simply the retrieval of a record accurately laid down at the time but are inevitably constructions, based on fragmentary impressions and significantly influenced by the circumstances and vantage point of the present. Why should the account I am offering here be any different?

If there is anything at all valid in my fundamental views of how the mind works, then my account of how I have come to those fundamental views must be powerfully biased and flawed. Conversely, if what I am writing in this chapter is accurate, then it is an accurate account of a life of error. Only if I am significantly deceiving myself, if my recollections are self-serving and self-protective, if I am misreading what I experienced then in the light of how I see things now, is there any possibility that the ideas I discuss in this chapter have any value. For such capacity for self-deception, such inability really to simply "remember," lies close to the heart of my thinking about human psychology, and (if I remember accurately!) it has lain at the heart of my views from the earliest years of my training as a psychologist.

We are here, of course, in the realm of paradox and contradiction, a realm that has been my comfort zone for quite a few years but that—in contrast to the views just expressed—probably was not a significant part of my thinking about psychotherapy in the early years of my career (although its cousin, conflict, already was). In what follows, I largely proceed as though I can offer accurate recollections and convey my earlier views untainted by the ways in which I now "know better." That will, of course, be a snare and a delusion, but this is all the warning, dear reader, that you will receive. From this point on, it is my job to play the role of omniscient (if first-person) narrator, and it is your job, in turn, to misinterpret and misconstrue what I say in light of your own biases, blind spots, hobby horses, favorite theories, and internalized objects (if you will). Rest assured, yours is an easy job; indeed, if this chapter is at all worth reading, it is a job at which you cannot fail.

LESSONS ORIGINALLY LEARNED

My interest in self-deception—an interest that persists strongly to this day—was part of a larger set of ideas that were part of the psychoanalytic approach in which I was originally trained. Some of those ideas remain compelling to me today, and others felt problematic even in my student days.

The version of psychoanalysis in which I was originally trained was primarily that of psychoanalytic ego psychology, modified by a simultaneous exposure to the stimulus–response learning theory of Clark Hull and its applications to psychoanalysis by John Dollard and Neil Miller, both of whom were at Yale University during the years I was in graduate school.

Whereas the psychoanalytic ideas took root immediately—if filtered through my seemingly constitutional skepticism about any versions of received wisdom—I was never even a closet Hullian. But aspects of the Hullian ideas predominant in the more academic side of Yale at the time did stay with me in certain respects, especially as they were translated by Dollard and Miller. Perhaps the most influential was the concept of extinction. Although I regard extinction as more a name for a phenomenon than an explanation, I continue to find the extinction metaphor extremely useful in my thinking about the therapeutic process. The idea that repeated exposure to an experience without the anticipated consequences can change the meaning of that experience guides much of my work, especially as applied to experiences that are anxiety provoking.

In the main, however, my focus and my identity in my graduate school years centered on psychoanalysis. Sid Blatt, who at various points was my professor, the head of my internship program (at the Yale Psychiatric Institute), and my dissertation adviser, was an empathic and impassioned guide to this realm. Also influential in those years were George Mahl, who taught an extraordinarily thorough course on psychoanalytic theory, and both Roy Schafer and Ernst Prelinger, each of whom taught a clinical seminar during the year I was on internship. The ideas of David Rapaport; of Anna Freud; and of Heinz Hartmann, Ernst Kris, and Rudolph Loewenstein were particularly emphasized by my teachers.

Also emphasized—and especially influential in my own thinking—was Erik Erikson. Erikson's thinking captivated me because it was much more "experience near" than that of the other thinkers just noted; it was much more concerned with people and their feelings and experiences than with "representations" and mental apparatuses. Erikson also, of course, paid much more detailed attention to culture and history, and his influence was no doubt significant in my own later choice to apply what I had learned in addressing psychotherapy and personality theory to addressing cultural trends and social problems (e.g., P. L. Wachtel, 1983, 1999). I got to meet Erikson a few times years later, when we were both members of the Rapaport–Klein Study Group, a relatively small group of psychoanalytic theorists and researchers that meets each year in Stockbridge, Massachusetts. I was a rather junior member of the group at that time, and he was, of course, a world-renowned thinker; but he conveyed a sense of respect and genuine interest that I appreciated enormously. In my own dealings with younger colleagues, I have tried to emulate his humane and respectful stance.

Erikson served as a bridge to my later thinking in another way as well. What one might call the geopolitics of psychoanalysis cast him as a member of the school of psychoanalytic ego psychology, the mainstream of American psychoanalysis at the time. That was the club he belonged to. But his ideas seemed to me to fit better with those of the interpersonalist or culturalist school of Karen Horney, Harry Stack Sullivan, Erich Fromm, and their followers. As my interest in the latter point of view grew over the years (see below), Erikson served as a link between these newer elements in my thinking and the point of view in which I was originally trained.

It seems to me in retrospect that my education as a psychologist at Yale was much broader than my education as a psychotherapist. Most of the elements of my later integrative thinking were in some form introduced or foreshadowed by the varied perspectives that I omnivorously devoured as a graduate student. But my early training in the practice of psychotherapy proceeded along rather traditional psychoanalytic lines, if couched (so to speak) in up-to-date theoretical terminology for the times. Indeed, one of the difficulties with psychoanalysis as a body of thought and practice is that it often has combined rather daring and innovative theorizing with rather conservative persistence in only glacially changing practice. New developments in theory and new incorporations of research findings have seemed to provide increasingly sophisticated and varied rationales and justifications for essentially the same way of proceeding. There are hopeful signs that this is finally beginning to change, but it is by no means an issue that has been rendered moot.

The approach to the therapeutic enterprise that I learned had a complex structure of interrelated assumptions—some explicit and carefully thought out, and others implicit, not necessarily acknowledged, but no less powerful or influential for that (a point, of course, which no self-respecting psychoanalyst ought to be inclined to dispute). Among the implicit but unmistakable assumptions was that psychoanalysis was unambiguously the most profound and effective of the psychotherapies and that even psychoanalytically oriented psychotherapy (in contrast to psychoanalysis proper) ought to strive to be as much like psychoanalysis as possible. Necessities of patients' limited time, motivation, or resources (whether ego or financial) might make psychoanalytic psychotherapy the treatment of choice rather than psychoanalysis, but the former would be most effective the more it could be made to resemble the latter (see P. L. Wachtel, 1987, chap. 12).

The more explicit features of the approach I was taught reflected the continuing evolution of the psychoanalytic vision. The idea of making the unconscious conscious originated in the earliest stages in the development of Freud's thinking, when what was to be made conscious was thought to be memories of actual traumatic events. As is well known and recently controversial, Freud concluded rather early in his career that most memories of traumas were not literal memories but recollections that reflected the traces of wishful fantasies. As psychoanalytic theory developed in response to this newer idea, the focus of what was to be made conscious shifted, but the aim of bringing to consciousness what had been repressed remained central. It was certainly a cornerstone of how I was taught to do therapy: Insight was the royal road to cure, especially to "structural change," that special kind of cure thought to be obtainable only by a full and rigorous analysis.

The conception of insight emphasized by my teachers, however, was a sophisticated one. The distinction between intellectual and emotional insight was addressed clearly, with only the latter thought to be significantly related to change. Moreover, a second organizing slogan, as it were, was added to "making the unconscious conscious." With the introduction of the concept of the ego and the beginnings of psychoanalytic ego psychology, Freud introduced a new principle for the process of psychoanalysis as a therapy: "Where id was, there ego shall be." This conception was rooted in the accruing observations about the importance and complexity of defensive processes. Making the unconscious conscious without altering the defensive efforts that made the experience unconscious in the first place would have little permanent benefit. The patient would again "forget" or "misunderstand" or in one way or another resubmerge the all too fragile and temporary insight. "Defense analysis" or "resistance analysis" became increasingly the centerpiece of the therapeutic enterprise. It was this approach to insight and working through that was emphasized by my teachers and characterized my practice at the beginning of my career.[1]

Other key features of the approach I was taught are closely related to the elements I have discussed thus far. Therapy was conceptualized as a largely interpretive enterprise. The therapist's task was in large measure to uncover or recover hidden meanings. In one sense, this is just another way of talking about making the unconscious conscious. But it does not completely overlap this idea. It can point as well, for example, to a trend that has become increasingly prominent in contemporary psychoanalytic discourse and, indeed, in the larger sphere of psychotherapy beyond the psychoanalytic tradition. I am referring to the constructivist bent that has become increasingly evident in recent years—the view that psychotherapy is in large measure a meaning-making activity. Patients today often are seen as suffering both from a sense of meaninglessness (in the depressive or existential sense) and from the confusion and lack of clear direction that come from not being able to "make sense" of their experience. At the time I was first learning to do psychotherapy, interpretation was almost universally understood to be a seeking after the "true" meanings that had been submerged or distorted by defensive processes. Today, however, increasing numbers of psychoanalytic therapists view interpretations as offering but one of a number of possible interpretations or constructions of events. An interpretation, from this vantage point, is therapeutic if it either (a) enables the patient to see things differently, giving him[2] a new handle on his experience that is less disturbing or more likely to lead to effective behavior, or (b) simply gives some meaning to a set of experiences that were experienced previously as chaotic or incoherent (see, e.g., Hoffman, 1991; and Spence, 1982).

Consistent with the earlier, more literal notions of interpretations as conveyors of truth, the therapist was cautioned, in the model I was first taught, to be "neutral," to strive for a kind of anonymity, to not talk too much, and to refrain as much as possible from answering questions directly or giving advice. There were a number of nested rationales for these recommendations, some ethical as much as technical, but they all related to the effort not to interfere with or muddy the material that supposedly was spontaneously emerging or unfolding from the patient's unconscious (see P. L. Wachtel, 1987, chaps. 11 & 12).

Especially central in this regard were the rules associated with a particular kind of interpretation—the interpretation of transference. For the patient

---

[1] See P. L. Wachtel (1993, especially chap. 7) for a more detailed discussion of this principle and my changing views of its implications.
[2] For clarity of meaning and construction, I use male pronouns to refer in the abstract to the "patient" and female pronouns to refer to the "therapist."

to see that his transferential perceptions of the therapist were distortions, it was essential that the therapist not really do anything that would "justify" the patient's perception. Then the patient could begin to recognize the ways he distorts in the present on the basis of imagos from the past and could begin, eventually, to correct those distortions. This view was given its most sophisticated articulation by Gill (1954), who, interestingly, a few decades later was among the leading figures promoting a rethinking of the nature of transference and criticizing the idea that the patient's perceptions were not related to the reality of the patient–therapist relationship (e.g., Gill, 1982, 1984).

STRENGTHS OF ORIGINAL ORIENTATION

As apparent below, over the years I had many bones to pick with the ideas and methods I was originally taught. But I am enormously grateful in many ways to have had the opportunity to begin my training with a strong psychoanalytic foundation. Messer (1992) argued that efforts at integration in psychotherapy largely are structured on an assimilative basis: One starts from a home orientation and assimilates new ideas into the original structure, changing in the process both the new ideas and the old. For me, that original structure was a psychoanalytic one, and the "cyclical psychodynamic" version of an integrative approach that I have developed (and is discussed in more detail below) does not come by its family name illegitimately.

To begin with, I have always thought that the psychoanalytic approach views the phenomena of human behavior and experience with both a subtlety and a breadth of vision that are significantly greater than that of most other approaches, which are more likely to stick to the surface of experience, to view the world through overly rationalistic lenses, or to exhibit considerably less daring in their aims. The advantages for psychoanalysis, however, do not come without significant costs. When it comes to studying human behavior and experience, there is often a trade-off between how clearly grounded in systematic research an idea is and how interesting or important it is. I have encountered disturbing complacency and epistemological flaccidity in much psychoanalytic discourse; the tendency to support a theoretical statement by citing a well-known author's (equally nonempirical) theoretical statement or to couch questionable ideas in the protective coloration of obscure language or jargon that substitutes for genuine critical thought can be embarrassingly prevalent. But knowledge often is advanced in important ways by attending to intuitively grasped coherences that are not yet accessible to operational definitions (Bowers, 1981; Polanyi, 1958). In addition, damn it, psychoanalytic discussions often are just plain more interesting!

Also of continuing value to me in the approach I initially learned is its emphasis on understanding individuals' lives in detail and in depth. It offered a particularly strong emphasis on understanding people's subjectivity and on discerning meaning and intentionality in human behavior and experience. It emphasized as well the value and importance of listening to people, of hearing the complexity of what they were conveying and not leaping to interventions or to offering advice on the basis of premature or simplistic understanding. This latter strength is the flip side of what is also a weakness; it can lead to a hesitancy to intervene at all, to a therapy that has become so good at asking still more questions that it has become phobic about providing answers.

I also am grateful for my original training for its emphasis on respect for configurational evidence. Here again, there is a flip side. Many analysts forget their own premises about the readiness with which we make our perceptions conform to what we need or expect; they exhibit little appreciation of the need to complement this methodology with attention to the kinds of evidence that are more the strong suit of academic psychology. But it is important to appreciate that attention to the types of configurational evidence that guide disciplines such as history can be of value not only in the context of discovery but also in the context of justification. Some phenomena cannot be studied rigorously without attention to such evidence, and failure to appreciate its significance can lead to superficiality and a constricted picture of the possibilities of psychological inquiry.

Finally, I especially value the attention to unconscious phenomena of many sorts and to conflict in particular, which is a central feature of the approach I originally learned. Although recent trends in psychoanalytic theorizing have at times seemed to make conflict less central, conflict is a crucial key to useful understanding. Many errors in therapeutic technique (both by therapists of psychoanalytic persuasion and by nonpsychoanalytic therapists) derive from insufficient attention to conflict (P. L. Wachtel, 1993).

LIMITATIONS OF ORIGINAL ORIENTATION

From the beginning, despite my fascination with the psychoanalytic way of viewing human behavior and experience, aspects of psychoanalytic practice seemed problematic to me. One crucial difficulty centered on the difference between insights that are merely verbal and those that are genuinely experiential. It seemed that notwithstanding the absolutely central role of emotion in psychoanalytic thought, in actual practice psychoanalysis often was too verbal and intellectualized.[3]

I was consequently attracted to the work of Franz Alexander (e.g., 1963) and Thomas French (e.g., Alexander & French, 1946), work that was unfortunately disparaged by the psychoanalytic community. I thought Alexander and French's idea of the corrective emotional experience was a valuable reconceptualization of how the psychoanalytic process really worked when it was effective. The emphasis on emotion and on experience was at once a corrective to a prevalent failing in standard psychoanalytic work and a distillation of what was valuable and effective in the best psychoanalytic practice. I agreed strongly with Alexander's view that psychoanalysis had become sidetracked by an excessive attachment to the clinical method that had been developed early in the evolution of psychoanalysis. I also agreed with his view that ironically such an attachment actually sold psychoanalysis short, failing to capitalize fully on the enormous potential inherent in psychoanalytic ideas and discoveries. Whereas most psychoanalysts viewed the method that had come to be called "psychoanalysis" (in contrast to psychoanalytic psychotherapy) as the Rolls Royce of therapies, Alexander in essence viewed the received methods as more equivalent to the Model T: an innovation of great historical importance but by no means the present state of the art—or, in the case of psychoanalysis, by no means the most effective application of psychoanalytic principles and of what had been learned from decades of psychoanalytic inquiry.

It is interesting to note that both Alexander (e.g., 1963) and French (e.g., 1933) were early proponents as well of the fruitfulness of viewing psychoanalytic ideas and methods from the vantage point of learning theory, thereby constructing a bridge, as Dollard and Miller did from a different vantage point, to the possibility of a more comprehensive and integrative therapeutic approach.

I also was strongly attracted to the work of the interpersonalists, especially that of Horney and Sullivan, as further correctives to the limitations I saw in the more mainstream psychoanalytic approach. Psychoanalysis seemed too internal in its focus. Its enormously valuable insights into the depths and divisions of subjectivity were limited by its failure to integrate the equally powerful impact of current interactions with other people and of the larger social order. The impact of social and economic position, of

---

[3]In later years, I had similar concerns about cognitive therapy. It was largely for this reason, to the surprise of many who knew and followed my work, that I continued to find the original versions of behavior therapy more congenial and useful to the integration I was forging than the newer, more cognitive versions, notwithstanding the latter's apparent closer match to the mediational and representational emphases of psychoanalysis. The introduction of a cognitive perspective was an advance for behavior therapy, but not necessarily for a behavioral–psychodynamic integration (see P. L. Wachtel, 1997, chap. 16, for a further discussion of this issue).

racism, privilege, social values, generational and peer influences, and so forth all seemed insufficiently woven into mainstream psychoanalytic thought, and the work of Horney and Sullivan, along with that of Fromm, Erikson, and others, provided a valuable foundation for reconstructing both psychoanalysis and social thought (see P. L. Wachtel, 1983, 1987, 1999). Psychoanalysis, it seemed to me, actually could be deepened if its conception of depth could relinquish the vision of an "internal world" sealed off from the larger world of social and societal interaction.

Finally, in an area related to the above considerations, I increasingly came to be dissatisfied with the way psychoanalysts conceptualized and understood the process of therapeutic change. The nature of those dissatisfactions became clear only gradually, but my encounter with behavior therapy (described below) was a crystallizing experience that led not only to the incorporation of methods and perspectives from that realm but also to a reexamination of precisely what my own understanding was of the nature of psychoanalysis itself—its discoveries, its assumptions, its essentials, its false starts and unnecessary features, and its implications for the process of change and healing.

HOW CHANGE OCCURRED

As in psychotherapy, change in the evolution of a theoretical point of view is rarely a matter of a sudden "aha" experience. Looking back, I can trace the roots of my current point of view, and even of its challenges to my original perspectives and commitments, in the very premises and experiences that eventually were reworked. Given that I am an advocate of integrative thinking, that path should not be surprising. I did not reject most of the ideas I was originally taught. Rather, I reworked them, casting them into a new form that enabled them to be combined with valuable ideas and observations that had been excluded from the psychoanalytic vision.

The process of change began well before I began to consider seriously the potential value of behavior therapy as a complement to the psychoanalytically oriented therapy I had been practicing. Even in graduate school, I was troubled by certain features of the psychoanalytic approach I was learning, especially its tendency to pathologize people and to categorize them as stuck at a particular developmental "level." This was part of the appeal of Erikson and of the interpersonalists. Erikson offered a way of thinking that was just as "deep" as the more prevalent psychoanalytic formulations but had a much more accepting tone and positive vision of human nature; along with Sullivan and Horney, he was much less disposed to treat the cultural and interpersonal realities a person encounters as superficial or irrelevant.

When I began my postdoctoral psychoanalytic training at New York University (NYU), I found myself still further drawn to the interpersonal point of view.[4] From my interpersonally oriented supervisors I learned to be much more active in my questioning, enabling me to notice coherences and connections that I had been able to overlook when relying more exclusively on free association and the patient's spontaneous outpourings. When I looked much more closely at the concrete details of the patient's interactions with others, I was increasingly struck by how regularly the patterns in my patients' lives could be seen as vicious circles, in which each party in the relationship brought out in the other precisely the behavior that would keep it going and internal states generated behavioral outcomes that tended to re-evoke those same internal states.

This was the first crucial step on my path to what I finally called "cyclical psychodynamics." The next step was a much larger and more difficult one. It required me to confront a set of taboos that were by then both internal and external. I had learned little about behavior therapy in my training up till then, but I had learned one crucial point: It was not worth learning more. Behavior therapy, I had picked up, was superficial, manipulative, insensitive to human complexity. It was technocratic, pseudo-scientific, and incapable of leading to genuinely profound or durable changes. It was thus more than a little surprising to find myself, in a few short years, an advocate of the clinical and theoretical value of integrating a behavioral perspective and behavioral interventions into psychoanalytic work.

That process began with my encounter with Walter Mischel's (1968) book, *Personality and Assessment*. I had been a staff member at NYU's Research Center for Mental Health while completing my postdoctoral psychoanalytic training. The Research Center for Mental Health at the time was perhaps the leading academic venue for psychoanalytically informed research and theory development. During my first year there, Mischel's book, which was harshly critical of psychoanalytic modes of thought and of the research that purported to support it, became a hot topic of conversation. As I studied it closely, I was struck by several intersecting and, at times, competing impressions.

The book was tendentiously tunnel visioned in certain ways (P. L. Wachtel, 1973b), but it made a number of important points that have

---

[4]More recently (see, e.g., P. L. Wachtel, 1997, chap. 15), I characterized the psychodynamic core of my approach as "relational" rather than "interpersonal." The term *interpersonal* at times has been confused by readers as implying something alternative to intrapsychic, an idea that was never my intention and that I do not believe was implied by Sullivan (e.g., 1953) either. The term *relational* points to an evolving contemporary psychoanalytic paradigm that incorporates the work of the interpersonalists but includes other perspectives and considerations as well (e.g., Mitchell, 1988). I do not endorse the ideas of every theorist who has been characterized as relational—few relationalists actually do—but I do identify with the broader paradigm shift in psychoanalysis to which the term *relational* applies.

continued to reverberate in my thinking (again, see P. L. Wachtel, 1973b, which was not simply a critique but a critical appreciation; see also P. L. Wachtel, 1997). In particular, Mischel's emphasis on the specificity of behavior, on the ways in which human beings behave differently in different contexts, pushed me to think more deeply about certain habits of thought in psychoanalytic discourse and the possibilities for psychoanalytic theorizing that were implicit in the interpersonal paradigm. Far from discrediting psychoanalysis, Mischel's central point converged with what I viewed as the versions of psychoanalytic thought that were most progressive and comprehensively attuned to the daily reality of human lives.

True to the proclivities I described above, I viewed (and continue to view) the psychoanalytic version of this shared vision as richer and more profound than the version offered by Mischel, which to my mind overvalued the contribution of artificial analogue experiments in the laboratory and failed to appreciate the ways in which such experiments could be misleading and distorting (see P. L. Wachtel, 1973a, 1973b). But wrestling with Mischel's arguments induced me to learn more about behavior therapy, and I found myself impressed on a number of levels with what I discovered. To begin with, I found the evidence for the effectiveness of behavioral methods, especially in reducing anxiety, substantial. The standard psychoanalytic view of the time—that behavioral methods would inevitably lead to symptom substitution or that any gains achieved would quickly succumb to relapse because the underlying issues had not been addressed—did not appear to comport with the evidence.

Moreover, as I began to reflect not only on the research evidence for particular behavioral interventions but also on what I was learning about the clinical uses of behavior therapy, I began to see surprising convergences with my evolving views and practices from a psychoanalytic vantage point. The emphasis of behavior therapists and social learning theorists on the ways in which behavior varied with different environmental input contrasted significantly with certain versions of psychoanalytic thought—those that in emphasizing the preponderant role of "psychic reality" regarded the impact of the events of daily life and present relationships as superficial or viewed people as "stuck" at particular developmental "levels" that organized their experience almost inexorably from within. With some reworking and crossing of linguistic boundaries, however, the observations of social learning theory were interestingly compatible with Erikson's depiction of the role of social and cultural influences, with Horney's account of how old patterns are maintained through their impact in the present, and with Sullivan's emphasis on the profound importance of the interpersonal field.

But the compatibility I was noticing was by no means a redundancy. The psychoanalytic perspectives did not simply replicate the behavioral account of the impact of the current environment. They attuned the sensitive observer to a rich array of subjective phenomena and dynamic influences that were only minimally considered (if at all) by most behavioral theorists and clinicians. Dollard and Miller (1950) demonstrated several decades earlier that concern with conflict, defense, unconscious motivation, and the complex clinical and social phenomena of interest to psychoanalysts was by no means inconsistent with the learning theory perspective that was the point of origin for behavior therapy or with the pursuit of rigorous experimental research. But their vision was not the vision that guided the evolving field of behavior therapy. There remained a wide gap between what behavior therapists paid attention to and what psychoanalysts paid attention to. The convergences I was seeing created a framework for bridging that gap and bringing the two sets of observations together; the existence of the gap itself created both a need and an opening for an integrative effort.

Excited by the clinical and theoretical possibilities I was beginning to envision, I contacted a number of leading behavior therapists to learn more about their work. I encountered great openness and generosity. Behavior therapists, I found, were less bound into the authoritarian structures within which psychoanalysis had evolved and less cowed by a vision of human nature in which one was in constant danger of inadvertently revealing something primitive, instinctual, or shameful; the individuals I contacted were prepared to let me observe their work firsthand. I am especially grateful in this regard to Joseph Wolpe, Arnold Lazarus, Alan Goldstein, Gerald Davison, and Marvin Goldfried.

My observations of these leading behavioral clinicians encouraged me further. Although, as might be expected, there were substantial differences among them in how they worked, they had in common both an activist bent that was in certain ways missing in psychoanalytic work and a clinical sophistication that belied the ideologically driven image of behavior therapy and behavior therapists that was common in psychoanalytic circles. At the same time, despite my enormous respect for their work, I also found that (at least in my view) they had as much to learn from psychoanalysis as psychoanalysis had from them. Even as I saw many ways in which my own work (and that of other psychoanalytically inclined clinicians who might be induced to pay attention) could be greatly enhanced by incorporating the methods and observations of behavioral clinicians, I saw many areas in which behavioral work could be enhanced by the psychoanalytic emphasis on discerning conflict; unconscious motivation; self-deceptions arising out of self-protection; and images of self, other, and relationship that differed substantially from both social clichés and the patient's own conscious vision of what he or she believed. The challenge was to create a theoretical framework that could pull all of these ideas together in coherent fashion. For me, the key to doing this lay in the identification and analysis of the vicious circles that seemed to lie at the heart of the difficulties that people bring to psychotherapy (P. L. Wachtel, 1987, 1993, 1997).

MY CURRENT APPROACH

When I began integrating behavioral methods into my work, I tried to use them in as faithful a manner as possible. I did this for several reasons. First, I introduced these procedures into my practice because I was impressed with their impact and therapeutic potential, and hence I wanted to "do it right" to ensure that the methods I was using were those for which the evidence had impressed me. Moreover, I was entering into territory in which I was not nearly as well trained as I had been in the psychoanalytic approach—another reason to strive to "do it right."

Before long, however, I realized that I was, in fact, not implementing these procedures in precisely the same way as the behavior therapists who had trained me. My experience in practicing therapy from a psychoanalytic vantage point gave a psychoanalytic "accent" to my behavioral work. Both in what I stated explicitly and in the more nonverbal dimensions of my interactions with patients, I conveyed an interest in their subjective experience, their associations, the feelings about me evoked by our using these methods, and so forth. Thus, from early on, procedures such as systematic desensitization became, in my idiosyncratic use of them, not just a complement or alternative to psychodynamic exploration but a means for such exploration as well. I described a number of instances of this in *Psychoanalysis and Behavior Therapy* (P. L. Wachtel, 1977).

Over time, however, the accent I gave to behavioral measures, combined with the further odd accent my experience with those methods sometimes gave to my psychoanalytic work, has seemed to yield a new dialect altogether. As I have described elsewhere (P. L. Wachtel, 1991), my work has become more "seamless." Compared with when I first began to experiment with a psychodynamic–behavioral integration, it is much more difficult now to find the boundary that separates the moments when I am being psychodynamic and the moments when I am being behavioral. Although it is certainly possible to find instances of my work even today in which I use a specific, discrete behavioral intervention, most of the time the behavioral dimension of the work is woven right into the way I go about engaging in an exploratory dialogue with the patient. The surface of the work mostly looks psychodynamic, but a closer look reveals distinctive currents underneath that reflect a second dimension to what I am doing.[5]

---

[5] A third dimension—systemic—is now a crucial part of my work as well (see later in the text).

Conceptually, this second dimension centers on two key themes: (a) extinction and exposure and (b) the impact of anxiety and patterns of avoidance on the development of crucial skills in the realm of social interaction and emotional expression. When I talk to my patients—when I make an "interpretation" or inquire into their feelings or their patterns of behavior—these two points of focus usually figure prominently.

The issue of self-deception with which I began this chapter (see also below) continues to seem crucial to me. The failure to understand or recognize our own motives and feelings, however, is not driven by perversity or sheer ignorance, but by fear. It is the ways in which we can become afraid of our own inclinations and feelings that lie at the heart of our psychological difficulties and account for our failures to recognize or acknowledge crucial aspects of our own experience. In countering that fear, in helping people reappropriate their own feelings, there is no substitute for direct experience. "Interpretations" do contribute to promoting insight and to helping the person clarify what he or she is feeling. But most of all, I now believe, good interpretations bring the person into contact with the previously avoided or warded-off feeling or inclination. What lies at the heart of the venerable distinction between intellectual and emotional insight is whether the patient is exposed to the full range of cues associated with the experiences that have been avoided or warded off. It is through the effects of repeated exposure that one of the most important links can be discerned between psychodynamic interpretations and the interventions of behavior therapists.

Characteristically, those latter interventions have been directed primarily toward exposure to external or situational cues. But incorporated into a psychodynamic format and with guidance from psychodynamic conceptualizations, they can be implemented equally effectively with regard to the internal cues (e.g., thoughts, images, sensed inclinations or affective proclivities) that have been at the heart of the psychodynamic understanding of people's difficulties (see Dollard & Miller, 1950). In my understanding of my patients' problems, I view both internal and external cues as potentially relevant. On the one hand, with complaints such as simple phobias, I am quite prepared to view the primary target as exposure to the particular stimuli reported as the object of the phobia. In this I differ from some psychodynamic therapists, who assume that there is always a "deeper" root that must be addressed. The evidence is overwhelming that phobias can be treated thoroughly and effectively (often most effectively and efficiently) with techniques that concentrate on exposure to the object of the phobia.

On the other hand, it also seems to me that most patients (certainly most patients who come to see me) seek help with a broad, pervasive, often vague set of complaints that center on their relationships with others and their feelings about themselves and their lives. For these presenting complaints, attention to the internal cues associated with the conflicts, anxieties, and self-and-relationship imagoes that have been central to psychodynamic theorizing continues to seem crucial. (Note, however, that I have learned a good deal from my observations of master behavioral clinicians about the value of attempting to break down vague complaints into quite concrete accounts of particular problematic reactions to particular psychologically relevant situations. Here again, my aim is not an endorsement of one point of view over the other but an enhancement of each point of view through the other.)

Turning from the dimension of exposure to that of lacunae in development and their alleviation, one finds another point of convergence in my work between psychodynamic and behavioral perspectives. The anxieties and avoidances that psychoanalytic theorists most of all have illuminated have reverberating consequences over the course of a person's life. Avoidance of frightening feelings or interpersonal situations brings short-term comfort at a high price. An enormously varied and complicated set of trial-and-error efforts is required to develop the skills necessary for living well in the complex, largely man-made environment in which modern humans live. We must learn how to engage and maintain relationships with others, communicate our needs, regulate our emotions, express our emotions, and—more important—recognize and know our emotions and desires to direct our efforts in ways that will bring genuine satisfaction. None of this is easily or quickly learned. The learning trials must number in the millions or, more likely, in the billions. When we protect ourselves against exposing ourselves to the perceived dangers associated with those trials, we fail to learn effectively how to make our lives work.

To some degree, we all show these lacunae. The conditions that nature has created for our first decade or so of life virtually assure this. We begin life small and helpless, dependent on giants whose decisions and actions it takes us years to learn to understand. In the meantime, we develop means of feeling safe that may serve us reasonably well at the moment they are introduced but limit in one way or another our ability to develop the full range of our potentials later in life. Some of us, more frightened either through temperament or experience, engage in these restrictions more than others. In addition, some of us are better than others at obscuring the very fact that we have engaged in self-restricting avoidances.[6] But none of us escape completely the consequences of our species' prolonged childhood.

Early in my integrative efforts, I was excited to discover that methods such as assertiveness training, social skills training, behavior rehearsal, and

---

[6] For example, the person whose defensive efforts entail always being assertive but never experiencing what it is like to relax or rely on others may appear to be a "fuller" human being, but he still may have restricted access to modes of being that are readily available—and useful—to others who are more comfortable with feelings of dependency or are more able to express vulnerability and elicit comfort.

graded practice could help address these lacunae. I continue to value these methods but again have found that over time, a hybrid has evolved in my work, in which my efforts to direct the patient to develop and practice various skills (e.g., assertiveness or expression of emotion) are voiced in a form that looks much like a psychodynamic interpretation, and my interpretations increasingly include a dimension that points to what the person can do. Exposure, skill development, repeated practice, attention to both behavior and emotion, and increasing clarification of what the person wants and feels all move in tandem, enhancing and even defining one another.

The key to this more "seamless" integration in recent years has been my concern with the therapist's language. The central focus of my clinical and theoretical efforts in the past decade or so has been the exploration of precisely what it is that therapists actually say and the implications of different ways of saying to the patient what might seem to be roughly the same content. In this I have been concerned especially about three themes. The first and most general has been the examination of the "metamessages" that invariably accompany the more focal messages that we think we are conveying to the patient (P. L. Wachtel, 1993). Second and more specifically, I have been concerned with the many ways in which these metamessages are unwittingly critical and accusatory (see also Wile, 1984, 1985) and with ways of phrasing our comments that confront the same truths but enhance, rather than diminish, the patient's self-esteem. Third, I have increasingly explored the ways in which the skillful, conscious use of language can enable the therapist not only to avoid the dangers of unwittingly accusatory comments but also to construct ways of proactively framing the patient's experience to enhance and promote change. I cannot go into detail here regarding the numerous ways in which these aims can be effectively pursued in therapeutic work, but the interested reader may find my book *Therapeutic Communication* (P. L. Wachtel, 1993) useful in this regard.

Finally, another key facet of my work develops a theme that was not originally part of my integrative efforts but has become increasingly important over the years. During the time I was completing work on *Psychoanalysis and Behavior Therapy* (P. L. Wachtel, 1977), my wife, Ellen, was undertaking postdoctoral training in family therapy at the Ackerman Institute. As we discussed the vision of psychoanalysis that was emerging in my work, it became clear that that vision, with its emphasis on vicious circles and the ways in which people elicit responses from each other that perpetuate the patterns and vulnerabilities learned earlier in life, converged significantly with many of the central tenets of family therapy. Several years later, we coauthored the book *Family Dynamics in Individual Psychotherapy* (E. F. Wachtel & Wachtel, 1986). I was primarily responsible for writing the theoretical discussions that addressed the convergence between psychodynamic and systems thinking, and Ellen wrote most of the clinical chapters, which described in detail her own innovative ways of bringing family members and other key figures in the patient's "cast of characters" into therapeutic work with individuals. One of the wonderful family dynamics that evolved (at least from my point of view) was that Ellen wrote the lion's share of the book.

CONCLUSION

I wish finally to return to the theme of self-deception with which I began. We live in an era in which the subtleties of psychological experience are increasingly subjugated to the economistic concerns that presently dominate in our society. Idolatry of the market and a singular emphasis on the "bottom line" are rampant. Managed care is but one symptom of a larger misreading and misunderstanding of human needs and human experience (see P. L. Wachtel, 1983). The hyperrationality of economic models—economists are perhaps the last pre-Freudians in the intellectual world—is largely matched by that of influential conceptions of human cognition that reduce the complexity of experience to what is rational, verbal, and syllogistic.

Psychotherapy is potentially a corrective to this impoverishing view of human mental life. Many patients come not so much to cure what they know is wrong but to discover what it is they wish to cure. We are often opaque to ourselves, and as a consequence, the ways in which we initially frame our complaints often are shaped by the very problems we are consulting the therapist to resolve. It is one of the serious failings of our market-dominated society that in the course of our lives, we are inclined to seek happiness more in the latest video game, technological doodad, gas-guzzling sports utility vehicle, or overpriced pair of sneakers than in the deepening of our relationships and our understanding of our own needs and desires. Managed care, which points us to save money on the latter so we have more to spend on the former, is itself a part of the systematic self-deception that lies at the heart of a society in which materialism trumps subjective experience (P. L. Wachtel, 1983).

It aids the bottom line to assume that all that bothers people is what they can tell us in the first session or two. The number of "legitimate" complaints is thereby drastically reduced, and the ones that remain tend, almost by definition, to be those that yield to a relatively small number of sessions. Transparency and rationality are convenient fictions that enable economists to justify both inequality and the despoliation of the environment (cf. Friedman & Friedman, 1980; P. L. Wachtel, 1983). In contrast, appreciation of the many ways in which we misrepresent both our experience and our needs holds a key not only to the enhancement of our individual lives but to the renewal of our society. From early on, my work as a psychotherapist has felt complementary to my concerns about the larger social order. Now, when the therapeutic professions are under increasing duress and the society at large seems even more entranced by the myth of the market and the seductions of materialism, it seems to me especially crucial not to trim our theories of psychotherapy to fit the corporate mold. The promise of integrative models of psychotherapy is that they can embrace the genuinely valuable interventions that achieve therapeutic change more rapidly than traditional methods without abandoning the critical perspective and the appreciation of complexity, conflict, and anxiety-driven misrepresentation of experience that have been central to the psychodynamic model from its inception. It is to such an integration that I remain dedicated, both as a psychotherapist and as a citizen.

REFERENCES

Alexander, F. (1963). The dynamics of psychotherapy in light of learning theory. *American Journal of Psychiatry, 120*, 440–448.

Alexander, F., & French, T. (1946). *Psychoanalytic therapy*. New York: Ronald Press.

Bowers, K. S. (1981). Knowing more than we can say leads to saying more than we can know: On being implicitly informed. In D. Magnusson (Ed.), *Toward a psychology of situations: An interactional perspective*. Hillsdale, NJ: Erlbaum.

Dollard, J., & Miller, N. (1950). *Personality and psychotherapy*. New York: McGraw-Hill.

French, T. M. (1933). Interrelations between psychoanalysis and the experimental work of Pavlov. *American Journal of Psychiatry, 89*, 1165–1203.

Friedman, M., & Friedman, R. (1980). *Free to choose*. New York: Harcourt Brace Jovanovich.

Gill, M. M. (1954). Psychoanalysis and exploratory psychotherapy. *Journal of the American Psychoanalytic Association, 2*, 771–797.

Gill, M. M. (1982). *Analysis of transference*. New York: International Universities Press.

Gill, M. M. (1984). Psychoanalysis and psychotherapy: A revision. *International Review of Psycho-Analysis, 11*, 161–179.

Hoffman, I. Z. (1991). Toward a social–constructivist view of the psychoanalytic situation. *Psychoanalytic Dialogues, 1*, 74–105.

Messer, S. B. (1992). A critical examination of belief structures in integrative and eclectic psychotherapy. In J. C. Norcross & M. R. Goldfried (Eds.), *Handbook of psychotherapy integration* (pp. 130–168). New York: Basic Books.

Mischel, W. (1968). *Personality and assessment*. New York: Wiley.

Mitchell, S. A. (1988). *Relational concepts in psychoanalysis: An integration*. Cambridge, MA: Harvard University Press.

Polanyi, M. (1958). *Personal knowledge: Toward a post-critical philosophy*. Chicago: University of Chicago Press.

Spence, D. P. (1982). *Narrative truth and historical truth*. New York: Norton.

Sullivan, H. S. (1953). *The interpersonal theory of psychiatry*. New York: Norton.

Wachtel, E. F., & Wachtel, P. L. (1986). *Family dynamics in individual psychotherapy*. New York: Guilford Press.

Wachtel, P. L. (1973a). On fact, hunch, and stereotype: A reply to Mischel. *Journal of Abnormal Psychology, 82*, 537–540.

Wachtel, P. L. (1973b). Psychodynamics, behavior therapy, and the implacable experimenter: An inquiry into the consistency of personality. *Journal of Abnormal Psychology, 82*, 324–334.

Wachtel, P. L. (1977). *Psychoanalysis and behavior therapy*. New York: Basic Books.

Wachtel, P. L. (1983). *The poverty of affluence: A psychological portrait of the American way of life*. New York: Free Press.

Wachtel, P. L. (1987). *Action and insight*. New York: Guilford Press.

Wachtel, P. L. (1991). From eclecticism to synthesis: Toward a more seamless psychotherapeutic integration. *Journal of Psychotherapy Integration, 1*, 43–54.

Wachtel, P. L. (1993). *Therapeutic communication: Knowing what to say when*. New York: Guilford Press.

Wachtel, P. L. (1997). *Psychoanalysis, behavior therapy, and the relational world*. Washington, DC: American Psychological Association.

Wachtel, P. L. (1999). *Race in the mind of America: Breaking the vicious circle between Blacks and Whites*. New York: Routledge.

Wile, D. B. (1984). Kohut, Kernberg, and accusatory interpretations. *Psychotherapy, 21*, 353–364.

Wile, D. B. (1985) Psychotherapy by precedent: Unexamined legacies from pre-1920 psychoanalysis. *Psychotherapy, 22*, 793–802.

III

PROFESSIONAL MEMOIRS OF COGNITIVE–BEHAVIOR THERAPISTS

7

THE PROFESSIONAL AUTOBIOGRAPHY OF A BEHAVIOR THERAPIST

HERBERT FENSTERHEIM

My experiences within the field of clinical psychology have been widely varied. I have gone from a psychoanalytic to a behavioral to an integrated behavioral orientation. I have worked overseas in a UN camp for people recently freed from concentration camps; worked in a physical medicine and rehabilitation setting; done clinical and community work in the East Harlem ghetto of Manhattan; been a sport psychologist for the U.S. Olympic Fencing Team; done motivational research for advertising agencies; taught at undergraduate and graduate levels in both academic and medical college settings; written professional papers as well as books for the general public; made radio and television appearances; and, for a 3-year period, had my own radio program on the human side of the newly emerging racial integration movement. I have been involved in both individual and group therapies (both dynamic and behavioral), had a continuing interest in chronic hyperventilation, and most recently have developed an interest in eye movement desensitization and reprocessing (EMDR), a visualization procedure used to treat people who have traumatic pasts. Throughout all this, I earned almost my entire livelihood through a private therapy practice with middle-class adults, most of whom have various personality disorders.

All of these experiences have influenced my understanding of psychotherapy and the way I actually practice. To these I also must add my student experiences. In those days, except for academic positions, few jobs existed in psychology. I went into the field because I loved all phases of it. I especially was absorbed in the area of animal behavior, and the influence of Ted Schneirla still dominates much of my thinking. Schneirla's (we never referred to him as Ted) area was as much theory as it was the study of the Panama army ant. He was a tough-minded scientist who was an antibehaviorist in a field dominated by stimulus–response thinking. In other words, he was a brilliant rebel. I was also lucky with my classmates, who were enthusiastic, industrious, and fun loving. Many of them eventually made their marks in social psychology, animal behavior, or statistics; we clinicians were not isolated from the other areas of psychology. This connection with the more academic areas was one of the major reasons that I eventually became immersed in the behavioral approaches to therapy. I have the vague fantasy that the major paradigm change in psychotherapy will be triggered by new findings in academic psychology, although I myself have lost contact with the new developments in psychology in general.

LESSONS ORIGINALLY LEARNED

I first started practicing in August 1950. I was a psychoanalyst, although not yet fully trained in that profession. I saw patients once, twice, or three times per week, depending on what the person could afford. There were no third-party payments then. The patient would lie on the couch and free associate. I would listen, attempting to be sensitive to my own feelings and those of the patient and being alert to all nuances of what the patient was saying, although I admit that at times my mind would wander. I would reflect feelings, raise questions, make insightful remarks, or be silent, depending on what I believed was called for at that particular moment. Not to keep a patient coming for years was a failure on my part; somehow I had done something wrong and had cheated the patient in those cases.

At that time this approach was not only the accepted way of doing treatment—it was the only way. The possible exception was Carl Rogers and his nondirective approach; although we clinicians always spoke respectfully of Rogers, no "real" clinician took his work seriously. The only true therapy was five-times-per-week, free-association-on-the-couch psychoanalysis. The core of psychoanalysis was in the correct formulation of the patient's dynamics and the observation of how those dynamics were played out in the transference reactions during treatment.

To really understand that psychoanalysis was the only choice, I must describe the limited state of clinical psychology back in the late 1930s when I first started my clinical studies. My own first "clinical" experience was at a small settlement house on Henry Street in Manhattan's Lower East Side. I was an undergraduate senior, and my client, who was just starting City College, wanted career advice. I knew I should take a case history, which I did in great detail, but then I did not know what to do with all that information. I consulted a first-year graduate student who also was interested in clinical psychology. He complimented me on the history I had taken and told me that the obvious next step was to find the discrepancies between what the client had said happened and what actually did happen. Those were the points to work on. I first felt considerable relief because now I knew exactly what to do. This was quickly followed by strong feelings of incompetence because I did not know how to start doing even this obvious and basic therapeutic task. (I must add that this counseling turned out to be a success. The person I counseled became a well-known clinical psychologist. At a meeting many years later, he told me that our work together was an important influence in his choosing psychology as a profession.)

To get some smattering of a therapeutic approach, I had to go outside of the academic university. I attended many lectures by the outstanding psychoanalysts of the time, and the core of those lectures all pointed to the need for the correct formulation of the patient's dynamics. Perhaps the extracurricular activity that had the most lasting influence on my focus on the case formulation was a series of case conferences at Columbia Medical College that I attended during my senior undergraduate year. David M. Levy, then a highly respected child analyst, led them. The model he presented was to draw a series of hypotheses about the patient's dynamics from the resident's presentation of the patient. Each hypothesis led to specific courses of therapeutic action. The most reasonable hypothesis was chosen, and the therapeutic action indicated would be attempted. If that did not yield the desired results, the hypothesis would be discarded and another likely dynamic hypothesis would be substituted in its place, leading to a different course of therapeutic action. The formulation and reformulation of a therapeutic hypothesis remain a major core of my approach to treatment to this day, even though I now may use a different content. Indeed, in a recent article on EMDR (Fensterheim, 1996), I paid considerable attention to the need to reformulate cases, a conscious remnant of these experiences.

The quest for the correct dynamic formulation continued after my time in the army, when I liberated North Africa and Italy during World War II. I also spent a year in southern Italy at a UN camp for people recently released from concentration camps. This experience sensitized me to the influence of social variables on individual behavior; the paper analyzing this experience (Fensterheim & Birch, 1950) is the one of which I am most proud. After returning home, I spent 4 years with the Veterans Administration Clinical Psychology Training Program. Three of those 4 were spent at the Northport Veterans Hospital on Long Island (NY). The patients all had schizophrenia, and we could do little for them in those days. We had insulin shock therapy, electric shock therapy, and lobotomies; rumor had it that our hospital had a 25% death rate for lobotomies (I never did find out if this last was true). In addition, we had individual and group psychotherapy. We received psychodynamic supervision for our therapeutic work from some of the best professionals in the area, who were on our visiting staff. At grand rounds and other lectures, the foremost psychoanalysts (mainly from the Columbia University Medical School) presented case formulations of patients with schizophrenia that were awe inspiring and beautiful. We staff therapists realized that treatment based on those formulations rarely worked on our patients, but we always hoped. We were certain that the psychoanalytic approach was basically the correct approach but that we just had not yet learned how to apply it correctly with these patients.

The same perspective dominated our training in diagnosis and therapy. The aim of students' psychological reports and of their supervised therapy was to present the dynamics of the patient's schizophrenic process with the same profundity, creativity, and aesthetic beauty that we heard at the grand rounds. We took great pride in the formulations we derived from those psychological tests; the fact that they did not influence patient treatment in any way did not create a state of dissonance. The patient's test scores and his responses, statements, behaviors, and interrelations with the therapist all were used to gain insight into the patient's motivations and dynamics.

After completion of this training, the only way to go if I wanted to become a competent therapist was further training in psychoanalysis. This required training in theory, therapy supervision, and my own analysis. I did all three. Analytic training sites for non-MDs were few, and I was lucky: I trained with the Flower analytic group as an unofficial student because I was not an MD. I went through the entire program and used their supervisors for my own work. The training was primarily strict Freudian, but several faculty were committed to the Sullivan approach; they kept my mind open to analytic alternatives. This training and supervision solidified where I was as a therapist, added many details to my understanding of psychoanalytic theory and practice, and deepened my commitment to the psychoanalytic approach. So great was my commitment to psychoanalytic theory that I was able to teach it at the graduate level at the New School for Social Research. Practice was different, however. My own practice offered no sense of adventure and no intellectual challenge when I was actually with the patient. Although I realized that I still had far to go, I felt a growing mastery of the area but a disappointment that more of my patients did not show major improvement. I coped with the latter problem by pompously proclaiming on several occasions that therapists could not become concerned with outcome but had to immerse ourselves in the process, something I had been told by one of my mentors and had heard several times in lectures. In retrospect, I was bored doing this kind of treatment. It was not for me.

My own analysis lasted 14 years and involved three analysts. My Freudian analyst was literally 100 years old when I started working with him. He had been with the original Freudian group in Vienna and was still bright, sharp, and open to new ideas. He did not help me, however, nor did the Sullivanian analyst whom I saw for several years. Most of my analytic time was with a Horney-based analyst, and I would say that he also had no effect on me except for one incident. Near the end of this analysis, while I was lying on the couch associating, an image came to me. It was an image of myself as a little boy. I won't go into the characteristics of the boy in the image, but I was at once that boy, fully and in all different sense modalities, and an onlooker. It was a shaking experience and one of its consequences was that the terrible headaches from which I had suffered since I was 8—headaches that had been diagnosed as "sinus headaches"— disappeared, never to return. I saw no other effects of any kind, and soon even the memory of this having occurred faded. Some 25 years later it returned. Several times a day the memory of the incident having occurred, not so much of the image itself, thrust itself into my mind. This went on for almost half a year; during that time major changes in me took place. The most dramatic of those changes was quitting smoking. After smoking three to four packs of cigarettes a day for almost 50 years, after numerous and futile attempts to give it up, I suddenly stopped smoking. I had no tension, no difficulty, no withdrawal signs. I simply stopped, and for 13 years now I have had only rare, mild, and brief impulses to smoke. I assume that after all those years, my analysis finally worked; but as to how this came about I still have no idea.

In my own practice I believed that change was brought about through acquisition of insight by the patient. From the initial interview on, even though I felt no challenge, I was constantly formulating, testing, and reformulating the unconscious dynamics that brought about and organized the patient's motivational network. By providing an atmosphere of nonpossessive warmth and accurate empathy as best as I could and by making challenging or interpretive statements, I would lead the patient toward an ever deepening understanding of himself. The content of those understandings varied; some were strict Freudian, whereas others were mainly based on Horney or Sullivan. I paid little attention to changes in real life, some attention to the changes in feeling, and most attention to the growth of understanding. It was primarily, I now see, a cognitive approach. Changes in real life sometimes did take place, anxieties disappeared, and good things began to happen. I attributed those changes to the emergence of insight and understanding.

I performed this therapy in my own practice. I also was an instructor in physical medicine and rehabilitation at the New York Medical College. Physical rehabilitation was an area that called upon the widest knowledge of many areas of psychology. A major goal of treatment was to teach patients with neurological or physical disabilities adequate modes of functioning within the limits of their difficulties. Many times, however, little or no progress was made toward this goal, the patient was labeled uncooperative or hostile, and I was called in. The attempts to solve such problems often involved an understanding of the patient's psychological organization, his or her biological characteristics, and the training situation itself. I quickly learned that the presence of psychopathology often was irrelevant in finding a solution, but current coping patterns were extremely important. A common problem among patients with brain damage is the inability to form concepts, to place things in categories. In occupational therapy the work situation was often disorganized, leaving such a patient swamped with seemingly unrelated stimuli. To avoid the catastrophic reaction that would result from trying to deal with this chaos, the patient would avoid the actual work situation through a variety of devices (such as getting into long conversations with the therapist) and be labeled as being unmotivated. Extensive simplification of the work situation usually brought about a sudden change in the level of the patient's "motivation."

In the early 1950s all of the clinical psychologists that I knew were completely immersed in the psychoanalytic approach. I recall reading a psychological report by the person who had preceded me in my job. The report, based mainly on the Rorschach, stressed the patient's masturbation guilt and nowhere mentioned that the person had just had both legs amputated. Although I, too, was immersed in the psychoanalytic approach, I did try to bring other psychological perspectives into my work. What psychological testing I performed was limited and problem oriented. I also performed some brief, goal-limited psychotherapy and some group therapy. This latter was with patients having similar disabilities, and the aim was to share coping methods and, more important, to help the people in the group feel less alone. Most of my time, however, was spent in the actual training situations. I would work with the physical and occupational therapists, suggesting changes in the training situation or pointing out patient characteristics that interfered with treatment and suggesting solutions. I published several clinical papers on this work, papers that actually were naive, pre-Wolpe illustrations of the behavioral approach (Fensterheim, 1953; Fensterheim & LaKritz, 1958; LaKritz & Fensterheim, 1953).

One illustration of this approach concerns a young man who, as the result of an accident, had a mild hemiparesis, which led to a scissors gait and constant falling. A great deal of training finally enabled him to walk well enough to go home. Whenever an authority figure happened to pass by, however, he would fall. It was obvious that he had extreme anxiety about authorities, and observation showed that he would fix his gaze on such authority figure when he or she was nearby. How was this connected to his falling? The hypothesis I formed was based on Witkin's (1949) studies of the perception of the vertical. Witkin had demonstrated that with some people (field dependent) the perception of the vertical was dominated by visual cues, whereas in others (field independent) kinesthetic cues were dominant. With this patient I assumed that prior to his injury, he had based his perception of the vertical on kinesthetic cues, that his injury had disrupted these cues, and that in his ambulation training he had learned to use visual cues and thus was able to keep his balance. When he stared at authority figures, however, he lost the cues and so would fall. Using this formulation we taught the patient that whenever he saw an authority figure he should quickly look around. The strategy worked. He stopped falling and was soon able to leave the hospital. Does that mean the hypothesis was verified? I did not care then, nor do I care now; I fixed the patient. I was proud of this work and yet felt somewhat guilty for ignoring deeper dynamic forces.

I was involved with this work for about 6 years and learned much from it. I became far more aware of the biological factors influencing maladaptive behaviors. Herb Birch, who was my mentor in much of this work, stated that he had never seen an inorganic patient, and I still find this an often useful concept (see Fensterheim, 1999). My work in rehabilitation also stressed the importance of outcome and of change in behavior, concepts that were usually considered only in abstract terms during those days of psychoanalytic dominance. It was in rehabilitation that I developed the idea that the validity of the working hypothesis was irrelevant; what mattered was whether it brought about the desired behavioral change. Although this experience laid the basis for my later work involving brief therapy in a psychiatric walk-in clinic and problem solving in sport psychology, it had no obvious effect on the analytic therapy I was then doing in my practice.

When I moved into psychiatry I worked at the Metropolitan Hospital, a city hospital located in the East Harlem section of Manhattan. Our population was mostly Hispanic, followed by African American and then White patients. At various times I worked on the inpatient and outpatient services. The work was fairly similar in both settings, consisting of psychological testing and dynamically oriented individual and group psychotherapy. Again I heard many profound, creative discussions of patient dynamics, but now, except for with the drug addicts, there was a genuine attempt to make use of those formulations. We therapists had much interaction with our community psychiatry section, and we became increasingly aware of how little we took cultural issues into consideration. I gathered some data (never published) on the initial intake diagnoses given by our attending psychiatrists on the outpatient service. Hispanic patients were most often diagnosed as hysterics, African American patients as having personality disorders, and White patients as either neurotic or psychotic. I also gathered some data on our inpatient service concerning length of hospital stay and outcome. I noted that the better educated, more verbal patients (usually White and female) were considered to be good candidates for psychotherapy and were referred to a psychiatric resident for training purposes. The others were placed on medication, which was only then coming into general use. No one doubted that the patients undergoing psychotherapy were receiving the superior treatment. However, the data revealed that the patients on medication had shorter hospital stays and showed greater improvement than did those on psychotherapy. I gathered data (again unpublished) on the dropouts in our outpatient service and discovered that most of the dropouts were our successes. They felt better and saw no point in coming to see the doctor; because they were not middle class, it never occurred to them to phone in. The data were not gathered carefully enough to warrant publication, but they did influence both attitudes and action within the department.

One incident illustrates my continued commitment to the interaction between biology and psychology. In the mid-1960s I presented a grand rounds where I reported on a patient with phobic anxiety and depression (the PAD syndrome—the term then used for the newly recognized pattern now known as panic disorder). I interpreted the symptoms as manifestations of hyperventilation; this realization, a full decade before Lum's identification of chronic hyperventilation, brought me to a major commitment to the study of hyperventilation. When I had finished my presentation, there was no reaction from the audience—no questions, no comments. I believe the entire behaviorally oriented approach was just too strange to that dynamically oriented audience. I did call on one senior analyst and asked how he formulated patients with such panic symptoms. He replied that in his many years of practice, he had never seen a patient with symptoms at all resembling those of this patient. To cite a maxim from field geology: "If you don't believe it, you won't see it."

Many other projects, such as my close involvement in the formation of one of the first psychiatric walk-in clinics in the country (Normand, Fensterheim, & Schrenzel, 1967; Normand, Fensterheim, Tannenbaum, & Sager, 1963) influenced my thinking and working. These experiences solidified my focus on treatment outcome; limited and problem-oriented psychological examinations; short-term, goal-oriented treatment; and the need to consider the cultural context of the patient. I became more aware of both the strengths and the limitations of dynamic formulations in actualizing this mode of functioning. I was aware at the time that all of my hospital experiences had just about no impact on how I conducted treatment in my own practice. I was most aware of the schism between hospital and practice and was finding my practice less and less satisfying. Then I heard about behavior therapy.

Behavior therapy (BT) seemed designed to meet my specifications both for clinical work and for psychotherapy. Suddenly I was with a group of clinicians and academicians who spoke of Pavlov and Skinner within a clinical context. Specific techniques were derived from the experimentalists; they were subjected to scientific testing and were found to work. There were academic people who actually listened to us clinicians and tried to devise methods to solve the problems we brought to them. An era of unlimited possibilities opened up to me.

This new information did influence my practice, but it was not easy to change perspectives while sitting with a patient. It took an uncomfortable but stimulating period of somewhat more than a year before I was over the hump. I was more alive during the session, less tired at the end of the day. This was my kind of therapy: I was now getting "real" results, real changes in my patients. I was taking on problems I would not have considered in my dynamic days, problems such as treating sexual impotency in a homosexual person without attempting to change the sexual orientation of that person. Each case became a challenge to apply findings drawn from a broad range of psychology to that patient's problems. I truly believed Wolpe's dictum that if the patient did not get better, the therapist was doing something wrong. At a professional meeting one of the then leading figures in BT was asked whether BT could cure schizophrenia. "You tell me," he said, "what behaviors the patient shows that make you call him schizophrenic. I will take those behaviors one at a time and modify each one. Then you will no longer be able to call the patient schizophrenic." The future was ours! It is hard to capture in words the excitement and optimism I felt at the time.

Of course, my psychoanalytic colleagues were not at all kind to me. Most of their comments were mocking or sarcastic. When my first book for the general public was published (*Help Without Psychoanalysis*; Fensterheim, 1971), I was soundly berated for influencing people away from "real" treatment. One analytic specialist in the field of homosexuality wanted me to "cure" a series of homosexual patients (he seemed to have no doubt that I could do it, nor did he doubt the desirability of that goal). He would then interview the patients and find out what really brought about the change. A more blatant incident occurred when I was invited as a behavior therapist to discuss a member's paper at a meeting of a major psychoanalytic group.

Less than halfway through my allotted time, the chairman cut me short and during the discussion period would allow no questions to be addressed to me and no discussion of any points I made. I must add that the secretary of the society telephoned me and apologized; my paper was published in full in their journal. Obviously, my clinical community was unfriendly to this exciting new approach.

So my original learning was within a psychoanalytic context. For me the theory was exciting, but the work was dull. Furthermore, the analytic approach stood apart from the fields of basic psychology that so interested me. When I found BT, it was like coming home; I took to it with all the ardor and conviction of the new convert. It turned my concept of treatment completely around. Before, everything came from the bottom up; what happened at the top was essentially trivial; it was the process that was important. Suddenly, everything was focused on the top—there was no bottom. The certain knowledge that this was psychology, that this was science, allowed me to stand up to the buffeting of my colleagues. Yet I still wonder whether BT would have been my first choice had it been available to me from the beginning. I might well have followed the urgings of my Pavlovian colleagues and chosen the psychoanalytic approach.

STRENGTHS OF ORIGINAL ORIENTATIONS

From the perspective of a more than three decades of involvement in a behavioral approach to therapy, I have even more regard for the psychoanalytic orientation as powerful and stimulating. For one thing, it begins to get at the essence of the humanity of each patient, of what makes that specific person so unique. Lehrman, in one of his critiques of the behaviorist position, points out how Skinner and his followers attempted to discover what behaviors different organisms have in common. In this way they ignored the unique characteristics that make an ant an ant, a rat a rat, and a human being a human being. Unlike behaviorism, the psychodynamic orientation emphasizes the individual attributes of each person, although it does recognize that different people have many things in common.

Furthermore, the psychoanalysts were keen observers of human behavior. Unfortunately, like the early zoologists, they often tended to combine observation and interpretation. Many of their observations, however, are extremely helpful in treating patients. Although the influence of the concept of the unconscious, the descriptions of defense mechanisms, and the role of early life experience may be exaggerated or magnified or may be tied to a specific theoretical perspective, they often are useful in helping to arrive at a formulation for the patient's problems. The analytic perspective also may be helpful in its notion of a psychological organization rather than the idea of discrete behaviors being maintained by a network of reinforcement contingencies. Although the identification of reinforcers that maintain an unwanted behavior is indeed important, I find the concept of a psychological organization most useful in formulating a patient's difficulties and selecting target behaviors for change.

The last of the strengths of psychoanalysis that I mention here has to do with the therapist as a person. The psychoanalytic approach does consider the person of the therapist. For example, it places great emphasis on counter-transference, on the therapist's own problems influencing reactions to the patient. There is the requirement that the therapist undergo his or her own analysis to better recognize and understand such reactions as well as his or her personal qualities. Despite the experimental methodologies that see the therapist as mechanically applying specified procedures, the analytic approach has no need to point out that the therapist is not a mere variable, that the therapist is a person. The therapy situation is not a mechanical one, easily put into the form of a manual. It is an interaction between two people. It is a humanizing experience for both. Indeed, a growing body of experimental findings shows that the person of the therapist may be an important factor in determining therapy outcome.

The strengths of my hospital experience and those of my first experiences with BT were similar. They concentrated on outcome, on behavior change. They drew on the wide body of general psychology rather than on the narrow motivational framework that characterizes psychoanalysis. The behavior therapist had greater flexibility in deriving the formulation and an almost unlimited range of fact and theory drawn from psychology in general to serve as the basis for the formulation. BT pays far greater attention to the person's external environment than did the analytic approach. Most important, BT involves a determined commitment to establish an experimental basis for therapeutic work.

LIMITATIONS OF ORIGINAL ORIENTATIONS

I found the psychoanalytic orientation too narrow an approach. Everything was motivated. The therapist had to be hypervigilant so as not to miss a possibly valuable cue to the operation of some motive; hence, everything was a potential federal case. Despite attempts at the formation of an ego psychology, in practice the ego was mainly ignored. Ethnicity, cultural background, and environment all were ignored. The biology of the patient was ignored, yet I did agree with one of my colleagues who stated that he had never seen an inorganic patient. Everything had to go from the bottom up, from the depths of the unconscious to feelings and behavior.

Treatment, too, was extremely narrow. Everyone was to be treated in the same way, through free association. Of course, some patients for a variety of reasons could not undergo such a process and so were treated through some form of psychotherapy. As I had been told many times, however, psychotherapy had nothing to do with psychoanalysis, and it was sad that those unfortunate people could not gain from the one true treatment. Interestingly, during the early days of BT many of my referrals came from psychoanalysts. They explained to me that because psychotherapy had nothing to do with psychoanalysis, they may as well refer the patient to the more effective type of treatment. Despite many different formulations, psychoanalytic treatment was primarily cognitive; the aim was for the patient to gain knowledge and understanding of his or her unconscious motives. Feelings, interpersonal reactions, and dream interpretations all were in service of achieving this cognitive goal of attaining insight.

These limitations were not the reasons I stopped doing psychoanalysis. Rather, a major reason was that I found it incompatible with my personality; it was not my métier. I found the theory (especially the Horney theory) fascinating but the actual work boring. The second reason was that I found BT, an orientation that initially appeared to be more in tune with my interest in psychology.

During my hospital work and the first years of my work in the behavioral mode, I was not truly aware of limitations—that awareness came later. At the time I was aware that sometimes, no matter how frequently one revised one's formulation and no matter how valid each formulation seemed to be, the patient just did not change. I attributed that problem to the fact that we still did not know enough and felt that the basic approach itself was solid. Although the seeds of doubt were there from the beginning, it took several years before I truly began to recognize the limitations of the BT perspective.

My honeymoon with BT lasted for several years, but doubts began to creep in. I could not quite go along with the idea that running rats through mazes was more important than gaining clinical experience, as many were claiming in the late 1960s. Psychological approaches were being replaced by an almost monolithic learning-theory orientation. Skinner was dominant, and I myself was brought up in a Pavlovian, anti-Skinner atmosphere. I well remember trying to counter this behaviorist trend when I was program chair of the Association for the Advancement of Behavior Therapy (AABT) annual meeting. I invited Gregory Razran, a noted Pavlovian, to address that meeting. Nobody paid any attention to his talk; throughout the remainder of the meeting, I heard no comment or discussion of what he had said.

Other changes were taking place. In my professional activities I had always been surrounded by clinic- or practice-based clinicians. Now university-based clinicians were beginning to dominate the AABT, and the hard realities of clinical practice were being minimized. I tried to reinforce the clinical orientation of the meetings by asking Mal Kushner to deliver a paper on his treatment of a case that had received much newspaper publicity, in which the newly developed aversion therapy had magically stopped a patient's uncontrollable hiccuping within a 24-hour period. After the newspaper coverage ceased, however, there was a relapse of symptoms, complicated family dynamics turned out to be involved, and years of further treatment were necessary. This had not been reported, even to the professional community. Fewer than 10 people preferred this presentation to a competing discussion of token economies.

The general atmosphere within the BT movement was influencing my therapeutic work. In my own practice I became increasingly aware that I was treating problems and not people and that I actually disapproved of such an approach. Along with these events, my academic colleagues, who were immersed in Pavlov, argued that Freud was closer to Pavlov than was Wolpe. They also argued that because BT was dominated by behaviorist perspectives, it also had the major theoretical weakness of ignoring Darwin. Helen Kaplan, with whom I worked closely during part of this period, pointed out to me how she incorporated dynamic concepts into her sexual treatments and urged me to do the same with BT. In my own practice, I increasingly used dynamic concepts to select target behaviors and began to write about phobic reactions to childhood memories fueling current anxieties and about the defenses that enabled a person to avoid these phobic memories (Fensterheim, 1993; Fensterheim & Glazer, 1983). Despite all of my doubts, I still appreciated the great therapeutic powers of the behavioral approach. My solution was to attempt to integrate the strengths of the two perspectives.

HOW CHANGE OCCURRED

Within the area of BT, assertiveness training (AT) most appealed to me. It seemed to be the most human aspect of BT as well as to offer the greatest opportunity to apply many different psychological concepts to helping people change. I soon learned that AT was not a simple matter of coaching and behavior rehearsal, although those methods are indeed important. It also involved identifying and removing the inhibitions that prevented the patient from acting assertively. Those inhibitions often involved fears and anxieties, many stemming from phobic reactions to present-day memories of childhood events. Cognitive distortions and inappropriate rules, passive attitudes, values and moral standards, and environments also encouraged the lack of assertion, as did many other variables. Assertion thus became the core of an integrated approach to behavior change. It took a number of years working with AT, however, to reach this point. Initially my approach was mainly coaching and behavior rehearsal, which were best carried out in a group setting. This approach also seemed to make the most sense to the general public; I taught several ministers in the East Harlem area how to conduct such groups with members of that deprived community, and they told me that they found it quite helpful. For example, they taught people that they had a right to—and how best to—assert themselves to the landlord to have repairs made in their apartments.

I also became involved in a second area of integration: hyperventilation. I always had been interested in that area as a biological–psychological interaction and integration. In the mid-1970s Claude Lum (1976) published a seminal article identifying the phenomenon of chronic hyperventilation, attributed its cause to a learned habit of incorrect breathing, and described some of its massive medical and psychological manifestations. It was published in an obscure book and does not appear to have had much impact on general clinical practice, but it did have a great impact on me. For almost 20 years, I have used the concept in my practice, have many times found it to be helpful, and have seen a number of patients who could not have been constructively formulated and successfully treated unless the condition of chronic hyperventilation had been taken into account. Even though I realize the great difficulties in diagnosing this condition (there is no "gold standard" for the diagnosis), I have felt frustrated that the field has not considered chronic hyperventilation more seriously.

Thus, although I still regard myself as primarily a behavior therapist, my theoretical orientation is so different from other behavior therapists that I feel somewhat alienated from that community. I rarely attend meetings of the AABT and have been looking for a home where psychotherapy has a broader base than that permitted by the generally accepted BT approach.

My practice of a pure form of BT was relatively short. I had great difficulty in keeping myself from thinking in terms of the psychological organization of behavior, the idea that behaviors grouped together in a gestalt whole that possessed characteristics that were more than the sum of the constituent behaviors. For example, a hierarchical structure within the organization led to some behaviors being peripheral and others central. These last behaviors—those that were central to the organization—would be selected as the targets for change. If we changed those, the entire organization would be expected to change and the problem behaviors to disappear. In formulating such organizations to help select target behaviors for change, I many times was forced to consider psychodynamic variables and formulations. This was the beginning of my interest in integrating the behavioral and dynamic approaches within a treatment framework.

The first result of this attempt was to somewhat alienate me from the more purely behavioral groups. Also, in the mid-1970s few practitioners could accept a combined behavioral–psychodynamic orientation. My professional social support came from my continuing case seminar at the medical college and, a bit later, from the Society for the Exploration of Psychotherapy Integration (SEPI).

The case seminar has been meeting weekly for more than 20 years. Some of the current participants have been members from the beginning; other participants come, stay for a semester or so, and leave. All are mature therapists and make their livelihoods mainly or exclusively from a private practice. Most have solid training in both the dynamic and the behavior therapies. Many also are trained in such areas as hypnosis, sex therapy, bioenergetics, neuropsychology, and psychopharmacology. More than half of the seminar participants have had advanced training in EMDR. The cases discussed usually are extremely difficult and complex and drawn from our own practices. At times, life-and-death issues have been at stake. The discussions are characterized by a playfulness and a humor along with the application of serious ideas to specific cases. Disagreements are expected, and the group offers respectful listening to differing formulations and differing therapeutic approaches. Seminar participants have influenced each other greatly. Although the seminar was initially centered on BT, the problems posed by our patients (interacting with our individual backgrounds) eventually led us to the more integrated perspectives. One book, a number of articles in professional journals, and a number of presentations at SEPI meetings have emerged from this seminar. In short, it was the seminar made possible my transition to the more integrated but still behaviorally based approach that I use today.

Several years after the founding of the seminar, SEPI was formed. The first annual meeting of SEPI took place in Annapolis, Maryland, and was one of the highlights of my professional life. We were a small number of involved clinicians meeting in a friendly atmosphere and eagerly listening and discussing perspectives that differed from our own. I vividly remember at that first (or perhaps second) meeting Arnold Lazarus presenting a case. Stan Messer, at a number of points during the presentation, gave another perspective on the ongoing treatment being described. At the end of this combined presentation, Ellen Wachtel presented the family-therapy perspective of the case.

This was an exciting and stimulating experience, and I wanted to hold on to the atmosphere it generated. My hope was that SEPI would remain a small group of clinical and academic therapists who were dedicated to and immersed in the concept of psychotherapy integration, who understood the problems of working therapists, and who were open to considering new perspectives. Despite its strong beginning, the organization soon became more and more academic. The organization's journal, for example, seemed to be more interested in exploring concepts then in sharing clinical experiences. This is now changing. The organization and the journal are making increasing attempts to integrate the clinicians, researchers, and academicians, and I truly hope those attempts succeed. Meanwhile, SEPI remains a major professional support for my attempts to practice an integrative therapy, a place for the exchange of new and meaningful ideas about the field.

MY CURRENT APPROACH

I see myself as a behavior therapist attempting to function within a Pavlovian framework and following the model set by Schneirla for understanding animal behavior. From the beginning to the end of treatment, I constantly attempt to form a picture of the patient's psychological organization. In the past, I would actually draw diagrams to show the interconnections between behaviors, but now I do it in my mind. The diagram may involve the organization of some specific behavior (e.g., a phobia or a loss of temper), or it may attempt to show the patient's overall psychological organization (Fensterheim, 1975). This formulation uses either behavioral (such as habits or conditioned reflexes) or dynamic (such as reactions to childhood memories or defenses against these memories) concepts. The aim is not to achieve a valid understanding of the patient; instead, it is to identify targets for change and thereby lead to a systematic series of approaches to the patient's problems. I have no investment in maintaining a formulation that is not bringing about the desired change. If treatment is not working, I am quick to reformulate. The relationship I form with the patient varies with the characteristics of that specific person. Most usually I strive for a relationship modeled after the doctoral candidate–thesis mentor relationship. I provide guidance, help resolve treatment difficulties that may arise, give technical suggestions, and furnish support when needed. But I realize that I will never know as much about what goes on inside the patient as does the patient himself or herself.

The most recent development in my approach has been my involvement with EMDR. Saul Raw, a colleague, a collaborator, and a member of the seminar, gave me a copy of Francine Shapiro's first published article, and I became immediately interested. First, it repeated many of the experiences I was having at that time. I had started to question my patients about their thoughts during the desensitization procedures and had found that instead of the patient focusing on one specific image, these procedures often brought forth a wide range of associations. Shapiro described findings similar to those I was obtaining. In addition, I had the impression that here was a truly Pavlovian procedure, an impression supported by Shapiro's support of Salter's Pavlovian-oriented conditioned reflex therapy. I received training in EMDR and began to use it in my practice for people with personality disorders. In formulating the psychological organization underlying a patient's problem,

I often find that the targets that emerge from this formulation have a core involving a series of childhood memories. This core serves as the basis for the EMDR approach. As the EMDR procedure continues, I get clues that allow me to reformulate the patient's problem and to select new target behaviors. I find that many times, the method does not work with personality disorders no matter how flexible I am at reformulating the patient's difficulty; I also find that it rarely works fast with such disorders. Using EMDR I also have obtained remarkable results with a number of refractory patients.

Thus much of my current therapeutic work involves using both behavioral and psychodynamic concepts to formulate the case and using mainly behavioral approaches in attempting to bring about change. I am extremely aware of the therapeutic relationship and of my own impact on this relationship, but I have not thought very deeply in this area. I do pay increasing attention to ego deficits. One concept I find useful is that of the passive ego: the ego that is passive in the face of feelings and impulses. This is a concept advanced by David Rapaport, and although I do not use the psychodynamic underlay he uses, I find the idea extremely helpful and use it as a target area. I also am sensitive to the presence of attention deficit disorder and other cognitive deficits. My experience in physical rehabilitation has shown me that even mild forms of these disorders may bring on huge behavioral consequences that in turn may influence internal psychodynamics and self-concept. I send an increasing number of patients to neuropsychologists for evaluation and ancillary treatment when indicated. The way I practice these days is far different from what I did at the beginning of my career, and I wonder how I will be practicing 10 years from now.

CONCLUSION

My career has been marked by restlessness, a desire to explore new territory. Although rarely in the first wave of a new approach, I was often in the close-following second wave. I was one of the first to study the Rorschach; one of the first to work in physical rehabilitation; one of the first in the country to establish a psychiatric walk-in clinic; one of the first in BT; one of the first in hyperventilation; and an early practitioner of EMDR. My main thoughts are of where to go next. Looming on the horizon are discussions about what makes the good life, about what strengths should be encouraged and how to develop them, and about how to help people self-actualize. That direction fits well with my long-term interest in assertive behavior and may lead to my next endeavor. In the meantime my main interest, my main motive, still is to help the specific person sitting in front of me.

REFERENCES

Fensterheim, H. (1953). Some psychological principles in the physical rehabilitation of aged patients. *American Archives of Rehabilitation Therapy, 5,* 1–6.

Fensterheim, H. (1971). *Help without psychoanalysis.* New York: Stein & Day.

Fensterheim, H. (1975). Behavior therapy of an obsessive–compulsive personality. In C. Lowe & H. Grayson (Eds.), *Three psychotherapies* (pp. 41–59). New York: Brunner/Mazel.

Fensterheim, H. (1993). Behavioral psychotherapy. In G. Stricker & J. R. Gold (Eds.), *Comprehensive handbook of psychotherapy integration* (pp. 73–85). New York: Plenum Press.

Fensterheim, H. (1996). Eye movement desensitization and reprocessing with complex personality pathology: An integrative therapy. *Journal of Psychotherapy Integration, 6,* 27–38.

Fensterheim, H. (1999). Comment on "The angry patient." *Journal of Psychotherapy Integration, 9,* 143–149.

Fensterheim, H., & Birch, H. G. (1950). A case study of group ideology and individual adjustment. *Journal of Abnormal and Social Psychology, 45,* 710–720.

Fensterheim, H., & Glazer, H. (Eds.). (1983). *Behavioral psychotherapy: Basic principles and case studies in an integrative clinical model.* New York: Brunner/Mazel.

Fensterheim, H., & LaKritz, J. B. (1958). An experimental study of the role of self-concept in the physical rehabilitation of aged patients [Abstract]. *American Psychologist, 8,* 348.

LaKritz, J. B., & Fensterheim, H. (1953). The psychologist therapist team in physical rehabilitation. *American Journal of Occupational Therapy, 7.*

Lum, L. C. (1976). The syndrome of habitual chronic hyperventilation. In O. H. Hill (Ed.), *Modern trends in psychosomatic medicine* (Vol. 3, pp. 196–230). Boston: Butterworth.

Normand, W., Fensterheim, H., & Schrenzel, S. (1967). A systematic approach to brief therapy for patients from a low socioeconomic community. *Community Mental Health Journal, 3,* 349–354.

Normand, W., Fensterheim, H., Tannenbaum, G., & Seger, C. (1963). The acceptance of the psychiatric walk in clinic in a highly deprived community. *American Journal of Psychiatry, 120,* 533–539.

Witkin, H. A. (1949). The nature and importance of individual differences in perception. *Journal of Personality, 18,* 145–160.

8

MAKING MEANING OF THERAPY: A PERSONAL NARRATIVE OF CHANGE OVER 4 DECADES

IRIS E. FODOR

© Amy Beilin

He who lives his life in genuine realizing knowledge, must perpetually begin anew, perpetually risk all anew; and thus his truth is not a having, but a becoming. (Martin Buber, 1913/1964, p. 90)

I consider myself an integrative therapist. This chapter describes my training and experiences in four different therapy modalities spanning the 4 decades that have formed the foundation of my work.

My original training as a graduate student in the late 1950s to mid-1960s featured a Freudian psychoanalytic orientation. From the mid-1960s to 1970s, following postdoctoral training and beginning work as a therapist, I learned behavior therapy and cognitive therapy while continuing psychoanalytic training. In the mid-1970s, I began integrating a feminist approach with cognitive–behavior therapy (CBT) and brought to this integration an experiential–gestalt focus from the 1980s on. Each phase of my training and work as a therapist has enriched my growth and provided me with an integrative framework to make meaning of the many changes in my own life and the broader culture.

In my private practice, in New York City, I work mostly with people in their mid-20s to mid-60s. They come into therapy experiencing anxiety and depression or dealing with trauma or loss. Many of my clients work too hard; feel stressed with all the competing demands on their time; and wonder why they are so anxious, tired, depressed, or unfulfilled. Many of them also are trying to create a life that enables them to pursue creative goals while struggling to earn a living and achieve recognition in the arts. In addition, they either are struggling with or are despairing of finding a special personal relationship. Recently, I have been working with older women in crisis after the death of their husbands, helping them deal with their bereavement issues. All of my clients, whatever their presenting problems, are trying to make meaning of their lives, and many are searching for spiritual understanding as well.

Through 4 decades of personal challenges, working with many people and sharing pieces of their lives and struggles, I am convinced that no one therapy has a monopoly on the truth for human experience. The essence of therapy is the personal encounter between the client and therapist. From my earliest work as a Freudian therapist, where I was the "special friend" for lonely children in pain, to my current work with adults, who come to me seeking some refuge from the loneliness, insensitivity, and abuse they experience in the outside world, I see the therapeutic encounter as an opportunity for clients to explore their experiences, learn about themselves, and learn how to cope in a safe place with someone who tries to understand them, who meets them as another human being, and who has struggled to cope and make sense of life.

In many respects, I am a lifelong student of personality theory and psychotherapy. As a professor, I teach personality theory and therapy. I also believe that one cannot teach about therapy without the ongoing experience of working with clients. Recently, I have become interested in bringing an integrative perspective into the classroom for work with children on emotional education.

LESSONS ORIGINALLY LEARNED

Each of us is born in a particular culture at a particular time and place and is part of an age cohort. As therapists, we receive graduate training and begin to acquire experience at a particular point in the development of the field. Through our families, relationships, and friends, we are exposed to fields outside of psychology. I did not choose my original therapy orientation. It was all there was at the time where and when I trained. I was very young when I became a psychologist, and I wanted to learn all about myself and other people as well as help others. I initially accepted the Freudian approach, but it was not until later, as I grew and society changed, that I began to question Freudian assumptions. I never asked whether this explanatory system fully fit my experience as a woman. I accepted the authorities (i.e., professors and supervisors) as they reinforced Freud's take on human experience. The changes in my work as a therapist occurred in the context of changes in the culture in general and in psychology in particular as well as of the changing nature of the clients and the issues they brought into therapy. In addition, growing older, listening to myself rather than others, luck, fate, and the challenges of my personal life and my responses to them also have been most influential in motivating me to change and shape the directions of my therapeutic work.

Exposure to New Experiences

I majored in psychology as an undergraduate at the City College of New York (CCNY) in the late 1950s. I lived in the Bronx and commuted from home. I was part of a generation who took advantage of free tuition with the hope of achieving beyond the level of our working-class parents. The depression and World War II marked my parents' generation. I am Jewish and was raised as a "red-diaper" baby, with a strong emphasis on concern and care for others' well-being and a focus on social justice. Men and women of my age in the United States are part of a generation who were raised for the most part with traditional gender role expectations. We were raised to be heterosexual and to marry early for life. Marriage was clearly for better or worse; divorce was rare.

I was in the second class of "girls" at CCNY. I was attracted to psychology, which was then more of a man's field, not to education, which was for women. I sought out female college teachers as role models. I had only two female professors at City College, however. One was an anthropologist, who spent a lot of time in places like Fiji, and the other was a psychology professor, who seemed to have a more balanced life. She taught, did research, and had a husband and four children. She was my role model; I became her research assistant to learn more about her and her life and what she did, and I decided to be a child psychologist.

CCNY in the 1950s was an exciting place. Gardner Murphy, the chair of the psychology department, was a well-known social psychologist who brought together an unusual psychology faculty. The social and experimental faculty had a gestalt orientation. I learned gestalt psychology, with its field-theory orientation, and it became the context for all my other thinking about the organization of experience and change. I was in college during the McCarthy era, and the campus was a focus of the House Un-American Activities Committee investigations into left-wing activities of faculty and students. As a member of the student council, I was involved in sit-ins and protests against the committee's hearings on campus.

Although social concerns were prominent at CCNY, all the clinical courses I took featured Freud and the classical psychoanalytic approach to clinical issues, and in New York and, later, in Boston, that was my major theoretical framework for clinical work. I was fascinated by clinical case studies, such as Robert Lindner's (1955) popular book *The Fifty-Minute Hour: A Collection of True Psychoanalytic Tales*, which features stories of unusual psychoanalytic cases. Psychotherapy is presented as a method akin to detective work; that is, the therapist hangs in there and, through caring work with the patient, unravels the mysteries of their bizarre symptoms.

I attended Boston University for graduate work in clinical psychology. Again, all the clinical faculty were Freudians. I had one woman professor, a developmental psychologist. Leo Reyna, who taught me experimental psychology, had just returned from South Africa, but he never spoke of his research with Wolpe and his role in the development of behavior therapy. I also had intensive training in projective techniques, and I learned even more how to see the world in Freudian terms.

At that time, clinical psychologists working in the Boston mental health centers mostly did comprehensive assessments, with reports organized according to Freudian theory. In my internship, however, and later as a staff psychologist at Children's Hospital, Harvard University Medical School, I was assigned child and adolescent therapy cases and was supervised by prominent psychiatrists who were members of the Boston Psychoanalytic Institute.

In my original training, therapy was viewed as a corrective emotional experience. The goal was related to undoing defenses, making the unconscious conscious through interpretations, and providing an environment to support in-depth psychodynamic exploration.

The big events of my work with these children were the clinical case conferences. I pored over the books and constructed a history and view of the child's dynamics. My psychoanalytic training focused on pathologizing children to come up with a Freudian story to account for the symptoms. Most of the creative work in therapy was in finding evidence for this story. As clinicians, we never really looked at how the child was changing or even took seriously the parents' complaints about lack of progress. It was more important for us to understand the dynamics. This same focus on diagnostics was present almost a decade later at Massachusetts General Hospital, when I worked on an inpatient ward with adult patients.

During my graduate school and internship training, I was taught how to do play therapy with children (mostly using dollhouse play and drawing) and to use my background and knowledge of psychoanalytic theory as a guide for making interpretations. What was stressed over and over again in child therapy was that the relationship with the child was central; change would occur through the healing inherent in the relationship. Also emphasized was that the child needed to get in touch with his or her feelings and that the play therapy was a form of catharsis, with the therapist providing interpretative guidance.

I often did not know what I was doing when I did therapy with children. I took extensive notes after each session, and my supervisor and I reviewed them. My supervisors never observed me doing therapy, but they assured me that in building the relationship I was doing good work. The children did improve, but I often felt that I was missing the mark by not directly addressing the presenting symptoms. I liked working with children, especially preschoolers and adolescents; too often, these children from large working-class families in Boston did not get enough adult attention. I believed that whatever change occurred was related to the "special friend," who listened and tried to understand.

My first phobic client was at Children's Hospital, a girl of 8 years who had a school phobia. My supervisor hypothesized that she was angry at her mother and had to stay at home to make sure her angry wishes were not realized (i.e., so that her mother did not die). I was skeptical of that explanation. I was told to engage in doll play to uncover the fantasy. Actually, the child was shy, and I think she was fearful of the school setting (what we would now call a social phobia). We drew and played with the dollhouse, and I gingerly spoke to her about school. I did not directly focus on the supposed anger toward her mother. The child subsequently was able to attend school.

In the mid-1960s, what was exciting in psychology and psychotherapy was happening outside of psychoanalysis. I was lucky enough to become active in the beginnings of two psychotherapy movements: CBT and feminist therapy. They have remained my core, much more so than psychoanalysis.

In the first decade of my training and career as a psychologist, many of the changes that occurred in my life were not actively sought but were the results of exposure to new experiences related to the life and moves of my husband as well as changes in the culture. Like many women of my time, my husband's career was more important than mine, and he, not I, chose where we lived and worked. The most important shifts for me occurred in these circumstances: Having to change jobs resulted in working with varied clinical populations and thus exposed me to other therapeutic modalities in settings as diverse as rural southern Illinois and Oxford, England. By the 1970s, however, when I was no longer married, I was actively seeking out new challenges for ways of working as a therapist.

Cognitive Science Beginnings

When I was applying Freudian theory to clinical work during the 1960s, my philosopher husband joined the psychology department at MIT, where Hans-Lukas Teuber had brought together linguists, philosophers, and physiological and experimental psychologists in what was one of the beginnings of the cognitive science movement. I attended courses and seminars and was intellectually excited by these new ideas. I lived in two worlds: the clinical world and the world focused on understanding language and the mind. I did not know how to bring them together at that time. I did my thesis on organization and memory with a population of patients recovering from head injury. My dissertation research and the work at MIT also seemed compatible with the gestalt orientation I had been exposed to in college. Later, it formed the basis for my adapting schema theory as a core organizing experience for the integration of cognitive and gestalt therapy (Fodor, 1996b, 1998).

When my husband was invited to the Center for Advanced Studies in Palo Alto, California, I took a postdoctoral fellowship at the Palo Alto Veterans Administration (VA) hospital. The year in Palo Alto was a pivotal experience that changed my life. It was the 1960s, and it was California. That year, I saw my first Beatles movie, the Free Speech movement at Berkeley began, and the flower children of the Haight–Asbury neighborhood were attracting attention.

At the hospital, I was assigned to the ward Ken Kesey drew on for *One Flew Over the Cuckoo's Nest*. It appeared that some of his patients were still there. On my first day, a patient tried to throw a chair through the window of the nurse's station. I knew that my previous training had not prepared me for work in this setting. Leonard Krasner was the director of training for the psychologists at the hospital, and we were taught behavior therapy. In addition, what I was exposed to included the following:

- an anti-Freudian bias: Once a week a Freudian psychiatrist would come to the case conference, and his interpretations would be cause for laughter.
- no psychodiagnostic testing: Instead, the focus was on individual therapy, weekly seminars, and a supervision group.
- therapeutic community: Patients and doctors met each morning to discuss ward happenings.
- a weekly family therapy supervision group run by Don Jackson. He taught us a systems approach to therapy, including the radical ideas of Bateson and other systems theorists.
- process group therapy, which was run by a psychiatrist who later joined the staff of Esalen
- a "token economy" ward
- hypnotherapy.

The most important influence on me that year, however, was psychotherapy supervision with Walter Mischel, a personality theorist who had been a student of George Kelly. Mischel taught me about a constructivist approach to personality and supervised me on my psychotherapy cases. My first case was a man who had attempted suicide one night and had not expected to wake up. In the therapeutic work, my supervisor and I had to find another way for this client to construe his life, beyond "I am a failure" and "I have no wish to live." In this, my first encounter with adults and a constructivist perspective, I found the meaning that the Freudian approach lacked, by giving a person responsibility for framing his or her life and choices. Mischel helped me understand how this depressed man was framing his experiences. Given the urgency of this man's plight, I appreciated not having to dig for root causes and make interpretations but instead focusing on realistic problem solving. In addition, under the supervision of Don Jackson, I worked with this client and his wife in couple's therapy, appreciating all the implications of the family system on his despair and recovery. I began to envision a way of working with clients' presenting problems directly, which was refreshing after my previous analytic training.

Another client had profound anxiety symptoms, and Mischel, a framer of social learning theory, encouraged me to learn behavior therapy. Teaching the client how to relax and learning systematic densensitization were profound changes for me. I could now work with clients on what seemed most important for them, develop a plan with them, and see changes related to the therapeutic work.

I arrived back in Boston in the summer of 1965 and tried to find a job that would enable me to continue to learn behavior therapy. A summer continuation of the postdoctoral fellowship provided me with a demonstration case for my colleagues in the Boston community. I worked with a man who had a severe transportation phobia of 18 years' duration and who had to be hospitalized for debilitating anxiety about a change in job that would require commuting. He had 3 years of psychodynamic therapy with no symptom relief. A Freudian formulation of the etiology of his symptoms was proposed, but the client was "resistant" to working on these issues.

The client was so anxious at the time I saw him that he could not even ride the hospital elevator. When I described the new therapy to him (i.e., he needed to learn to how to relax), he was delighted. We began relaxation and desensitization to the hospital elevator, coupled with graduated in vivo practice. The client was a middle-aged working-class man, and he reminded me of many of the men I grew up with. He was so pleased with his ability to master the elevator fear that he asked to work on his biggest fear, riding trolley cars. Again, together we drew up a plan and took small steps; I was his coach. What was apparent is that his early success on the elevator prompted a desire to seek out more challenges. His self-esteem increased as he mastered his fears. After a month of treatment, he boarded a trolley car for the first time in 20 years. Many at the VA hospital heard about his treatment and hung out the window cheering him on. He got better, and I was hooked on behavior therapy.

I was offered a job in the inpatient unit of Massachusetts General Hospital doing traditional psychodynamic assessment but was told that I would have the opportunity to experiment with behavior therapy with children. I discovered a group of other mental health professionals interested in behavior therapy. We met regularly, reading articles, teaching each other, presenting cases, working on projects together, and supporting each other's endeavors. Many of these people were instrumental in the further development of behavior therapy.

I began seeing clients privately for behavior therapy, mostly women with phobias and weight problems. The big issue in Boston, as we presented our behavioral approach to the traditional psychodynamic community, was over the problem of treating the symptom. The analysts said that one could not treat symptoms without dealing without the underlying pathology. But we behaviorists did. We also did research, and our treatments worked. I presented the transportation phobia case at grand rounds at both Massachusetts General Hospital and Children's Hospital, and because I was "one of them," some analysts were open to this new therapy.

Furthermore, dynamic issues would emerge from this work as well. For example, an overweight woman was referred by one of my former supervising psychiatrists, who said "she is successfully analyzed, but still overweight." By doing a behavioral analysis, I honed in on her eating patterns, which the analyst never did, and could see dynamic issues emerging from this work.

STRENGTHS OF ORIGINAL ORIENTATIONS

Psychoanalytic

I was only 22 years old when I began learning Freudian therapy; naturally, I liked the completeness of the Freudian system. There was an explanation for everything; the whole system fit together. I also have a historical bent and a love for the archeological dig. I was well trained in assessment, and I especially enjoyed the case conferences, where we put our heads together and tried to figure out the dynamics of a case. Anna Freud's elegant elaboration of the theory of the ego and mechanisms of defense made sense to me. I also appreciated the emphasis on fantasy symbols, dream interpretation, and meaning making. I still lecture on classical psychoanalysis and appreciate its developmental focus. Even though I now focus on present concerns, I want to know the client's view of her history; background; relationship with her mother and father; and other relevant information. I also like the complexity of psychoanalytic theory and practice. People are ambivalent: They love and they hate the same person, they have conflicts, and one part wants to do one thing and the other something else. Also, psychoanalytic theory accepts the dark side.

I liked and still believe what I learned from the interpersonal focus, the centrality of the relationship. While in postdoctoral analytic training, I also had a positive experience with an interpersonal analyst who came out of the Sullivanian tradition. We worked face-to-face, and he showed me what relational work could be. He was accepting and empathetic, and he encouraged me to explore my own sense of what was going on. I was having a difficult time in my personal life after my marriage ended (with symptoms of depression and anxiety), and I felt cared about and respected by him. He was clearly himself in the therapy. He provided me with a way of being that I strive to emulate to this day.

Cognitive–Behavioral

The social learning perspective appealed to me. In the 1960s, behavior therapy was part of the movement away from viewing emotional problems as a sickness or abnormality or as evidence of some mysterious underlying pathology. Instead behavior therapists viewed emotional problems as maladaptive learning. What was learned could be unlearned.

What I liked about behavior therapy was being able to take seriously the client's presenting problem or symptom and to focus the assessment on learning as much as possible about the patterning of the symptoms. I liked the role of the therapist as a consultant or teacher who was there to help clients learn about their patterns and devise opportunities and strategies for new learning. As cognitive therapy developed, I appreciated the constructivist perspective as well as the focus on the irrational thought pattern or dysfunctional thinking that appeared tied to the problematic behaviors. I enjoyed highlighting this cognitive–behavioral interplay in the therapeutic work.

The here-and-now and experiential focus of behavior therapy also was appealing, as was the custom tailoring of treatment. For example, I once treated a woman with a butterfly phobia. She was unable to walk in parks or go into the countryside. Because butterflies are rare in the city and her avoidance behavior was strong, I had to be creative in the exposure therapy. She brought in colored pictures of the butterflies she was most afraid of; I pasted them on my fingers and acted as a butterfly in the office. Eventually, she was willing to go for summer walks with me in the country and remained symptom free and appreciative of my willingness to be creative in helping her.

I also appreciated the research focus of cognitive–behavior therapists—the effort to try to understand the patterning of symptoms, what worked and what did not—as well as the emphasis on posttreatment assessment and follow-up. I enjoyed participating in the creative, energetic CBT community of the late 1960s and 1970s and focused on applying CBT to a multitude of clinical problems.

As I became transformed by behavior therapy, I became interested in preventive mental health and took an academic position in a school of education. I began teaching graduate students who were working with children and adolescents in schools. CBT provided an ideal psychoeducational model for work with children and adolescents, and I wrote and did research with my students on anxiety as well as assertiveness and social skills training in school settings (Fodor, 1992). My current teaching and research on emotional education for school psychologists still take this perspective.

LIMITATIONS OF ORIGINAL ORIENTATIONS

Psychoanalytic

As I became a behavior therapist, I continued to work in psychodynamic settings. (It was where the work was at that time.) Because I generally was the sole behavior therapist, I became interested in integrating psychoanalysis and behavior therapy and became a candidate in a postdoctoral program in psychoanalysis. In spite of the positive aspects of the psychoanalytic approach, this experience fostered misgivings about the possibility of such an integration.

At the time I was in training, there was too much focus on the intrapsychic and not enough attention paid to the actual interpersonal relations of the client or social context. Nor in my experience was there enough emphasis on the actual ongoing relationship between the therapist and the client. I still do not buy into the analytic assumption that we cannot really know ourselves, that central issues are out of our awareness and governed by unconscious forces.

I did not like the role of the analyst as the interpreter of the client's experiences. In my first analysis, my Freudian analyst too often discounted my experience. She appeared through her interpretations to know better than I what was happening with me. After 3 years on the couch, this attitude prompted a change to an interpersonal analyst.

I did not like the arrogance, pathologizing, and arguing among analysts at case conferences as to who is "right" about the dynamics or interpretation of a case. The long-term focus of analysis also was problematic. I once heard a famous analyst state that "it was only in the 13th year of the analysis that the true nature of the transference became apparent." (Do we have forever to figure out our issues?) Furthermore, the focus on analysis and transference as the vehicle for change was problematic. I had a negative experience with one supervisor when I commented in supervision on my frustration about my client's "choking on his anger"—with the wish that I could find a method to help him express it better. She told me I was too invested in change and that my job was just to "analyze."

Most important, I had trouble accepting the limited psychoanalytic perspective on female development that was still dominant at that time. Despite the large number of women analysts, the developmental framework for women still featured a "phallocentric" perspective, that is, viewing female development from a male perspective that mirrored the sexist societal view of women. Women were prone to "penis envy"; had a less developed "super ego"(moral sensibility); and needed to accept their femininity—notions that implied a second-class status to men (Freud, 1925/1956; Strouse, 1974). Cultural factors were not highlighted in my analysis or psychoanalytic training. Within psychoanalytic programs in the 1970s, women students began to form study groups, which were critical of the traditional perspective and provided fertile ground for the development of a feminist psychology of women within psychoanalysis. At NYU, I participated in such a group, but given what I considered the core limitations of the theory and practice, I chose to work on female development outside of psychoanalysis.

Cognitive–Behavioral

As I became more experienced with CBT and was seeing more and more people with complex problems, I began to realize the limitations of just working within the cognitive–behavioral model. I have presented these criticisms in several articles (Fodor, 1983, 1987, 1988b).

First, the focus on symptoms as targets for change became problematic as I began working with more complex problems. Often the treatments did not work, despite well-designed assessments and interventions. I had difficulty helping overweight clients maintain their weight loss, and many of my phobic clients, despite initial treatment success, relapsed. I also began to see clients, who were initially successfully treated, returning a year later for therapy with another problem. Often the system continued to break down as I worked piecemeal on anxiety management, assertiveness, and self-control while not addressing the larger pattern of their response to changing stressors. By maintaining a focus only on symptoms rather than on patterns and process, I was failing to enable the clients to understand some of the redundancies that contributed to their persistent problems.

For the most part, the focus on the dyadic interaction between therapist and client was not attended to in CBT. For example, a client who formerly had agoraphobia who, after 1 year of hard work in therapy, was now traveling on her own insisted that she had not been helped at all by the therapy (because she still felt anxious while driving) and berated me for thinking she had been. In the act of carrying out specific procedures, many of the problematic patterns experienced by my clients in their lives were repeated in their interactions with me.

Another problem for me was the acceptance of the client's goals at face value. Not enough attention was paid to conflict or splits. Resistance to treatment did occur (e.g., an overweight client reported eating three candy bars just after a session in which she had worked up a plan to reduce caloric intake). Another client became more anxious as her phobias subsided. Clearly, the exploration of conflicts about goals or feared consequences about the changes needed to be explored.

As cognitive therapy developed, we practitioners were optimistic that emotions could be handled by focusing on maladaptive beliefs. Too often, however, emotions had a life of their own and were not so easily controlled by cognitions. Eliciting emotions and understanding their patterning were downplayed.

Although behavior therapists spoke of social learning theory, the onus of change was still on the client, rather than on changing society. The message to the client was, "It's up to you to change! We can help you learn how to overcome prior conditioning and so forth if you work hard enough and learn these new behaviors." Such optimism, however, discounts both the difficult reality of many people's lives and the ongoing practices that exist in our society that make it hard for clients to change (e.g., sexism, racism, ageism, poverty). Not enough emphasis has been placed on techniques for addressing societal prejudices.

In the late 1960s, I became active in the antiwar movement and became concerned with social issues and the impact of society on individuals. The social activism of the 1960s was a spur to the women's movement of the 1970s. As I moved away from psychoanalysis, I became interested in seeing therapists move beyond the focus on the individual client's concerns toward the wider social context of the client's problems. Feminism and gestalt therapy provided a framework for such work.

HOW CHANGE OCCURRED

I have found that my own womanhood is a very important factor in my work as a therapist. With some women it adds an expectation of being understood in a way no man could understand them. . . . I do know how it is, I have been there and I am still there. (Miriam Polster, 1974, pp. 261–262)

When my generation was in their early adult years, fulfilling their traditional roles, the feminist movement began and altered the lives of many of us traditionally raised women and men. For my generation, it meant forging a new path—with excitement and anxiety—and a good deal of personal upheaval, as the old paradigms no longer fit the lives we were living.

I was no exception; sadly, my marriage ended. By the early 1970s, I was living in New York, a single parent with a baby girl and a 4-year-old son and an academic job in the school psychology program at NYU, where I had been hired to teach the traditional psychodynamic assessment courses and to develop a behavior therapy practicum sequence. I began to do research and writing and began a New York psychotherapy practice doing what is now called CBT, mostly with agoraphobic women.

I felt lost without the traditional script that I had been following, and I had a hard time financially. Early on, in the many lonely evenings at home with the children asleep, I read every feminist book that came out. I was particular impressed with Simone de Beauvoir's *The Second Sex* (1953), her existential framing of woman as the "other" and descriptions of her personal struggles to become an independent woman. I began to construct a new view of myself and what my life as a woman was about. I also joined a consciousness-raising group.

Many of my women clients and students at that time also were experiencing similar struggles. At the same time, I joined with other women therapists in studying women's lives and began to think and write about women's mental health issues. Many of the problems of my clients appeared to relate to their socialization into the female role. I also joined with other women faculty to start a women's studies program at NYU, where I developed (and still teach) a course on women and mental health.

I became a leader in the feminist therapy movement even before I had a firm sense of my new identity. I was a candidate in a psychoanalytic institute and had the goal of integrating psychoanalysis and behavior therapy. I had gone into a personal analysis with a female Freudian analyst but, like many women of my generation, found the traditional analytic approach at that time to be too restrictive toward the new way of thinking about women. Some of my psychoanalytic colleagues who stayed with psychoanalysis became leaders in developing the new psychology of women. I took a different path and found a male interpersonal analyst who provided support and encouragement for moving beyond analysis. By that time, I no longer believed it was possible to integrate psychoanalysis and behavior therapy.

I moved further away from psychoanalysis to behavior therapy as I became a feminist. I saw behavior therapy as providing a model for women to take charge of their lives and to learn new ways of behaving. My first clinical publications appeared in 1972. The first was an article titled "Sex Role Conflict and Symptom Formation in Women: Can Behavior Therapy Help?" (Fodor, 1972b). When I had presented this work at a conversation hour at the behavior therapy convention the previous year, Violet Franks asked me to contribute a chapter to her and Vasanti Burtle's book *Women in Therapy*, which I titled "The Phobic Syndrome in Women" (Fodor, 1972a). In these two publications, I proposed a link between stereotypic female socialization (to be dependent and helpless and the development of phobic symptomology) and that behavior therapy could help women to become less fearful and more self-sufficient and assertive. I became an advocate for behavior therapy beginning to better address women's issues and began speaking and writing about its applicability for the new generation of women seeking change (Fodor, 1980).

Women therapists began working together to create a feminist approach to working with women. We also began using the same techniques, with the support of other therapists in our consciousness-raising groups, to reparent ourselves. I specialized in assertiveness training and body-image and self-esteem problems as well as in helping women taking charge of their lives, overcoming their fears and phobias to move beyond the model of helpless woman.

The behavior therapy community provided support for this work, and I was invited to present at conferences and universities. There was an excitement and freshness about behavior therapy at that time, and I felt fortunate to be able to integrate the behavior therapy and feminist modalities. Through this work, I met many behavior therapists who influenced me and are still my close friends.

By the 1970s behavior therapy had became more cognitive, as had my own orientation. I brought the feminist perspective to my beginning work in cognitive therapy. I built on prior training in constructivism and saw the major change process in CBT for women as cognitive restructuring, envisioning other ways of being, and then developing new behaviors for change.

At NYU, Janet Wolfe, a graduate student in clinical psychology who was actively involved in clinical work and training at the Institute for Rational Emotive Therapy (now the Albert Ellis Institute), asked me to work with her on her dissertation, thus launching a long-term collaboration. She reintroduced me to the cognitive approach, this time in the form of rational–emotive therapy (RET). We began to work together to develop, conduct and do research on women's assertiveness groups.

We proposed that woman's lack of assertion was tied to cognitions stemming from sex role socialization messages:

> For many women, the stereotypes about the "shoulds" and "oughts" of sex role behavior and assertiveness function as internal belief systems or schemata through which their own and others' behaviors are evaluated. And when their behavior deviates from what they believe they ought to be, or from what others expect them to be, feelings of anxiety, guilt and confusion may follow. (Wolfe & Fodor, 1975, p. 45)

The assertiveness training usually was carried out in women's groups. These groups focused on

- helping women become aware of their beliefs related to assertiveness, the sex role socialization messages tied to these beliefs, and their role in the continued construction of these beliefs
- directing women to test their beliefs about the negative consequences of assertiveness against their real-life situations
- teaching women to adapt new attitudes and experiment with new behaviors in the group, with the feedback and support of the group and leaders.

When they were ready, the women were encouraged to try out these new behaviors at home, work, and other settings and to provide feedback to the group about what worked and did not work (Fodor, 1980). Women's assertiveness training groups in the mid-1970s became an important part of the women's movement, were adapted by the public, and contributed to women's empowerment (for a fuller discussion of the personal becoming political for women, see Fodor, 1988a; and Fodor & Epstein, 1983).

I also brought the feminist perspective to my work with women with phobias. I addressed the social context of anxiety and phobias in women, with an emphasis on socialization as a key factor in their developing and maintaining phobic avoidance behavior. At that time, I believed that behavior therapy, by developing techniques to enable women to face their fears, provided remediation for prior social conditioning (Fodor, 1972a).

In a similar vein, after failing to help overweight women lose weight with behavioral techniques and seeing low self-esteem and body image issues in too many adolescents as well, I began to stress that behavior therapists need to consider societal messages about attractiveness and weight in designing their treatments (Fodor, 1983). Body image, self-esteem, and eating behavior and media influences continue to be an ongoing interest in my therapeutic work with women (Fodor, 1996b).

Almost all of my specialty areas have emerged from my own struggles. My work with women has focused on assertiveness training, weight and body image, and mother–daughter relationships. I was trained to be unassertive and to put others' needs before my own: Hence, I realized from my personal life the need to be assertive. Body image and weight concerns mirrored my family's concern that I be thin and attractive and not like other overweight family members, whose struggles I recalled from childhood. (I graduated from the Barbazon School for modeling as a teenager.) Coming to terms with my mother, the choices she had made for herself, and my desire to pursue a different path set me to work on these issues with other women. When I brought my 11-year-old daughter to a mother–daughter assertiveness workshop and identified more with the mothers than the daughters, I realized that I was working these issues from both sides.

As I further focused on assertiveness issues in the mid-1970s, highlighting the interpersonal aspects and building on what I learned in relational psychodynamic therapy, I became increasing dissatisfied with what I viewed as the limitations of CBT in dealing with interpersonal issues. The approach too heavily emphasizes the internal ideational system and assumes that the clients' major relationships consist entirely of the self-statements they are generating within their own heads. I felt that too often, those internal dialogues focused on messages, appraisals, or evaluations of or by significant others. As I continued to work with women and the array of their interpersonal relationships, I became convinced that therapists needed to look beyond the individual focus.

I also was not convinced that changing cognitions themselves led to significant change. My clients were more complex and were resistant to substituting the therapist-generated rational–adaptive thinking for their own persistent maladaptive beliefs. After watching the emotional upheavals in many of my clients, I became convinced that emotions cannot always be controlled by cognitions and that affective patterns need to be explored more fully as routes into deep structures that organize behavior.

In the mid-1970s, I began working more experientially in the assertiveness groups to access the affective patterns and their relations to cognitions as well as to highlight interactions within the group. One participant noted that my work resembled gestalt therapy, especially with its emphasis on emotional awareness. I decided to seek some gestalt therapy training. Gestalt therapy was then outside of the psychotherapy mainstream and was taught mostly in intensive workshops or by individual trainers at Gestalt Therapy Institutes. As I discovered more about gestalt therapy, it became clear that gestalt therapy was a rich, theoretically based system of therapy that addressed the very issues I felt needed further development in cognitive therapy. It is a learning-based therapy that focuses on present experience, enhancing awareness, and facilitating dialogue. Gestalt therapy, with its foundation rooted in field theory, addresses social issues as well. What gestalt therapy and behavior therapy have in common is the concept of the "therapist as educator." They both believe that the role of a therapist is to teach clients how to learn about themselves, although they approach the task differently.

Gestalt therapy, following existentialism, has no explicit goals for therapy except increased awareness. It also addresses the complexity of individual experience by highlighting polarities. Having people become aware of what they are experiencing in a moment of time is the primary focus of the therapy. Gestalt therapy posits the paradoxical theory of change (i.e., having clients stay where they are and both own and explore their present experience; Beissmer, 1970). In espousing organismic self-regulation, gestalt therapy presents a positive view of people's ability to take charge of themselves once they become aware of and own where they are, what they need, and the choices and resources that are available to them (Perls, Hefferline, & Goodman, 1951).

I began my gestalt therapy training in the summer of 1977, in a 10-day intensive workshop conducted by the Gestalt Therapy Institute of Los Angeles in what was then Yugoslavia. The trainers from the Los Angeles Institute all had been trained by Fritz Perls or Jim Simkin. I am thankful that I was trained by the second generation of gestalt therapists because I am not sure I would have been able to tolerate the initial confrontational style of Fritz Perls. By the time I began training, and much more since then, the style has become less confrontational and more focused on dialogue. Since then, I have been to more than a dozen of these workshops and to training in New York and Los Angeles. The gestalt trainers who had the most impact on my personal work and training include Bob Martin, Lynn Jacobs, Irving and Miriam Polster, Laura Perls, Jannette Rainwater, Robert Resnick, and Gary Yontef.

The first gestalt workshop in Yugoslavia was unlike anything else I had ever experienced and, like the Palo Alto experience 12 years earlier, had a profound effect on me both personally and professionally. In the 1977 training group, the trainers did therapy demonstrations with the group members. They worked with a precision and depth I had never seen before. When I was in the "hot seat" as a client in the gestalt training doing personal work, I accessed emotional experiences that I never had touched in personal analysis. In addition to the hot-seat work, there was training in awareness, body work, tracking process, and meditation, among other things. Spirituality and Buddhism were a focus of some of the trainers.

What attracted me and continues to hold my interest in gestalt therapy training is its process focus, dealing with what is actually going on in the session at the time. Gestalt therapists have developed a sophisticated system of therapy training. The training typically occurs in groups with live demonstrations. Many of the participants in the training groups are experienced therapists from various orientations and cultures. In training, a student therapist does "a piece of work" in front of the group with a volunteer "client." The group members discuss their reactions to the work, and the volunteer client relates his or her experience of the work as well. Supervision by the trainer occurs on the spot, and the group discusses how the work represents an aspect of gestalt theory. As I continued to train in gestalt therapy, what impressed me most was the excitement and energy among trainers and group members: a willingness to be open, to experiment, and to use creative modalities in therapeutic work. There was encouragement to honestly express what one was experiencing and to communicate this to group members. We learned about feelings, emotions, and "working from the inside out." The process emphasizes unfolding at the moment of experiencing. This powerful process of tracking makes for a depth of focus and often elicits a strong emotional response. We were encouraged to allow the powerful emotions to emerge and be present with the client in this state.

In psychoanalysis, I learned about my issues from personal history. In CBT, I learned about how I construct my beliefs and their impact on my emotions and behaviors. In gestalt therapy, I experienced these emotional patterns and behaviors in my interactions with other group members. I learned how to focus on myself—become aware of what I was experiencing as I worked with a client, to learn to deconstruct the nuances of relating and be able to explore how others experienced my relational style. In working with a client, I learned to explore, from moment to moment, our experience of each other.

Another important aspect of the European residential training program was its international focus. Most of the participants were from other countries, including Australia, Brazil, Israel, and South Africa. More recently, increasing numbers of participants have been coming from Eastern Europe. Hence, cultural differences and misunderstandings, as well as contextual issues, become a part of the training process. In addition, social issues are addressed related to therapeutic and clinical issues (e.g., changes in Eastern Europe following breakup of Soviet Union). This experience has enriched my work with culturally diverse populations in New York City.

MY CURRENT APPROACH

The Integration of Gestalt Therapy and CBT

From my first gestalt training to the present, my intent has been to integrate gestalt therapy and CBT. I thus brought the gestalt therapy process focus and the relational perspective to my work as a cognitive–behavior therapist. For the past 15 years, I have been writing and conducting workshops about the possibilities for such an integration for both the cognitive–behavior and the gestalt communities. Since I began training in gestalt therapy, CBT itself has changed and now places a greater emphasis on schematic processing and attending to the cognitive–emotional interface. In moving toward integration today, I highlight schema theory and the schematic interplay between our sensed experiences and the meaning-making process (Fodor, 1987, 1996a, 1996b, 1998).

In my teaching, I now use experiential methods for training school psychologists. For example, I teach my first-year graduate students to attend to their experience when they enter a school on the first day of their field placement: the sights, sounds, and smells; their own experience as children in school; cultural differences; and the meaning they are making of this experience. As they learn to work behaviorally, they are encouraged to continue with this focused awareness of their experience as well as to attend to the child's perception of what is happening.

In clinical work, the integrative cognitive–behavioral–gestalt approach begins by attending to the clients' view of their problems, taking account of the social context of their lives, their gender issues, family relationships, where they are in their life cycle, and their cultural and spiritual values. The central thrust of this integration, however, is a focus on awareness of process. As I listen to their view of their problems, I try to facilitate their awareness of what they are experiencing as they tell their story and how they engage me in the process. By beginning with a gestalt focus for the presentation of the issues, I slow down the assessment process.

In the beginning of therapy, I also am interested in learning how the client constructs his or her view of the world and what other worldviews might be possible. In later sessions, when I have a clearer understanding of what the issues are from their point of view, I might become more active in introducing experiments and homework assignments to foster new learning. I view the process of change in this integrative model as providing a new meaning or information context to enable the client to reappraise what they are experiencing.

I see therapy as a personal encounter, and my work as a woman therapist and feminist informs this work. My presence itself and the questions I ask influence the patterned process that emerges. I want to examine my client's experience of what it is like to be with me. At each step, I also stop and become aware of what I am experiencing as I hear my client's experience. Even in the therapeutic work in accessing the emergent schematic patterned process, by being part of the inquiry, I am affecting what is attended to and what is not. At best, we are cocreating the reality of that moment of experience.

An Illustration

> Rose, age 50, a recently separated landscape painter, comes for help because she is frightened about being alone. She has begun to have panic attacks while walking on the street and in stores. I approach the beginning stages of therapy over several sessions. (adapted from Fodor, 1998)

I begin with her story about herself (the larger narrative about where she is in her life cycle and the larger meaning of her symptoms). She did not want the separation and believed she could not function competently without her husband's support. Her children are grown. Her husband had helped her to organize shows. Her income is erratic, and she worries about making enough to support herself and deal with her husband and the lawyers in working out the settlement. She cannot stand being alone and is afraid that she will not be able to take care of herself. My role is simply to be present, ask questions, and try to understand how she construes her experience. I also am aware of the social context of her new life: Working out details of a separation is hard. Life is more difficult for an older woman alone, and our culture does not provide support for artists; this is a profound role shift for her. I have been there myself. I want to know more about her work as an artist, the readjustment issues in her life, her economic situation, and other social factors and their relation to the anxiety. This illustration, however, focuses mainly on the patterning of anxiety symptoms themselves.

What does she know about the schematic patterning of anxiety? When does she get anxious, and when does she not feel anxious? Does she know the triggers? What does she do or not do when they occur? What is her theory about how and when the panic begins and when it eases? What happens when the panic emerges? How does she take care of herself? Who is there for her? How does she ask for help? What is she aware of in her body as she speaks of her symptoms? Is she aware of her breathing, racing talk, fluttering hands, impressionistic view of what is happening as she tells me about her panic attacks? What does she say to herself? (e.g., "I can't stand it." "I can't take care of myself." "I'm going to die or go crazy."). I ask questions about what she knows about her patterns and observe what emerges in our process work together.

At the beginning of the fifth session, Rose comes in and appears distant. She is talking in a rushed way about all the problems of the week and her meeting with her lawyer, and she looks away as she fires off the events of the week. I am feeling pressure to deal with all the problems of the week, and I do not feel in contact with her.

Therapist:	"Look at me and try to tell me what's going on. I'm finding it hard to reach you. What are you feeling?"
Rose:	"I'm not sure. It's hard to feel anything, I have so much to deal with."
Therapist:	"Take a few minutes to sit with yourself. When you feel ready, tell me what you feel."
Rose:	"I'm feeling numb."
Therapist:	"Tell me how numb feels."
Rose:	"It's just numb, empty."
Therapist:	"Stay with numb and empty. Describe its shape, color. Where it is in your body?"
Rose:	(looking at the therapist) "It's just black, empty, cold." (Her hands start to shake.)
Therapist:	"I see you shaking."

Rose: (looking away again) "I'm so scared." (She starts to wring her hands.)

Therapist: "I feel you are having a hard time staying with me right now. What's happening to your hands? I see that you are scared."

Rose: (looking at her hands and making teary eye contact with the therapist) "They are shaking, I feel so scared!"

Therapist: (taking the client's hands) "I know you're scared. It's hard to really focus on the fear. Let me stay close to you while you tell me about your fear."

(Rose shares her terror about being alone, her being overwhelmed, and her experience of abandonment.)

Therapist: "I see how terrified you are. How do you feel right now with me?"

Rose: "Not so alone."

Feeling more in contact, I can now begin to better work with her on these fears and her feelings of being alone and overwhelmed.

In later sessions, we explore all the triggers and patterning of the anxiety attacks and the feelings of being overwhelmed. We process an anxiety episode she had in a store. By retelling me about the situation, she becomes anxious again. This time, she is willing to dive into her experience of an anxiety attack with me at her side. We focus on what's happening in her body (her breathing), her runaway anxiety, what contributes to the feeling of being overwhelmed, and what she is saying to herself while all of this is happening. In particular, we examine together her awareness of how she is processing information about her anxiety and coping. I am both supportive and interested in what she is finding out about her process. We explore possibilities for other responses to her anxiety.

As therapy progresses, she begins to develop a different narrative and appraisal of her anxiety and her life situation. From "I can't stand the anxiety," she develops a mastery narrative: "I can do it, if I work on breathing and do not scare myself. Meditation helps me stay calm and to be less afraid of feeling anxious and overwhelmed. If I can do this, allow the anxiety to emerge and handle it, I can live alone. I do not have to be so scared. I can take care of myself."

We also attend to her stressful life situation and her anger, sadness, grief, and economic readjustment as well as the problems of being an artist in our culture. For example, we study the interrelation between the anxiety triggers and anger with her separated spouse and the pattern of anxiety when she picks up a brush and looks at the blank canvas.

Of course, this therapeutic work is much easier said than done. But the focus of the work is always on the experience in the moment and what the person is feeling, what she is saying to herself and her actions. I am there to facilitate this process of self-awareness. All along, I am also revealing how I am experiencing her anxiety and her challenge to master her fright and despair over the panic. We talk about her feelings of dependency on me. What is relying on me like for her? And what is it like for me? I am there to facilitate a dialogue about where she is in her learning about the anxiety–panic schema; to hear about what works to facilitate calmness and does not; and to feel sad, worried, or delighted with her as she goes through these processes. As two women, we also talk about what life is like for a middle-aged woman alone—its problems and its possibilities.

During the year of therapy, Rose did develop an appreciation of her patterns and how she contributed to making things better or worse. What she reported helped her most in the therapy was my just being there—being interested, supportive, and caring and being willing to talk about my own struggles when I had found myself in a similar situation. She viewed the therapy as a process of self-discovery, and she said she had a much clearer sense of how to take care of herself. As she began painting again, we shifted the focus to her creative concerns and possibilities for earning a living.

CONCLUSION

In reflecting on my personal and professional life over the decades, what seems clear is that I have been challenged by the changes in the therapy community and our culture, my work as a therapist, and the personal changes of my own life. At this point, making meaning of all the changes is still a central focus of my life. As I get older, I appreciate my psychoanalytic training (ironically as I moved away from psychoanalysis to seek a relational perspective elsewhere, psychoanalysis has become more relational). What I enjoy most is teaching an integrative perspective to my students; continuing to enjoy the many friendships I have made in the cognitive–behavior, feminist, and gestalt communities; and seeking out new learning (a recent focus has been Buddhist spiritual training). I feel privileged to continue to work with clients who are creatively seeking to make sense of their lives and to teach new generations of students. My commitment to my family, husband, friends, students, and clients remains the center of my life.

Today, I consider myself an integrative therapist with specialties in both cognitive–behavior and gestalt therapy. As an integrative therapist, I bring a gestalt perspective to CBT and a cognitive perspective to gestalt therapy. I teach, write, and give workshops in these modalities for the cognitive–behavioral, gestalt, and integrative communities (Fodor, 1987, 1998). Gender issues are still central to my work with clients whether I am working with a man or a woman. As I get older, I more fully appreciate a life-cycle perspective. The sudden death of my mother, and the deaths of all my aunts and a beloved mother-in-law, led me to an interest in mid-life issues, aging, and dealing with loss. Many of my clients now are dealing with such losses as well. I have also remarried and am dealing with the complexities of later life relationships and adult children and stepchildren.

In addition, preventive mental health, urban education, and social change still remains a focus for me. At NYU, in teaching and supervising first-year graduate students, I present an integrative framework for these beginning therapists to learn CBT, gestalt therapy, and psychodynamic therapy. I also am interested in bringing this integrative work back into the classroom and am currently developing modules using both cognitive and gestalt concepts in emotional education for children and adolescents (Fodor & Collier, in press).

REFERENCES

Beissmer, R. (1970). The paradoxical theory of change. In J. Fagen & I. L. Shepard (Eds.), *Gestalt therapy now* (pp. 77–80). Palo Alto, CA: Science and Behavior Books.

Buber, M. (1964). *Daniel: Dialogues on realization*. New York: Holt, Rinehart & Winston. (Original work published 1913)

de Beauvoir, S. (1953). *The second sex*. New York: Bantam Books.

Fodor, I. (1972a). The phobic syndrome in women. In V. Franks & V. Burtle (Eds.), *Women in therapy: New psychotherapies for a changing society* (pp. 132–168). New York: Brunner/Mazel.

Fodor, I. (1972b). Sex role conflict and symptom formation in women: Can behavior therapy help? *Psychotherapy: Theory, Research, Practice, 2*(1), 22–29.

Fodor, I. G. (1980). The treatment of communication problems with assertiveness training. In A. Goldstein & E. Foa (Eds.), *Handbook of behavioral interventions* (pp. 501–603). New York: Wiley.

Fodor, I. (1983). Behavior therapy for weight disorders: A time for reappraisal. in M. Rosenbaum & C. Franks (Eds.), *Perspectives on behavior therapy in the 80's* (pp. 378–384). New York: Springer.

Fodor, I. G. (1987). On integrating gestalt therapy to facilitate personal and interpersonal awareness. In N. Jacobson (Ed.), *Psychotherapists in clinical practice: Cognitive and behavioral perspectives* (pp. 340–410). New York: Guilford Press.

Fodor, I. G. (1988a). Assertiveness training in the 80's: Moving beyond the personal. In L. Walker & L. Rosewater (Eds.), *Handbook of feminist therapy* (pp. 257–265). New York: Springer.

Fodor, I. G. (1988b). Cognitive behavior therapy: Evaluation of theory and practice for addressing women's issues. In M. Douglas & L. Walker (Eds.), *Feminist* psychotherapies: Integration of therapeutic and feminist systems (pp. 91–117). Glencoe, IL: Haworth.

Fodor, I. (Ed.). (1992). *Adolescent assertiveness and social skills training: A clinical handbook*. New York: Springer.

Fodor, I. (1996a). A cognitive perspective for gestalt therapy. *British Gestalt Journal, 5*, 31–42.

Fodor, I. (1996b). A woman and her body: The cycles of pride and shame. In R. Lee & G. Wheeler (Eds.), *The voice of shame: Silence and connection in psychotherapy* (pp. 229–265). San Francisco: Jossey-Bass.

Fodor, I. (1998). Awareness and meaning making: The dance of experience. *Gestalt Review, 2*, 50–71.

Fodor, I., & Collier, C. (in press). A model for adolescent assertiveness and conflict resolution. In M. McConville & G. Wheeler (Eds.), *The heart of development*. Hillsdale, NJ: Analytic Press.

Fodor, I., & Epstein, R. (1983). Assertiveness training from women: Where are we failing. In P. Emmelkamp & E. Foa (Eds.), *Failures in behavior therapy* (pp. 137–158). New York: Wiley.

Freud, S. (1956). Some psychological consequences of the anatomic distinction between the sexes. In J. Strachey (Ed.), *Sigmund Freud: Collected papers* (Vol. 5, pp. 186–197). London: Hogarth Press. (Original work published 1925)

Lindner, R. (1955). *The fifty-minute hour: A collection of true psychoanalytic tales*. New York: Bantam.

Perls, F. S., Hefferline, R. F., & Goodman, P. (1951). *Gestalt therapy*. New York: Julian Press.

Polster, M. (1972). Gestalt therapy. In V. Franks & V. Burtle (Eds.), *Women and therapy* (pp. 247–262). New York: Brunner/Mazel.

Strouse, J. (1974). *Women and analysis*. New York: Grossman.

Wolfe, J., & Fodor, I. (1975). A cognitive/behavioral approach to modifying assertive behavior in women. *The Counseling Psychologist, 5*(4), 45–52.

9

REFLECTIONS OF A
BEHAVIOR THERAPIST

ALAN J. GOLDSTEIN

Like most professionals in training during the mid-1960s, I was introduced to the prevailing models of psychoanalytic psychotherapy and Rogers's client-centered psychotherapy. Psychoanalytic psychotherapy was the exclusive choice in psychiatry, and Rogers's model held sway in university counseling centers. The bedrock model of most psychology doctoral programs was psychoanalytic theory, with some family and couple's therapy training, and the occasional Skinnerian advocate using reinforcement techniques when working with inpatients or with children. At the same time, there was a lot of excitement about the new models growing out of the counterculture movement of the late 1960s and early 1970s, which were being developed outside of university-based programs. These included gestalt therapy (which involved active attempts to increase a person's awareness of thoughts and feelings) and encounter groups (in which there was direct interpersonal confrontation), both of which I found of interest. While on a rotation at the university student health center, I had a gestalt-trained supervisor, and I read a good deal about encounter groups and gestalt therapy.

LESSONS ORIGINALLY LEARNED:
THE GRADUATE SCHOOL EXPERIENCE

With the exception of Rogerian and Skinnerian models, theory that informed practice was absent, and practitioners most often described psychotherapy as an art form—an art that seemed formless. Consequently, most of my earliest attempts at therapy were rudderless and largely conducted by trial and error. I gleaned some useful information from supervision, case conferences, and rare opportunities to observe experienced therapists and kicked around ideas with fellow graduate students. I managed to get all the way through graduate training and internship with only one supervisor ever actually listening to therapy tapes. To his credit, he did so regularly, but he then provided little guidance. Surely I wasn't doing everything perfectly. The Skinnerian supervisor watched most of my sessions with a child client and provided good feedback about my reinforcement skills, but this model seemed of little help with adults in therapy, my primary area of interest. Not surprisingly, in this milieu, observations of practitioners, the limited information that they provided, and random but striking happenings had profound effects upon my developing attitudes toward schools of psychotherapy.

Early on I attended a psychiatry case conference at which a psychiatrist presented a patient with so-called hysterical blindness. He introduced the case in the usual way, telling us the patient's age, gender, marital status, and so forth, and noted that the patient lacked psychological sophistication and was not informative. Nevertheless, the presenter was confident that he understood the dynamics of the case. He pointed out that the patient worked in a road repair crew and was often the flag man, holding traffic and then waving the waiting cars through when the road was clear. While working, the patient surely would be able to see female drivers with their skirts pulled up. (It was hot in Florida.) This stimulated forbidden impulses, and the symptom of blindness was the patient's solution to the resulting conflict. When questioned about evidence to support this hypothesis, the presenter seemed to think none was required. This was of a piece, as it seemed at the time, in that for all psychodynamic practitioners Freud was king, and all psychological symptoms were obviously related to the Oedipal complex. It galled me that the professional was all knowing, whereas the patient was lost in the morass of his or her parent-induced sickness.

Among other difficulties I found with psychoanalytic practice were the insistence upon medical model diagnosis and the arbitrary rules about how one related to the patient. The diagnosis provided no help in the treatment, because all patients were treated essentially the same regardless of diagnosis. The rules included the necessity for the therapist to stay distant and avoid self-revelation; the importance of sticking to the 50-minute hour;

the patient's paying as large a fee as possible; the need to enforce prompt arrival for the session; and habitual interpretation of any conflict between the patient and therapist as the patient's problem. Although these rules supposedly were for the patient's benefit, it seemed that they were, more often than not, in the service of the therapist's need for control, convenience, and protection of ego. I came to think of psychoanalytic psychotherapy as "therapist-centered" therapy. The nonfalsifiability of the theory, the arrogance underlying the rules of practice, and the one-sided search for pathology in diagnosis and treatment that often became nothing more than name calling turned me off to psychoanalytically based psychotherapy. I was further distanced from psychoanalytic practice by the seemingly antiscientific attitude and simplistic, noncritical thinking of the psychoanalytic practitioners as well as the frustration of finding no way to translate theory into interventions in the therapy hour. Although I found the theoretical notions of the unconscious and defense mechanisms interesting and of use personally, on the whole I was unable to separate the message from the messengers.

I was introduced to Rogerian client-centered therapy (CCT) when on a counseling center rotation. CCT provided a theoretical model that guided the conduct of therapy sessions. It also had the virtues of face validity: It directed the therapist's attention to what the client was experiencing; trusted the client's capacity for self-healing; and implicitly reinforced clients' view of themselves as worthy, acceptable, and lovable rather than sick. I was heartened by this alternative view of human nature. However, from the beginning of my attempts to provide CCT for the students seeking services at the counseling center, the results were mixed. Some clients seemed to get a great deal out of our interaction, whereas others left me feeling helpless. CCT seemed to work well with college students who had problems related to developmental stresses and minor interpersonal difficulties but who otherwise were functioning well. Unfortunately, things did not go so well when I was confronted with clients who would today be considered to be suffering from such problems as anxiety disorders; personality disorders; and other, more ingrained patterns of maladaptive behaviors and feelings. Yet there was much I treasured from exposure to this model. I was fortunate to have the opportunity to learn it through practice while there were as yet no competing models pulling at me. My experience with CCT furnished me with a solid appreciation for the necessary therapeutic conditions for effective psychotherapy.

During my third year in graduate school, I ran across Joseph Wolpe's (1958) first book, *Psychotherapy by Reciprocal Inhibition*. I was primed for a system that flowed from learning theory. From the beginning year of graduate school, I was enthralled with learning theory and research on conditioned emotional responses and their reversal. My exposure to the Boulder model of training in psychology—which provided skills in both research and practice—also held me in its sway. At this time, however, there was only Dollard and Miller's (1950) translation of psychoanalytic theory into learning theory terminology to offer some hope for the development of a scientifically based system of psychotherapy. I found Wolpe's book to be an answer to the shortcomings of the models to which I had thus far been exposed. It was based on laboratory research and a learning theory model that seemed to be the best hope for a research-driven theoretical alternative to the existing models. Wolpe's model for treatment of neurosis was internally consistent and logical and could be operationalized in the consulting room. In addition Wolpe's book promised clinical efficacy and applicability to the full range of psychological problems that at that time were described as neurotic. This book introduced me to the process of looking at the presenting problem contextually and, unlike anything I had yet encountered (with the exception of Harry Stack Sullivan's work), paid specific and detailed attention to the situations in which presenting complaints occurred.

Wolpe's operating assumption was that fear, anxiety, guilt, and so forth were not pervasive symptoms but, instead, were triggered by specific cues. A second assumption was that these maladaptive, cue-generated responses were learned and could be unlearned. My constant question in response to supervisors' descriptive comments about the personality of the client ("Okay, so now what do we do about it?") was at last answered. Wolpe described techniques based on learning theory and, most important, emphasized techniques for unlearning conditioned emotional responses, allowing the therapist to generate new interventions that could be validated quickly by the client's response. Imagine my excitement: a theoretical system that could be individually tailored to the specific complaints of the client! I was sold on the spot.

In the summer of 1966, while still in graduate school, I attended the first of what was to become an annual summer training course in behavior therapy. Wolpe was at the University of Virginia Medical School at that time, and he invited eight psychologists and students who had been in touch with him to spend a month training in behavior therapy at the Department of Psychiatry. We attended daily lectures and daily case conferences and observed Wolpe working with patients. We worked in pairs, each pair seeing one to two patients on a daily basis. It was my good fortune to be paired with Joseph Cautela, who was already developing a form of behavior therapy based on covert processes. The opportunity to watch two excellent clinicians, Wolpe and Cautela, helped counteract the highly vocal criticism of those who damned behaviorism as being mechanical, dehumanizing, and ineffective except for treatment of specific phobias in otherwise psychologically healthy people. These clinicians were clearly dealing with complex cases in a sensitive, respectful way, and to good effect.

For example, Cautela was applying his covert conditioning techniques with a woman in her mid-20s who had a history of severe eating disorders, depression, and interpersonal problems. When she began treatment with Cautela, she was still severely bulimic, had lost all of her teeth as a result, and was depressed. She had been in psychoanalytically oriented therapy for 8 years and for the past 3 years had been in treatment with a highly respected psychoanalytic faculty member in psychiatry at the University of Virginia. She had been the subject of many case conferences in which Wolpe had suggested behavioral interventions and had been referred to Wolpe for treatment during the 1-month training as a way of putting behavior therapy to the test with a complex case. Bulimia was the focus of the daily 1-month treatment. Within 3 weeks the client went from daily binge eating and purging to no binge eating and no purging. Moreover, she experienced a noticeable decrease in body image-triggered anxiety and a considerable shift away from her tendency toward distorted evaluation of her weight. Her depression lifted with her growing sense of control over the compulsive eating that had dominated her life since early adolescence. Although the treatment was tightly focused, it was in no way mechanical. On the contrary it was done with great sensitivity and within the context of a skillfully developed therapeutic relationship. This was my first introduction to a therapist's establishing a working partnership with a client in which they appeared to be equals working together. The problem was "out there" and a result of unfortunate experiences that could happen to anyone, rather than "in there," in the patient as part of her personality, poor genes, developmental inadequacies, and so forth, as other models seemed to imply.

STRENGTHS OF ORIGINAL ORIENTATION

This early behavioral training provided me with an internal structure, a way of organizing and understanding the heretofore overwhelming amount of information and attending affect that clients provide in the early sessions of their therapy. To this day, I find that having a coherent internal structure that leads to a concrete treatment plan is vital to providing effective treatment. For me this structure is an expanded behavioral analysis, a point to which I return later.

Other aspects of my early training in behavior therapy that have stood the test of time include the importance of understanding clients to be contextual responders, rather than the victims of fixed, internally driven personality characteristics, and the power of the therapist's and the client's working on the problem as a team, rather than the therapist doing something to the so-called patient. I still value flexibility over inviolable rules about the conduct of therapy. Flexibility includes openness to reevaluation of my conceptualization of the client's problem and, as a result, the treatment plan. I use changes in the day-to-day world of the client as the major criteria for judging the effectiveness of the therapy and, consequently, as a determining factor in changing what I do in the session. This approach does not imply that I need not monitor the quality of process, for it is well known that some within-session processes correlate well with change outside sessions. I particularly was attracted to many of these behavioral principles because they seemed to flow from an underlying respectful attitude toward the client rather than the superior stance that was adopted by many of the professionals whom I had encountered early on.

Another strong influence on my development as a clinician was my acceptance of scientific method as a legitimate approach to psychopathology and treatment. Findings from therapy research on process and outcome and from research on psychopathology have shaped my approach. From observing many therapists of diverse backgrounds, I concluded that some clients will improve regardless of their therapists' specific theory (or lack thereof) and no matter what interventions their therapists use. Therapists thus are on an intermittent reinforcement schedule (i.e., the same treatment will sometimes be rewarded and sometimes not); as we know, such a reinforcement schedule leads to behavior that is hard to change and may lock therapists into suboptimal practices. This observation has strengthened my allegiance to the scientific method, which I believe has paid off in the consulting room. I see clinical observations, scientific inquiry, and diagnostic schemes all interacting to support development of stronger theoretical models and more valid assumptions underlying our view of clients' problems. This change in our understanding then feeds back into and influences clinical observations, diagnostic schemes, and scientific inquiry.

If scientifically derived evaluation is absent in this loop, as it generally was as late as the 1970s, there is no corrective mechanism, no motivation to do the difficult work of casting theoretical postulates into testable form, and we therapists are locked into the star system that existed when I began my training. We studied the stars—Freud, Rogers, and Perls—and their pronouncements were taken as truth with no agreed-on standard for disconfirmation. Practice was a matter of faith. We owe Carl Rogers a great debt for his groundbreaking work in fostering psychotherapy process and outcome research. Behavior therapists took up this work eagerly, and research on psychotherapy has been part of my work for my entire career. Research on treatment is still driving changes in behavior therapy. Thus, the years since graduate school have been exciting ones because I have been fortunate enough to have been part of and influenced by a paradigm shift that is still in progress.

At the beginning of my career, no appropriate scheme for diagnosis existed. The *Diagnostic and Statistical Manual of Mental Disorders* (2nd ed. [*DSM-II*]; American Psychiatric Association, 1968) was based on psychoanalytic theory. Under the influence of early focused research efforts based on descriptive categories of client complaints (in my area, anxiety, this research mostly came from England) and widespread dissatisfaction in the field, the *DSM* diagnostic scheme moved to descriptive classification and, as a result, has been far more useful in treatment and research. Following the old system, researchers lumped heterogeneous populations into single categories, such as neurosis. However, clinicians noticed that subcategories of the neurotic population fared better than did others. For example, behavior therapists noticed that systematic desensitization worked well for simple phobias, less well for social phobia, and not at all for agoraphobia. These observations prompted reconsideration of our understanding of phobias as an unitary phenomena and, in the case of agoraphobia, for example, led to a reformulation that emphasized fear of internal cues associated with panic rather than external ones. This shift, in turn, allowed for development of new interventions and created further pressure for change in the diagnostic system. We began to reframe the question "Does psychotherapy work?" to "What treatment for what problem works best?"

Undoubtedly, I have found the resulting treatment outcome research to be extremely helpful. First, it is a way of shaking me out of complacence with what I think that I already know about treatment of various disorders. Second, it serves as a map to treatment of problems with which I have not had extensive experience. Third, the research prompts me to constantly consider the impact of new findings on my theoretical understanding of particular disorders. It is true that packaged treatment interventions are not sufficient as a blueprint in the treatment of many individual cases; however, one ought not to expect that learning how to drive by reading a description of how to do it on the salt flats sufficiently prepares one to be a race car driver or to drive a stick shift through New York City traffic. Nonetheless, the treatment manuals developed for research offer skilled clinicians definite opportunities to improve their treatment of the next client and, for neophytes, an enlightened set of guidelines for the trip. We still have a long way to go in determining how best to match treatments to clients, particularly how to take into account the effects of clients' personality characteristics on their response to treatment. Research on finding whether a treatment is differentially effective for clients with a particular characteristic is proceeding but as yet is insufficient to guide clinical practice.

LIMITATIONS OF ORIGINAL ORIENTATION

My first position was at the Behavior Therapy Unit of the Temple University Medical School Department of Psychiatry. Wolpe had joined the department the year before and was in the process of building the Behavior Therapy Unit as a training facility. Arnold Lazarus and Michael

Serber were already on board, and there were several postdoctoral psychologists in training. These were exciting times because the highly contentious debates between the psychoanalytic majority and the small but vocal group of behavior therapy pioneers were being played out in the microcosm of the Department of Psychiatry and on a national level in the journals, conferences, and psychiatric and psychological associations' publications. The solid opposition and our own revolutionary fervor drove us behavioral true believers into extreme positions in defense of behaviorism and in our rejection of all else.

At about this time I had the good fortune to meet Paul Wachtel, who changed my view of psychoanalytically trained professionals. Here was a man who was a model of openness to the value of seeking growth through exposure to divergent views. He seemed completely free of the narrowing influence of blind loyalty to one school of psychotherapy. Conversations with Wachtel led me to revisit psychoanalytic concepts and to be aware of how much that school of thought had already influenced my thinking. Among many pioneers in the behavioral movement, there was a growing, if behind the scenes, awareness that radical behaviorism had thrown out the baby with the bathwater. Although in the literature, behaviorists wrote only about behavioral theory and techniques, the really skilled practitioners were modeling a good deal more and talking to one another about the importance of other factors, such as the therapeutic relationship, in getting positive outcomes. At the time it just was not politically correct to put this conversation in writing, and when we behaviorists did, we changed the language to behavioral metaphors and pretended to have just discovered these concepts.

In 1976, Goldfried and Davison published *Clinical Behavior Therapy*, in which these two prominent behavior therapists openly acknowledged the contribution of other psychotherapy models. The revised edition of the book (Goldfried & Davison, 1994) remains an excellent resource for those who are open to exploring other factors and how they may be integrated in clinical practice within a behavioral framework.

HOW CHANGE OCCURRED

I continued to value the humanistic and client-centered aspects of Rogerian therapy that I had come to see as necessary but often insufficient. While embracing behaviorism, I continued to explore the offerings of the humanistic movement. I attended workshops and encounter groups, read what I could find, and experimented with the practice of gestalt therapy. I found the humanistic therapies to be both misleading and useful in the long run. In the short run, this experience was personally challenging and professionally frustrating. The personal challenge of the humanistic approaches stemmed from my need to understand them by experiencing them through participation in gestalt and encounter groups. I sometimes felt brutalized and sometimes warmly supported, but I always felt challenged. In these groups therapists heavily emphasized confrontation and getting out feelings. Their primary notions seemed to be that if one expressed feeling fully and was confronted with his or her unacceptable behavioral patterns, then psychological health would follow. Instead, I observed that encouraging clients to fully express their feelings often reinforced endless anger and blaming others and sometimes justified rather sadistic group and therapist pressure for participants to conform. I concluded that the behavioral approach to helping clients develop adaptive patterns of behavior, rather than harsh confrontation, was actually the more humanistic choice. I witnessed a number of psychological casualties among participants in encounter groups and was pleased to see this form disappear along with bell-bottom pants.

Gestalt therapy, although weak theoretically, seemed to have more to offer in that it provided some techniques for moving clients through intense feelings to insight and resolution of painful past experiences. Through my experiences with humanistic therapies, it became clear that expression of feelings is just the beginning of change. One must also come to think and feel differently about the causative events and then begin to take the chance of trying out new behaviors in the present. Expression of feelings was a high for many, but it often did not lead to change (unless it was part of the process of self-disclosure for those whose avoidance of such disclosure was inherent to the patterns they wished to change).

After some years at the Behavior Therapy Unit, I was intrigued by the notion of developing a treatment facility based on the model of psychotherapy integration rather than a rigid adherence to behavior therapy. I was able to convince the department chairman to support a separate program for treatment of panic disorder and agoraphobia. From the outset, I hired staff with diverse theoretical backgrounds. As the program grew, I was able to add experienced therapists with gestalt, psychoanalytic, humanistic, and family systems backgrounds. It was a major challenge to integrate all of these models, and there was a good deal of experimentation in the process.

I provided intensive training in behavioral interventions for panic disorder and agoraphobia to each staff person as he or she came on board, and the staff had weekly case conference meetings that focused on integration issues. For the experienced therapists, the integration seemed to take place at the technical level. They did well learning the techniques from other models (generally, this meant that nonbehavioral therapists were learning to use behavioral approaches, such as relaxation and exposure), but most were not able to integrate at the theoretical level. Thus, they had trouble generating behavioral interventions for atypical cases. The young people that we brought on staff during their formative stage did much better at integrating the various models to which they were exposed and, as a result, were able to be more creative when later faced with unusual clinical problems. By the time they had several years of experience in the program, they were the most versatile among us and able to handle all phases of therapy with most clients.

The years of struggling in the trenches with integration provided invaluable opportunities for broadening my perspective. At the personal level, this experience created intense interpersonal bonds and an enhanced respect for the power of shared diversity.

MY CURRENT APPROACH

My current thinking about what makes for effective psychotherapy includes establishing and maintaining a sound therapeutic relationship and having an internal structure that enables me to organize the information that the client provides into a multilayered understanding of the client's complaints, present circumstances, needs, and blocks to fulfilling these needs. In addition, I must have at my disposal both process and change interventions from a variety of schools of therapy.

The Therapeutic Relationship

My understanding of the requirements for a positive working relationship is based on CCT principles and further enhanced by the recent work of Safran (1993). I have made reference to these factors above and will simply summarize here. I try to bring to the work a warm, accepting, validating, attentive openness to understanding the client's view of him- or herself and the presenting problems. Because the first necessity is to create a safe place for the client to explore, reveal, and struggle with change, I do not attempt interventions until a climate of trust is established and the client feels that I understand him or her well enough to have an informed base for suggestions. I attempt to present myself as an equal partner in the search for answers to the problems and respect the client's need to be the final arbiter. I share whatever I believe to be relevant to help clients understand the development and solutions of their predicaments. At first I attempt to adapt to the client's style of processing (e.g., intellectual, intuitive, feeling, or factual) and suggest changing that style only when the client comes to see that an overly restrictive style is part of the problem. For example, I do not insist that clients talk about feelings or painful historical events while they still see doing so as irrelevant. I take clients' dissatisfaction with me or with the therapy seriously. Often such dissatisfaction points to my own errors and leads to a change in my stance.

I have learned many times over that it usually is necessary to concentrate on symptom reduction in the first phase of therapy. Symptom-focused treatment, such as anxiety-management techniques, "flooding" to obsessive worries, or exposure to feared cues, usually does proceed well up to a point. As the client gains a sense of control over the symptoms and is able to experience periods of relative calm, the client and I are able to see more clearly how certain cues, such as interpersonal interactions, awareness of unfulfilled needs, and events that trigger negative affect and avoidance patterns, were developed as a result of painful early life experiences. Gradually the foreground content for the client shifts to the deeper response networks that will then become the focus of the work.

My most common mistake is attempting to get at the underlying networks when the client's energy and motivation are elsewhere, usually on reduction of symptoms. In the case of anxiety disorders, for example, when the client enters therapy, therapists usually deal primarily with fear and avoidance response networks triggered by obvious cues, such as those that are made up of social situations, body sensations, or contact with things perceived to be contaminated. In response to the helplessness and incapacitation that occur after onset of these debilitating problems, the client usually has developed chronic anxiety or depression. A good therapeutic relationship, therapist-provided structure, and agreed-on concrete goals established in the early stage of therapy often will provide relief from secondary anxiety and depression.

Structuring the Information Provided by the Client–Therapist Interaction

My approach to case conceptualization is the most important step in effective therapy because it informs long- and short-term goal setting as well as the choice of interventions. Through the years, I have had the opportunity to do extensive training of professionals with varied backgrounds and have found that a great many lacked an internal structure. Accordingly, when I train students and interns, I begin by attempting to inculcate such a structure. The content of the structure must be concrete enough to allow for disconfirmation and must be relevant to the development of a clear treatment plan that includes specific interventions. The more information that can be consistently accommodated by the structure, the more useful it becomes.

My own current operating model is the result of an integration of the behavioral stimulus–response model with aspects of the notion of conflict taken from psychoanalytic thinking; it includes an understanding of normal human behavior as unobstructed cycles of seeking and fulfilling needs as expressed in gestalt theory. I attempt to understand the client's past and present circumstances, feelings, and overt and covert behavior in the context of striving to satisfy basic needs for love, intimacy, validation, affiliation, and sense of worth. These needs include the need to face and finish normal processes, such as grief and other reactions to the inevitable assaults that life visits upon us. Maladaptive coherent chains of covert and overt behavior and feelings form in response to a critical mass of negative experiences with efforts to fulfill needs. These chains form in the service of avoiding recurrences of anxiety, fear, guilt, or painful evaluation by others and the self. I see these patterns as thematically organized and contextual in that they are activated in response to events, whether internal or external, and think of them as *response networks*. I see the cues that trigger a particular response network as forming a *cue network*, which is also thematically coherent. To the extent that they obstruct the client's flow toward self-actualization, the response networks are maladaptive and lead to distressing symptoms, such as anxiety and depression. I find that this way of organizing information helps me to better attend to the whole person, to define priorities in therapy, and at the same time allows me to focus interventions on a specific aspect of the client's presentation. Therapy proceeds with processing response networks one or two at a time, allowing the client to see change in some part of life rather quickly.

If permitted to do longer term therapy, I may find that I have to work with what Teasdale (1996) called "implicational networks." A discussion of this rather complex model is beyond the scope of this chapter, but any therapist should recognize the general concept. The client who may or may not be objectively functioning well describes a felt sense of the self that is negative—incompetent, defective, unlovable, and the like.

Considerations Guiding the Delivery of Therapy

Establishing Goals

In the beginning phase of therapy, I share my case conceptualization with clients to help normalize their reactions by putting difficulties in a cause-and-effect model. I strive to develop a story about how the client got to this point in life and how and why the problems developed, so that the client feels that anyone who had similar genetic makeup and had the same experiences would be experiencing similar difficulties. I also attempt to cast genetic contributions in a positive light by pointing out their advantages (e.g., introverted people may tend to be socially anxious, but they are rarely bullies and are often sensitive and creative). The conceptualization becomes the basis for a shared agreement on the goals of treatment. In addition, I find it useful to share what I know about how people change, both to help the client maintain changes we accomplish in therapy and to draw on when new problems arise later in life.

Although establishing and maintaining a good therapeutic relationship are necessary in every case, they usually will not be sufficient, at least not for the cases in my practice. For example, someone presenting with agoraphobia certainly does require a good therapeutic relationship, but he or she also requires particular exposure-based interventions. In addition to helping clients cope with what are now called Axis I problems—where the focus is on symptoms—I also typically have to address more embedded characteristics. These include clients' distrust, maladaptive ways of processing information, developmental issues, and, perhaps most important, psychological defense patterns formed in the service of avoiding painful feelings. The personality characteristics I am addressing here are usually referred to as aspects of personality disorders; however, I find the present way of thinking of personality disorders to be of little use. My preference is to think about the personality characteristics as specific cue-and-response networks that began to develop early in life, cause the client grief, and interfere with the client's ability to accomplish important life goals and with therapy. Although these networks have infiltrated many aspects of the client's life and, therefore, appear to be global in nature, I believe them to be contextual and subject to change, albeit more slowly than more limited networks.

How Are We Doing?

I attempt to avoid complacency and to monitor my progress with a case. Questions I ask myself include the following:

- Am I being respectful of the client's motivation for seeking treatment?
- Am I planning interventions that are compatible with the client's present motivation for change and present understanding of problems?
- Is change occurring in the client's satisfaction in everyday life, in his or her ease of performing previously blocked behaviors and freedom from debilitating feelings?

These are my external criteria for determining whether therapy is effective. On the basis of the client's response to therapy, I modify my understanding of the problem and my consequent treatment interventions.

What about within-session criteria for effective therapy? All therapy systems I have encountered seem to agree that change takes place only when the client is emotionally involved in the process. I see this emotional involvement as a necessary element in change but as insufficient in and of itself. Change requires that the feelings aroused are part of the personal-meaning network to be changed, and that new information is incorporated into and restructures that network (Foa & Kozak, 1986; Teasdale, 1996). A good session includes the following:

- Early in the session, the client and I determine the work to be done, balancing the client's immediate needs with the importance of pursuing work already in progress.
- The client is affectively involved (i.e., the relevant response network is activated).
- The client has some sense of resolution by the end of the session.

The resolution may take many forms, such as finding a probable solution to an immediate interpersonal problem, no longer experiencing guilt in response to particular memory, repairing a breech in the therapeutic relationship, shifting perspective, or feeling hopeful where there was hopelessness.

To illustrate the intrasession process and how it fits into longer term goals, I present the case of a 21-year-old college student coming into therapy as a result of an aborted rape attempt. She reported that all was well in her life before the incident but that she had suffered considerable distress ever since. She was constantly anxious, depressed, and unable to be alone. She was unable to study and feared that she would have to drop out of school. She also felt confused and could not understand why she was unable to get over the incident as well as other victims that she met in a support group for rape survivors. The cue network that developed after the attack included memories of the incident, experiencing sexual arousal with her boyfriend, seeing a man with similar characteristics to those of the perpetrator, walking in particular areas in the town and on campus, and lying in bed in the dark. The response network included fear, guilt, keeping lights on at night, and complex avoidance behaviors such as ritualistically checking locks and staying away from certain objectively safe areas of town.

In her fifth session, the client complained of not being able to get enough sleep because the light in the room was keeping her awake. In addition, if she started to drift off, she awoke with a start, wondering if the door was really locked. As a result, she checked the locks through the night and suffered from the cumulative effects of sleep deprivation. In this session we decided to work on resolving the sleep problem. To activate the response network, I asked the client to imagine being in her bed with the lights out and thinking about the door's being unlocked. I judged whether I was on the right track by noticing whether the exercise provided enough of the cue network to trigger affective aspects of the response network. To modify the response network, I continued to flood the client with content from the cue network, following associations that caused fear. I repeated the relevant scenarios until she was able to effectively hold them in mind without feeling frightened and was obviously feeling a great deal of relief. This was my within-session cue that today's work was done. I spent the last part of the session eliciting the client's view of the work that we had done, discussing any problems that she may have had with it, and suggesting that she follow up by no longer checking the door after 10:00 p.m. and turning out the lights when ready for bed.

In the next session, the client provided extrasession information important to my session planning. She still had difficulty with sleep. Consequently, during this session we continued to work with the same networks by ferreting out overlooked cues and subjecting them to the same process. After this session, she was sleeping through the night with the lights out. We continued over the coming sessions to tackle other cue-and-response networks related to the rape attempt until we reached a plateau of about 80% improvement.

At this point, the client shared with me that her life, in fact, had not been fine up until the point of the attack. Rather, from childhood she had seen herself as incompetent and unable to cope with life's challenges. This was a rather vague sense of inadequacy, which the client could logically reject as untrue. Nonetheless, she felt it, a sure sign of an implicational network. This is more difficult to change in that, as Teasdale (1996) described it, it is an abstraction of many life experiences and is not linked to one specific cue network. I often find that the client and I can achieve a breakthrough on the implicational network, but I lack a road map for doing this reliably.

CONCLUSION

This has been an oversimplified view of the process of therapy but one that I hope conveys the essence of what I consider to be the core of effective therapy—or at least today's thoughts on that subject! From time to time I have been convinced that I have found the true way, but I have come to find instead that I had a hand on the elephant somewhere and would have been well advised to feel around some more. In fact, I must remind myself that it may not even be an elephant and that more than one of them may be out there.

REFERENCES

American Psychiatric Association. (1968). *Diagnostic and statistical manual of mental disorders* (2nd ed.). Washington, DC: Author.

Dollard, J., & Miller, N. E. (1950). *Personality and psychotherapy: An analysis in terms of learning, thinking, and culture.* New York: McGraw-Hill.

Foa, E. B., & Kozak, M. J. (1986). Emotional processing of fear: Exposure to corrective information. *Psychological Bulletin, 99,* 20–35.

Goldfried, M. R., & Davison, G. C. (1976). *Clinical behavior therapy.* New York: Holt, Rinehart & Winston.

Goldfried, M. R., & Davison, G. C. (1994). *Clinical behavior therapy* (rev. ed.). New York: Wiley.

Safran, J. D. (1993). Breaches in the therapeutic alliance: An arena for negotiating authentic relatedness. *Psychotherapy, 30,* 11–24.

Teasdale, J. D. (1996). Clinically relevant theory: Integrating clinical insight with cognitive science. In P. M. Salkovskis (Ed.), *Frontiers of cognitive therapy* (pp. 26–47). New York: Guilford Press.

Wolpe, J. (1958). *Psychotherapy by reciprocal inhibition.* Stanford, CA: Stanford University Press.

10

FROM INSIGHT AND REFLECTION TO ACTION AND CLINICAL BREADTH

ARNOLD A. LAZARUS

The year is 1956. The setting is Johannesburg, South Africa. It has been 8 years since the fanatically pro-apartheid Nationalist Government has come into power, and the conservative political outlook seems to have permeated most aspects of society. The "brain drain" has accelerated—innovative thinkers in science and medicine are emigrating abroad. Liberal or progressive ideas are being stifled. Many books are on an official and large banned list. I am 24 years old, have completed my BA degree (majoring in psychology and sociology) and am enrolled in intensive postgraduate psychological training preparatory to embarking on my master's thesis and doctoral dissertation. The school I am attending, the University of the Witwatersrand, is an English-speaking university (as opposed to institutions that were predominantly Afrikaans speaking) that is reputed to have high standards. In retrospect, the bar indeed was set rather high, but the many hoops and hurdles we students jumped through and over achieved mainly one thing—they tested our persistence and endurance.

The emphasis throughout most of my undergraduate and graduate courses was directed at understanding the history of psychology, with theories of social psychology also figuring quite prominently. The most useful courses, in my opinion, examined psychological theories; in those classes, we studied Spence, Tolman, Meehl, Allport, Hull, Thurston, Lewin, Koffka, Guthrie, Skinner, Miller, and Mowrer. We also were heavily exposed to the writings of Freud. There was no specific program in clinical psychology. The South African Medical and Dental Council had recently established a register, where master's- and doctoral-level psychologists who had completed an approved internship could serve as medical auxiliaries. The clinical training was left up to the discretion of the internship facility. And who were the clinical trainers and supervisors? Psychiatrists and one bachelor's-level psychologist who had been recruited into the army during World War II and had worked with psychiatrists at a military base. After the war, he was invited to join a psychiatric firm, and he was the primary clinical psychologist in Johannesburg. He declared himself a Sullivanian.

Another important event took place in 1956, one that had a far-reaching impact on my professional trajectory. A maverick senior lecturer at my alma mater had invited Joseph Wolpe to lecture to us on what he termed "behavioristic conditioning therapy," and I learned about relaxation therapy, systematic desensitization, and assertiveness training. This was followed by one-way mirror seminars in which we witnessed Wolpe doing therapy on actual clients. Subsequently, I joined a coterie of professionals who had regular off-campus meetings with Wolpe. His work was perhaps the polar opposite of the strict Rogerian approach that was predominant at two of my practice sites.

Toward the end of 1957, after obtaining my master's degree, I spent 3 months as an intern at the Marlborough Day Hospital in London. There, the orientation was Adlerian. Their humane, practical, educational approach was most appealing to me. I then returned to Johannesburg and continued my internship at the pre-eminent facility, Tara Hospital. My principal training, both in London and Johannesburg, was in group psychotherapy, with some supervision in individual psychotherapy. Also at both hospitals, the supervisors in charge of individual psychotherapy were bona fide psychoanalysts. Thus, by the time I was awarded my PhD in 1960, I had been exposed to Freudian, Sullivanian, Rogerian, Adlerian, and conditioning theories and methods in my clinical training. I also had been taught to apply a wide range of psychometric and projective tests.

LESSONS ORIGINALLY LEARNED

Many therapists start out by learning one or two specific orientations. As they gain in experience, many discover gaps and lacunae and expand their repertoires. As the foregoing introduction points out, I was exposed to several different orientations in quick succession. My formal training had taught me that insight was the sine qua non of effective living and that psychological suffering stemmed mainly from a lack of insight. I also was led to believe that good therapists provide a "blank screen" on which their patients can project their wishes, needs, and perceptions. A nondirective stance was recommended for all comers. Thus, my initial forays into therapy were a combination of Freudian and Rogerian methods. After seeing Wolpe working behind a one-way mirror, I was slowly won over to more pragmatic methods and subsequently joined his camp. I became firmly convinced that active procedures are usually superior to passive or reflective approaches (a view that I still embrace). Nevertheless, I always have acknowledged that although some clients need no more than empathy and warmth, in most instances, directive methods will win out.

In the early 1960s, my clients almost always were subjected to numerous psychological tests. In addition to measures of IQ when supposedly indicated, I administered tests of persistence, personality inventories (e.g., the Willoughby Personality Schedule and the Minnesota Multiphasic Personality Inventory), and projective tests (e.g., the Thematic Apperception Test, the Rorschach Inkblot Test, and sentence-completion tests). It took perhaps a couple of years for me to conclude that these tests, by and large, were not providing me with useful or valid clinical data. I came to realize that careful history taking, occasionally supplemented by a straightforward pencil-and-paper psychometric test, enabled me to derive far more effective treatment plans.

As I grew more behavioral (it was I who first used the terms *behavior therapy* and *behavior therapist* in a professional publication; Lazarus, 1958), I adopted Wolpe's viewpoint that most emotional disturbances resulted from phobia-like clusters or hypersensitivities. For example, after undergoing a functional behavioral analysis, clients who presented with complaints of anxiety or depression would evince several discrete, phobia-like overreactions in each instance—fears of criticism and rejection figured prominently. What was the solution? Administer systematic desensitization based on relaxation. Back then, I followed Wolpe's desensitization procedure rather slavishly. In fact, I outdid the master. When developing a specific hierarchy of a client's specific fears or hypersensitivities, I would obsess over the calibration of each item. Just how many subjective units of disturbance did each entry warrant? In this era long before the advent of personal computers, a friend found paper or light cardboard ladders in a stationery store that enabled me to write out each item on a separate rung or tier and then easily change its position on the hierarchy as needed. Like Wolpe, I became an arch desensitizer.

I would train clients in deep muscle relaxation and then have them picture the easiest items on a hierarchy, slowly proceeding up the scale.

They were instructed to signal by raising their right forefinger if they felt any anxiety or discomfort. When they did so, the scene would be withdrawn (i.e., I would say, "stop picturing that event") and the relaxation would be deepened ("go back to the relaxation, breathe in and out, and feel yourself becoming even more calm and relaxed"). If the anxiety did not attenuate after another two visualizations, I would revert back to an easier scene. In this manner, incidents would be presented over and over until the one on the top of the hierarchy evoked no anxiety. I used desensitization individually as well as in groups. In fact, I published an article, "Group Therapy of Phobic Disorders by Systematic Desensitization" (Lazarus, 1961), which was an excerpt of my doctoral dissertation.

As I reflect on the oversocialized clients I saw in my private practice, a combination of desensitization and assertiveness training seemed to be quite effective in many instances. Certainly, in terms of initial outcomes, they surpassed the results I had obtained when offering little more than empathy, understanding, and insight.

STRENGTHS OF ORIGINAL ORIENTATION

Whereas my initial orientation was Freudian and Rogerian, I rapidly grew disenchanted with this laid-back, reflective, psychoarcheological approach and embraced Wolpe's reciprocal–inhibition orientation. Thus, I regard the latter as my original orientation. Nevertheless, there was something to be gained from the strongly nonjudgmental, active-listening skills that I learned from my Freudian and Rogerian teachers. In my opinion, it is imperative to be an excellent listener if one wishes to function as a truly effective clinician.

One of the major strengths of my original way of practicing that has held me in good stead over the past 40 or more years is the behavioral emphasis on conducting a thorough functional analysis. Careful history taking in terms of antecedents, ongoing behaviors, and their consequences often has enabled me to pinpoint subtle problems in my clients that had eluded the attention of their previous therapists.

To this day, when I watch videotapes of nonbehavioral clinicians with clients, I am struck by the fact that they tend to gloss over events that, from my perspective, call for careful scrutiny. For example, a client refers to a somewhat distressing incident at a party. I have seen clinicians who do not share my orientation offer little more than an empathic reflection or even less—a head nod or noncommittal "uh-huh." Although "uh-huh" could be deemed an appropriate response at times, it is more likely that what we used to call a *stimulus–response analysis* would yield more pertinent information; simply stated, the stimulus–response analysis would focus on the questions who, when, what, where, how, and, only occasionally, why. For example,

- "When were you at the party?"
- "Who were you with?"
- "What were you thinking?"
- "What happened at the time?"
- "How exactly did you feel?"
- "Where did you go afterward?"
- "And then what did you do?"
- "How did this change the way you felt?"

These questions are not presented in a staccato fashion but are woven into the tapestry of an ongoing but clearly focused dialogue. As a relevant aside, I should mention that the analysis of *response couplets* is a most valuable clinical training procedure: The client makes a response—she or he asks a question or makes a statement. The therapist has to respond—he or she may say "uh-huh," remain silent, render an interpretation, give advice, and so forth. When watching videotapes or listening to audiotapes of clinical exchanges, one stops the recording at judicious points to analyze a range of good, bad, or indifferent interventions.

LIMITATIONS OF ORIGINAL ORIENTATIONS

If my memory serves me, one day during a desensitization session, when a patient signaled distress or anxiety by raising his forefinger, instead of doing what Wolpe had taught me to do (withdraw the scene and reinstate deep relaxation), I spoke to the client and inquired what had elicited his discomfort. The dialogue might have proceeded more or less as follows:

Therapist: "What were you thinking or feeling when you raised your finger to signal anxiety or other distress?"

Client: "I had a flashback to an unhappy event."

T: "Would you please share the details with me?"

C: "I'm not sure of the connection, but I suddenly saw myself being ridiculed by one of my teachers in front of the class."

T: "Did this actually happen to you?"

C: "Yes."

T: "How old were you at the time?"

C: "About 12."

T: "So this occurred about 20 years ago."

C: "Yes. I don't know what made me think of that. You and I were dealing with my fear of hospitals."

T: "Well, there may or may not be a tenuous connection, but regardless, let's talk about being ridiculed. It never came up before."

C: "Well, I've always been afraid of public speaking, of looking foolish in front of a group of people. I never brought it up because I believe that almost everyone has similar fears and that they are quite normal."

T: "Well, I guess it depends on the extent of the fear. Let's continue the desensitization to your fear of hospitals, but I will make a note to examine the issue of ridicule at our next session."

C: "Okay."

I pointed out to Wolpe that a finger signal, head nod, or whatever prearranged sign of distress had been agreed on merely indicated that discomfort or displeasure was being experienced. It did not speak to the content of the uneasiness or anxiety. By examining the meaning behind the finger signal, one often sheds light on hitherto unknown components and associations. Wolpe claimed that to conduct discussions in the middle of the desensitization procedure would dilute the process and interrupt the relaxation. This was perhaps the first indication that within a few years, an extensive parting of the ways would take place between us.

The aforementioned procedural shift was the harbinger of a significant modification in my thinking. My understanding of the process of change had gone from "insights into putative unconscious complexes" to "reciprocal inhibition, counterconditioning, and extinction." At this juncture, I started to view cognitive restructuring as one of the primary psychotherapeutic change agents. I was influenced by Ellis's (1962) *Reason and Emotion in Psychotherapy* and London's (1964) *The Modes and Morals of Psychotherapy*, and I began to embrace the notion that the power of a person's beliefs often can override his or her operant or respondent conditioning. When I stated that in addition to focusing on behavior, elegant therapy called for attention to cognitive processes—beliefs, attitudes, values, and opinions—my behavioral peers were unimpressed. They saw it as an atavistic regression to mentalism, and I was wrongly accused of being a closet psychoanalyst.

In retrospect, it was largely when dealing with couples that I became aware of the limitations of viewing change in terms of Pavlovian conditioning and behavioral contingencies. It became clear that many distressed couples had value clashes, divergent expectations, incompatible desires, and other cognitive components that called for specific attention. These findings, along with the fact that follow-up inquiries revealed a fairly high relapse rate, led me to realize that the rigid and somewhat narrow behavioral methods I had embraced needed to be expanded. I wrote a series of articles on what I termed "broad-spectrum behavior therapy"; they culminated in my 1971 book *Behavior Therapy and Beyond* (Lazarus, 1971/1996). This book emphasized the notion that "effective psychotherapy must teach people to think, feel, and act differently" (p. 166) and was the beginning of an even broader application of treatment dimensions.

HOW CHANGE OCCURRED

The changes that have taken place over the years in the way that I work with clients result first from my direct clinical observations and follow-ups and then from various readings and the influence of several esteemed colleagues. Perhaps a fundamental question concerns the extent to which my clinical work has been shaped by the reports of researchers working in laboratories versus clinicians or practitioners. I strongly believe that innovations by clinicians are the lifeblood of advances in the development of new therapeutic interventions, a point that G. C. Davison and I have emphasized and have elaborated on (Davison & Lazarus, 1994, 1995; Lazarus & Davison, 1971). Workshops that I attended on gestalt therapy, psychodrama, and Ellis's rational–emotive therapy extended my technical repertoire. Three books that take a clinical rather than an experimental viewpoint had an enormous influence on my thinking.

The first book, by Standal and Corsini (1959), described 23 *critical incidents*, in which therapists deviated from their standard methods and orientations. Thus, a psychoanalyst became uncharacteristically authoritarian and forbade a woman who was having indiscriminate and unprotected sex from continuing to do so; a committed nondirective therapist, instead of remaining reflective, took an uncharacteristically active stance. Twenty-eight experts of the day offered their comments. To the practitioners' dismay, several therapists reported that by deviating from their ingrained training, the results were positive rather than detrimental. To my mind, this opened up the need to step outside delimited or circumscribed theoretical boundaries.

Second, Ellis (1962) addressed the significance of direct changes in self-talk and cognitive processes in achieving therapeutic results. His emphasis on changing irrational ideas and the importance he attached to "four fundamental life operations—sensing, moving, emotion, and thinking" (p. 39) helped pave the way for the multimodal orientation I subsequently developed.

Finally, London's (1964) book emphasized the virtues of several psychotherapeutic approaches and contained an observation that had a profound effect on my thinking: "However interesting, plausible, and appealing a theory may be, it is techniques, not theories, that we actually use on people. Study of the effects of psychotherapy, therefore, is always the study of the effectiveness of techniques" (p. 323).

The workshops and books coalesced into a broad-based perspective that placed techniques in the ascendant over theories. I wrote a brief article stressing the need for technical eclecticism and eschewing theoretical integration (Lazarus, 1967). I have emphasized the virtues of technical eclecticism (Lazarus, 1992; Lazarus, Beutler, & Norcross, 1992) over the dangers of theoretical integration in several publications (e.g., Lazarus, 1989, 1995; Lazarus & Beutler, 1993). The major criticism of theoretical integration is that it inevitably tries to blend incompatible notions and only breeds confusion. Two personal clinical events also played a significant role in changing my thinking.

Behind the Mirror

The first event occurred at the Palo Alto Veterans Administration Hospital in 1964. I was treating three clients behind a one-way mirror using the then new methods of behavior therapy. Each week, a large audience from the San Francisco Bay Area observed the treatment sessions. Most of them came week after week to study the methods. They saw me administering relaxation and hypnotic methods, systematic desensitization, and assertiveness training. After the sessions, a discussion would follow regarding the methods employed. After about 10 to 12 sessions, all the patients had made considerable progress. Nobody disputed that observation. However, when it came to explaining why the clients had benefited or what processes or factors had played a part, there was virtually no consensus.

The group consisted mainly of practitioners from widely different backgrounds and theoretical orientations. Participants argued vociferously for the accuracy of their observations and impressions. Some psychodynamic thinkers explained the gains in terms of transference factors; others referred to specific introjects, or insights that had inadvertently been achieved. Gestalt therapists, transactional analysts, and clinicians who embraced other theories each offered a different interpretation. At that time, I was firmly committed to reciprocal inhibition as a unifying theory, as exemplified by Wolpe's (1958) general principle: "If a response antagonistic to anxiety can be made to occur in the presence of anxiety-evoking stimuli so that it is accompanied by a complete or partial suppression of the anxiety responses, the bond between these stimuli and the anxiety will be weakened" (p. 71). I fought for the supremacy of my beliefs no less ardently than the rest of my colleagues. It then occurred to me that given the fact that widely incompatible and divergent hypotheses were being offered, we all could not be correct—but we all could be incorrect. Perhaps a superior, more accurate and encompassing, and yet-to-be-specified theory could identify what was really behind the process of change. It was then that I started focusing on what works rather than dwelling on why I thought it might be effective. Thus, the seeds of technical eclecticism were sown.

The Woman With Agoraphobia

The second clinical event that played a pivotal role in my outlook occurred in 1966. I was treating a severely agoraphobic and fearful 35-year-old woman. She was a cooperative and highly motivated client who responded well to a standard range of behavioral techniques, which consisted of imaginal and in vivo desensitization, behavior rehearsal, and assertiveness training. After 5 months of therapy, she was able to enjoy taking long walks alone, shopping, visiting, and traveling without distress. Important changes had accrued above and beyond the client's capacity to venture out of her home—her marriage relationship and sexual experiences were more gratifying, she was no longer socially submissive, and she enjoyed a wider range of social outlets. Nevertheless, although the client was delighted by her newfound ability to remain anxiety free while traveling and engaging in the niceties of social interaction, she continued to view herself as a worthless person. She referred to herself as being like a 12-year-old who was now able to cross the street alone but was contributing nothing to society. At this juncture, what is now called "cognitive therapy" was clearly indicated, and we launched into an assessment of her more fundamental attitudes and beliefs. She concluded, "if you want to feel useful, you have to be useful." Consequently, she founded an organization that distributed basic essentials, such as food and clothing, to impoverished people. This behavior, which was based on her attitudes and self-concept, led her to view herself as "eminently worthwhile." In a follow-up interview, she stated "thanks to the fact that I exist and care, thousands of people now derive benefit." This case is described in greater detail in my book *Behavior Therapy and Beyond* (Lazarus, 1971/1996).

That client led me to realize that behavior therapy alone might be insufficient (to use a football analogy) to take people into the end zone. It soon became quite apparent that it often was necessary to venture beyond the customary parameters of behavioral interventions into such territory as values, attitudes, and beliefs. Although the early books on behavior therapy discussed the need to "correct misconceptions" (Wolpe, 1958; Wolpe & Lazarus, 1966), the focus was solely on erroneous ideas and did not address the realm of the client's self-talk, his or her basic values, or other cognitive processes. When I emphasized the need to explore and modify such concerns and drew a distinction between broad-spectrum behavior therapy and "narrow-band behavior therapy," the reactions from Wolpe and many of my fellow behavior therapists were less than positive. Eysenck (1970), who was, after all, a theorist who had never treated a patient in his life, wrote a strident criticism and said that my ideas would lead to "nothing but a mish-mash of theories, a huggermugger of procedures, a gallimaufry of therapies, and a charivari of activities having no proper rationale, and incapable of being tested and evaluated" (p. 145). It took about 10 years before the need to add cognitive interventions to standard behavioral methods became widely recognized. Goldfried and Davison, in their updated edition of *Clinical Behavior Therapy* (1976/1994), stated that

> one no longer needs to argue for the admissibility of cognitive variables into the clinical practice of behavior therapy. Indeed, more than two-thirds of the membership of the Association for Advancement of Behavior Therapy now view themselves as "cognitive–behavior therapists." (p. 282)

As an aside, I took Eysenck thoroughly to task in a chapter I called "On Sterile Paradigms and the Realities of Clinical Practice" (Lazarus, 1986).

MY CURRENT APPROACH

The culmination of all the preceding events and experiences, together with several series of careful treatment outcomes and follow-ups, resulted in what I have termed "multimodal therapy" (MMT). Broadening the base of behavior therapy appeared to be insufficient. Despite the addition of cognitive restructuring to the usual repertoire of behavioral methods, relapses were not uncommon in many instances. Clients would emerge significantly improved, only to revert back to their old habits within a few months. It appeared that something was lacking in the A–B–C treatment formulation (affect–behavior–cognition). At first, I wondered if my psychodynamic confreres might be correct—that some hidden, unresolved, intrapsychic complex called for exploration and resolution. But further sessions with people who had not maintained their gains revealed a far simpler reason.

Although standard cognitive–behavior therapy (CBT), in addition to assessing and modifying untoward affective, behavioral, and cognitive issues, also dealt with imagery, sensory, and interpersonal factors, it did so rather cursorily. It became evident that clients had been treated and discharged without learning adequate methods to quell a variety of sensory discomforts or how to mitigate subtle but highly intrusive mental images. Nor had they become socially competent in a manner that transcended assertive skills. Biological determinants also had been glossed over. This was the early 1970s, and biological psychiatry had yet to exert its powerful influence—no wonder that many patients failed to maintain the initial benefits they had derived. In addition to evaluating clients' affective, behavioral and cognitive issues, equal attention had to be given to their sensory, imagery, and interpersonal modalities, and the biological substrate often was crucial.

The foregoing considerations gave rise to MMT, a psychotherapeutic approach predicated on the assumption that most psychological problems are multifaceted, multidetermined, and multilayered and that comprehensive therapy calls for a careful assessment of seven parameters or "modalities"— behavior, affect, sensation, imagery, cognition, interpersonal relationships, and biological processes. The most common biological intervention is the use of psychotropic drugs. The first letters from the seven modalities yield the convenient acronym BASIC I.D.—although it must be remembered that the *D* modality represents the entire panoply of medical and biological factors, not just drugs. MMT emphasizes the fact that at base, we are biological organisms (neurophysiological–biochemical entities) who *behave* (act and react), *emote* (experience affective responses), *sense* (respond to tactile, olfactory, gustatory, visual, and auditory stimuli), *imagine* (conjure up sights, sounds, and other events in our mind's eye), *think* (entertain beliefs, opinions, values, and attitudes), and *interact* with one another (enjoy, tolerate, or suffer various interpersonal relationships).

To reiterate, the multimodal approach developed mainly from clinical follow-ups that showed a fairly high relapse rate in patients who received standard CBT. Addressing the usual A–B–C variables (affect, behavior, cognition), as many systems do, tends to overlook or omit significant sensory, imagery, interpersonal, and biological issues. Untreated excesses and deficits in these areas of human functioning may leave patients vulnerable to back-sliding.

It is assumed that the more a patient learns in therapy, the less likely he or she is to relapse. In other words, therapeutic breadth is emphasized. Over many years, my follow-ups have revealed more durable treatment outcomes when the entire BASIC I.D. is assessed and when significant problems in each modality are remedied (Lazarus, 1989, 1997).

MMT is, in a sense, a misnomer because there is no actual treatment method that is totally distinctive to this approach. There are, however, distinct assessment procedures that tend to facilitate treatment outcomes by shedding light on interactive processes and by pinpointing the selection of appropriate techniques and their best mode of implementation. In MMT, one endeavors to use, whenever possible and applicable, empirically supported methods (Chambless et al., 1996). Thus, its practitioners are at the cutting edge of the field, drawing on scientific and clinical findings from all credible sources. This technically eclectic outlook is central and pivotal to MMT. It is important to understand that the MMT approach sees theoretical eclecticism—or any attempt to integrate different theories in the hope of producing a more robust technique—as futile and misguided (see Lazarus, 1992, 1997).

The BASIC I.D. and Its Various Applications and Spin-Offs

Fundamentally, by separating sensations from emotions, distinguishing between images and cognitions, emphasizing both intraindividual and interpersonal behaviors, and underscoring the biological substrate, the multimodal orientation is both focused and comprehensive. By assessing a client's BASIC I.D. one endeavors to "leave no stone unturned." A multimodal assessment addresses the following types of issues:

- B *(Behavior)*: What is this person doing that is getting in the way of his or her happiness or personal fulfillment (e.g., self-defeating actions and maladaptive behaviors)? What does the client need to increase and decrease? What should he or she stop doing and start doing?
- A *(Affect)*: What emotions (i.e., affective reactions) are predominant? Are the therapist and client dealing with anger, anxiety, depression, or combinations thereof, and to what extent (e.g., irritation vs. rage; sadness vs. profound melancholy)? What appears to generate these negative affects—certain cognitions, images, interpersonal conflicts? How does the person respond (i.e., behave) when feeling a certain way? It is important to look for interactive processes; what effects do various behaviors have on the person's affect, and vice versa? How does they influence the other modalities?
- S *(Sensations)*: Does the client have specific sensory complaints (e.g., tension, chronic pain, or tremors)? What feelings, thoughts, and behaviors are connected to these negative sensations? What positive sensations (e.g., visual, auditory, tactile, olfactory, and gustatory delights) does the person report? This BASIC I.D. category includes the client as a sensual and sexual being. When called for, the enhancement or cultivation of erotic pleasure is a viable therapeutic goal (Rosen & Leiblum, 1995). (The importance of the specific senses, often glossed over or even bypassed by many clinical approaches, is spelled out by Ackerman, 1995).
- I *(Imagery)*: What fantasies and images are predominant? What is the person's "self-image?" Are there specific success or failure images? Are there negative or intrusive images (e.g., flashbacks to unhappy or traumatic experiences)? How are these images connected to ongoing cognitions, behaviors, affective reactions, and the like?
- C *(Cognitions)*: Can the therapist and client determine the client's main attitudes, values, beliefs, and opinions? What are his or her predominant "shoulds, oughts, and musts"? Are there

any definite dysfunctional beliefs or irrational ideas? Can we detect any untoward automatic thoughts that undermine his or her functioning?

- *I (Interpersonal)*: Interpersonally, who are the significant others in this person's life? What does he or she want, desire, expect, and receive from them, and what does he or she, in turn, give to and do for them? What relationships give him or her particular pleasures and pains?
- *D (Drugs–biology)*: Is this person biologically healthy and health conscious? Does he or she have any medical complaints or concerns? What relevant details pertain to diet, weight, sleep, exercise, alcohol, and drug use?

A patient requesting therapy may point to any of the seven modalities as his or her entry point:

- Behavior: "I have this habit of pulling out my hair."
- Affect: "I feel anxious most of the time."
- Sensations: "I have these tension headaches."
- Imagery: "I can't get the picture of my father's heart attack out of my mind."
- Cognitions: "To me there are two ways of doing things—the wrong way and the right way."
- Interpersonal relationships: "I hate my sister."
- Drugs–biology: "I take antihypertensive medicines, and I should start exercising more."

It is more usual, however, for people to enter therapy with explicit problems in two or more modalities (e.g., "I'm having problems at work, and I frequently have stomach aches that my doctor assures me are due to tension. I'm also not getting along too well at home with my wife. All of this makes me feel kind of depressed"). Any good clinician first addresses and investigates the presenting issues and then fleshes out the details. However, a multimodal therapist goes further. She or he carefully notes the specific modalities across the BASIC I.D. that are being discussed and which ones are omitted or glossed over. The latter (i.e., the areas that are overlooked or neglected) often yield important data.

As mentioned near the beginning of this chapter, I have found the usual run of personality tests and assessments to be of limited value. Several instruments, however, have proved to be extremely useful. A comprehensive problem identification sequence is derived from asking most clients to complete a Multimodal Life History Inventory (Lazarus & Lazarus, 1991, 1998). This 15-page questionnaire facilitates treatment when conscientiously filled in by clients as a homework assignment, usually after the initial session.

Seriously disturbed (e.g., deluded, deeply depressed, highly agitated) clients obviously are not expected to comply, but most psychiatric outpatients who are reasonably literate find the exercise useful for speeding up routine history taking and readily provide the therapist with a BASIC I.D. analysis. This questionnaire not only helps to identify a range of potentially salient problems throughout the BASIC I.D. but also generates a valuable perspective regarding a client's style and treatment expectations.

The use of a 35-item Structural Profile Inventory (SPI) yields a quantitative BASIC I.D. rating of a person's degree of activity, emotionality, sensory awareness, imagery potential, cognitive propensities, interpersonal leanings, and biological considerations (see Lazarus, 1997). The SPI is particularly useful in couple's therapy, where differences in the specific scores reflect potential areas of friction. Discussion of these disparities with clients can result in constructive steps to understand and remedy them. Herman (1992) and Landes (1991) have established the reliability and validity of the SPI. Herman (1991, 1994, 1998) also has shown that client–therapist similarity on the SPI is predictive of psychotherapy outcome. Multimodal therapists use several other assessment instruments (e.g., the Expanded Structural Profile and the Revised Marital Satisfaction Questionnaire), which are printed and discussed in Lazarus (1997).

Second-Order BASIC I.D. Assessments

The BASIC I.D. format has resulted in several specific assessment methods. They were developed solely on pragmatic grounds—they tend to enhance treatment understanding and facilitate psychotherapeutic outcomes. Second-order BASIC I.D. assessments may be conducted when therapy falters. For example, an unassertive person who is not responding to the usual social skills- and assertiveness-training methods may be asked to spell out the specific consequences that an assertive modus vivendi might have on his or her behaviors, affective reactions, sensory responses, imagery, and cognitive processes. The interpersonal repercussions also would be examined, and if relevant, biological factors would be determined (e.g., "If I start expressing my feelings I might become less anxious and require fewer tranquilizers"). Often this procedure brings to light reasons behind such factors as noncompliance and poor progress. A typical case in point concerns a man who was not responding to role-playing and other assertiveness-training procedures. After traversing a second-order BASIC I.D. assessment, he revealed a central cognitive schemata to the effect that he was not entitled to be confident, positive, and in better control of his life because doing so would only show up his profoundly reticent and inadequate father. Consequently, the treatment focus shifted to a thorough examination of his entitlements.

Tracking the "Firing Order"

A method called *tracking* may be used when clients are puzzled by affective reactions (e.g., "I don't know why I feel this way." "I started becoming anxious for no apparent reason."). The client is asked to recount the latest untoward event or incident. He or she then is asked to consider what behaviors, affective responses, images, sensations, and cognitions come to mind.

Using the tracking method, a client who reported having panic attacks "out of the blue" was able to put together the following string of events. The client initially had become aware that her heart was beating faster than usual. The heartbeat brought to mind an episode where she had passed out after imbibing too much alcohol at a party, a memory or image that still occasioned a strong sense of shame. She started thinking that she was going to pass out again, and as she dwelled on her sensations, this cognition only intensified and culminated in her feelings of panic. Thus, she exhibited an S–I–C–S–C–A pattern (sensation, imagery, cognition, sensation, cognition, affect). Thereafter, she was asked to take careful note of whether any subsequent anxiety or panic attacks followed a similar "firing order." She subsequently confirmed that her two "trigger points" were usually sensation and imagery. This finding alerted the therapist to focus on sensory training techniques (e.g., diaphragmatic breathing and deep muscle relaxation) followed immediately by imagery training (e.g., the use of coping imagery and the selection of mental pictures that evoked profound feelings of calm).

Bridging

The BASIC I.D. lends itself to another assessment tactic that keeps the clinician on track and enables him or her to address issues that might otherwise have been glossed over. I refer to it as *bridging*—a shift of focus from one modality to another. Bridging is a strategy that is probably used by most effective therapists, and it can readily be taught to novices through the BASIC I.D. format.

Suppose a therapist is interested in a client's emotional responses to an event and asks, "How did you feel when your parents showered attention on your brother but left you out?" Instead of discussing his feelings, the client responds with defensive and irrelevant intellectualizations: "My parents had strange priorities, and even as a kid I used to question their judgment. Their appraisal of my brother's needs was way off—they saw him as deficient, whereas he was quite satisfied with himself." Additional probes into his feelings only yield similar abstractions. It is often counterproductive to confront such clients and point out that they are evading the question and seem reluctant to face their true feelings. Bridging is usually effective in situations of this kind. First, the therapist deliberately tunes into the client's preferred modality—in this case, the cognitive domain. Thus, the therapist explores the cognitive content: "So you see it as a consequence involving judgments and priorities. Please tell me more." In this way, after perhaps a 5- to 10-minute discourse, the therapist endeavors to branch off into other directions that seem more productive. "Tell me, while we have been discussing these matters, have you noticed any sensations anywhere in your body?" This sudden switch from cognition to sensation may begin to elicit more pertinent information (given the assumption that in this instance, sensory inputs are probably less threatening than the affective material for the individual). The client may refer to some sensations of tension or bodily discomfort, at which point the therapist may ask him to focus on them. "Will you please close your eyes, and now feel that neck tension. (Pause). Now relax deeply for a few moments, breathe easily and gently, in and out, in and out, just letting yourself feel calm and peaceful." The feelings of tension and the associated images and cognitions then may be examined. The therapist next may venture to bridge into affect. "Beneath the sensations, can you find any strong feelings or emotions? Perhaps they are lurking in the background." At this juncture it is not unusual for clients to give voice to their feelings. "I feel a lot of anger and sadness." By starting where the client is and then bridging into a different modality, most clients become willing to traverse the more emotionally charged areas they had been avoiding.

BACK THEN AND TODAY

Practicing multimodally is different from the Freudian, Adlerian, Sullivanian, and Rogerian approaches that were taught to me as a student and trainee. It is much closer to, yet different from, the instructions and training I received from Wolpe and the methods and ideas I learned from Ellis and other clinicians. The evolution and changes in my professional approach over the years can perhaps be conveyed by the following scenarios:

The 1950s

Client: "I feel a lot of resentment toward my mother."
Therapist: (We have an Oedipal issue here.) "You feel resentful toward your mother."
C: "She puts me down and treats me like a child."
T: "She treats you like a child."

The 1960s

C: "I feel a lot of resentment toward my mother."

T: "Please elaborate."

C: "She puts me down and treats me like a child."

T: (Sounds like a lack of assertiveness on his part.) "Let's try out some role-playing. I'll be your mother, and let's see how you dispute her put-downs."

The 1970s and Beyond

C: "I feel a lot of resentment toward my mother."

T: (This can be a result of many factors.) "What seems to be the main reason behind your resentment?"

C: "She puts me down and treats me like a child."

T: "Let's run through what I call a BASIC I.D. After we examine exactly how you act or respond to these put-downs, we'll explore your feelings, sensations, images, and thoughts."

CONCLUSION

The foregoing vignettes are, of course, simplistic parodies, but I think they capture the essence of the changes that accrued to my therapeutic stance and tutelage. I work the way I do because I have found that it yields better outcomes and follow-up results. But aren't all clinicians results oriented? Not according to many conversations I have had over the years. I often have asked colleagues of different persuasions, "Why do you work the way you do?" The answers usually have been variants of "because it makes sense to me," "because I enjoy working this way," "because I was helped by this form of therapy," or "because this is what I have been taught to do." These types of answers may soon fall by the wayside.

Wilson (1995) pointed out that many more clinical psychologists need to be trained to use empirically supported methods. He emphasized that "such training is rare among psychiatrists and other mental health professionals" (p. 189). In the years to come, as our colleagues discover more robust ways of working with specific problems, develop better manual-based procedures (see Wilson, 1998), and find empirically supported methods of choice for various conditions, there will be many changes. Perhaps one day all clinicians will say, "I do what I do because there are data-based studies to support the way I work." As the current trend in psychotherapy toward multidimensional, multidisciplinary, multiform, multifactorial, and multifaceted interventions becomes more widespread, it is to be hoped that rigid adherents to narrow-based schools of thought will recede into a minority.

REFERENCES

Ackerman, D. (1995). *A natural history of the senses.* New York: Vintage Books.

Chambless, D. L., Sanderson, W. C., Shoham, V., Johnson, S. B., Pope, K. S., Crits-Christoph, P., Baker, M., Johnson, B., Woody, S. R., Sue, S., Beutler, L. E, Williams, D. A., & McCurry, S. (1996). An update on empirically validated therapies. *The Clinical Psychologist, 49,* 5–18.

Davison, G. C., & Lazarus, A. A. (1994). Clinical innovation and evaluation: Integrating practice with inquiry. *Clinical Psychology: Science and Practice, 1,* 157–168.

Davison, G. C., & Lazarus, A. A. (1995). The dialectics of science and practice. In S. C. Hayes, V. M. Folette, R. M. Dawes, & K. E. Grady (Eds.), *Scientific standards of psychological practice: Issues and recommendations* (pp. 95–120). Reno: Context Press.

Ellis, A. (1962). *Reason and emotion in psychotherapy.* New York: Lyle Stuart.

Eysenck, H. J. (1970). A mish-mash of theories. *International Journal of Psychiatry, 9,* 140–146.

Goldfried, M. R., & Davison, G. C. (1994). *Clinical behavior therapy.* New York: Wiley. (Original work published 1976)

Herman, S. M. (1991). Client–therapist similarity on the Multimodal Structural Profile Inventory as predictive of psychotherapy outcome. *Psychotherapy Bulletin, 26,* 26–27.

Herman, S. M. (1992). A demonstration of the validity of the Multimodal Structural Profile Inventory through a correlation with the Vocational Preference Inventory. *Psychotherapy in Private Practice, 11,* 71–80.

Herman, S. M. (1994). The diagnostic utility of the Multimodal Structural Profile. *Psychotherapy in Private Practice, 13,* 55–62.

Herman, S. M. (1998). The relationship between therapist–client modality similarity and psychotherapy outcome. *Journal of Psychotherapy Practice and Research, 7,* 56–64.

Landes, A. A. (1991). Development of the Structural Profile Inventory. *Psychotherapy in Private Practice, 9,* 123–141.

Lazarus, A. A. (1958). New methods in psychotherapy: A case study. *South African Medical Journal, 32,* 660–664.

Lazarus, A. A. (1961). Group therapy of phobic disorders by systematic desensitization. *Journal of Abnormal and Social Psychology, 63,* 505–510.

Lazarus, A. A. (1967). In support of technical eclecticism. *Psychological Reports, 21,* 415–416.

Lazarus, A. A. (1986). On sterile paradigms and the realities of clinical practice: Critical comments on Eysenck's contribution to behaviour therapy. In S. Modgil & C. Modgil (Eds.), *Hans Eysenck: Consensus and controversy* (pp. 247–257). London: Falmer Press.

Lazarus, A. A. (1989). *The practice of multimodal therapy: Systematic, comprehensive and effective psychotherapy* (rev. ed.). Baltimore: Johns Hopkins University Press.

Lazarus, A. A. (1992). Multimodal therapy. In J. C. Norcross & M. R. Goldfried (Eds.), *Handbook of psychotherapy integration* (pp. 231–263). New York: Basic Books.

Lazarus, A. A. (1995). Multimodal therapy. In R. J. Corsini & D. Wedding (Eds.), *Current psychotherapies* (5th ed., pp. 322–355). Itasca, IL: Peacock.

Lazarus, A. A. (1996). *Behavior therapy and beyond*. Northvale, NJ: Jason Aronson. (Original work published 1971)

Lazarus, A. A. (1997). *Brief but comprehensive psychotherapy: The multimodal way*. New York: Springer.

Lazarus, A. A., & Beutler, L. E. (1993). On technical eclecticism. *Journal of Counseling and Development, 71*, 381–385.

Lazarus, A. A., Beutler, L. E., & Norcross, J. C. (1992). The future of technical eclecticism. *Psychotherapy, 29*, 11–20.

Lazarus, A. A., & Davison, G. C. (1971). Clinical innovation in research and practice. In A. E. Bergin & S. L. Garfield (Eds.), *Handbook of psychotherapy and behavior change* (pp. 196–213). New York: Wiley.

Lazarus, A. A., & Lazarus, C. N. (1991). *Multimodal Life History Inventory*. Champaign, IL: Research Press.

Lazarus, A. A., & Lazarus, C. N. (1998). Clinical purposes of the Multimodal Life History Inventory. In G. P. Koocher, J. C. Norcross, & S. S. Hill (Eds.), *Psychologists' desk reference* (pp. 15–22). New York: Oxford University Press.

London, P. (1964). *The modes and morals of psychotherapy*. New York: Holt, Rinehart & Winston.

Rosen, R. C., & Leiblum, S. R. (Eds.). (1995). *Case studies in sex therapy*. New York: Guilford Press.

Standal, S. W., & Corsini, R. C. (Eds.). (1959). *Critical incidents in psychotherapy*. Englewood Cliffs, NJ: Prentice-Hall.

Wilson, G. T. (1995). Empirically validated treatments as a basis for clinical practice: Problems and prospects. In S. C. Hayes, V. M. Follette, T. Risley, R. D. Dawes, & K. Grady (Eds.), *Scientific standards of psychological practice: Issues and recommendations* (pp. 163–196). Reno, NV: Context Press.

Wilson, G. T. (1998). Manual-based treatment and clinical practice. *Clinical Psychology: Science and Practice, 5*, 363–375.

Wolpe, J. (1958). *Psychotherapy by reciprocal inhibition*. Stanford, CA: Stanford University Press.

Wolpe, J., & Lazarus, A. A. (1966). *Behavior therapy techniques*. Oxford, England: Pergamon Press.

11

BEHAVIORISM, COGNITIVISM, AND CONSTRUCTIVISM: REFLECTIONS ON PEOPLE AND PATTERNS IN MY INTELLECTUAL DEVELOPMENT

MICHAEL J. MAHONEY

Change has been the most constant theme in my life's work. My focus in this writing is my "intellectual" history. I put the word *intellectual* in quotation marks to indicate at the outset that my intellectual and emotional (or personal) lives are inseparable. I feel (as much as think) that I have lived a life of good fortune and that I have changed substantially within and across several dimensions of interests. What seems to have changed least are some basic themes of values and styles of inquiry in my life.

People have been and continue to be the major events of my life. My children, Sean and Maureen, always have been among my most influential teachers. I will say no more about them in this chapter because I have not focused on personal and family particulars. I freely admit that my attempted contributions to theory, research, and practice clearly reflect themes that are close to my heart. I also admit that I am an inveterate explorer and organizer. I enjoy getting lost. I enjoy creating and re-creating. I episodically rearrange my physical life space, usually for no conscious motive other than the change and novelty that it affords. My mother used to call it *nesting*— a kind of combination of transition (the new nest arrangement) and anchoring (the nest is home to a life, a physically stable center of safety and other life preferences). I am attached to the past (e.g., my most treasured possessions are my great-grandfather's Blackthorn walking stick from Ireland and my grandmother's special ivory rosary with pictures inside the cross). At the same time, however, I am preoccupied with and fascinated by what is novel. New ideas, new developments, and new technologies are constant sources of enjoyment in my life. I feel fortunate to be enjoying a life in which many days are rich with appreciation and adventure.

How have I changed in my more than 30 years of work in the profession of psychology? I have been a behaviorist, a cognitivist, and (currently) a constructivist. Cutting across my involvement in these traditions have been interests in basic human change processes; history and systems of ideas and practices; self-relationships (including control, esteem, and perception); issues and experiences of embodiment, exercise, and sport psychology; and science and complexity studies (Mahoney, 1976, 1985, 1991b; Mahoney & Moes, 1997; Mahoney & Suinn, 1986; Thoresen & Mahoney, 1974).

My earliest work dealt with self-change—what was then called "behavioral self-control"—and my more recent work focuses on how professional helpers are changed by their lifelong work in the realm of helping people to change (Mahoney, 1972; Radeke & Mahoney, 2000). I am sure that I have changed in the process of my studying and attempting to facilitate change in others. The factors involved in my changing are probably multiple and complex. I also believe that they are inseparable from the processes that have remained fundamentally stable in my life.

This chapter is organized around the themes suggested for each of the contributors to this volume. As I try to elaborate in the final sections, I have come to view my own development and that of others (whether clients or not) as expressive of fundamentally dialectical (contrast-generated) activities. In other words, I see development in complex systems as both gradual accumulation of small changes and a punctuated revolution in basic activities of being. I view development as a lifelong process of complex self-organization in which core processes change less, change more slowly, and change more fitfully (i.e., nonlinearly) than other life processes. But now I am ahead of myself, and I should perhaps begin at the beginning.

LESSONS ORIGINALLY LEARNED

My first impressions of the mental health profession were not positive, and they preceded my receiving any formal training in psychotherapy. In retrospect, I should perhaps be surprised that my initial experiences did not dissuade me from pursuing the career that I did. These early impressions came from my work as a psychiatric aide (now sometimes termed a "psych technician") on a 30-bed locked psychiatric ward in a general hospital. I was working my way through community college when I was hired as a minimum-wage assistant. My responsibilities depended on which shift I was on and the current needs of the nursing and psychiatric staff. Sometimes I was asked to lead or assist in group discussions with some of the "higher functioning" patients. As situations demanded, I also served as a fill-in recreational therapist, occupational therapist, crisis interventionist, empathic listener, and assistant in the administration of electroconvulsive therapy (ECT).

Assisting in the administration of ECT was my least favorite responsibility (even lower than crisis interventions with violent or suicidal patients, who inevitably received ECT). My role was to walk with the psychiatrist, two or three nurses, and another psych aide as we wheeled the ECT apparatus from room to room. At times as many as half the ward was receiving ECT treatment. I assisted in hundreds of administrations to people ranging from a 14-year-old adolescent to a woman in her 70s.

Early in the sequence my responsibility was to help hold patients down while 140 volts surged across their temples and their body went into spastic convulsions of whole-body tetany. They were receiving oxygen through a mouthpiece that also prevented them from biting their tongue, but their arms and legs had to be restrained to prevent bone breakage during the trauma. It was a gruesome spectacle. At some point in the sequence of administrations to different patients, I would be asked to stay with a patient after the treatment and to remain in the room until he or she regained consciousness. My memories of sitting next to those unconscious people and witnessing their confusion and pain as they regained consciousness are among the most poignant of my life. Coming "back to reality" seemed like it was most often a process of questioning. Different pacing and different questions, but mostly questions and silence. Sometimes I felt like I was supposed to be a watchful usher waiting to show them back to their life.

At Joliet Community College, where I first enrolled in college (on a probationary basis because I had no high school diploma), I took more coursework in philosophy than I did in psychology. That being the case, it is perhaps not surprising that I first tried to reason with patients about their beliefs and problems. I elsewhere have described some of my naive first efforts at cognitive therapy (Mahoney, 1974); a sense of compassionate humor helped me endure some of those early lessons. Two incidents that I relate to my students occurred when we had two men on the locked ward, each of whom believed that he was Jesus Christ. This was a Catholic hospital, and the head psychiatric nurse was a nun. One of our Jesus patients was verbal and bright, and he seemed to enjoy reminding this nun that she was technically his bride. He also taught me a thing or two about the idiosyncrasies of personal logic. When I challenged him to perform the miracle of making me disappear, he eagerly met the challenge by closing his eyes and announcing "Ok—you're gone!"

The other Jesus figure was diagnosed with catatonic schizophrenia. He lay in bed all day in a cruciform position, arms out at his side. One night, however, he began a new pattern that upset the entire ward. As soon as it became dark outside, he began to moan at the top of his lungs, making sounds that were disturbing to the other patients and the staff. When I arrived for my turn at the night shift, the ward was in near chaos. The other patients could not sleep, and some were frightened by his painfully endless moaning. There was a long line of patients at the nursing station—some were crying, some were yelling, and many were demanding tranquilizers or sleeping pills. The switchboard to the patients' rooms was alight with signals from the nonambulatory patients who wanted attention, assurance, or medication. When I arrived, the head nurse and nun (who could have passed for Nurse Ratched of Ken Kesey's *One Flew Over the Cuckoo's Nest*) was telling the night nurse that the catatonic Jesus already had been injected three times with Thorazine and that he had reached the maximum dose for the evening. Clearly near her own wits' ends, Sister Psyche threw up her hands and abandoned us—storming down the hall with her keys jingling against her rosary and saying, "It's in your hands now!"

The night nurse and I looked at each other in horror—we were the only staff on duty, and the situation was desperate. She gave the other patients medications as she could, and I rushed around to the rooms where the call lights had been activated, trying to offer reassurances that I had trouble believing myself. After perhaps an hour of making little progress and having our own patience taxed, I came up with an idea. The night nurse—who happened to be married to one of my philosophy professors—was on the verge of tears herself, and our shift had just begun. I told her I had an idea, but I wasn't sure if she would like it.

"If it's legal and medically ethical, I don't care!" she replied. "We have got to do something, or this is going to get worse."

The moaning Jesus continued to bellow out his pain as if to underscore her point, and I said, "Well, if you will step into the medication closet for a minute, I will try something."

She looked at me suspiciously. "You won't touch him?"

"No," I said. "I won't even go into his room."

"How can you . . ." Her voice drifted off in desperation, and I knew that she trusted me. "All right, I don't want to know. One minute—that's all!" With this, she entered the small medication closet and closed the door behind her. I felt anxious, and my idea was still poorly formed. I walked to the switchboard inside the nursing station, flipped the switch that connected me to the room of the moaning Jesus, and mustered the deepest voice that I could: "This is God the Father . . . GO TO SLEEP!"

The echo of my own voice down the hall was eerie. Our catatonic Jesus was immediately silent. Seconds later, the night nurse came out of the medicine closet. She seemed startled by the sudden silence on the ward. She rushed down to the patient's room and found him breathing quietly, his eyes closed. She rapidly swept past all rooms on all four corridors before returning to the nursing station. Smiling, she said to me "I don't even want to know how you did it." I never told her, and at the morning staffing meeting, we simply said that the situation had been resolved. I wondered whether I should have told Sister Psyche, but I was afraid that she would have found it sacrilegious. It was, I thought, the same strategy Robert Lindner (1955) used in his case of "The Jet-Propelled Couch" in *The Fifty-Minute Hour*, which I was reading for my first course in abnormal psychology.

Respiratory problems made it increasingly difficult for me to endure the harsh winters of northern Illinois, and my allergist recommended that I move to a dry climate like that in Arizona. I was so naive about college that I did not realize that an application was required. After learning that there were two state universities in Arizona, I decided to flip a coin as to which one to attend. My coin came up Arizona State University (ASU) in Tempe, and I was fortunate that they indeed accepted me. What happened thereafter is an illustration of "chance encounters in life paths" (Bandura, 1982). When I tried to register for summer school at ASU, I was informed that I had to declare a major "by Monday." Not feeling prepared for such a decision that Friday, I was absorbed in an existential panic that rivaled my earliest encounters with ambiguity and helplessness. I decided to ask for professional help. I went to a public telephone booth in downtown Phoenix and looked up psychotherapists in the *Yellow Pages*. There were hundreds of listings, and I have no idea why I dialed the number that I did. It was my good fortune that he had an opening that Friday and was willing to see me. Having only $60 in life savings, I told his receptionist that I could only see him once but that it was important to my future. He was kind enough to give me two hours of his time, and he advised me with compassion and wisdom. The details of that encounter are elaborated elsewhere (Mahoney, 1997a). I owe a deep debt of gratitude to my first therapist, Milton H. Erickson, for giving me the permission I apparently sought for declaring psychology as a major.

The following week I was assigned to David C. Rimm as my academic adviser. He and John Masters were first-year faculty members at ASU, both having just graduated from Stanford. At the time, the psychology department at ASU was thoroughly Skinnerian: Art Bachrach was the chair, Tom Verhave and J. Gilmore Sherman were on the faculty, Fred Keller had set up the self-paced lab courses in animal learning, Skinner had debated Rogers there (among other places), and Wolf had recently graduated and helped establish (with Baer and Risley) the *Journal of Applied Behavior Analysis*. Undergraduate ASU psychology majors were then required to pass two animal learning labs (one with rats and one with pigeons) and to read the behavioral classics: Bernard, Pavlov, Ryle, Sidman, Watson, Ullmann and Krasner, Keller and Schoenfeld, and, of course, everything that Skinner had written.

ORIGINAL VIEW OF THE CHANGE PROCESS

I was an enthusiastic and dedicated student. Dave Rimm helped me learn to cope better with my considerable anxieties about getting into graduate school, and in so doing he became my first mentor in relaxation techniques. I later would have the privilege of further refining those skills under John Marquis at the Palo Alto Veterans Administration Hospital. Dave was a liberal thinker relative to the Skinnerian mainstream in the department. He introduced me to Bandura's early work on social learning processes and self-regulation; it was Dave, in fact, who introduced me to Al Bandura during a colloquium visit. My first publication resulted from a study that Dave and I did comparing the effects of token reinforcement and participant modeling on snake avoidance behavior. Dave also introduced me to the writings of Ellis, Lazarus, Wolpe, and Yates, and he was the first to show me how mathematical principles could help to refine questions about change and its determinants.

My original view of human change processes was probably an incomplete mixture of classical and operant conditioning combined with vicarious learning and self-regulatory processes. When I arrived at Stanford in the summer of 1969 I didn't have an integrated "big picture" of change. The ASU enthusiasm for pursuing experimental science remained with me, but the inadequacy of conditioning models was becoming apparent. That fall I was awed by and grateful for the publication of Bandura's (1969) *Principles of Behavior Modification*. That book, in my opinion, was a tour de force challenge to traditional views of conditioning and learning. It documented the need for a better understanding of cognitive processes in change and thereby helped to usher in the "cognitive revolution" that was sweeping through psychology. Bandura was on sabbatical my first year in grad school, which allowed me the honor and genuine pleasure of working with Gerald ("Jerry") C. Davison, who was a recent Bandura graduate and already a leading thinker and researcher in clinical psychology. He was and is a true *mensch*, and he taught me invaluable lessons about psychotherapy, science, and their responsible relationship. We still remain close friends 30 years later.

In those days, cognitive psychology was called "information processing." My first idea for a term paper in graduate school was on the implications of information processing for behavior modification. My proposal was declined by a teaching assistant as being empirically premature. I have forgotten now what I wrote my paper on, but my interest in the interface of cognitive science and clinical services endured. A graduate course from Atkinson and Bower suggested that the literatures in cognitive psychology were rich with relevancies for practical applications. My earliest research in graduate school was on self-regulated thought control (the term *thought* was then deemed less scientific than the term *cognitive behavior*; changing thought patterns amounted to "cognitive behavior modification").

Since thoughts are followed by a range of events, I wondered about the forces influencing thought patterns and the effects of thoughts on a person's feelings and actions. It seemed that thinking processes were important and influential and that they did not follow the linear associationism that had been the dominant paradigm at ASU. I wrote to Skinner, hardly expecting a response. I expressed my doubts about the possibility that thoughts were "automatically" shaped by the valence of events that succeeded them in time. Much to my delight and surprise, Skinner responded with a brief note that he, too, doubted automaticity in the effects of reinforcement on thoughts. He did not elaborate. But his response presented me with both encouragement and challenge.

Carl Thoresen arranged for us, Fred Kanfer, and Skinner to have dinner during the joint meeting of the American and Canadian Psychological Associations in 1973. That evening was an influential one for me. Being "up close and personal" with someone like Skinner was an invitation to reflect and challenge. I came away from our evening together feeling both Skinner's encouragement of my work on behavioral self-control and his stern warnings about the misguidance of my interest in thoughts and thought patterns, an interest that he considered the "blind alley of mentalism." I had just finished a summer of teaching in Brazil, where one of the organizers had thanked me for "giving them permission" to study and talk about the inside of the person. I wondered what was so powerful about this domain that it brought such emotional reactions, and I wondered what a review of the existing research would reveal. I was teaching a special-topic graduate seminar that fall at Penn State on human belief systems. During that seminar I wrote *Cognition and Behavior Modification* (Mahoney, 1974), in which I attempted to evaluate the theory and evidence relevant to conditioning and cognitive models of learning. I concluded that there was warrant for cautious optimism regarding the promise of cognitive models. Others in the field were voicing similar opinions at the time, and a polarity began to develop within behavior therapy around the issue of cognition.

I cannot specify a particular event or year when I stopped considering myself a behaviorist (or, for that matter, when I became a cognitivist or a constructivist). Some of the changes within me came from my reading and research, but there were many lessons from clinical practice that forced me to reconsider the adequacy of orthodox behaviorism. While I was a graduate student I worked as a live-in "teaching parent" in a community-based treatment program for predelinquents. It was a live-in laboratory as well, and those children taught me a lot about the complexities of change. They did not react the way the textbooks said they would. I remember one boy who threw temper tantrums every night at bedtime. We tried all the behavioral techniques we knew: time out for tantruming, praise for approximations to more acceptable behavior, token rewards and fines, and so on. Then one evening he went to bed without a problem, much to our surprise. In trying to figure out why, I realized that I had unwittingly offered him a choice between the two available bathrooms for his shower. During subsequent evenings I offered him his choice of color in towels, and that also seemed to help! In a somewhat related instance, another child refused to accept any candy when we offered it around one evening (free of tokens). I knew she liked the candy, so I asked her why she declined. She said, "because you just want to control me." Slowly, with the children's help, our program began to drift toward one that invited them to communicate and collaborate with us.

I am sure that another factor in my disillusionment with behaviorism came from the reactions that my cognitive colleagues and I received for venturing into realms of research and practice that lay beyond those condoned by some of the more conservative behaviorists. Davison had tried to interest me in reading Kuhn's (1962) book *The Structure of Scientific Revolutions* while I was in graduate school, but I wasn't then ready for it. After a couple of years on the conference and colloquium circuit, I was more than intrigued by Kuhn's notions about the social psychology of scientific developments. Indeed, my 1976 book, *Scientist as Subject: The Psychological Imperative*, was probably motivated by my needs to process the harsh attacks I received from Skinnerian loyalists when I suggested the relevance of cognitive sciences for clinical services.

Skinner himself became increasingly intolerant of the growing popularity of the cognitive sciences and therapies in the 1970s and 1980s. Toward the end of his life, he launched an attack on cognitive psychology, humanistic psychology, and psychotherapy in general (Skinner, 1987). These, he said, represented the greatest obstacles to a truly scientific psychology—a science of behavior rather than a pseudoscience of consciousness. Reluctantly and apprehensively, I responded with a proposed differentiation between radical behavioristic ("scientistic") and traditionally scientific psychology (Mahoney, 1989)—suggesting that an important difference involved the dimension of dogmatism and openness of inquiry. Implicitly, I challenged Skinner's intolerance of criticism and the isolationist tendencies of his followers. Skinner was apparently angered by my response, although he never contacted me about it. Instead, he encouraged Catania to organize an attempt to pressure the editor of the *American Psychologist* to print a scathing letter of attack on me, cosigned by scores of radical behaviorists (Catania, 1991). I documented these events elsewhere (Mahoney, 1996b). To counteract the adversarial polarization process that ensued, I organized a collective tribute to Skinner signed by many of the cognitive scientists, humanists, and psychotherapists that Skinner had identified as enemies (Mahoney, 1991a).

STRENGTHS OF BEHAVIORISM

Although I strongly challenge the adequacy of conditioning models of learning, I have continued to embrace elements of the behavioral tradition. Behavior therapy is transforming, and its valued contributions are being incorporated into integrative approaches, including constructivism (see below). In my opinion, the major strengths of behaviorism include

- an emphasis on agency and the activity of the organism
- an emphasis on contrast and directionality
- an emphasis on the wisdom of working with small steps in the direction of desired change
- an emphasis on accountability and the evidence of experience.

In a brief elaboration, human change processes involve changes in the activity patterns of the person. Something that behaviorism and behavior therapy highlighted was the need to do more than talk about a problem. The "corrective emotional experiences" proposed by early psychodynamic and contemporary integrative therapists require that the person become an engaged agent in their own development. Talking about one's fear of flying usually is not as powerful as actually approaching an airport with a ticket in hand. Behavior therapists were among the first truly experiential therapists in the profession, and their emphasis on this dimension is borne out by many studies of "exposure" and "participatory" therapies.

Contrast and *directionality* refer in part to immediate goals, and behaviorism emphasizes the importance of structure and clarity in many programs of personal change. But getting from here to there requires more than a sense of direction. It also requires patient and persistent movements that capitalize on the person's abilities to maintain an existential balance in their life movement. *Shaping* (or "successive approximation") is a valuable skill in teachers, parents, and therapists. It requires recognizing small (sometimes awkward) movements in a desired direction and an appreciation for the noncontinuous (i.e., nonlinear) nature of learning. What may seem like a small step to the counselor may be a giant step for the client, and the size of the step (or its appearance) may vary from moment to moment or session to session. What is important is an appreciation for maintaining a viable sense of balance between familiar (refined) skills and new challenges (Mahoney, in press).

Finally, the tradition of behaviorism has contributed significantly to our current appreciation for the role of scientific research and accountability in informing our services and responsibilities as helping professionals. It is ironic and, indeed, unfortunate, that a dogmatic interpretation of what it means to be scientific also has been at the heart of some of the limitations of behaviorism.

LIMITATIONS OF BEHAVIORISM

Briefly, I would say that the major limitations of behaviorism (and there are now several "behaviorisms," so I should say, perhaps, radical or orthodox behaviorism) would include

- the attempt to press associationism beyond its warrant
- the tendency to either deny cognitive processes or to redefine them as relatively simple connections between presumably isolated events (whether defined as "stimuli," "responses," or whatever)
- the claim that a pattern (habit) can be totally eliminated from a person's repertoire
- an authoritarian and dogmatic tendency that denies the meaningfulness or warrant for knowledge claims that fall outside of a positivist (or logical positivist) approach to epistemology.

The first two limitations, which are related, are dealt with at length in other sources (Bandura, 1969; Mahoney, 1974, 1991b). They essentially involve the oversimplified notion of how human experience organizes itself. As Hayek (1952) pointed out in his classic treatise, one cannot reduce the complexity of our "sensory order" to an accumulation of pairings (associations). The human nervous system (which is embedded in and influenced by other bodily, social, and symbolic systems) is essentially classificatory in nature, and any semblance of an adequate theory of human experience needs to address the complexity of our central symbolic processes. As it turns out, these central processes have now been shown to be inseparable from the phenomenon of embodiment, making untenable the Pythagorean–Platonic–Cartesian dualism between mind and body.

The oversimplifying tendency of some behaviorist doctrines has led to claims that activity patterns can be permanently eliminated from a person's repertoire; this assertion is one of the more irresponsible and damaging claims in 20th-century therapeutics. One does not (and cannot) totally eliminate the behaviors that constitute "bad habits." Although one can change the likelihood of patterns, the person must remain an active agent in his or her expression (e.g., exercising, dieting, not smoking). Indeed, to promise such an achievement is tantamount to jeopardizing a person's ability to navigate the warp and woof of developmental dynamics. In the course of biological evolution, nervous systems rarely eliminate any structure or functional pattern that has served the survival of the system in its past. When early mammals developed a protocortex and what we now call the limbic system, they did not eliminate the reptilian complex on which it was built. Humans show the vestiges of their reptilian heritage—a heritage that serves us well in the protection of basic life-support networks. Leaping here to more clinical examples, the person who has suffered from anxiety, panic attacks, and episodes of depression always is going to be capable of experiencing those patterns (particularly in the face of fatigue, trauma, and novel challenges). The occasional reappearance of old patterns of coping does not necessarily signify relapse or recidivism so much as the self-protective conservatism of the surviving organism.

The last limitation listed above touches on issues of epistemology. Positivism was a perspective proposed by Auguste Comte (1798–1857), who also proposed to render science as a natural religion. This first version of positivism declares that all scientific statements must be capable of public inspection. Although there is some wisdom to its appeal to consensual evaluation, it essentially splits off all forms of personal or private experience from the realm of scientific discourse. The second form of positivism is called *logical positivism*, largely because it attempts to wed the formal requirements of logic with the realm of observations. In this sense, at least, it is a kind of "shotgun marriage" between the rival positions of rationalism and empiricism in theories of knowing (Mahoney, 1976). Regrettably, both forms of positivism—which are vigorously endorsed by most behaviorists—encourage a "scientistic" dogmatism. I elaborated on this in my 1989 response to Skinner, and I do not belabor it here. Suffice it to say, radical behaviorism, at least in its evangelical forms, came to take on religious trappings.

HOW CHANGE OCCURRED:
THE COGNITIVE REVOLUTION

I find it interesting that one of the recurrent questions about human change is whether it occurs suddenly or gradually. Dressed in various terminological garments, that same question has been asked in studies of human personality, biological evolution, and the quest for conscious enlightenment. I used to think that sudden changes were less common and less enduring. Slowly—and in punctuated bursts—my thinking about change has changed. When I look for turning points in my own change processes, I tend to find them in several realms. My clinical work clearly has been a catalyst for much of my change. When I first began teaching and developing a private practice in the early 1970s, I was not prepared for the challenges and complexities that my clients presented me. None of them fit the neat textbook examples or diagnostic categories, and they were not as easily changed as I had expected. I often felt like I was barely navigating through the emotional rapids of their and, hence, my life, and I realized that I needed more training, experience, and some personal therapy.

I entered personal therapy with an existential–humanist who introduced me to the work and, later, the person of Jim Bugental, who has remained one of my therapeutic heroes and mentors ever since (Mahoney, 1996a). I learned the central importance of the therapeutic relationship, and I began to relax some of my needs to understand everything that was taking place in my life and my clients' lives. I began to enroll in experiential workshops that stretched me beyond my behavioral and cognitive base camps, including bodywork, creative dance, gestalt techniques, restricted environmental stimulation, and a variety of approaches to meditation. On one retreat in the Mojave desert, I felt particularly accelerated. Our 2-week stay included 3 days of fasting and silence, during which I was amazed at the deepening I felt in my awareness of how extensively I actively construct a world inside myself. To help accelerate my clinical skills, I sought more peer supervision and decided to be more selective in the clients whom I treated.

From 1975 to 1985, I restricted my small private practice to difficult clients—clients who might now be labeled as "borderline" or "personality disordered." Since 1985, I have tried to confine my practice to mental health professionals—partly because I believe that we therapists need a lot of support in what we do and partly because I believe that personal change processes are accelerated and amplified in practitioners (which makes them challenging—but edifying—clients).

The cognitive revolution was sweeping through clinical psychology in the 1970s, and many of us who were on the early waves of that phenomenon also were going through revolutions in our own lives, personally and professionally. I remember fondly the first panels on cognitive approaches at meetings of the Association for the Advancement of Behavior Therapy. By 1976 many of us who were pursuing cognitive themes wanted a forum for networking. I served as founding editor of *Cognitive Therapy and Research*, which first appeared in 1977. At the time, I was making regular visits to Beck's Center for Cognitive Therapy in Philadelphia and having regular dialogues with Albert Ellis and Don Meichenbaum.

During this time, I felt myself to be changing at a rate that felt like it would leave stretch marks. As a young faculty member at Penn State, I had met Walt Weimer, Dale Harris, and Don Ford, all of whom influenced my reading and thinking. Weimer introduced me to the writings (and later the people) of Friederich Hayek (Mahoney & Weimer, 1994) and William Bartley. Bartley's *The Retreat to Commitment* (1962/1984) left me sleepless for weeks, and Hayek's *The Sensory Order* (1952) is probably the most underlined book in my personal library. We converged on a New York meeting of Friends of the Open Society honoring Karl Popper's 80th birthday, and I discovered that Don Campbell had left factorial designs in his own dust as he and Popper had moved into *evolutionary epistemology*—the study of the development of knowing systems (Mahoney & Agnew, 1996).

MY CURRENT APPROACH

Opportunities to travel became rich opportunities to experience different cultures and to interact with colleagues whose experiences helped stretch my own. In 1980, I made the first of many trips to Italy and Portugal, where I encountered the version of cognitive therapy then being practiced by Vittorio Guidano and Luis Joyce-Moniz. I say "version" because it struck me as different from what I had seen in North America. Guidano and Gianni Liotti were combining the epistemological writings of Lakatos with the findings of ethological research on primate behavior and Bowlby's attachment theory. I presented a paper in Rome on "the structure of personal revolutions," which was patterned after Kuhn's classic on scientific revolutions. Guidano and I were struck by the parallels in what we were doing, and we began a friendship and professional collaboration that is now in its 20th year. On that same trip, I stopped in Lisbon to meet Joyce-Moniz, who was drawing on his work with Piaget and the drama therapy of Moreno to conduct a much more experiential approach to personal counseling. Guidano, Joyce-Moniz, and I began to exchange visits. I eventually spent a sabbatical in Rome, taught a summer in Lisbon, and had the pleasure of knowing and working with the likes of Giampiero Arciero and Óscar Gonçalves.

In 1981, I met Viktor Frankl at an Adlerian conference in Vienna, and we began correspondence about the search for meaning and therapeutic strategies. I remained in contact with him until shortly before his death (Mahoney, 1997b). He was a close friend of constructivist Paul Watzlawick, who edited a classic volume on *The Invented Reality* (Watzlawick, 1984). As I began to move into dialogues with people like Neil Agnew and other epistophiles, I learned of the incredible writings of Humberto Maturana and Francisco Varela, which also influenced the directions I saw myself taking. A few years later, I met Bob Neimeyer at the first meeting of the Society for the Exploration of Psychotherapy Integration, and we began to talk about an emergent interest that would eventually be called "constructivism" (Mahoney, 1995; Neimeyer & Mahoney, 1995).

The label of constructivism may be new, but the tradition itself dates back at least as far as Giambattista Vico in the early part of the 18th century. Some of my spiritual and Buddhist friends (especially Frances Vaughan, Roger Walsh, and Ken Wilber) have reminded me that the opening line of the Dhammapada (*The Sayings of the Buddha*) is "mind is the forerunner of all things." Constructivism, at least as I construe it, is a view of human beings that emphasizes their active participation in creating the meanings around which they organize their lives. Much of that construction is socially embedded, of course, and it is powerfully influenced by symbolic processes like languages and mathematics. I met Sophie Freud in 1996, and she has helped me discover and appreciate the constructivist developments in psychodynamic theory (primarily in the writings of such people as herself, George Atwood, Merton Gill, Irwin Hoffman, Stephen Mitchell, Donald Spence, Charles Spezzano, Donnel Stern, and Robert Stolorow). I also found feminist theories to be rich with contributions to constructivist views of knowing, learning, and human relationships.

As I understand it, constructivism emphasizes five overlapping themes:

1. the inherent activity of the organism
2. the directedness of that activity toward self-organization (and most of this goes on at levels far beyond our capacities for consciousness)
3. the centrality of processes associated with "selfhood," or personal continuity in referencing and organizing experiences
4. a social embeddedness (what analysts call "intersubjectivity" and others call "interbeing") that is predominant in humans and inseparable from our symbolic capacities
5. a view of development that is dialectical (i.e., contrast generated) and dynamic.

Among other interesting features, constructivism connects the processes of memory and anticipation (which share a time-transcending function). It also challenges the neat separation of experience into thoughts (cognition), feelings (emotions), and actions (behavior). For the constructivist, all of these are organizing activities that contribute to the creation of "personal realities" that make sense to the idiosyncratic logic of each person.

How this translates into practice is itself highly individualized, but some common themes exist. Constructive therapists tend to respect and honor the phenomenology of clients and to trust that personal realities have developed out of the clients' best efforts to survive their unique life circumstances. They emphasize exploring personal meanings and core ordering processes (which include both explicit and tacit assumptions about what is real and necessary, what is good or bad, what is possible and impossible, who clients have been and are, and what clients are capable of). Exploratory processes are encouraged at the individual pacing of the client. Indeed, at the heart of constructive therapy is the human relationship that is psychotherapy. Within that context, which serves as a safe and secure base, the client is encouraged to explore and experiment with new ways of experiencing themselves and their worlds. Because development is contrast generated, progress is usually nonlinear and punctuated by episodes of "expansion" and "contraction." These are normal parts of a healthy and self-protective process that is attempting to balance individual needs for coherence (familiarity) and challenge (novelty). One of the primary tasks of the constructive therapist is to coordinate and collaborate with the client in such a way that comfort (i.e., support, or "holding") and challenge are paced according to changing personal needs.

So how is constructive therapy different from any other kind? I do not think of constructive therapy as a separate school, and it certainly is not manualized or defined by distinguishing techniques. In a sense, constructivism is a philosophy of human knowing with a broad spectrum of expressions and subtheories. Indeed, this integrative and transtheoretical capacity of constructivism appeals to me, as does the fact that it is inherently an organic philosophy (i.e., one that is both capable of and dedicated to growing in response to the challenges it faces). The approach offers some refreshing alternatives to the pathologizing that has dominated clinical psychology and psychiatry for more than a century. In this sense, at least, it is well attuned to the contemporary "positive psychology" movement.

At the time of this writing, I am executive editor of the journal *Constructivism in the Human Sciences*, which is read in more than 30 countries. It is a publication devoted to exploring views of "human beings as actively complex, socially embedded, and developmentally dynamic self-organizing systems." I have just finished a manuscript, *Constructive Psychotherapy* (Mahoney, in press), and I have begun work on another dealing with the role of the body in psychotherapy. My research on the personal life of the psychotherapist continues, and I have begun to explore the changing meanings and perceived correlates of spirituality. I continue to be intrigued by the history of ideas and believe that promising relevancies for our understanding and practice of psychotherapy exist in the developing dialogues about dynamic self-organizing systems and the sciences of complexity.

CONCLUSION

That is my life so far. Have I changed? Most definitely. If asked to specify how and when, I cannot point to more than some themes, and in those themes I see continuities that have remained throughout all the shifts in terminology and theoretical assumptions. Labels (e.g., behaviorist, cognitivist, constructivist) are much less important to me now, particularly when compared with the importance of opportunities for genuine dialogue with others in and beyond the profession. I have come to believe strongly that diversity lies at the heart of development and that open dialogue allows us to exchange ideas and experiences in more enriching ways. I feel fortunate to have been able to follow some of the many chance encounters that have unfolded along my life paths.

How have I changed as a therapist and teacher and supervisor? Probably in many more ways that I realize. The ones that come to mind, however, are that I am more patient now and much more tolerant of ambiguity. I am not in as much of a hurry to change clients' presenting concerns (which often evolve into other concerns as our work together continues). I am more flexible; I can now do single-session, time-limited, episodic, or intensive long-term therapy with some degree of confidence in my potential helpfulness. I am less technique oriented and feel much more comfortable working in the moment (with its many unknown challenges and trajectories). I have a deeper respect for individual differences, for human resilience and resourcefulness, and for the importance of relationships in the quality of our lives. I now view emotions as healthy and adaptive processes, rather than part of the problem, and believe that many difficulties in change (or "resistance to change") are expressions of a basic self-protective process by which the adapting person attempts to preserve a precious balance of familiar order (i.e., systemic coherence) while exploring changes that challenge that order.

I trust both my intuition and that of my clients much more than I once did. I am more comfortable with not understanding why things happen the way they do, and I am more emotionally nurturing (or more forthright about it). I speak from the heart and to the heart as often as I can, and I encourage my clients to do the same. I feel grateful for the privilege of participating in their lives, and I enjoy my work now more than ever. If my life patterns continue as they have over the past 30 years, I will continue to explore and expand in ways that I cannot now anticipate. I look forward to that adventure.

REFERENCES

Bandura, A. (1969). *Principles of behavior modification*. New York: Holt, Rinehart & Winston.

Bandura, A. (1982). The psychology of chance encounters and life paths. *American Psychologist, 37*, 747–755.

Bartley, W. W. (1984). *The retreat to commitment* (2nd ed.). LaSalle, IL: Open Court. (Original work published 1962)

Catania, A. C. (1991). The gifts of culture and of eloquence: An open letter to Michael J. Mahoney in response to his article, "Scientific psychology and radical behaviorism." *The Behavior Analyst, 14*, 61–72.

Hayek, F. A. (1952). *The sensory order*. Chicago: University of Chicago Press.

Kuhn, T. S. (1962). *The structure of scientific revolutions*. Chicago: University of Chicago Press.

Lindner, R. (1955). *The fifty-minute hour*. New York: Bantam Books.

Mahoney, M. J. (1972). Research issues in self-management. *Behavior Therapy, 3*, 54–63.

Mahoney, M. J. (1974). *Cognition and behavior modification*. Cambridge, MA: Ballinger.

Mahoney, M. J. (1976). *Scientist as subject: The psychological imperative*. Cambridge, MA: Ballinger.

Mahoney, M. J. (1985). Open exchange and epistemic progress. *American Psychologist, 40*, 29–39.

Mahoney, M. J. (1989). Scientific psychology and radical behaviorism: Important distinctions based in scientism and objectivism. *American Psychologist, 44*, 1372–1377.

Mahoney, M. J. (1991a). B. F. Skinner: A collective tribute. *Canadian Psychology, 32*, 628–635.

Mahoney, M. J. (1991b). *Human change processes: The scientific foundations of psychotherapy*. New York: Basic Books.

Mahoney, M. J. (Ed.). (1995). *Cognitive and constructive psychotherapies: Theory, research, and practice*. New York: Springer.

Mahoney, M. J. (1996a). Authentic presence and compassionate wisdom: The art of Jim Bugental. *Journal of Humanistic Psychology, 36*, 58–66.

Mahoney, M. J. (1996b). Narrative truths about behaviorism. *History of Psychology Newsletter, 28*, 3–12.

Mahoney, M. J. (1997a). Brief moments and enduring effects: Reflections on time and timing in psychotherapy. In W. J. Matthews & J. Edgette (Eds.), *Current thinking and research in brief therapy: Solutions, strategies, narratives* (pp. 25–38). New York: Brunner/Mazel.

Mahoney, M. J. (1997b). Viktor E. Frankl, 1905–1997. *Constructivism in the Human Sciences, 2*, 31–32.

Mahoney, M. J. (in press). *Constructive psychotherapy: Exploring principles and practices*. New York: Guilford Press.

Mahoney, M. J., & Agnew, N. M. (1996). Donald T. Campbell: 1916–1996. *Constructive Change, 1*(2), 13–15.

Mahoney, M. J., & Moes, A. J. (1997). Complexity and psychotherapy: Promising dialogues and practical issues. In F. Masterpasqua & P. A. Perna (Eds.), *The psychological meaning of chaos: Translating theory into practice* (pp. 177–198). Washington, DC: American Psychological Association.

Mahoney, M. J., & Suinn, R. M. (1986). History and overview of modern sport psychology. *The Clinical Psychologist, 39,* 64–68.

Mahoney, M. J., & Weimer, W. B. (1994). Friederich A. Hayek (1899–1992). *American Psychologist, 49,* 63.

Neimeyer, R. A., & Mahoney, M. J. (Eds.). (1995). *Constructivism in psychotherapy.* Washington, DC: American Psychological Association.

Radeke, J. T., & Mahoney, M. J. (2000). Comparing the personal lives of psychotherapists and research psychologists. *Professional Psychology: Research and Practice, 31,* 82–84.

Skinner, B. F. (1987). What ever happened to psychology as the science of behavior? *American Psychologist, 42,* 780–786.

Thoresen, C. E., & Mahoney, M. J. (1974). *Behavioral self-control.* New York: Holt, Rinehart, & Winston.

Watzlawick, P. (Ed.). (1984). *The invented reality: Contributions to constructivism.* New York: Norton.

IV

PROFESSIONAL MEMOIRS OF EXPERIENTIAL THERAPISTS

12

FROM EXPERIENTIAL TO ECLECTIC PSYCHOTHERAPIST

LARRY E. BEUTLER

It is February 1965. As I look out on the quad at Utah State University (USU), I can see the sun beginning to peek from behind fluffy clouds. But it belies the cold. Students struggle against a cold wind and blowing snow to walk to the new library.

As I sit in the university counseling center, however, I am warm. I can hear the steam heater hiss and the wind whistle through a crack in the window. I am well covered with a sweater and a jacket, under which is the obligatory starched shirt and tie. I have not yet taken the risk of adopting the broad tie that is a reincarnation of the 1940s, and I feel safe with my 2-inch black tie that no one can see beneath all my warm clothing.

I am waiting for my first psychotherapy client. He will be here in 10 minutes, so I thought it would be a good idea to spend a little time getting ready and meditating. I am working on a master's degree in counseling psychology while researching concept formation in deaf children under a university fellowship. My real love, I have discovered, is psychotherapy. I do not know that from experience, but I have certainly been doing my share of reading and studying, role-playing, and practicing in front of the mirror.

LESSONS ORIGINALLY LEARNED

My mentor, Wayne Wright, worked with Carl Rogers in Chicago; he has spent hours teaching us the differences among a reflection, an interpretation, a restatement, and a question. I can identify the quality of an empathetic statement along a 9-point continuum. But this is different. In this first session, I have an assignment, one to which the client will be only partially privy. I must communicate through the entire session without using verbal language. I can use sounds, expressions, and silence. This exercise is to teach me the power of such interventions and help me avoid the constant trap of the graduate student—trying to do too much, too quickly.

My client arrives. After brief introductions, I invite him to be seated and ask him to tell me why he's here. From this point on, the ball is in his court. I use my best "Mormon missionary" (caring and soulful) expression to evoke further responses; there are long silences—"periods of thought"— and there are rushes of emotion as he tells me of marital problems and school difficulties. The session ends; it seems likes hours. With a rush of adrenaline, I reschedule when he surprises me by agreeing to come back. My commitment to client-centered therapy is sealed; forever after, it will be my place of refuge whenever I become uncertain about what to do.

I spend the remainder of my postbaccalaureate year at USU learning more about the client-centered tradition. I'm also working to earn a school psychology certificate, one component of which involves learning play therapy. I learn the nondirective methods of Virginia Axline, a student of Carl Rogers, and the similar psychoanalytic methods of Hyam Ginott. Every Thursday evening, I go to the local mental health clinic and work with a group of adolescents; John, a small boy with a behavioral problem; and two adult clients. The work is fun, and I recommit to my career goal of being a professional practitioner.

My introduction to clinical work left me with a deep commitment to the importance of the *personal* in interpersonal processes. I left USU with a commitment to the development of personal "authenticity" and a faith in the healing nature of interpersonal exchanges built on this type of relationship. Much of that faith survived my subsequent doctoral training.

In 1966, I entered the doctoral program in clinical psychology at the University of Nebraska at Lincoln. The training there was multifaceted; and it is difficult to identify a specific theoretical leaning from my years there, although client-centered, rational–emotive, and psychodynamic philosophies all were represented. The main focus of the Nebraska program reflected the 1960s. It was in something called "community clinical psychology," and it adopted values that were consistent with the Great Society ideals: opportunity for all, freedom, and flexibility. My client-centered views were consistent with this perspective. Stimulated by my dissertation research on persuasion in psychotherapy, I began to consider the possibility that nondirection and unconditional (i.e., value-free) acceptance on the part of the therapist were a myth. My early research convinced me that psychotherapy was value laden and could not be nondirective. My dissertation revealed that patients became converted to therapists' value-laden perspectives in successful treatment, even when therapists remained oblivious to this occurrence.

I left the University of Nebraska in January 1970 to assume a faculty position at Duke University Medical School, Highland Hospital Division. In a few short months, I became the first psychologist, to my knowledge, to treat psychiatric inpatients independent of medical supervision, writing orders and arranging for admissions and discharges. I worked with seriously distressed but largely neurotically oriented patients. My real love had become research, but my clinical orientation remained largely client centered, assuming the larger view of being person centered in the emerging Rogerian model. I spent a weekend with Carl Rogers, which solidified my orientation, and then another weekend with a student of Fritz Perls that again raised the question of how directive a therapist can be without sacrificing the value of human freedom. During this period, I remained enthralled with the debates at the meetings of the American Psychological Association between Carl Rogers and B. F. Skinner on the nature of free will. I found myself, by choice, decidedly on the side of Carl Rogers in emphasizing the importance of free will and relationship therapy. Although I was drawn to the experiential and humanistic movement of the early 1970s, I was guiltily repulsed by the 100-person nude march and the confessional group held to commemorate the death of Fritz Perls in Miami during that period.

STRENGTHS AND LIMITATIONS OF MY ORIGINAL ORIENTATION

Client-centered therapy seems to have lost a distinct identity. Many of the principles of the client-centered tradition have been incorporated into general psychotherapeutic practice. Indeed, these principles are the basis for most of the "nonspecific" factors that are thought to facilitate change. Although there are some variations in what is assumed to be a working or therapeutic relationship, they all approximate the concepts of empathy, regard, acceptance, and authenticity originally discussed and formulated by Rogers. These factors are considered to be the backdrop against which specific procedures work in most treatments.

If these nonspecific factors were all of what contributes to psychotherapy benefit, however, graduate training would be of little value; some people have argued that this is indeed the case (Christensen & Jacobson, 1994).

Certainly, we have had precious little success in training psychotherapists at the graduate level to enhance these qualities, and there is some evidence that highly focused training augurs to reduce the therapist's ability to deliver these therapeutic qualities (Beutler, Machado, & Neufeldt, 1994; Henry, Strupp, Butler, Schacht, & Binder, 1993).

Faced with the complex, serious, and recurrent problems that characterized the patients I saw at Highland Hospital—along with increasing evidence from my own research that therapists exert a powerful, though often unacknowledged, persuasive influence on patients to adopt their own favored value position—I had to eventually face the reality that caring is not enough. Neither unconditional nor nondirective caring is likely to be possible if one is interested in helping other people. As I have come to see it, the task is to know when and how to direct, when and how to be conditional, and when and how to express one's own values.

At some point, it occurred to me that "free will" may be not a reality but an important perception that is implicated in behavior change. I reasoned that free will is a cognitive experience that serves as a stimulus event in the causal chain of behavior. In retrospect, it is clear that I was the originator of cognitive therapy, although I graciously have allowed people like Aaron ("Tim") Beck and Al Ellis to take the credit for this role (stated tongue in cheek). Although I eventually came to blend cognitive, behavioral, experiential, and many other procedures in my therapeutic work, I never have lost sight of my roots in the client-centered tradition of the relationship. To wit, I still believe that

- the perceptions of an empathic and accepting therapist are cardinal in facilitating change
- the therapist is best served by learning, knowing, and working within the phenomenological perspective of the patient
- change often is a by-product of a healing and caring relationship rather than a direct result of therapeutic techniques and manipulations.

HOW CHANGE OCCURRED

Change occurred for me through a combination of three factors: (a) my own research, (b) colleagues who have solidified my commitment to research findings generally, and (c) personal experiences that have cemented my commitment to remain open to information and change. The latter two factors are intertwined intimately with my experiences with important people in my life. My change did not all occur at once but has been a process that is still in evolution.

Elsewhere (Beutler et al., 1991), I have traced the development of my research from its initial foundation in the client-centered tradition and the passive persuasion role of the therapist to a focus on the specific factors that affect different people at different points in time. This research has moved from addressing the question of what therapist factors contribute to how the efficiency of treatment can be improved by knowing when what tactic can change which people. This change was initiated by a growing appreciation of and investment in science as an avenue to knowledge and my growing awareness that change is not a passive process but a process of persuasion. Given that so many patients become converted to the values and beliefs of their therapists, therapy must be considered a process to which the therapist contributes actively, like it or not.

Faced with the inescapable truth that therapists seemed capable of developing an unending variety of new theoretical approaches, that all of these approaches produced average effects, and that many people got worse in any and all treatments despite the therapeutic qualities of the therapist, I gradually turned my attention to the questions of psychotherapy's differential effects. I wondered about and then enthusiastically endorsed the view that all therapies and therapists are good for some people but not for all people. Naturally, my research turned to discovering the defining conditions that would predict when a given treatment would work best. Eventually, my work came to address the bigger issue of how we can design and manage the treatment we offer to maximize those effects.

In the course of this academic work, personal experiences and contacts with important figures in my life taught me that we live and die in chunks. That realization came to full bloom only recently, when I suddenly and serendipitously transitioned from a state of nearly perfect health to one of hospital and physician dependency in a matter of weeks, a chunk of my body dead. It became clear at last that decline is not part of the smooth growth-curve function that was described to me in the developmental psychology textbooks. It is more like a Burger King commercial: a bite here and a bite there, the remainder appearing relatively oblivious to the loss until the fate of the whole is sealed.

But it also came clearly to my mind that if we die in chunks, so do we grow in chunks. Cognitive powers do not accumulate in a linear, progressive fashion with each new memorization; rather, they do so with chunks of data—gestalts—that comprise concepts and abstractions. Professionally, we do not make our mark on the world according to a linear function of how many publications and presentations we make or how many successes we have with our patients and clients. We move in chunks, leaps, and through key events.

In these professional events, a few rare individuals give some of the rest of us some chunks of professional development. In my career, there have been many signal people, but three such people stand out because they have had this type of influence in my career—one early on, and two later. Those people are Sol Garfield, Kenneth I. Howard, and Pat Parelli. Sol and Ken were important because they taught me the value of allowing research findings to determine my clinical orientation. Ken also was important because he provided me with therapeutic support at the time when I needed to find a way to keep myself moving and open to change. Pat is important because he showed me how to integrate my research into my practice at more than an academic level.

Sol Garfield

Sol had the unforeseen misfortune and poor judgment to take me under his wing early in my career. In the spring of 1974, I happened on an advertisement for a meeting of the Society for Psychotherapy Research (SPR). It was to be held in June in Denver, Colorado. Over the previous 3 years, I had published five papers in the *Journal of Consulting and Clinical Psychology*. Nobody at the University of Nebraska studied psychotherapy. A psychotherapy dissertation stood out like a neon sign among studies of eyelid conditioning, Hullian learning models, dissonance theory, and studies of experimenter bias. My modest effort investigated and compared social judgment theory and dissonance theory in the prediction of psychotherapy outcomes, as moderated through the assimilation by the patient of the therapist's attitudes and values. My mentors (James K. Cole and Monte Page) were extremely helpful to me, but they did not know psychotherapy research, nor did they know psychotherapy research methodology. I had to read the masters, so I read Garfield, Bergin, Strupp, Luborsky, Rogers, Patterson, Gendlin, and Thorne and even the controversial Albert Ellis and Joseph Wolpe.

But meeting Sol Garfield at the 1974 meeting of SPR overshadowed all that reading. I first met Sol outside of a meeting room, following a stimulating presentation on nonspecific effects and therapist-facilitated conditions. Sol was a paradox. He morphed before my eyes from an aggressive and devastating critic of the previous presentation and presenter to a kindly and acknowledging father–supporter. He actually recognized my name and obviously had read what I had written. He was encouraging. He invited me to a small gathering of guests and authors who were contributing to a book being edited by Alan Gurman and Andrew Razin, *Effective Psychotherapy* (1977). He asked me about my research; he appeared interested and invited me to correspond with him. I was overwhelmed. Sol became my first mentor and role model.

In 1975, he appointed me to the editorial board of the *Journal of Consulting and Clinical Psychology*. Two years later, I submitted a particularly important (in my opinion) paper to the journal. Sol was the editor-in-chief. I had worked on that paper for the better part of 3 years, fine-tuning and honing it. It was a paper that I knew was going to set my own research agenda and would, I was convinced, change the face of psychotherapy research for the next 2 decades. My article, "Toward Specific Therapies for Specific Conditions," was a box-score reanalysis of Luborsky, Singer, and Luborsky's (1975) famous *Archives* article that established the Dodo bird verdict, "All Have Won and All Must Have Prizes."[1] Sol rejected it; I protested; Sol invited me to revise and resubmit.

There followed a 14-month period in which that paper underwent four different reviews with critiques, each returned with a kindly rejection letter and an invitation to revise and resubmit the paper. After protest and struggle as well as shame and fear—and humiliation—but buoyed by righteous indignation, I identified the author of the critiques from his writing style and finally simply returned a revision with a suggestion to Sol that he invite Allen E. Bergin to assume the role of coauthor on the paper. That paper was finally accepted for publication.

Indeed, the article was published in 1979 (Beutler, 1979). Researching and writing it convinced me that no theoretical model had a singular hold on the truth. It occurred to me that the proliferation of psychotherapy theories signified the failure of all to be universal. I was both impressed and chagrined by the realization that a patient entering psychotherapy was likely to be indoctrinated with whatever favored value system and theory the therapist held, whether they were useful or not. In my daily life, if I needed a nail, I went to a hardware store; if I needed bread, I went to a bakery; but if I was depressed, I went to a unspecified psychotherapist and got whatever philosophy he or she accepted as truth. It was akin to going to a bakery when I needed a nail and coming home with the assurance that bread is what I really needed.

In the years subsequent to that cardinal event in my history as an author and theorist, Sol opened many other doors for me, all of which continued to expose me to the importance of allowing research results, rather than favored philosophy or my reverence for signal individuals, to dictate the nature of my clinical practice. I learned to revere the solidity of science and began thinking intensively about the implications of extant research knowledge. The uneven course of this process is represented in the transition of my own views. My first effort to express this emerging viewpoint placed me decidedly in the eclectic camp.

Sol's influence in this process was central: It was he who best taught me that ideas are to be valued more highly than the people who voiced

---

[1] This refers to the race in *Alice in Wonderland*, where the Dodo concludes that all must be recognized as having won.

them. To Sol, ideas were sacred in their own right; they were objects to be debated openly, independent of the status of those who expressed them. To Sol, science was not like art. As I say this, I am reminded of the disputed Van Gogh painting "Flowers." This is a one-production painting whose value varies precariously by millions of dollars, depending on whether the latest expert has determined whether Van Gogh or someone else is the actual creator. The painting is the same. The beauty of the work does not change—only its value, and then only by virtue of who did it, not by virtue of what it is. To Sol, science was about the discovery of truth. It is not one's status that makes one's ideas good; good ideas form the foundation for one's status. Furthermore, each idea must stand on its own apart from the reputation of its creator.

But even then, still early in my career, Sol intuitively knew that I was not yet ready to make that leap of separating ideas from people. Thus, that experience in 1979 was not the only time that Sol was called on to practice patience and empathy in his effort to mentor me. In subsequent years, he challenged me on many occasions to rethink my clinical viewpoints in light of extant research. The result was a rather narrow but innovative view of technical eclecticism entitled *Eclectic Psychotherapy: A Systematic Approach* (Beutler, 1983).

Later, with the influence of John Clarkin, I was convinced that I should practice the eclecticism that I was beginning to preach and thus formed a practice that was not only empirically informed but empirically led. My original extension to simple, technical eclecticism was supplanted by the broadened view presented as a second-generation eclecticism (Beutler & Clarkin, 1990). The most recent evolution of this movement toward a research-guided and clinically useful model for practice has recently been published (Beutler, Clarkin, & Bongar, 2000). The book makes a concerted effort to make mental health treatment more sensitive to research findings and more easily prescribed than it has traditionally been. The research-informed values of making principles of change explicit, ensuring that procedures and relationship qualities can be measured and monitored, and identifying points at which one makes differential treatment decisions all are represented in this volume.

Kenneth I. Howard

I met Ken Howard at the same meeting where I met Sol Garfield. Like Sol, he was a founding member of the SPR. His low-key humor initially failed to impress me, although it proved to be a decided asset in later years.

Ken's influence has been much more personal than Sol's and was most pronounced at a time when I particularly needed that personal touch. I was a professor of psychiatry at the University of Arizona. I directed the psychology programs in the College of Medicine, and we had been successful: By some counts, our programs were ranked among the top half-dozen in productivity, and psychologists in the department sustained most of the research and earned all of the federal research dollars within the department. Our place was assured—I knew I was indispensable.

In 1989, the medical school went through a reorganization. One change was to replace the chair of the Department of Psychiatry and to seek an individual who would help establish a program of biological research, a common value at the time. To prepare for this change, two major review groups evaluated the department's strengths; one comprised highly regarded psychiatrists from across the nation, and the other was made up of faculty members from the university itself. Both groups acknowledged the weaknesses in the research programs of the department, and both groups pointed to the Psychology Division as being the leading light that could serve as a model for the development of the department. Accordingly, I was asked to assume the role of acting chair of the department to guide its search for a chair. I declined, electing instead to serve as director of the extensive outpatient programs, a position that promised to advance my research programs.

I was scheduled to go on sabbatical leave on July 1, 1989. A psychiatrist from Harvard University had agreed to assume the role of department chair that June. I had never had a private, face-to-face meeting with him. Two days before I was to leave on my 6-month sabbatical, I received a telephone call from him in which he informed me that I should find another job because there was no place for psychology in his future plans for the department. I was astounded, but when I told people of his comments, no one believed my story. I protested that I was a tenured professor and could not be fired. He acknowledged that this was true but pointed out that he controlled the resources of the department and would ensure that I never received support for secretarial assistance, research, or clinical work again. Moreover, he promised to block my grant applications, and he immediately reassigned my laboratory space even though it was then the center of a large, federally sponsored study.

The ensuing months were strenuous. I began a job search in the midst of being depressed and feeling defeated—a failure. The university was caught off guard but felt obligated to respect the wishes of their new appointee. They immediately returned my laboratory space, but their compensatory job offer, which proposed that I shift my appointment to the Department of Psychology, was inadequate. There was a catch: The Department of Psychiatry would continue to control my salary and advancement, leaving me in the control of my dedicated enemy.

I secured several job offers, one from the University of California, which I eventually took. I returned from sabbatical in January and was gone by June. But I had to leave my family behind. My wife, devastated by the recent loss of her mother and searching for her own way, could not comprehend the nature of the struggle that I was experiencing. She wanted me to forsake my career and find a place as a clinical practitioner in the Tucson community. It was not a choice that I could make.

The separation proved to be too much for our relationship. I worked and commuted to try to maintain the marriage, but it soon became clear that our lives and values were becoming too different to support the relationship. As I lost the great love of my life, I became seriously depressed. That is when my friends came through.

Ken Howard invited me to his home in Chicago and provided the support and direction that I needed. He shared stories of his own struggles and offered his kindness and love. He laughed at his own four marital misadventures and got me to laugh about my two marriages. He and John Clarkin traveled to Santa Barbara to watch over me and continually called and offered assistance. I found support and experienced the care of trusted friends. Ken offered a large chunk of his own life and experience to help me learn to cope with my struggles. From him I learned the fine line between professional and private experience and absorbed the strength to carry on in the midst of tremendous hurt and pain. He helped me find reasons for living at the darkest time of my life and eventually taught me that even in the midst of darkness, a light can be found and opportunities realized.

I cannot diminish the strong influence Ken has had in supporting the emergence of my valuing of research findings in my practice. His research acumen always overwhelms me, and his work has confirmed my view that psychotherapy is an effective intervention. Ken has reinforced my early faith in the power of the treatment relationship. Incidentally, he also confirmed the importance of treatment change as a sequential process that includes and incorporates long-term changes and, correspondingly, supports the role of long-term psychotherapy for some people. However, it is his personal support that I have valued the most because it provided me with the incentive to keep going and the motivation to keep myself open to the possibility of being wrong. Ken constantly challenged my views of myself, my relationships, and, indirectly, my concepts of my own clinical practice. Ken's examples reinforced the value of the principles underlying these views. I never have known anyone who was able to accept research data so well, even when it disagreed with his own views. This principle undergirds my own form of prescriptive psychotherapy and guides my clinical practice.

Pat Parelli

Pat Parelli is, without a doubt, the most intelligent and creative man I have ever met, bar none. To try to keep up with him is to run backward:

It is impossible. Yet readers of this volume have probably not heard of him. Why is this? Because he is not a clinical psychologist but a Colorado–Australian cowboy and horse trainer. He is a true horse whisperer who has something to shout about. He is the founder of Parelli Natural Horsemanship and the executive director of the Parelli International Study Center in Pagosa Springs, Colorado. He taught me how to be a true behavioral scientist—an integrated behavioral scientist–clinician—and to put into practice my commitment to blend the science with practice. Although his influence on how I practice my eclecticism is undeniable, Pat has had an even larger influence on how I teach psychotherapy skills to others. I did not really know, on an emotional level, what it meant to blend science and practice in these activities until Pat showed me by his example.

From Pat Parelli, I learned the six keys to success and later successfully applied them to training psychotherapists. From Pat, I learned what we have done wrong—the errors of the "germ theory" of education (i.e., if you're exposed to it, you'll catch it; Beutler, 1995). As formulated by Pat and his equally astute wife Linda, the six keys are designed to be sequentially mastered and then forgotten—what they call becoming "unconsciously competent."

Attitude is the first key; whether horse or human, attitude is central to a relationship on which a partnership is framed. Respect, communication, understanding, sensitivity, and patience are attitudes that are the foundations for partnership; and without partnership, man and horse (or patient) remain distanced from one another by their roles as prey and predator. A psychotherapist does well to understand that a frightened, anxious patient approaches therapy as a prey animal does a predator, wary and uncertain of the danger awaiting. No technique will suffice. Attitude, patience, and listening are the tools that bridge the gap. We have largely given up, I believe, on the task of training attitudes, assuming prematurely that these are preformed and static. I find this approach to be a fallacy, one that can be overcome only by tremendous creativity, a limitation that is attributable only to the teacher.

Knowledge is the second key and rightly should follow, not precede, attitude development. I learned late in my career that psychological training usually gives the knowledge key precedence over attitude, to the detriment of the field. We train principles and knowledge first, making our students rely on these qualities rather than a therapeutic attitude. In the process, they often become sterile and unfeeling technicians. Pat convinced me that when facts about behavior are thought to be more important than attitude, we may be doomed to forget the importance of partnership and vulnerability. Without vulnerability, all things are labor intensive and emotionally costly. When I met Pat, I knew how to be right but had not yet acquired the attitude that allowed me to be wrong. Traditional training in professional psychology teaches students to "be right and bright" at any cost. We often justify what we do to make it appear planned. We can explain what we do whether we actually do it or not. I have become convinced that without a receptive attitude, one has no patience, no ability to be wrong, no willingness to experience change. That is, such a person is a technician, not an artist or craftsman. In contrast, when embodied within an attitude of respect, teachability, trust, and love, knowledge provides direction. Knowledge of technique is not as important as the principles of behavior and change. Pat convinced me that principles are more important than techniques and required me to reconnect to my Rogerian roots, to reestablish my faith in the healing power of relationship.

Tools—the selection of the right procedures—are the third key to success. Whether psychotherapist, horse trainer, or lover, the tools of one's trade include communication and implements that facilitate listening from the other's perspective. In Natural Horsemanship, we use a "carrot stick"— a stick that can be either a stick or a carrot. In psychotherapy, we use confrontation, enactment, and questions as sticks and support; we use affirmation and reassurance as carrots. The "sticks" create stress, and the "carrots" relieve it. The arousal of defense followed by support and relief through the relationship supports—reinforces—change and sustains motivation. Pat does not help people or horses. He trains people to help horses. Psychotherapy students who learn tools within the context of principles of change open a world of art and creativity that is unsurpassed. They become the epitome of an artistic practitioners who can swing with the vagaries of each new patient and problem.

Techniques are the fourth key; together with the right tools, they allow the emergence of skill. The tools are created to support the use of techniques, but techniques are not the essence of either psychotherapy or horse training. They are, however, a means of facilitating communication and selecting interventions. As in horse training, in psychotherapy one selects techniques to fit problems and people, not diagnoses. One does not treat diagnoses; one helps people through relationships that are imbued with trust and bonding and provide technical tasks that advance change. In both horse training and psychotherapy, success comes when we create a bond in which the predator (trainer or therapist) becomes partner and guide. Pat points out that in working with horses, every day is election day. Each day, a horse takes a vote about who is the alpha—the boss of the herd. With patience and skill, the trainer who is willing to not act like a predator wins most of the elections. With patients, a good 1st, 2nd, or 20th session is not sufficient to ensure that the trust is and will always be there. It is torn and repaired, rebuilt, and made stronger by the process. It is magic, and its influence is both mystical and spiritual. Faith in the therapist, as much as anything else, causes healing.

"If you keep doing what you've always done, you'll get the results you've always gotten." "Things take the time they take." "More time now means less time later." Such is the sage wisdom of Pat and Linda Parelli about the use of *time*, the fifth key.

I have sat, fascinated, watching Pat talk with his developmentally delayed son or work with a 9-year-old girl who wants to teach her horse to jump a table. In each case, Pat always allows the development of the person's own initiative and creativity, letting the audience stand patiently, learning vicariously. I would be "taking care of " and "taking charge" of them, all in the name of "protection." Parelli, however, places his method on the line, nondefensively inspecting and evaluating his results as the work unfolds, like a process researcher. He genuinely seems to be seeking to uncover the flaws in his own thinking and methods. Thus, he develops principles from scientific data but then analyzes the effects of application in individual practice in front of and with the critical inspection of colleagues and students.

Patience is part of this key. Let things happen that happen. Let people find their own comfort. Allow them to learn through struggle. Don't rescue, just support. Let yourself receive feedback. I have learned all of these lessons from Pat and from work with horses, not from my profession—although, as I've observed, my failure was not for lack of available models. At last, I am learning not to be right, but to be better; not to do things for the praise (a predatory attitude), but to value work when it only matters to my horse (patient) and me. No need to shout or pronounce it to others. That is the essence of horse whispering.

Imagination is the last and most difficult key to master. Imagination is creative foresight. It is seeing things as they have never been seen before, knowing how to position elements in a unique pattern to allow the desired effect—what a challenge! If only I could show my doctoral students how to do this. At best, I can plant the seed so that they eventually will release their own defenses enough to experience those rare moments of insight and creativity that place them near the world of the gods. To create, produce, lead, and allow life are the noblest of callings but the most difficult of tasks.

Through imagination, the other keys come together, and the technician becomes an artist. Although painters may use the same tools, the same colors and color blends, and the same brush strokes, it is the creative thought that gives the painting value. Van Gogh's *Flowers* has worth only if it was his idea. If it was copied, no matter how well and how exact, it is just a technical work and valueless. In truth, it is the creative idea that has value, whoever creates it. The therapist who repeats by rote what his or her mentor has said or who performs technically proficient procedures has only the limited success of the moment. The procedures lack generalization, breadth, and class. Imagination creates true skill, the blending of attitude, knowledge, tools, and techniques, fermented by time and flavored by imagination. The product is a true therapist, healer, academic, or horseman.

Others

Sol Garfield, Ken Howard, and Pat Parelli represent a small, albeit significant, portion of those who have contributed to my professional evolution. Through direct or indirect contributions, John Clarkin, David Orlinsky, Richard Shavelson, Bruce Bongar, John Norcross, Marvin Goldfried, and Arnold Lazarus, among others, have helped me along the way by giving me chunks on which to build my professional practice. The support of these acquaintances and friends has been invaluable and has added needed dimensions to my life. These other people of influence invariably came to me at times of need and reinforced a view that I have come to prize—that there is no adversity without hidden opportunity. Other people in my life, including my significant others and children, have made quite indirect but nevertheless important contributions to my transition on a personal level.

MY CURRENT APPROACH

The reader, by this point, has a general view of my particular therapeutic approach. Its name has changed over the years from client centered to technical eclectic, to prescriptive, although the last term is shared and was borrowed from my good friend John Norcross. The approach is based on a process of identifying the best treatment to provide for a given person, a process I call *systematic treatment selection* (Beutler & Clarkin, 1990).

In its current form, systematic treatment selection focuses on four domains in which treatment decisions are made: (a) determining what patient and environmental variables are relevant to planning effective treatment; (b) assigning the context (i.e., the intensity, modality, and format) of the treatment; (c) establishing a therapeutic relationship that is conducive to the growth of this patient; and (d) the fitting of strategies and techniques to the needs of the particular patient. The particular patient dimensions and methods of assessing them are in constant flux as we explore promising leads from research. At present, I believe that the most promising patient qualities to consider in selecting treatments include functional impairment level, social support structure, level of subjective distress, chronicity or complexity of the problem, patient coping style, and level of likely patient resistance. Each quality leads to the selection of a distinct aspect of treatment, ranging from the intensity of treatment to the modality, format, focus, level of directiveness, and the like.

More recently, our research group has been attempting to consolidate a finite number of principles that can be used to guide the selection and use of therapeutic procedures. Some of these principles are true to my client-centered roots and pertain to establishing and maintaining a solid and supportive therapeutic relationship, whereas others direct the therapist toward making a decision as to whether the interventions should be cognitive, behavioral, or insight oriented. In all cases, the therapist's personal theory of psychopathology, his or her value systems, and his or her beliefs about good mental health are considered to be tentative maps in treatment. They are not rigid truths, but they nonetheless can guide the content, objectives, and direction of the interventions. The therapist provides a theory about what constitutes good mental health and the strategies that facilitate this process, always within the context of a relationship that serves both as a stick and a carrot, to induce change.

My current model does not lose sight of the therapeutic relationship while it blends specific interventions and strategies for instigating change. A central tenet toward which I have always looked as a beacon is the pursuit of truth. The adage "the truth shall set you free" is one to which my professional life has been committed. Although science is not the only avenue to truth, the method of science provides the best opportunity for pursuing and discovering stable truth, and I have found it freeing. If science cannot provide a guide that will help people live better, more complete lives, it has no value. I have always discovered that the integration of science and practice is not only possible but extremely rewarding. Surprisingly, unlike many of my academic colleagues, I never have found it hard to let science direct my clinical work. Because I strive to remain relatively atheoretical, as applied to psychopathology, the boundaries among intervention models perhaps have been easier to bridge. My challenge, from time to time, has been the opposite: to keep from being so open minded that the truth disappears. My theoretical view is one of eclectic integration. It combines principles that cut across theoretical allegiances and that auger for enhancing change. Fundamental to this viewpoint, however, are some of the basic chunks that have served as the building blocks in my professional life. I continue to respect the power of goodwill and faith, the power of relationship. The first things to change in patients are hope and optimism (Kopta, Howard, Lowry, & Beutler, 1994). Long before one can attribute changes to the specific things that therapists do, patients acquire a point of view and sense of hope from their clinician. Like Rogers, I came out of a religious, moralistic tradition, rebelled against the external controls imposed by that viewpoint, and, paradoxically, found in the rigors of science a faith to which I could adhere. It has been said that the enemies of truth are not the liars, but the convinced. I believe that is true. Strong belief, in the absence of evidence, is damning to truth, as is the belief that there are truths that never change.

We live in a dynamic world; by its nature, truth is constantly changing. Any truth that promises to be forever is suspect. I long ago became convinced that searching for some static, unchanging truth was an error. I think it was when I heard a research report describing peanut butter as a carcinogenic agent. Whether it was carcinogenic depended on what study and newspaper report one heard. I concluded with another observer that it was "research that causes cancer." To mix a metaphor, I would rather have a clock that was persistently fast by 3 minutes than one that is stopped. Even though the latter gives the correct time twice a day and the first does not, one never really knows what time it is. It is in understanding change that people find hope. A farmer does not need to know that the weather will be the same from day to day, but he or she does need to know when the weather will change. Change is the nature of life. Each event, each moment, determines a change in the next. The prerogative and strength of science are its skepticism of things that are not expected to change.

I find comfort in knowing that truths can be discovered as principles of change and that they can be applied to enhancing the human condition. My professional heritage is the client-centered tradition, and this tradition has bridged the time and evolution of new treatment procedures. I never have lost the fundamental perspective, however, that one must seek understanding through one's phenomenological perspective. Experience is not the same as reality, but it is perception that guides one's decisions and life, not reality.

CONCLUSION

In this chapter, I have identified people in my life who have touched and boosted my development, who have given me chunks on which to build. Of the many chunks provided by these people, I count as most important the knowledge that people are interdependent. We rely on one another. For our safety, comfort, and well-being, we must be connected and loved, and we must develop the capacity to express those emotions of attachment, whether therapist or patient. Any of us who denies our reliance on our patients are blind. These lessons are well-to-be learned by patients as well. This all confirms my belief that the processes of change are interpersonal and rely on kindly persuasion and partnership. Patients learn through many means, not usually closely tied to a therapist's favorite theory, to share their day and expose their preylike fears. This process is a healing one if it takes place in an interpersonal environment and the therapist uses the six keys described earlier.

REFERENCES

Beutler, L. E. (1979). Toward specific psychological therapies for specific conditions. *Journal of Consulting and Clinical Psychology, 47,* 882–897.

Beutler, L. E. (1983). *Eclectic psychotherapy: A systematic approach.* New York: Pergamon Press.

Beutler, L. E. (1995). The germ theory myth and the myth of outcome homogeneity [Special section]. *Psychotherapy, 32,* 489–494.

Beutler, L. E., & Clarkin, J. F. (1990). *Systematic treatment selection: Toward targeted therapeutic interventions.* New York: Brunner/Mazel.

Beutler, L. E., Clarkin, J. F., & Bongar, B. (2000). *Systematic guidelines for the treatment of the non-bipolar depressed patient.* New York: Oxford University Press.

Beutler, L. E., Engle, D., Shoham-Salomon, V., Mohr, D. C., Dean, J. C., & Bernat, E. M. (1991). University of Arizona Psychotherapy Research Program. In L. E. Beutler & M. Crago (Eds.), *Psychotherapy research: International programmatic studies* (pp. 90–97). Washington, DC: American Psychological Association.

Beutler, L. E., Machado, P. P. P., & Neufeldt, S. (1994). Therapist variables. In S. L. Garfield & A. E. Bergin (Eds.), *Handbook of psychotherapy and behavior change* (4th ed., pp. 259–269). New York: Wiley.

Christensen, A., & Jacobson, N. S. (1994). Who (or what) can do psychotherapy: The status and challenge of nonprofessional therapies. *Psychological Science, 5,* 8–14.

Gurman, A. S., & Razin A. M. (Eds.). (1977). *Effective psychotherapy.* New York: Pergamon Press.

Henry, W. P., Strupp, H. H., Butler, S. F., Schacht, T. E., & Binder, J. L. (1993). Effects of training in time-limited dynamic psychotherapy: Changes in therapist behavior. *Journal of Consulting and Clinical Psychology, 61,* 434–440.

Howard, K. I., Moras, K., Brill, P. L., Zoran, M., & Lutz, W. (1996). Evaluation of psychotherapy: Efficacy, effectiveness, and patient progress. *American Psychologist, 51,* 1059–1064.

Kopta, S. M., Howard, K. I., Lowry, J. L., & Beutler, L. E. (1994). Patterns of symptomatic recovery in psychotherapy. *Journal of Consulting and Clinical Psychology, 62,* 1009–1016.

Luborsky, L., Singer, B., & Luborsky, L. (1975). Comparative studies of psychotherapies. *Archives of General Psychiatry, 32,* 995–1008.

13

THE EVOLUTION OF AN INTEGRATIVE EXPERIENTIAL THERAPIST

ARTHUR C. BOHART

My path to client-centered therapy (CCT) started in 10th grade. It was 1959, and we were being socialized to be good middle-class citizens. We were supposed to get solid, well-paying jobs; get married; buy a house in suburbia; have the same kind of car as everyone else; go to church; hate communists; mow our lawns; and, above all, fit in. I was rebellious. I joined a group of three other boys who were the young rebels of Marshall Junior High School. We fancied ourselves the beatniks of Pasadena and read Allen Ginsberg, Lawrence Ferlinghetti, and Jack Kerouac. We planned to publish a book of poetry called "Protest From Pasadena." Regrettably, 40 years later, it remains not only unpublished but also mostly unwritten.

We were attracted to existential literature and philosophy. We read Camus, Kierkegaard, Nietzsche, Sartre, Husserl, and even Heidegger (slowly). I planned to be a novelist and live on the Left Bank of Paris. We wanted to be creative. We viewed the middle-class life of our parents and teachers as sterile. We did not want to be little robots that dressed like everyone else, held the same values as everyone else, and lived like everyone else. Existentialism fit us perfectly. It suggested that we had to challenge the "right" way to be and to find other, more authentic and personally meaningful ways of being.

In college, I could not decide what I wanted to do. I ended up double majoring in mathematics and psychology: math because I was good at it and thought it could lead to a sure-fire job if I decided not to be a writer, and psychology because I thought it was closer to my literary and philosophical interests. I was dismayed, however, to find that the psychology department at the University of California, Santa Barbara, in the grips of a reductive operationalism derived from logical positivism in philosophy, dismissed psychoanalysis and existentialism as "antiscientific." I had had enough philosophy to know that logical positivism had been discredited and that the simple operationalism I was being taught was naive, so I was able to resist their indoctrination.

When I entered graduate school at the University of California, Los Angeles (UCLA) in 1965, I considered my approach to therapy as existential psychoanalytic. I accepted much of psychoanalytic theory, believing that psychological problems were significantly based in early childhood experiences. I put those ideas in an existential framework: The negative impact of early childhood and repression had more to do with the loss of a sense of choice than it did with sexuality.

My first clinical experience was at a Veterans Administration (VA) inpatient hospital. There I was turned off by the subtly dehumanizing way I saw most of the patients treated. The hospital was not a place that showed any interest in understanding the individuality of people or what it was like to be them. Instead, the primary goal seemed to be to label and stereotype the patients based on the staff's prejudices about how people ought to be and then try to shape them back into social conformity. It seemed to be a case of one group of people with power imposing their truths on another group. I could see no difference between psychiatric labeling and racist and sexist stereotyping. All three took away parts of people's humanity and portrayed them as "less than." Labeling set the professional up as the guardian of truth and put the patient in the role of the one "in error," whom the professional was going to "correct."

The main theoretical framework of the hospital was psychoanalytic, and although I initially had an affinity for psychoanalysis, I also found that psychoanalytic concepts were used to dehumanize patients. I disliked the way patients were described in ways that made them sound like self-deceptive cowards who were always up to no good at an unconscious level. I was much more interested in empathically listening to and understanding my patients, whom I found quite interesting and, for the most part, far more sane than insane. I wanted to get to know my clients, and I found that the concepts I was learning got in the way of that.

I also found dehumanizing the traditional psychoanalytic method that some of the ward psychiatrists instructed us to use. We did not make patients lie on couches, but we were supposed to maintain a strict atmosphere of abstinence. We were not supposed to "gratify" patients by letting sessions go on too long or by self-disclosing. If the patient was "resistant" and did not want to talk, we were not supposed to do anything but sit there and interpret. The atmosphere was one of distrust: Patients were up to no good, and the therapist had to be sure he or she did not get deceived by their unconscious maneuvers.

Fortunately, I had a great supervisor. One client was a 19-year-old boy who had been hospitalized because he was hearing voices after having taken a few LSD trips (and consequently was diagnosed with paranoid schizophrenia). I found that when I tried to do therapy with him in my office using this psychoanalytic approach, nothing happened. With my supervisor's blessing but without the ward psychiatrist knowing, I began to take him for walks on the hospital grounds. We would sit on the lawn and talk. I related to him more as a big brother. We would even "tease" and "bullshit." Through this modality, I was able to connect with him, and he opened up to me. Hearing voices was an isolated part of him, and other than that, he was just a somewhat confused 19-year-old who needed a big brother, not a "therapist." Our talks seemed to help significantly, and he moved from being isolated and rebellious to volunteering to help around the hospital with more disabled patients. He was on the road to discharge when my internship ended.

The experience in this hospital reinforced my early existential ideas, only now it was the mental health profession that was the source of pressures toward conformity, judgmentalism, and labeling. It was when I met my clients as human beings that I was able to be helpful to them.

In the meantime, I was going through personal crises (see Bohart & Tallman, 1997). Off and on, from my senior year in college through my third year in graduate school I had been troubled with severe, pervasive anxiety. I had started seeing a psychoanalyst on a once-a-week basis. We tried to understand how the roots of my anxiety were in my relationship to my parents. I saw this therapist for 2 years. I have documented elsewhere this experience (Bohart & Tallman, 1997). Briefly, although it was somewhat useful, I also found it limited. I liked the therapist, but I disliked the "blank-screen" method that he used. In addition, the approach was highly intellectual. I found gaining insight to be of little use. Toward the end of therapy, I actually began to find it harmful. My insights into my "defenses" became paralyzing and, contrary to being liberating, led to self-criticism.

I began to doubt my motives for doing anything after learning over and over that what I thought were my motives were not my "real" motives.

In my third year of graduate school, I switched to another therapist, a Jungian, who practiced in a largely nondirective way. This therapist had less of a preset agenda, and I began to discover that my self-criticism itself was primarily my problem and it did not have that much to do with my parents. Furthermore, although he did not self-disclose much, he was more willing to be there as a real person, and I found that stance helpful and refreshing. I saw this therapist for about a year and overcame my anxiety problem. As I began to trust myself more and more, my anxiety went away. This experience fit with what I was learning in my clinical placement: Trusting and prizing clients and relating to them as human beings were most helpful to them.

My experiences fit with the zeitgeist of the 1960s, which were in full bloom. My burgeoning philosophy, which was that psychological problems were caused by the rigid imposition of "shoulds" about how one was to be— whether by parents, school, society, or psychiatry—fit the hippie philosophy of the 1960s. The hippie movement experimented with different ways of being and, philosophically at least, valued spontaneity, intimacy, connection, liberation of the artist in oneself, and diversity. Virtually everyone in graduate school had become a hippie. Students who had come into the program with short hair now had long hair. People were wearing every possible variation of colorful clothing. Many were smoking marijuana and taking LSD. Some students were trying social experiments, such as communal or quasicommunal living, and others were engaging in group sex and body painting. There was an emphasis on acceptance and tolerance of diverse lifestyles and of trying to get inside the experiential world of each person and appreciating it.

At the same time, my distrust of psychiatric labeling was being mirrored in the community psychology movement, which held that psychological problems were embedded in society's problems, such as racism, legal oppression, sexism, and other social conditions. The goal of the psychologist was to help people by correcting these conditions. The therapist was to be a social change agent, helping people by going to court with them, interfacing with welfare agencies, and so on. This point of view fit nicely with existential–humanistic theories that prized helping people break free from social oppression.

Some radical theorists saw traditional psychiatry and psychology as oppressive agents of society. *Diagnostic and Statistical Manual of Mental Disorders* diagnoses in particular were seen as social oppression—in essence, a form of blaming the victim. One of the slogans of radical therapy was that paranoia was "heightened awareness." R. D. Laing (1967) viewed schizophrenia as an attempt to break through toward health. His approach to therapy was to help people with schizophrenia find meaning in their experience rather than to drug them or try to therapize them out of it. Traditional methods were viewed as barbaric, as butchering people's experience rather than trying to understand and help them.

This philosophy of tolerance, acceptance, and understanding, found in both the hippie movement and in some of the alternative approaches to mental health at the time, had much to say for itself. It certainly appealed to me. I am sorry that the spirit of this time has been largely lost. Because schizophrenia is now routinely seen as a biological disorder, for instance, the possibility that some people could grow from episodes of it is no longer taken seriously. Yet there are documented cases of people who did seem to grow from psychotic experiences (Epstein, 1979; Kaplan, 1964), even if the psychosis was biologically based. Some evidence indicated that deterioration in schizophrenia was heightened by traditional methods of treatment, including hospitalization (Vaillant, 1978). Finally, a controlled experiment along the lines of Laing's ideas had met with some success (Matthews, Roper, Mosher, & Menn, 1979).

I had a general philosophical home in existentialism, but I still had no clear idea of what I was doing as a therapist. One of the problems was that the existential approach had no method. In my fourth year of graduate school, I had a gestalt therapist as a supervisor. He portrayed gestalt therapy—an approach that actively encourages patients to become more aware of their internal experiences—as an existentialism with method. I not only became a gestalt therapy adept, I also entered therapy with my supervisor (boundaries were different in those days), along with my girlfriend.

I learned a lot from my gestalt experience but ultimately found that gestalt therapy was not for me, either. One of my enduring struggles with therapy has been over "who owns truth." I had been turned off by the psychiatrists and psychoanalysts I had encountered who claimed they owned truth about their patients. In contrast, the gestalt therapist was supposedly a liberator who helped clients find and follow their own truths. I found, however, that even they were not averse to imposing their truths on their clients (Fritz Perls, in the Gloria series, is a good example). For instance, at one point I had read an article by Eugene Gendlin (1968) on experiencing. From Gendlin's client-centered point of view, statements like "I feel you don't like me" are (or at least can be) statements of feelings. Yet I was told by my gestalt therapist that such a statement was a "thought," not a feeling, predating cognitive ideology in this regard. He was adamant about this: He was not going to allow me to believe that they were feelings. We argued, but it was the beginning of the end for me with gestalt therapy, because I began to realize that an "official version of truth" was being imposed on me—I was not being allowed to have my own opinion or get in touch with what I believed. Of course, to this day I adamantly believe that statements like "I feel you don't like me" often are statements of feelings. They are not thoughts (Bohart, 1993).

I also ran into this contradiction in the encounter group movement. Most encounter groups practiced from a humanistic–existential ideology, but some of them were highly judgmental and confrontational (not unlike many alcoholism programs today, in which clients are confronted with their "denial"). Some participants were told they were talking "shit" (Lieberman, Yalom, & Miles, 1973); they were judged as not being real or authentic and were told they were inhibited or uptight if they did not want to take off their clothes, and so forth. For the life of me, I could not understand how one person could judge another person's "realness." This contradicted the philosophy they were supposedly following. One form of oppression was being replaced by another form. I was ready for a point of view that practiced what it preached and had a method consistent with the empathic nonjudgmental philosophy I was evolving.

ON BECOMING A CLIENT-CENTERED THERAPIST

An article by Gendlin (1968) finally led me to my client-centered point of view. I was rejecting points of view that were applied in an expert, "I know better than you" way, but I had found no alternative. I had previously read Carl Rogers but had found his ideas too vague. I agreed that the therapist should be warm, empathic, and genuine, but when the therapist is being those qualities, what is the therapist supposed to do? I found a book edited by Emanual Hammer (1968) with a chapter by Eugene Gendlin (1968). I had never heard of Gendlin, but when I read his chapter entitled "The Experiential Response," it literally turned me into a good therapist overnight. The next day I put his ideas into practice with a 10-year-old client with whom I had been floundering for some time. The session went extremely well, and my supervisor, watching through a one-way mirror, was exhilarated, saying "Now *that* was therapy!"

In his chapter, Gendlin (1968) provided a step-by-step model of empathic responding, tying it to a theory of why it should be helpful. The theory synthesized the collection of ideas and perceptions I had gathered to that time. Gendlin postulated a tacit, bodily process of meaning construction that he called "experiencing." This process is the source of personal creativity and growth. By tuning into it, people are able to carry forward their experiencing in productive ways. There is no "real self" underlying a false social self; people are always being their real selves. (This idea gets away from the problems involved in judging whether people are being authentic.) But we each have a potential for personal evolution that can be tapped into. This potential leads to the development of new ways of being and behaving that are more productive. All humans have this built-in capacity for further meaning construction, no matter how disturbed they are. This process is facilitated by empathic responding, but not by just any empathic responding. Instead empathy responses must be specific and tune in to what Gendlin called clients' "felt meanings."

Gendlin argued that there was something beyond our typical Western dichotomy of cognition and affect. The body is not merely a source of sensation but also a source of meaning. Those meanings are more felt or sensed than thought. I refer readers both to Gendlin's (1964, 1968, 1996) work and to one of my own articles (Bohart, 1993) for examples. Therefore, there is a bodily meaning system that differs from emotion and from cognition as typically conceived. A statement like "I feel you don't like me" literally can be a feeling—not an emotion but a feeling of someone not liking you—a complex bodily knowing state. Humans have such "feelings of" all the time—a feeling of understanding something, of being detached, or of something fitting. Einstein had had a feeling of—a direction that guided his work on relativity theory (Holton, 1971). Feelings of are neither beliefs nor emotions.

When we are struggling with a problem, we have a bodily felt sense of it, including a sense of its implicit complexity—all the elements of which it is composed. This bodily felt sense is often preverbal. We often know more than we can say about the nature of our problems (essentially what is now called *tacit* knowing or *implicit* knowing). Tuning in to this felt sense allows an unfolding or discovery process to occur, through which clients make experientially relevant discoveries that not only give them self-knowledge but actively shift their experience in productive ways. Experiential responding consists of tuning in to the felt meaning of the client in the moment and then framing a response that tries to capture that felt meaning in such a way that it carries forward the client's experiencing. The criterion for the usefulness of a therapist's response is how it was received by the client. The only useful truths are the truths that ring true to the client experientially. A brilliant insight by the therapist is useless unless it is actually experienced as true or relevant. This requirement does not mean that therapists cannot offer their own perspectives. They can, but they must be offered rather than imposed on the client as the voice of authoritative truth. In this regard, in a second article, Gendlin (1967) provided an effective model of how to self-disclose and offer one's own perspective in an attuned fashion.

In his articles, Gendlin provided specific ideas on how to be a genuine, empathically facilitative listener. His ideas combined my existential ideas on helping clients find their own voices, with the emphasis on acceptance and respect I valued, and supplied a philosophy and a method. I now saw

Carl Rogers's writings in a new light and suddenly discovered that my orientation was client-centered.

As I started putting Gendlin's method into practice, the boy I was working with, who had been showing no progress, began to make significant progress. His mother called my supervisor and reported that he was behaving much better at both home and school. Yet all I was doing was really listening to him, in the careful, specific way Gendlin prescribed.

The next year, my internship was at a VA outpatient clinic. My clients were the ones who would be seen as difficult nowadays. I had several *ambulatory schizophrenics* (what a horrible term). My other clients had what would now be seen as seriously disturbed personality disorders. Yet working with them, I felt the most effective I ever have felt as a therapist. I was totally committed to my radical client-centered philosophy. I completely rejected diagnosis, and my whole approach was to empathically listen, empathically self-disclose, and contact and prize the humanness in my clients. My clients, most of whom felt totally ineffective and had been judged, labeled, and diagnosed in the past, responded productively to someone who primarily related to them as if they had some sanity and really listened to them.

The other experience that confirmed my belief in the client-centered method and philosophy I had adopted was that to make a little extra money, I became a hotline worker for the Suicide Prevention Center. Every other Sunday, I handled suicide calls, and it was probably my single best training as a therapist. I found that I could significantly help a person in crisis in 15 minutes, simply through empathic listening and disclosing. Using this method, I was rated as one of the center's top two telephone counselors.

As the commercials say, But wait! That's not all! I had an integrative bent even then. I struggled with the issue of using procedures from other approaches, but I didn't want to adopt the authority role and prescribe for my clients. CCT provided an answer. During this time, CCT was developing from a specific method into a philosophical point of view (eventually renamed the "person-centered approach"). The point of view allowed for widely different modes of therapy practice (Hart, 1970) and was one of the first integrative models for doing therapy. In 1957, Carl Rogers argued that the key to being an effective therapist was to provide a warm, empathic and genuine relationship, no matter what point of view one followed. Evidence was accumulating to support the contention that these facilitative conditions were associated with effective therapy (Truax & Mitchell, 1971). Therefore, if one was warm, empathic, and genuine, one could use procedures from other approaches.

Gendlin's experiential philosophy also provided a basis for integration. Gendlin (1969, 1974) argued that any technique or concept from any theory could be used if it was used in an experiential manner (i.e., in a manner relevant to the client's experiencing process). For something to be experientially relevant, it had to address a concern that was "alive" for the client in the moment, which meant that the client had to be experientially in touch with it, not just abstractly thinking about it; and the proposed technique had to fit experientially with the client and with the problem—that is, it had to feel right to the client. The client had to be experientially open to trying it, not just intellectually because it should work or made sense. I give an example below.

Incorporating ideas from both Gendlin and Rogers, I decided that if I was warm, empathic, and genuine (Rogers's conditions) and if whatever I did was experientially relevant in the moment (Gendlin), I could use any procedure. As an example, one client was talking about some of his leftover fears from Vietnam, and I suggested systematic desensitization to him. In doing the relaxation part, however, it was clear that the relaxation was not experientially right for him at that moment. He was resisting, although intellectually he agreed that it would be good to learn how to relax. Finally he said he was "too defensive" to let down his guard. So we stopped trying to do relaxation and explored his defensive feelings. This approach turned out to be much more productive.

STRENGTHS AND LIMITATIONS OF ORIGINAL ORIENTATION

I consider my original orientation to be CCT, although I played around with existentialism, psychoanalysis, and gestalt psychology on the way to that orientation. I had learned that treating my clients humanly (not humanely)—prizing them, being interested and curious in their ways of experiencing, carefully listening to them, and empathically self-disclosing—seemed to provide a context in which they moved toward more proactive forms of behavior. To provide this context I had to eschew the role of the paternalistic authority (the "golden presence," to use Gerald Goodman's phrase), give up a claim to superior truth, and be willing to learn from my clients. My primary expertise was as a listener; I also felt free to be integrative, as long as I offered procedures in an experientially relevant fashion and did not impose them on clients. I cannot honestly say, therefore, that I saw any limitations in my approach as of 1970 because it provided a complete integrative base for doing therapy. I personally was limited, however. I tended to stick to an emphasis on empathic listening and distrusted techniques.

HOW CHANGE OCCURRED

My experience at the VA outpatient clinic in the academic year 1969–1970 was my last clinical experience for a while. The next year, I got a part-time teaching job and worked on my dissertation, which was a therapy analogue study (Bohart, 1977). I compared the gestalt role-play procedure to a catharsis procedure and to an intellectual insight condition for the reduction of anger and aggressive feelings. The role-play procedure, hypothesized to be more effective than the others because it combined cognitive insight and emotional experiencing, was indeed more effective.

My first job was as an applied social psychologist at the University of California, Riverside. For the next 5 years, I taught and did research, which centered on my interests in experiencing and catharsis and in community psychology. I continued my analogue research on catharsis, finding evidence that emotional expression by itself without cognitive insight was not therapeutic (Bohart, 1980). I did no clinical work. Instead, my clinical energies were invested in community psychology in the form of training paraprofessional counselors and supervising a student-run crisis clinic.

Unfortunately, my research did not turn into publications fast enough for a publish-or-perish university, so I perished. In 1976, I moved to California State University, Dominguez Hills. I resumed my clinical training and began to accumulate hours for my license. Over the next several years, my general philosophy stayed the same, but the way I did therapy began to shift. First, I had always found that the client-centered empathic listening mode of therapy worked best with more disturbed clients and people in crisis, the populations with whom I had worked in graduate school. In 1978, when I started my postdoctorate clinical internship, I was mostly working with more well-adjusted clients, and I did not feel that staying primarily or exclusively in an empathic listening mode worked as well with them. Some of my clients, who were not hurting that much, did not value having someone really listen to them. Instead, they wanted me to come up with techniques and procedures that were going to "fix" their problem. One depressed man, a successful businessman whose depression largely centered on conflicts over whether he should stay with his wife, leave her for his mistress, or keep them both, was insistent that I come up with some procedures that would resolve his conflict. At that time, my armamentarium was limited, and he left for a therapist who did have techniques and procedures.

Along those lines, a significant learning experience happened around 1978, when I was teaching summer school at UCLA and had Christine Padesky as my teaching assistant. She introduced me to cognitive therapy and gave me a copy of the manual that was to become *Cognitive Therapy of Depression* (Beck, Rush, Shaw, & Emery, 1979). Cognitive therapy appealed to me. First, Beck advocated a warm, empathic relationship. Second, the way Beck practiced was in a rather nondirective cognitive way. He let clients challenge their own dysfunctional cognitions, instead of him doing it (in contrast to Ellis). I borrowed several ideas from cognitive therapy, such as the use of Socratic questioning to help a client evaluate beliefs, the cognitive role-play technique, and graded task suggestions. I incorporated these into my humanistic frame in that I used them when they were experientially relevant. Although I did not become an entirely cognitive therapist, I saw cognitive procedures as highly useful in helping clients liberate themselves from dysfunctional thinking so that they could come to trust themselves more (e.g., Bohart, 1982).

Second, I began to doubt the client-centered position that warmth, empathy, and genuineness were all that was needed for therapy. Was I not shortchanging my clients by not using techniques? The research seemed to have supported the importance of those conditions (Truax & Mitchell, 1971), but by 1978, reanalyses of the data were casting doubt on these findings (Mitchell, Bozarth, & Krauft, 1977). The new findings shook my confidence, as did a continual bombardment of messages from other professionals that it was ridiculous to assume that just being warm, empathic, and genuine was enough. Demonstration of the usefulness of various behavioral techniques seemed to support this stance.

Third, there had been a shift away from the liberation philosophy of the late 1960s and early 1970s to a more conservative view of therapy. I slowly began to be socialized into the view that I was an expert interventionist who had powerful techniques and procedures to effect change in the client. I now call this the "medical model of therapy" (Bohart & Tallman, 1999). The medical model is pervasive in the view of therapy today. In medical practice, physicians use drugs, surgery, and other treatments to remediate physical conditions in patients. Similarly, therapists apply techniques and procedures to remediate psychological conditions in clients. Therapy techniques and procedures are treated as analogous to drugs (Stiles & Shapiro, 1989) or other medical procedures.

A linear, causal assumption underlies the medical model of therapy: It is assumed that the therapeutic technique or procedure causes the effect of change in the client. This assumption is mirrored in the favored research method for investigating therapy, that of the randomized controlled clinical trial. In this design the independent variable is the therapy procedure or approach. It is applied to the dependent variable (the client and the condition in the client), and change is measured. The goal is to demonstrate that the independent variable causes change in the dependent variable— the client.

This model is pervasive, and therapists from virtually all persuasions have assimilated their models to it, probably for economic reasons. In the medical model, therapeutic techniques and procedures become primary. The ideal is to find specific techniques that in an efficient, causal way change conditions in clients; therapy would become more and more like medicine. For each disorder, there would be a specific treatment or drug (metaphorically speaking) for that disorder. The therapist is an expert interventionist who diagnoses the client's problem and applies the proper procedures. In this model the therapist once again becomes the owner of truth. The client's position recedes to that of the role of the patient in medicine—the ignorant one who will be saved by the knowledgeable professional.

This model began to subtly influence me. I began to view myself as an expert who could intervene to make things happen in the client. I still thought of myself as client centered, however: I did not authoritatively lay truth on clients as to what was wrong with them or how they should live their lives. But I did stimulate, or liberate, the processes that would lead clients to finding their own solutions. Gendlin's (1969, 1974) view of experiencing has the potential to be interpreted this way. Gendlin argued that therapy worked through the facilitation of an experiential process. Therefore, many client-centered and experiential therapists began to set out to deliberately raise the level of the client's experiencing.

I became a "mechanistic Rogerian" (to coin a phrase). I believed that I could initiate productive client change processes through my interventions, which included raising their levels of experiencing; empathic responding to initiate a self-propelled exploration process inside them; framing empathic responses in deliberately chosen, specific ways; accessing emotion; and using empathic self-disclosure to model the kind of process I wanted. In the context of this mechanistic Rogerianism, I also thought I could liberate clients' creative processes through challenging their dysfunctional cognitions, teaching them assertion skills, desensitizing them, and so on. I even developed an interest in strategic therapy. Strategic therapy, based on Milton Erickson's work, held that therapeutic solutions were forged by the client's creative unconscious, which had to be liberated through the use of clever, therapist-chosen techniques, such as reframing and paradox.

Development of My Integrative Model of Psychotherapy

By the late 1980s, I had begun to develop my own common factors model of therapy (see the latest version in Todd & Bohart, 1999). Before the first version was published (as part of an undergraduate clinical psychology text), I had sent a draft of the chapter to Marv Goldfried, who did not know me from Adam (at that point I had published very little). He was kind enough to read it and send back an encouraging letter.

Briefly, the chapter had framed the issue of psychotherapy integration around the topic of "access." The problem of psychotherapy is, Why is it so hard for simple, corrective information to get into the person's system? If this were not the case, there would be no need for psychotherapy—clients could simply tell themselves what to do and do it. People with anxiety disorder could say to themselves, "calm down, there is nothing to be afraid of," and people with impulse control problems could think, "be sure to stop after only two drinks," and do it. Personal correction would simply be a matter of listening to rational, logical information. Dear Abby would suffice.

Yet this is clearly not the case; we (Todd & Bohart, 1999) argued that all therapies are built around the fact that simple, rational corrective information does not create change. We also contended that each therapy was ultimately an answer to the question of why simple corrective information does not work. Psychodynamic therapy assumed that it did not help because the problem was unconscious and based on avoidance. Behavior therapy assumed that information did not help because bad habits have been learned through reinforcement and practice and cannot be modified by simple cognitive insight. Cognitive therapy assumed that simple corrective information did not help because the problem stemmed from habits of thinking, which only change with rigorous and repeated practice. Family systems therapy assumed information did not work because the problem was implicit in the network of the family system. Humanistic therapies assumed it did not work because people were not operating holistically—listening to feelings and trusting experience.

We focused primarily on experiencing as the major way therapies encouraged access. We (Todd & Bohart, 1999) argued that all therapies incorporate an experiential component to flesh out cognitive knowing or to directly change behavior. Learning had to be experiential. This was accomplished through experiential responding (Gendlin, 1968) and various experiential exercises, such as those used in gestalt therapy, behavior therapy, and cognitive therapy.

We also identified other ways in which therapists create access. We suggested that rigid, top-down cognitive thinking was seen as dysfunctional by virtually all theories. In psychoanalysis, the strong superego helps maintain repression. In CCT, the shoulds learned from parents block self-trust and access to experiencing. Rigid either–or thinking is the cause of problems in cognitive therapy, and rigidly held cognitions block unconscious creativity in strategic therapy. Therefore, another therapeutic commonality was that different points of view all used ways of either suspending or circumventing dysfunctional cognitive monitoring. They might encourage clients to adopt a phenomenological attitude, such as in free association, meditation, behavioral and cognitive tracking, or suspending judgment in humanistic therapy. Strategic and solution-focused therapies try to befuddle the conscious, cognitive monitoring system through the use of paradox, teaching stories, and suggestion (e.g., Watzlawick, 1978).

These ideas fed into my therapeutic practice. I saw myself as an expert interventionist who liberated client creativity by facilitating learning experientially and by suspending, challenging, or disrupting the dysfunctional cognitive self-monitoring system.

A Personal Paradigm Crisis and the Journey Back Home

I soon began to encounter experiences that challenged my view of the therapist as expert interventionist. First, in 1988, I attended an International Conference on Client-Centered and Experiential Therapy in Leuven, Belgium. I was surprised to discover that some traditional client-centered therapists objected to the idea of deliberately trying to make an experiential process happen (Brodley, 1990). The whole idea of mechanistic Rogerianism, in which the therapist deliberately tried to make a process happen, even if the goal was to facilitate clients coming up with their own answers, was rejected as antithetical to what Carl Rogers had really believed (e.g., Bozarth, 1998; Brodley, 1990).

Over time, the traditional client-centered therapists convinced me they were right. For Rogers, therapy was never intervention, and he would have objected to those who tried to analyze his responses as interventions. In fact, traditional Rogerians rejected the whole concept of intervention. To see Rogers's responses as interventions was to look at what Rogers was doing through the lens of the medical model of therapy, a model that Rogers rejected. The arguments and complexities are beyond the scope of this chapter. Suffice it to say that I have come to agree with my traditional colleagues that interventionism is antithetical to Rogers.

The second source of conflict with my beliefs came from experiences I had with some clients. I discovered that intervening did not always work in the linear, causal way in which it was portrayed. One could raise experiencing levels, get clients to challenge their dysfunctional cognitions, practice relaxation, or do the gestalt chair procedures, and still no change might occur. One example from my practice was a 45-year-old married woman who was experiencing generalized anxiety. She was wealthy and did not have to work. She was used to spending money on the best doctors to fix whatever problem she had. She was quite intelligent, and other than being anxious, she was a functional person. But I never could break through her attitude that I was supposed to fix her. I would empathically reflect, and even if I was on target, she would never pick up the ball and carry it forward, like my more dysfunctional clients would. I tried relaxation with her, but she never learned to relax. Elsewhere (Bohart & Tallman, 1999), I noted that she acted as if she believed the interventionist model of therapy. When I was teaching her relaxation, she would do all the things I suggested, but then she would wait as though they were supposed to relax her. Although she complied with the "treatment," believed in it, and did it, it did not work—in my opinion, because she was expecting it to do the work. Over a 2-year period, I tried almost everything with her: I challenged dysfunctional cognitions and used strategic, behavioral, and gestalt techniques as well.

She made some progress, but I would rate her therapy as only a modest success at best.

In contrast, I had other clients who did nothing right and changed anyway. One woman broke all the rules. She did not access any deep emotion, she did not seem to achieve any insight, and she did not get into challenging dysfunctional cognitions; if she had been rated on the experiencing scale (Klein, Mathieu-Coughlan, & Kiesler, 1986), she would have been rated as functioning below the point minimally necessary for change to occur. All she did, in my view, was come in week after week and gossip and complain and externalize about her problems. Yet after a few months, she proceeded to make several major changes in her life that she had been having trouble making, took some really productive job risks, and improved her relationship. When she finally decided to terminate, she praised me and told me how much help I had been. I have heard from her periodically over the past couple of years, when she has called to tell me how well things are going for her and to once again thank me for all I did for her! Yet in my view, I was totally ineffective by all the standard criteria of what good therapy is supposed to be. Although I did not know it at the time, these experiences began to undermine my belief that powerful interventions changed people.

I was therefore prepared for a paradigm revolution when the third challenge to my model arrived, in the form of an article by Christensen and Jacobson (1994) in *Psychological Science*. Christensen and Jacobson summarized a wide body of research and suggested that therapist experience or professional training did not matter in terms of effectiveness and that self-help and computer-therapy approaches were nearly equally effective to professionally provided therapy. This summary, by two radical behaviorists, seemed to be a call back to my roots. It suggested that the special expertise of the therapist was not a potent variable in therapeutic change, an idea that fit with other conclusions from research. For instance, Bergin and Garfield (1994) said, "with some exceptions, . . . there is massive evidence that psychotherapeutic techniques do not have specific effects" (p. 822), and Orlinsky, Grawe, and Parks (1994) noted that "the quality of the patient's participation in therapy stands out as the most important determinant of outcome" (p. 361). Clearly, all the professional paraphernalia we cherished did not seem to amount to much in terms of therapeutic effectiveness, echoing Carl Rogers's claim from so long ago. I felt a bit like I had awakened from a dream.

That spring I was invited to give the keynote address to the California State University Undergraduate Psychology Conference. My topic was "Is therapy a dance or an operation?" Perhaps calling therapy a dance was a bit romanticized, but the main thrust of the talk was that therapy was not an operation. The linear, causal model of therapy, which assumed that "therapist operations" caused change, was misguided, as was the medical model of therapy. I began to think that the active role of the client was the most important variable in therapy. Bergin and Garfield (1994), in their summary overview on psychotherapy research, concluded that

> another important observation regarding the client variable is that it is the client more than the therapist who implements the change process. If the client does not absorb, utilize, and follow through on the facilitative efforts of the therapist, then nothing happens. Rather than argue over whether or not "therapy works," we could address ourselves to the question of whether or not "the client works"! In this regard, there needs to be a reform in our thinking about the efficacy of psychotherapy. Clients are not inert objects upon whom techniques are administered. They are not dependent variables upon whom independent variables operate. . . . As therapists have depended more upon the client's resources, more change seems to occur. (pp. 825–826)

This line of thought led to the development of my current view.

MY CURRENT APPROACH

Along with Karen Tallman, I began to develop a view that the most important healing force in therapy was the client (Bohart & Tallman, 1996, 1997, 1999; Tallman & Bohart, 1999). To paraphrase Prochaska, Norcross, and DiClemente (1994), therapy was actually professionally coached self-help. The change processes used by therapists are ones that clients use in their everyday lives (Prochaska et al., 1994). Most of the common factors identified by various writers on therapy (e.g., Goldfried & Pawader, 1982; Grencavage & Norcross, 1990) were actually client self-healing processes (Bohart & Tallman, 1999).

Our conclusion from the research was that the therapist's expertise at applying the right intervention to the specific problem mattered little to therapeutic outcome most of the time. This seemed a fair conclusion from studies showing that therapist training or experience made, at best, only a modest difference in effectiveness; that self-help materials worked about as well as professional therapists; and that different therapies all seemed to work about the same. It seemed to myself and my coauthor that the most reasonable conclusion was that Carl Rogers was correct way back in 1957: Clients are the primary self-healers in therapy, and their power to self-heal, mobilized by any decently provided therapist procedure in any decently helpful relationship, transcends special theories and techniques.

Others were thinking along similar lines. Jerry Gold (1994) had written an article on the client as the integrative therapist. Barry Duncan and his colleagues (e.g., Duncan, Hubble, & Miller, 1997) were developing a client-centered model of therapy in which interventions were chosen on the basis of what fit with the client's frame of reference and the client's theory of change.

Our conclusion was that the client, not the therapist, is the engine that drives the therapy. The therapist provides structure, tools, and a good working atmosphere. The most important variable in therapy is not client diagnosis or therapist intervention, but client involvement and participation. Clients who are openly involved and willing to participate will be much more likely to change than clients who are not. Contrary to medications, interventions have no power in themselves. Any power they have comes from the client's investment of energy, ingenuity, curiosity, willingness to learn, and intelligent participation. If a client does not actively "inhabit" a procedure (rather than merely comply and do it), the procedure will have no life to make anything happen. This is not true in medicine, where presumably, patients need not believe in the medication or be enthusiastic about it. Even if lukewarm about it, patients who comply and take the medication are likely to find it helpful.

This is not to say that procedures and techniques are useless or irrelevant. Different clients may prefer or take to different approaches, just as different people prefer different forms of exercise to attain physical fitness. Clients can use may different approaches and techniques to "scaffold" their self-healing efforts (they also need some kind of scaffolding). Clients can scaffold their efforts to overcome depression with cognitive–behavioral techniques (Elkin, 1994; Hollon & Beck, 1994), a client-centered empathic listening relationship or gestalt procedures (Greenberg & Watson, 1998), interpersonal therapy (Elkin, 1994), or even self-help procedures (Arkowitz, 1997). Clients can scaffold their attempts to overcome anxiety with cognitive–behavioral procedures (Hollon & Beck, 1994) or gestalt techniques (Johnson & Smith, 1997). They can overcome traumatic experiences with cognitive–behavioral procedures (Foa & Rothbaum, 1997), experiential procedures (Paivio & Nieuwenhuis, in press), or eye movement desensitization and reprocessing (EMDR; Shapiro, 1995).[1]

At this point, the reader might ask, "but doesn't everyone believe that the client is the agent of change?" Therapists of all persuasions emphasize the importance of client collaboration; however, I found that those in our field neither act nor write as though they really believe it. Instead, virtually all books on therapy and all conference presentations depict the therapist

---

[1] In EMDR, the client focuses on a traumatic experience while following bilateral stimulation provided by the therapist. Typically, the client follows the therapist's moving fingers with his or her eyes. This process is repeated until the traumatic experience shifts and changes in a productive direction.

as the hero of the therapy drama. As Bickman and Salzer (1996) said, our discussions of therapy are "therapist centric." The template for evaluating treatment guidelines from the American Psychological Association (Task Force on Psychological Intervention Guidelines, 1995) assumes that it is the job of the professional to select the treatment and that clients' opinion is only to be used when other criteria are lacking. Clients are relegated to the role of recipients of authoritative therapists' choices of interventions.

Similarly, at conferences the discussion is all about therapists and their choice of interventions. Rarely is any kind of dialogue with the client mentioned in terms of treatment selection or implementation. Clients are treated as dependent variables. For example, at a recent conference one presenter talked about the innovative intervention he had designed for a client and how effective it had been. What interested me was the fact that the brilliance of the intervention did not matter until the client decided to use it, and it took the client a couple of weeks to decide to do that. In deciding to use it, the client had to confront some of the very fears the intervention was supposed to help her confront. In other words, it was the client who thought about the intervention over a period of time, changed, and then decided to use the intervention. This was interesting—the client, as an active self-healer, had worked to change in order to use the intervention—so I raised my hand to comment on this. It is difficult to convey the depth of the indifference with which my comment was met; one could almost say it that was treated as random noise in the background. The discussion immediately turned back to the cleverness of the therapist and the intervention itself.

What most therapists mean by client *collaboration* is really client compliance with the therapist's treatment regimen. If clients do not comply, they are labeled *treatment resistant* (a phrase that reminds one of the development of resistance to antibiotics). Then the therapist must "treat" the resistance. None of this language portrays therapy as a genuine collaboration between two intelligent beings in dialogue with one another.

It is clear that despite everyone saying the client is the ultimate agent of change, most professionals act and talk as though their interventions are primarily responsible for change. But if the idea of the client as active self-healer is right—that therapy is professionally coached self-help—then intervention is not primary; rather, client participation and involvement are. When I look back at clients such as the middle-aged woman described earlier, what I notice is that my "potent interventions" did not work because the clients did not actively take them and invest life in them. They may have passively complied with them, but they did not really participate. They were like students who take notes, maybe even memorize the material, but never really invest in the learning. Such students never get a feel for or understanding of the material, so they do not learn in a way that allows them to put the material into useful operation. My guess is that a highly motivated client who actively participates in the tasks of cognitive–behavioral therapy, experiential therapy, or psychodynamic therapy will be able to mine those tasks for progress; the nature of the task does not matter except to the degree that the client prefers one approach to another.

Drawing analogies to both education and parenting can help. Across cultures, parents can be good parents in many different ways, because children are capable of thriving and growing in different parenting atmospheres. Similarly, in education there have been endless debates about the best way to educate children: Should teachers use phonetics and drill, or should they use whole language learning? Certainly something makes learning more or less effective in different countries, but no compelling evidence shows that any one teaching philosophy is truly better than another. Once again, success most likely has more to do with the degree to which the children are motivated and involved. Things like poverty, classroom size, and parental support seem to matter most. Motivated and involved children most likely can learn under the umbrella of many different philosophies. It is likely that cross-cultural differences in educational results have as much to do with the consistent structure of motivation provided students in different countries as they do with specific teaching methods.

Widely different learning environments, as long as they are reasonably supportive of learning, then, all can be effective. It is no wonder that the *Dodo bird verdict*—a term taken from the *Alice in Wonderland* race in which it was declared that all had won and all must have prizes—applies to psychotherapy, which is essentially a learning situation, as I argue below.[2]

My current position on psychotherapy is expressed in a book (Bohart & Tallman, 1999): *How Clients Make Therapy Work: The Process of Active Self-Healing*. I reject the idea that I am the physician-like authority who is supposed to diagnose the client's problem and then apply treatment. Rather, what I do is provide a climate in which clients can creatively learn how to cope better with their lives. I see the client as my full collaborator. Therapy is two intelligences in dialogue: It is neither one extreme of the expert therapist owning truth and deciding for the client what is best, nor the other extreme of the therapist only following the client. Each party has expertise. I have expertise on a variety of ways to facilitate learning. The client is the expert on his or her life and, ultimately, on what will work for her or him. Therapy has to be a meeting of minds, an intelligent dialogue or conversation.

---

[2] Parenthetically, an informal survey I conducted shows that the Dodo bird verdict holds in most areas of learning: For instance, there is no one way to train actors, widely differing coaching styles and philosophies can work in sports, and different college professors use different teaching styles effectively.

I assume that clients have the capacity to decide for themselves what the best procedures are for them, although they may not know this and may not initially use this capacity. More so than in medicine, psychological problems involve expertise on the part of the client. In medicine, patients do not have sufficient knowledge of their own bodies and how they work to decide for themselves what the best treatment is. But in psychology, psychological problems are intimately connected with clients' goals and experiences in a way that only clients can understand. The therapist is the expert on the use of certain techniques and procedures, which can be laid out in the service of the client, as a home decorating consultant puts his or her expertise in service of the client.

Therapy is a diverse collection of different kinds of learning experiences—supported creative self-exploration by the client, coached learning experiences, guided or structured exploration, and philosophical dialogue. Medical models that view therapy as treatment and intervention have obscured the learning nature of therapy, despite an emphasis on learning in cognitive and behavior therapy. If one thinks of the client not as someone who is coming to therapy to be treated for a condition, but as someone coming to learn (a much more active stance), then therapy becomes the provision of different kinds of learning opportunities, analogous to the different kinds of learning opportunities provided in school. For example, in a good mentoring environment, a graduate student may have a good idea for a research study. The mentor may primarily listen and help the student think it out but may not intervene to alter the student's trajectory as long as it is going in a profitable direction. Analogously, in therapy, some clients need nothing more than the empathic workspace provided by a client-centered therapist to grow. In that empathic workspace, many clients can productively think through their problems and grow with nothing but a platform of supportive listening; this is the first of five learning opportunities that therapy provides.

A second learning opportunity provided in school comes through interaction. A student can learn a great deal through interacting and participating with others. Likewise, therapy provides a learning opportunity of direct interaction. Through their interaction with the therapist (but without therapist guidance), clients can spontaneously learn new ways of being and behaving by testing things out, as both psychodynamic and humanistic therapists have argued. Clients can learn that they can be trusted by experiencing the therapist's trust. They can learn that they are worthy of respect by experiencing the therapist's respect and that they are worth listening to by having the therapist listen to them. This condition is the same kind of learning opportunity provided by both good teachers and parents.

The third type of learning opportunity is provided through feedback and dialogue. In school, students learn through getting feedback from their

teachers and fellow students. This feedback can be informational or corrective. Feedback also can stimulate thinking: A teacher can provide a new
perspective to a student on a problem they are having trouble solving, give
the student information the student does not have, or stimulate the student
to think things through by asking carefully timed, thought-provoking questions (as in cognitive therapy). Similarly, therapists can provide grist for
the client's mill through information; corrective feedback, such as interpretations in psychoanalysis; or Socratic dialogue, as in cognitive therapy.

The fourth type of learning opportunity provided in school is the use
of exercises to stimulate the student's creative development. In acting classes,
students may do improvisational exercises, and in music and creative writing,
they may complete structured exercises to write pieces in the form of Bach
or Hemingway. In therapy, this kind of learning opportunity is best represented by the exercises and procedures used in experiential therapies. These
exercises and procedures are designed to foster experiential and emotional
involvement, but focusing on those dimensions (as most theoreticians and
researchers do) misses the point that the exercises provide an opportunity
for self-discovered creativity and learning through enactment. Thus in the
empty-chair procedure in process–experiential therapy (Greenberg & Watson, 1998), clients get to imaginatively role-play a dialogue; in doing this
exercise, they creatively develop their own ideas about themselves and
another person. Getting experientially and emotionally involved is the
consequence, not the cause, of full participation in a creative learning
activity.

Finally, the fifth kind of learning opportunity provided in school is
direct tutoring. In this kind of learning, students develop basic skills, from
reading and writing to playing a guitar or dancing. Cognitive–behavior
therapy, whose primary methodology is to tutor clients in skills, most resem-
bles this process. Even exposure therapy could be thought of as providing an
opportunity for skill building, if one takes Bandura's (1997) and Goldfried's
(1995) view of why it is successful as raising a sense of self-efficacy.

CONCLUSION

Because it provides a series of learning opportunities, therapy is a
matter of collaboratively helping clients use different kinds of opportunities
at different times rather than the treatment of psychological conditions. At
times, the client needs an opportunity for exploration and creativity; at
other times, he or she needs the kind of relationship that often exists
between a dissertation mentor and a graduate student. Sometimes, directly
tutored skills training may be needed.

For example, Fred came to therapy because he was experiencing severe and pervasive anxiety. Fred worked in business but always had secretly wanted to be an artist. He had gone into business when he had gotten married because he wanted to support his wife. Now he had three children. His anxiety started when he was promoted into a position of authority; he began to feel that he had to say goodbye to his dream.

Fred came to therapy because he had heard the idea that anxiety may have to do with people not being true to themselves and thought his anxiety might have to do with his early experiences. Based on what he wanted, he and I engaged in a thorough exploration of his life trajectory. He had read about gestalt therapy and wanted to do some two-chair work to deal with his internal conflicts, so we did some of that. Much of this work seemed highly significant. Fred had a number of deeply emotional discoveries and seemed to gain understanding of many of his feelings and choices. But he still felt anxious. An important family reunion was approaching, and Fred was supposed to take his family and travel across country to attend it. He wanted to feel secure that he could handle the situation. I began to give him several practical cognitive–behavior techniques to handle his anxiety. Fred tried out the techniques and liked them. Despite his earlier interest in the psychodynamic–experiential activities, Fred decided that he wanted more techniques, and so for several sessions we focused on cognitive–behavior procedures.

Should I have started with the cognitive–behavior approach, using the voice of authority to convince Fred that it was the proper treatment? In my view, no. Fred definitely wanted a certain kind of therapy. He only came to the point of wanting the cognitive–behavior techniques after he had done some of the things he thought he had wanted. Moreover, after he had mastered some of the here-and-now problems using the cognitive–behavior procedures, he wanted to return to the psychodynamic–experiential exploration of the deeper issues of his life direction. As he gradually gained control over his anxiety, the exploration of these issues began to bear fruit. In fact, one of the best sessions came when he and I had a philosophical discussion about the best way to live life. I brought in my knowledge of philosophy and self-disclosed about some of my own philosophical conflicts. Fred became deeply involved. He began to realize that although he did want to do something more meaningful with his life than what he was doing in business, the deepest meaning at the present time came from his commitment to his family. So he began to see his work in business as part of what was most meaningful to him. His anxiety over his fear that he was choosing an inauthentic existence diminished.

This case was not one of an expert therapist treating a condition in Fred. Rather, it was two intelligent beings in dialogue. I brought in all my expertise and laid it at the service of the client. The client brought in his expertise on his own life and decided what he most needed at a given time. I used my knowledge to offer different kinds of learning opportunities at different times. The client was the one who used the various learning opportunities to meet his needs. It was our collaborative work that was most important.

REFERENCES

Arkowitz, H. (1997, April). Clients as cognitive therapists for their own depression. In A. Bohart (Chair), *The client's active role in change: Implications for integration.* Symposium conducted at the Convention of the Society for the Exploration of Psychotherapy Integration, Toronto, Ontario, Canada.

Bandura, A. (1997). *Self-efficacy.* New York: Freeman.

Beck, A. T., Rush, A. J., Shaw, B. F., & Emery, G. (1979). *Cognitive therapy of depression.* New York: Guilford Press.

Bergin, A. E., & Garfield, S. L. (l994). Overview, trends, and future issues. In A. E. Bergin & S. L. Garfield (Eds.), *Handbook of psychotherapy and behavior change* (4th ed., pp. 821–830). New York: Wiley.

Bickman, L., & Salzer, M. S. (1996, August). Dose-response, disciplines, and self-help: Policy implications of *Consumer Reports* findings. In Consumer Reports *Mental health survey results—Practice and policy implications.* Symposium conducted at the 104th Annual Convention of the American Psychological Association, Toronto, Ontario, Canada.

Bohart, A. (1977). Role playing and interpersonal conflict reduction. *Journal of Counseling Psychology, 24,* 15–24.

Bohart, A. (1980). Toward a cognitive theory of catharsis. *Psychotherapy: Theory, Research and Practice, 17,* 192–201.

Bohart, A. (1982). Similarities between cognitive and humanistic approaches to psychotherapy. *Cognitive Therapy and Research, 6,* 245–250.

Bohart, A. (1993). Experiencing: The basis of psychotherapy. *Journal of Psychotherapy Integration, 3,* 51–67.

Bohart, A., & Tallman, K. (1996). The active client: Therapy as self-help. *Journal of Humanistic Psychology, 36,* 7–30.

Bohart, A., & Tallman, K. (1997). Empathy and the active client: An integrative, cognitive–experiential approach. In A. Bohart & L. S. Greenberg (Eds.), *Empathy reconsidered: New directions in psychotherapy* (pp. 393–418). Washington, DC: American Psychological Association.

Bohart, A., & Tallman, K. (1999). *How clients make therapy work: The process of active self-healing.* Washington, DC: American Psychological Association.

Bozarth, J. (1998). *Person-centered therapy: A revolutionary paradigm.* Ross-on-Wye, England: PCCS Books.

Brodley, B. T. (1990). Client-centered and experiential: Two different therapies. In G. Lietaer, J. Rombauts, & R. Van Balen (Eds.), *Client-centered and experiential psychotherapy in the nineties* (pp. 87–107). Leuven, Belgium: Leuven University Press.

Christensen, A., & Jacobson, N. S. (1994). Who (or what) can do psychotherapy: The status and challenge of nonprofessional therapies. *Psychological Science, 5*, 8–14.

Duncan, B. L., Hubble, M. A., & Miller, S. D. (1997). *Psychotherapy with "impossible" cases: The efficient treatment of therapy veterans.* New York: Norton.

Elkin, I. (1994). The NIMH Treatment of Depression Collaborative Research Program: Where we began and where we are. In A. E. Bergin & S. L. Garfield (Eds.), *Handbook of psychotherapy and behavior change* (4th ed., pp. 114–142). New York: Wiley.

Epstein, S. (1979). Natural healing processes of the mind: I. Acute schizophrenic disorganization. *Schizophrenia Bulletin, 5*(2), 313–321.

Foa, E. B., & Rothbaum, B. O. (1997). *Treating the trauma of rape: Cognitive behavioral therapy for PTSD.* New York: Guilford Press.

Gendlin, E. T. (1964). A theory of personality change. In P. Worchel & D. Byrne (Eds.), *Personality change* (pp. 100–148). New York: Wiley.

Gendlin, E. T. (1967). Therapeutic procedures in dealing with schizophrenics. In C. R. Rogers, E. T. Gendlin, D. J. Kiesler, & C. B. Truax (Eds.), *The therapeutic relationship and its impact* (pp. 369–400). Madison: University of Wisconsin Press.

Gendlin, E. T. (1968). The experiential response. In E. Hammer (Ed.), *Use of interpretation in treatment* (pp. 208–227). New York: Grune & Stratton.

Gendlin, E. T. (1969). Focusing. *Psychotherapy: Theory, Research and Practice, 6*, 4–15.

Gendlin, E. T. (1974). Client-centered and experiential psychotherapy. In D. A. Wexler & L. N. Rice (Eds.), *Innovations in client-centered therapy* (pp. 211–246). New York: Wiley.

Gendlin, E. T. (1996). *Focusing-oriented psychotherapy: A manual of the experiential method.* New York: Guilford Press.

Gold, J. R. (1994). When the patient does the integrating: Lessons for theory and practice. *Journal of Psychotherapy Integration, 4*, 133–158.

Goldfried, M. R. (1995). *From cognitive–behavior therapy to psychotherapy integration.* New York: Plenum Press.

Goldfried, M. R., & Padawer, W. (1982). Current status and future directions in psychotherapy. In M. R. Goldfried (Ed.), *Converging themes in psychotherapy* (pp. 3–50). New York: Springer.

Greenberg, L. S., & Watson, J. (1998). Experiential therapy of depression: Differential effects of client-centered relationship conditions and process experiential interventions. *Psychotherapy Research, 8*, 210–224.

Grencavage, L. M., & Norcross, J. C. (1990). Where are the commonalities among the therapeutic common factors? *Professional Psychology: Research and Practice*, *21*, 372–378.

Hammer, E. (Ed.). (1968). *Use of interpretation in treatment*. New York: Grune & Stratton.

Hart, J. T. (1970). The development of client-centered therapy. In J. T. Hart & T. M. Tomlinson (Eds.), *New directions in client-centered therapy* (pp. 3–22). New York: Houghton Mifflin.

Hollon, S. D., & Beck, A. T. (1994). Cognitive and cognitive–behavioral therapies. In A. E. Bergin & S. L. Garfield (Eds.), *Handbook of psychotherapy and behavior change* (4th ed., pp. 428–466). New York: Wiley.

Holton, G. (1971). On trying to understand scientific genius. *The American Scholar*, *41*, 98–99.

Johnson, W. R., & Smith, E. W. L. (1997). Gestalt empty-chair dialogue versus systematic desensitization in the treatment of a phobia. *Gestalt Review*, *1*, 150–162.

Kaplan, B. (Ed.). (1964). *The inner world of mental illness*. New York: Harper & Row.

Klein, M. H., Mathieu-Coughlan, P., & Kiesler, D. J. (1986). The experiencing scales. In L. S. Greenberg & W. Pinsof (Eds.), *The psychotherapeutic process* (pp. 21–71). New York: Guilford Press.

Laing, R. D. (1967). *The politics of experience*. New York: Pantheon Books.

Lieberman, M., Yalom, I., & Miles, M. (1973). *Encounter groups: First facts*. New York: Basic Books.

Matthews, S. M., Roper, M. T., Mosher, L. R., & Menn, A. Z. (1979). A non-neuroleptic treatment for schizophrenia: Analysis of the two-year postdischarge risk of relapse. *Schizophrenia Bulletin*, *5*(2), 322–334.

Mitchell, K. M., Bozarth, J. D., & Krauft, C. C. (1977). A reappraisal of the therapeutic effectiveness of accurate empathy, nonpossessive warmth, and genuineness. In A. S. Gurman & A. M. Razin (Eds.), *Effective psychotherapy: A handbook of research* (pp. 482–502). New York: Pergamon Press.

Orlinsky, D. E., Grawe, K., & Parks, B. K. (1994). Process and outcome in psychotherapy—*Noch einmal*. In A. E. Bergin & S. L. Garfield (Eds.), *Handbook of psychotherapy and behavior change* (4th ed., pp. 270–376). New York: Wiley.

Paivio, S., & Nieuwenhuis, J. (in press). Efficacy of emotionally focused therapy for adult survivors of child abuse. *Journal of Traumatic Stress*.

Prochaska, J. O., Norcross, J. C., & DiClemente, C. C. (1994). *Changing for good*. New York: Morrow.

Rogers, C. R. (1957). The necessary and sufficient conditions of therapeutic personality change. *Journal of Consulting Psychology*, *21*, 95–103.

Shapiro, F. (1995). *Eye movement desensitization and reprocessing*. New York: Guilford Press.

Stiles, W. B., & Shapiro, D. A. (1989). Abuse of the drug metaphor in psychotherapy process–outcome research. *Clinical Psychology Review*, *9*, 521–544.

Tallman, K., & Bohart, A. (1999). The client as common factor: Clients as self-healers. In M. A. Hubble, B. L. Duncan, & S. D. Miller (Eds.), *The heart & soul of change: What works in therapy* (pp. 91–132). Washington, DC: American Psychological Association.

Task Force on Psychological Intervention Guidelines. (1995). *Template for developing guidelines: Interventions for mental disorders and psychosocial aspects of physical disorders.* Washington, DC: American Psychological Association.

Todd, J., & Bohart, A. (1999). *Foundations of clinical and counseling psychology* (3rd ed.). New York: Addison-Wesley.

Truax, C. B., & Mitchell, K. M. (1971). Research on certain therapist interpersonal skills in relation to process and outcome. In A. E. Bergin & S. L. Garfield (Eds.), *Handbook of psychotherapy and behavior change* (pp. 299–344). New York: Wiley.

Vaillant, G. E. (1978). Prognosis and the course of schizophrenia. *Schizophrenia Bulletin, 4*(1), 20–24.

Watzlawick, P. (1978). *The language of change: Elements of therapeutic communication.* New York: Basic Books.

14

MY CHANGE PROCESS: FROM CERTAINTY THROUGH CHAOS TO COMPLEXITY

LESLIE S. GREENBERG

I started my therapeutic career as a client-centered therapist, but the first therapy approach I remember being attracted to, while still an undergraduate engineering student, was Glaser's reality therapy. At that time I was reading Sartre and Camus, having decided that existential philosophies made most sense to me. What appealed to me most in existentialism and in Glaser was the idea that people are responsible for their actions. Influenced by existential readings, I believed that will and choice were the final arbiters of action. These beliefs, formulated in late adolescence, foreshadowed things to come.

My wife had completed a degree in psychology at the University of the Witwatersrand, a home of many behaviorally oriented therapists, so I had been exposed to the ideas of behavior therapy informally, through her, while we were still students in South Africa. I remember believing early on that behaviorism was an oversimplified approach that certainly did not much help me understand myself or others. At this time I also was opposed to notions of a dark Freudian unconscious, which I had been exposed to by general reading. I had as an adolescent developed a romantic rather than a tragic view of human nature; this came about in part through my youthful idealism, which was fired by my involvement in student protest against the South African government. There I learned not only about the importance of values and ideas in fighting against oppression but also about the role of power and its abuses in social interaction. Growing up in this political context, I developed images of people (myself included) as free agents who could choose to strive for values higher than self-gain, even when society promoted prejudice and oppression to hold on to privilege. These were important formative lessons in the type of therapist I was to become.

In 1970, having left South Africa and completed a master's degree in mechanical engineering in Canada (specializing in the design of complex systems), I was seeking greater social relevance in my work than that offered in engineering. It was the end of the 1960s, and everything was open to redefinition—myself included. I decided to change to psychology in order to study much more complex systems: human beings.

In seeking a program to attend, I heard that a person named Laura Rice had recently come to the psychology department at York University. I learned that she had been a student of Rogers and believed that curiosity was important in human motivation; it was this motivation that guided people to explore and change themselves in therapy. This positive view of human nature appealed to me. It matched my belief that people were highly self-directed agents and that some inherent motivation kept people curious and striving toward self-actualization. The image of the explorer seeking knowledge was strong in my realm of fantasy and in my ideology. Of course, this was how I saw myself—as a self-determining explorer seeking new experiences, knowledge, and higher values.

LESSONS ORIGINALLY LEARNED

I completed an undergraduate course in counseling with Rice, in which I learned about and practiced how to establish the conditions of a client-centered helping relationship. On entering graduate studies in psychology in 1971, I rapidly identified myself as a phenomenologist and humanist, and I reverberated with Rogers's view of the helping relationship, as taught by Rice. She emphasized the role of empathy as an aid to the creation of new meaning. Early in my training, I also became immersed in encounter groups, and there learned many lessons about the importance of the genuine relationship and the use of self in helping people change.

I was assigned my first client in my first year as a graduate student, and I saw six clients that year under the close supervision of Rice. The training at that time was based on a model of learning by doing, and it drew on people's natural talents in producing a helping relationship. Under her tutelage, the wonders of the world of the therapeutic process were opened up to me. I knew intuitively from my life experience that each moment of interaction influenced the next, and she was studying this process with great subtlety, showing that the kinds of vocal quality and the expressive stances used by both therapist and client were reciprocally influential and were related to distant outcomes. This training was like an experience of arriving home for the first time. All my years of inchoate relational experience were now being explicitly articulated, investigated, and clarified. The foundation of both my clinical practice and my research interests for the next 30 years were laid by my early graduate student experience, built on the bedrock of my life experience.

As a graduate student, I viewed myself as a client-centered purist and practiced accordingly. I was not just learning how to set up a good relationship with clients as a basis for further invention. No, I held to the radical view that the relationship itself was curative and that people had internal resources that in the right environment would propel them toward growth and development. I believed in Rogers's view that growth in the other could be facilitated by empathic understanding, unconditional positive regard, and therapeutic genuineness. I was a true believer and initially would not tolerate any breach in this stance. At this time, in addition to being influenced by Rogers and Rice, Gendlin's writings were important to me, and I rapidly came to see therapy as producing change by promoting deeper experiencing in the client. Influenced by Gendlin's view, I saw deeper experiencing as a common ingredient of all change processes. To this day the importance of experiencing has remained a cornerstone of my view of how change occurs in therapy.

Thus, I learned early on that the relationship was the crucial ingredient of therapy and that experiencing was the client process that led to change. I believed that much distress was caused by the anxiety of being with people and that this anxiety could be cured by being in an accepting relationship. I believed that what was formed in human relationships—identity—could be changed in a human relationship. Acceptance, both intrapersonally and interpersonally, seemed to be key to helping overcome anxiety produced by conditions of worth, whereas experiencing personal material deeply, rather than "talking about" it, seemed essential to producing perceptual shifts that led to changes in one's view of self and other as well as in behavior.

Within this framework of beliefs, with Laura Rice as my mentor, I began a rigorous course of learning how to listen with exquisite differentiation to the nuances of people's meanings. Practicing in this way was an incredibly fertile learning ground. Rather than intervening in a directive way or attempting to diagnose, interpret, or modify, what I learned to do was listen and to check my understanding with my client. I learned to use such phrases as "sounds like you felt sort of trapped" or to reflect "just feeling all washed up." The more evocative, sensory, and metaphoric the responses, the more they might catch the implicit felt meaning and its connotations and help clients experience what they were saying more deeply. This deeper experience then helped generate new meaning. This was by no means a passive process—it was a highly active form of listening and responding.

STRENGTHS OF ORIGINAL ORIENTATION

In client-centered therapy, I learned the importance of "being" attitudes. The ability to be present with my clients and with myself. The strengths of client-centered therapy lay in elevating acceptance to an art. It taught me how to be present with people in their distress, how to understand their complex meanings in a finely differentiated way, and how not to try to change people but rather to accept them as they are. Empathic understanding, as I learned it, also involved imaginatively entering the internal frame of reference of the other; sensing, almost tasting, his or her experience; and reflecting back to the other one's moment-by-moment understanding of his or her experience and implicit meanings.

The concept of attending to the "leading edge" of experience was a crucial concept. The leading edge of experience can be understood as coming from a concept of mind proposed by William James, in which certain things can be clear and in the center of awareness, while others can be vague and at the edge of awareness. James's concept of the importance of the vague in consciousness was put into practice by listening for the leading edge— the not yet known, but on the periphery of awareness—and by paying attention to background as well as to central meanings. The background (or the implicit) often was conveyed as much by manner of expression, by vocal quality and style, and by nonverbal expression as by content and often could be captured by focusing on a bodily felt sense. I thus learned to form empathic responses that would begin by reflecting aspects of what was said but would end by pointing to the leading edge of experience. Statements such as "So your husband walked away with his friend and you were left sitting there, just feeling, I don't know, sort of empty or hollow?" left the client's attentional focus not simply on internal experience but also on the vague edge of that experience. Such statements directed the clients attention to the not-yet-articulated but present sense—the vague leading edge of consciousness. In addition, my empathic response was modeling an internal search process. I was a coexplorer, trying to search out the edges of my experience of what it must be like to be my client in the situation described.

My statements provided the client with a model of a style of processing I hoped the client would adopt. My colleagues and I later came to call this the *experiential search process* (L. Greenberg, Rice, & Elliott, 1993), which was done with absolute acceptance, respecting the client as an authentic source of experience.

The power of being authentic and congruent in the therapeutic relationship was another one of the great strengths of the client-centered approach. Genuineness did not mean talking about myself or reacting impulsively; rather, it meant being authentically present, in the moment, attempting to listen and understand without extraneous thoughts or intents. This approach was a disciplined form of being facilitatively genuine. In this view, because one's genuine goal is to facilitate the other in a nonexploitive manner, one can be authentic, which in turn will be facilitative. Thus, the facilitativeness of genuineness depends on its intent. I learned to pay attention to my own in-therapy experience and reactions to clients and to use them therapeutically. I learned a disciplined form of facilitative genuineness that involved exploring further, in myself, any negative experience of my client I may have had until I reached my most authentic experience, which usually related to my needs or concerns; I then spoke from this experience using "I" language. This use of self involved sharing what I felt (when my experience seemed to reflect on the interaction in important ways) and disclosing when it seemed like disclosure would be helpful. Being authentic in this way involved, for both therapist and client alike, striving toward being responsibly open with each other; acknowledging and taking responsibility for our own actions, thoughts, and feelings; and working toward accepting the inevitable consequences of our own humanness.

I learned in this approach that empathetically understanding clients in a genuine manner reduced their interpersonal anxiety, which in turn strengthened their sense of self and allowed the self to tolerate more intrapersonal anxiety. This increased tolerance allowed people to explore further their own anxiety-provoking experience and to face the previously disowned.

In my last years of graduate school, I entered a 3-year gestalt therapy training and began to develop skills in active intervention and the use of awareness experiments. This was a major change from a client-centered approach because gestalt therapy was not simply a talking cure. Here people were asked to do things—to enact their conflicts, risk new behavior, and imagine doing things in a new way. Intervention involved "try this" followed by "what do you experience?" It was a behavioristic phenomenology, in which one worked with in-session behavior and experience. Clients were asked to do something and then focus on their present experience. If they were unable to complete the proposed task, their avoidances and their blocks became the focus of attention. This was a revolutionary way to bringing issues alive in the session.

Promoting awareness of present experience, including sensations, feelings, thoughts, desires, and behavior, became a new goal of mine in therapy. In retrospect I see that gestalt therapy included a number of behavioral elements as well as elements of what was to become cognitive therapy. Relaxation, desensitization, and assertiveness training all were done, less systematically, in gestalt therapy under different names. Behavioral experiments to test assumptions, cognitive restructuring to change beliefs, and awareness of attributions also were a part of the approach. These behavioral and cognitive elements were encompassed under the gestalt notions of sensory awareness, overcoming avoidance, promoting risk taking, and increasing awareness.

Probably the most significant aspects of this training in helping me change as a therapist was my personal work. In this process I became more aware of my own experience, interruptive processes, and avoidances, and I became more comfortable with experiencing and expressing my own emotions. I came to acknowledge my competitiveness and my insecurities, and I risked being more open and vulnerable and letting go of control. In addition, I learned to take more risks in relation to my fear of rejection or disapproval. I learned, too, that trust came from trusting oneself as much as from trusting the other.

Most, if not all, of the training was personal work: Concepts, interventions, and processes were learned by experiencing them as a client and then trying to apply them to others. The training encouraged creativity and use of self, and there was an intense focus on being aware and following the client's process. A real limitation, however, was that there was little systematic training, just a directive to be aware and follow the process. Other weaknesses in the gestalt approach at that time were the lack of focus on the relationship between client and therapist, and the often overconfrontational nature of the approach. Clients often were viewed as manipulative, and frustration of their manipulations was a favored intervention. A major limitation of the approach was the overly individualistic view of people that Perls promoted in his practice. Although gestalt theory was based on a highly interpersonal, field-theoretic view that saw the organism and environment as an interdependent whole, many of the practices saw the individual as totally self-determining and responsible to the point of isolation and pathology. Doing one's own thing, autonomy, and separateness were clearly valued over connectedness and interdependence.

I experienced two other important early influences in graduate school. Both Laura Rice and I were influenced as early as 1971 by Juan Pascual-Leone, a neo-Piagetian, to adopt the Piagetian notion of action-producing schemes as a core theoretical construct and a constructivist view of human functioning. We also had been influenced by Neisser's (1967) view of constructive information processing. We thus were highly interested in what cognitive science might contribute to further understanding of human change. At a theoretical level, I was becoming a cognitive theorist interested in the person as a meaning-creating, active processor of information who controlled his or her attentional resources and focus and developed internal schemes that organized perception, cognition, and action. At the level of practice, however, I did not see myself as a cognitive therapist; awareness and acceptance were my major goals, not modification, rational disputation, or cognitive restructuring.

Of historical interest is a conversation between Tim Beck and Laura Rice in 1974 at a Society for Psychotherapy Research meeting. He raised with her the similarities between his emerging cognitive views and her views on the role of schemata in human functioning. He suggested to her that she was a cognitive therapist. I was a part of this conversation, and afterward, she and I discussed the issue quite thoroughly. We felt that despite the overlap in viewing schemata as important, Beck's rationally oriented form of practice was quite different from the evocative form of client-centered therapy we were practicing.

I also was exposed to another important influence in my final year of graduate school. One that broadened my theoretical perspective. I took a course from Morris Eagle on British object-relations theory (Fairburn, 1952; Guntrip, 1969), which was my first positive exposure to psychodynamic theory. Fairbairn's idea that people's primary drive was toward contact with others and Bowlby's attachment theory were highly compatible with my views of human nature, and I began incorporating their ideas into my humanistic, cognitive theory of functioning.

At this point, leaving graduate school, I defined myself as an experiential therapist who integrated Rogers's client-centered therapy and Perls's gestalt therapy within a constructivist, cognitive information-processing view. Within this emerging humanistic cognitive framework, I also began looking for ways of theoretically incorporating emotion, initially without much success. I was, however, a process-oriented therapist who listened for and followed what was most poignant or alive in the client's present experience rather than having a content theory of dysfunction or a goal-setting or problem-solving form of intervention. For a decade or so, this remained my clear therapeutic identity. Later came an identity crisis.

LIMITATIONS OF ORIGINAL ORIENTATION

The greatest limitation in the client-centered view was that the therapist's influence was regarded as nontherapeutic. Therapist interpretation or direction was seen as robbing the client of an opportunity to discover a self-direction and actualize the self. The problem was that this view could become a straightjacket, preventing one from offering or doing different things at different times. Although the principle of genuineness allowed one to be present in a variety of different ways, a client-centered orthodoxy emerged that became too restrictively opposed to therapist interventions that might impose or influence. The approach came to suffer from a "one-size-fits-all" problem, which hampered development of differential treatment and theory. Its great strength—that of capturing an essence of helping—became its weakness: the uniform assumption that the same approach was all that was necessary for all clients.

While training in client-centered therapy, I discovered Buber's view of the I–thou relationship and came to value his perspective. He differed from Rogers, although only subtly, in offering a more interpersonal view of the therapeutic process. He saw the therapist as confirming the other, whereas Rogers saw therapeutic understanding as facilitating the other's ability to affirm himself or herself. In Buber's view the healing occurred in the meeting, whereas in Rogers's view the relationship created an environment for the person to self-actualize. This was probably my first change in view—one of recognizing the more influencing presence of the authentic therapist. This more interpersonal view of the growth tendency—seeing therapists' confirmation of clients' experience as growth producing—came to be articulated more clearly later in viewing the growth tendency, not as in the client alone but as coming into being *between* client and therapist (L. Greenberg et al., 1993). In this view, it is the seeing of the growth possibility in others that helps it strengthen, and it is focusing on the growth tendency that helps it to act as a guide rather than believing that growth simply is released in an empathic environment. Although this early change in my view was not that explicit or noticeable in practice, it was important, and it set the direction of further developments in my view.

The first explicit change I made was related to the issue of influence. I adopted some aspects of Carkhuff's (1969) expansion of Rogers's view. Although I did not agree with Carkhuff's view of empathy as a skill, rather than an attitude, I did add the skills of immediacy and confrontation to my repertoire, again slowly moving to a more interpersonal view. Adding confrontation to a client-centered approach was a major change for me because in my view, it diverged substantially from Rogers's practice and therefore demanded a change in both theory of human functioning and theory of practice. It emphasized the therapist's role as an agent of change and threw into question the idea that growth always would occur without some interpersonal influence. It also used a style of interacting that at times involved responses offering more than understanding alone.

In recognizing the value of confrontation, however, I favored only positive confrontations, believing in their power to help mobilize client resources. I saw that confrontations that involved pointing out discrepancies between clients' positive resources and negative self-views helped them focus on their strengths. I was much more interested in identifying strengths than in pointing out discrepancies to increase clients' awareness of their avoidances or incongruence. In fact, I saw confronting discrepancies between verbal and nonverbal behavior, a favored intervention in gestalt therapy, as doing more harm than good. Doing so often made the client either more anxious or more self-conscious, and it set up the therapist as a detective or expert searching for what was hidden. I generally saw therapy as involving listening for what was being said rather than what was hidden or not being said.

HOW CHANGE OCCURRED

Leaving Toronto: Destabilization

Change occurred for me through four major influences: practice, life experience, research, and conceptual clarification. After completing graduate school, I went to the Department of Counseling Psychology at the University of British Columbia and began teaching, training, supervising, and private practice. Leaving my mentors behind gave me the opportunity to differentiate and create my own identity.

I struggled for a number of years to integrate my client-centered and gestalt views. I trained and supervised counselors and practiced group and individual therapy, trying to harmoniously integrate the more empathic, relational aspects of the client-centered approach with the more active, experimental methods of gestalt. I had a strong client-centered top dog that would criticize me when I was being too gestalt (i.e., being too directive, too unsupportive, not sufficiently empathic, and too influencing). I was continuing to do process research, investigating the effects of gestalt two-chair dialogue and other aspect of the process of change. I found from this research that gestalt dialogues, in which clients openly articulate their unspoken thoughts and feelings, could be helpful and that other specific interventions and the processes they produced seemed related to change. What was important was that the research necessitated specifying not only what the therapist did but also when it was done. I came to clearly see that specific interventions worked best at particular times for specific problem states. This was the beginning of a view of differential in-session intervention, and it laid down some of the seeds of how I would change from being a purist to being more integrative. I also began to develop and do some research on systematic methods of training students to use gestalt interventions, which took me beyond the teaching of "being" skills (i.e., empathy and relational attitudes) toward teaching "doing" skills. I also began a concerted effort to clarify my understanding of the role of emotion in human functioning and psychotherapy. I recognized more and more from my practice and research that moments that involved intense feeling seemed important in change. At this time my research activities at the Society for Psychotherapy Research also brought me more into contact with cognitive, cognitive–behavior, and dynamic therapists, and I began assimilating some ideas from these points of view.

The most crucial factor in my change, however, came from learning to be a couple's therapist, which occurred in conjunction with learning to be a parent and a marital partner with children. This change in life stage and in my practice precipitated a major change, forcing me to expand and adopt new theoretical perspectives and new therapeutic possibilities. After seeing a number of couples in my private practice, I felt that using purely intrapsychic, experientially oriented approaches to couples was not sufficient. Bill Pinsof, a close friend from graduate school, was a strong proponent of family therapy, and at graduate school he had impressed on me the value of working with families. Lacking children of my own and being only recently married at that time, however, I had been too intimidated by the prospect of working with families. I always thought that I needed to work from my own experience, so I believed that I needed my own adult experience with marriage and parenting before I could understand and work with families. I had done some training with Virginia Satir in family therapy; this experience had led me to working with couples and reading more on family systems. My wife, who was now a social worker, had trained in family systems, and she once again was important in exposing me to new areas of knowledge, as she had in our undergraduate years. Through her I was exposed to developments in family systems.

My wife and I twice had been in brief couple's therapy: once in 1975, soon after our first child was born, and once while on sabbatical in Berkeley in 1980. The first therapy, with an object relations-oriented family therapist, was to work on improving our relationship once we had a child. The second, with a Satir-oriented couple's therapist, was to try to deal with the effects of having two children! Both therapies were somewhat useful and certainly helped me to see more of my role in our couple's issues. I came to see that couple's work involved more than facilitating good communication skills and that the issue of power—and whose rules govern the interactions— was as important as good communication. Above all, however, was the ability to disclose underlying attachment-related feelings and needs and have them understood and accepted. Being in couple's therapy gave me the experience of couple's work, promoted my understanding of such ideas as family structure and interactional cycles, and helped me gain confidence to practice with couples and families. So did having my own family: Parenting— and marriage in the context of parenting—changed my view of myself and others. The image of myself and others as autonomous, self-actualizing beings did not fit that well with my experience of raising a family. I began to see that parenting required more than the Rogerian conditions and that although acceptance and positive regard were crucial, limits were also important. In addition, much social influence and learning occurs, for better and for worse. I learned that partners' needs and demands often come second to the children's needs and demands. I had to learn to subordinate personal goals, on a daily basis, to those of my family. I became much more aware of myself as part of a highly interconnected system.

By the end of the 1970s, feminist views of therapy also had begun to influence me. My wife, my female colleagues, and my students exposed me to ideas of consciousness raising and feminist views of interdependence. My wife, in fact, had constantly been raising my consciousness! I was being painfully transformed from a man who always needed to be right into a slightly more vulnerable, androgynous human being. I saw feminist approaches as offering an important view on the influence of sex roles, and I added consciousness raising to my repertoire of intervention skills.

A crucial moment of change occurred around 1979, when I attended a workshop with Minuchin on structural family therapy. I was impressed with both his theory and practice. I construed some of the family enactments he used as gestalt-type experiments, but with an important difference: These were not psychodramatic enactments with imagined others but actual interactions with the people themselves. Rather than imaginal confrontations, to resolve unfinished business, clients were being asked to change behavior and experience in vivo with their significant others. I began reading voraciously in this area and attending training workshops in family systems. I decided to spend my first sabbatical in 1980 doing a family therapy externship at the Mental Research Institute (MRI) in Palo Alto under Carlos Sluzki; there I learned much more about interactional and systemic therapies. I began to see much of what was being done as a form of behavior therapy in context. Structural family therapy seemed most clearly behavioral, where therapists were not only getting people to engage in new behaviors but also attempting to modify how the people in the environment would respond. This seemed far more powerful than working with individual behavior alone, without access to the context of the behavior. I thus trained in a variety of systemic and interactional approaches, saw context as important in determining behavior and experience, and was impressed with interactional cycles as important targets of change. Also important was that this form of treatment involved goal setting, planning, and influencing. This was far different from my initial nondirective process orientation. Once I expanded beyond my adherence to a single-school approach into thinking about behavior and context and moved from a purely facilitative, process orientation into becoming an unabashed influencer of interactions when working with families, I stopped being a purist experiential therapist and began opening myself to other views.

I also spent part of my sabbatical year at the Langley Porter Institute in San Francisco, getting further exposure to psychodynamic approaches, and I sat in on Paul Ekman's seminar on emotion. Mardi Horowitz's more scientifically based approach to psychodynamic therapy, which attempted to incorporate cognitive science and used states of mind and configurational analysis, appealed to me and opened me to trying to understand how dynamic therapists thought and practiced. I also was interested in seeing if I could apply Ekman's facial coding system to process research. I decided that it was too complex for my purposes but that the exposure to emotion theory and issues was helpful. At the same time, I visited the Mount Zion group in San Francisco and learned more about their new control mastery theory of therapy, which posited that clients set up tests of their pathogenic beliefs in therapy in attempts to have them disconfirmed. Therapists could pass or fail these tests, depending on how they responded to their clients. I incorporated those ideas into my view of how the relationship could be curative. Connecting with these groups had been made possible by my association with them through the Society of Psychotherapy Research. Contacts through professional associations definitely were important in helping me change as a therapist, as was an opportunity on my sabbatical to retrain and be exposed to different points of view.

On my sabbatical I also gave birth to the book *Emotion in Psychotherapy* (Greenberg & Safran, 1987), which was my first theoretical effort and an attempt to place what I knew about working with emotion into an emerging scientific psychology of emotion. Jeremy Safran, a graduate student in my classes at the University of British Columbia, visited me in Berkeley, and we planned the book with great excitement while sitting at a coffee table in an outdoor cafe. Clarifying my ideas on emotion through writing this book was an important element in my change as a therapist because it took me out of the domain of school-based theories of therapy into an attempt at understanding therapeutic phenomena in terms of general psychological theory. It helped free me from the edicts of practice of any particular approach and allowed me to experiment on my own with working with emotion. The experience led me to sharpen my focus on the elements of emotion: appraisal, action tendency, need, and embodied experience. I thus returned from my sabbatical a changed therapist.

Prior to my sabbatical, I had been working with Adam Horvath on developing the Working Alliance Inventory for his doctoral dissertation. This effort grew out of my exposure to Ed Bordin on a panel that he organized at the Society for Psychotherapy Research on the working alliance between therapist and client, which involved agreement between the two on the therapeutic goals and methods (tasks) as well as the interpersonal bond between them. Laura Rice had been on this panel, and I had worked with her on her paper, which focused on the role of "tasks" in humanistic therapies, a perspective that we had been developing in our research program. Although we saw tasks as important, we still believed the bond between therapist and client to be the core element. When the results of our first study on the alliance (Horvath & Greenberg, 1989) came back showing that task alliance was a stronger predictor of outcome than the bond component of the alliance scale (Horvarth & Greenberg, 1994) or than the Barrett-Lennard (1962) Perceived Empathy Scale (as part of the Relationship Inventory), I reached an intellectual crisis. (In dynamic systems terms, this crisis would be described as being in a critical state, on the edge of chaos.) I was ready for a theoretical change. I had been exposed to much new information, and now one of my core beliefs, that empathy was the core condition of helping, was being disconfirmed by my own research.

Returning from sabbatical, I began focusing more on the role of emotion in therapy and ventured more fully into couple's therapy, developing a new integrative model of couple's therapy. I began integrating my newly acquired systemic and interactional views with my intrapsychic experiential views and my growing understanding of the role of emotion in human functioning. I put together the idea that accessing partners' underlying emotions and unmet adult attachment needs led to a change in interactions and a transformation of negative interactional cycles. Together with my doctoral student, Sue Johnson, I developed a theory and manual of emotionally focused couple's therapy (L. Greenberg & Johnson, 1988), and we conducted the first study comparing this treatment with a cognitive–behavioral marital therapy (Johnson & Greenberg, 1985). The study demonstrated the effectiveness of our newly devised affective–systemic treatment. Being more directive in couple's therapy—assessing negative cycles and targeting them for change—helped me further learn how to integrate process-oriented "being" attitudes with change-oriented, "doing" skills. This also was my first experience of doing comparative outcome research, and from it I saw with my own eyes that treatments other than the ones I believed in did actually work. This was a confronting and broadening experience.

In my individual therapy practice, I predominantly practiced intrapsychically, as an experiential therapist, using the empathic I–thou relationship (being) and gestalt chair dialogues (doing). Simultaneously, however, I was doing something completely different: running a family therapy team in a school-based community clinic using a variety of interventions based on a systemic framework. For example, I became skilled at sending messages from behind a one-way mirror, going into the room and delivering expert interventions, and devising Milan-style messages to read to families at the end of sessions. I was not working with the internal experience of the individuals in the family but rather with changing people's behaviors in their family contexts as well as reframing the meanings of their interactions. To integrate this diversity in my own practice, I began to view intrapersonal work as applicable at one level and interactional systemic work as useful at another level. I saw these levels as relating to each other like chemistry and physics might relate in solving an engineering problem: One would ask which was the better level of intervention for solving the problem rather than which was the truer view. I thus adopted a more pragmatic view: Instead of focusing on which explanation was true, I focused on which was most useful in helping to solve a problem.

In about 1984, I caught wind of the formation of the Society for the Exploration of Psychotherapy Integration (SEPI), providing me with the last bit of input that sent my pile of beliefs, already in a "critical state" near chaos, cascading into a new organization. SEPI produced an avalanche in my worldview. The idea of integration, along with the social support of a group of colleagues espousing this idea, provided me with a new elegant solution, one that helped simplify the growing complexity of my beliefs. My developing personal relationships with such people as Marv Goldfried, Hal Arkowitz, and Stan Messer—each having a view different from mine— also helped further this change in my perspective. I could integrate all of my increasingly unwieldy ideas into a new view of myself as an integratively oriented therapist. This approach produced a change in my identity and helped broaden my practice significantly. I now felt free to practice in a more varied manner without guilt.

Thus by this point in the 1980s, having practiced independently for about 10 years and having been exposed to sufficient individuals, couples, and families in my practice, I realized that no one treatment fitted everyone and became more deliberately pragmatic and integrative. I asked myself what type of intervention best seemed to fit a given case, and even more specifically, what intervention best fitted the moment. I had by now been exposed more fully to the actual practice of humanistic, psychodynamic, and systemic therapies, not just their theories. I had not yet seen much cognitive–behavior individual therapy practice, although that situation changed as cognitive–behavior therapy practice grew in prominence. My systemic work began to be assimilated into my individual therapy. In individual therapy I would at times reframe or prescribe the problem and use direct or paradoxical homework. I saw that therapist influence was acceptable when working with behavior. I began trying to work out how I decided to approach a problem intrapsychically or interactionally. Escalating cycles were primary indicators for thinking and intervening interactionally; enduring impasses, or "stuckness," also seemed like good opportunities for the paradoxical intervention of prescribing the stuckness. Combining my intrapsychic views with systemic interventions, it seemed that when someone was stuck, the no-change forces were stronger than the change forces and that identifying with the forces of no change was an act of acceptance and of re-owning the disowned experience of not wanting to change. The way I worked, I saw no-change interventions as being acceptance- and awareness-oriented (rather than power-based) therapist manipulations. I had developed and tested a systemic couple's treatment (Goldman & Greenberg, 1992) based on prescribing that couples continue their negative cycles. The rationale for continuing to quarrel was based on an exploration of the dangers of improvement, a paradoxical strategy I learned at MRI (Fisch, Weakland, & Segal, 1983). Over time, I came to see this intervention as helping people become aware of their underlying experience and the reasons they were stuck or distanced as well as respecting the partner's anxiety about change. I saw a real wisdom in couples' going slowly in reestablishing intimacy because negative cycles evolve as attempted solutions to protect the partners from pain. Getting close again could open them to the hurt and disappointment that led to the cycle in the first place. I thereby assimilated strategic interventions into my humanistic view of functioning.

I now began to conceptualize my individual practice as one that used experiential theory to focus on the clients' present, in-session experience; psychodynamic object relations theory to focus on influences of past relationships on present relationships; cognitive–behavioral views to promote between-session homework involving practice or new behavior; and systemic views to understand and work with the interactional context of the problem. In addition, with my original interest in constructivism, I had become interested in the epistemological issues that had emerged in the 1980s in the family systems domain and was trying to conceptualize my views within an overarching constructivist framework. On my family therapy externship at Palo Alto, I had been introduced to the ideas of Maturana and to the notion of self-organizing systems and was interested in combining this with Pascual-Leone's neo-Piagetian views (Pascual-Leone, 1987). I was interested in the development of a constructivist metatheory. I did not believe in a radical constructivist view, however, or the more recently articulated social constructionist view that all meaning comes from language and culture. Instead, I became aligned with a moderate view that our constructions progressively approach and are constrained by features of a reality that exists beyond our constructions.

I also was becoming increasingly interested in developing an integrative approach to therapy based on my emerging view of change-process research. In this research view, the best way to study change was to isolate key change events, which consist of markers of client problem states, therapist interventions, and specific change processes relevant to the problem state induced by the intervention. If particular interventions were found to be most effective for particular states, then they could be combined in a treatment if or when each became relevant. This approach suggested a type of systematic technical eclecticism, in which particular interventions would fit particular in-session states. I thus began to vary my practice according to the client's state or problem. With a client with agoraphobia, I did in vivo exposure, challenged catastrophic beliefs about the future when they arose, and made interpretations of underlying dynamics when they seemed to be governing present experience.

I was troubled, however, that the technically eclectic approach lacked a comprehensive theory of functioning. What seemed particularly important was that it lacked a theory of the therapeutic nature of the relationship and recognition of the importance of relational variables.

Returning to Toronto: Restabilization

In 1986 I returned to York University as a professor. I had a far broader view than when I had left the university as a new PhD in 1975. I had believed from the beginning in the importance of the client-centered relationship conditions but had begun to assimilate different types of interventions into this basic relational stance. I still believed that an empathic, client-centered relationship was curative in and of itself in individual therapy because it promoted an internalization of the therapist's empathy and acceptance that led to self-empathy and self-acceptance, but now I believed in adding a variety of interventions to this relationship. The only limitation on what interventions could be assimilated into my new integrative approach were those that would violate the empathic relational stance and disrupt the process of internalization. Thus, for example, interventions from rational–emotive therapy, gestalt therapy, or some short-term dynamic approaches that were too disrespectful or unsupportive and such manipulations by the therapist as paradoxical prescriptions done within a power-based view seemed too disjunctive to incorporate into the basic empathic I–thou relationship. In addition, I believed that an interpretive stance, in which interpretations of unconscious material were delivered authoritatively with the intention of giving clients "news" of things they did not know, would destroy the atmosphere of promoting client agency and interfere with my efforts to help clients access their internal resources.

My new integrative view, however, now allowed me to use interventions from many approaches. Influenced by cognitive therapy's explicit identification of the role of dysfunctional thoughts and beliefs, I more intentionally began to use interventions that helped clients increase their awareness of their negative thoughts, catastrophic expectations, and maladaptive beliefs. This approach was a combination of what I had been doing in gestalt therapy—focusing on awareness of shoulds, introjected views of self, and projections (attributions of thoughts and feelings)—with the clarity of a cognitive therapy view of the importance of thoughts, assumptions, and beliefs. I also began to use more homework, getting people to practice things that occurred in sessions or to try on new behaviors for which the motivation had emerged in the session. I was thus assimilating the use of homework and practice from systemic and cognitive–behavior therapy. The experience of giving homework to couples and families helped me to do so more easily in individual therapy.

Morris Eagle was still at York when I returned, and I taught a graduate theories of psychotherapy seminar with him. He recently had written his book (Eagle, 1984) on advances in psychodynamic therapy, and I read his as well as J. Greenberg and Mitchell's (1983) book; I found myself quite comfortable with much of object relational and self psychological views of human functioning. Psychoanalytic practice, however, was still a bit of a mystery to me, but with the research-based specifications of Luborsky and Strupp, and increased specification of other brief dynamic approaches, it became clearer that transference and linking interpretations were at the heart of much psychodynamic practice. So I began slowly to experiment in my own practice with linking interpretations. In individual therapy I began, much more explicitly, relating people's present experience to their past and identifying patterns in their experience across situations. However, I was often not too comfortable offering transference interpretations, especially in briefer treatments because doing so clashed with my view that the real relationship was an important vehicle of "healing." Seeing my clients' inter-action with me as a projection of the past onto the present seemed to miss what was occurring between us and appeared to be an overly reductionistic simplification of our interpersonal experience and interaction. I also used linking interpretations as a way of evoking experience more than as a way of promoting insight. Transference interpretations seemed to work best in long-term therapies, but even there, the more fragile the client, the more the transference interpretations seemed to produce a rupture in the alliance, which then needed to be healed by empathy.

I am left today still puzzling over whether transference interpretations with fragile people are helpful in my practice, whether the tear and repair of the alliance that generally ensues is a curative process, or whether it is better to remain empathic throughout. My views on transference have clarified, however. I use transference interpretations more freely now because I see them as one marker-guided intervention among many (van Kessel & Lietaer, 1998). I make the interpretations when a strong interpersonal pull emerges in the therapy or when the client fails to let go of a view of me in the face of contrary evidence. I also focus on both my client's and my own experience of our relationship when it appears as though it might help deal with an obstacle that is interfering with the relationship or deepen the client's experience of a manner of interaction that is strongly getting in the way of my being empathic. Rather than constituting the fabric of the treatment, transference work occurs only occasionally in my therapies.

At this point in my career, in the mid-1980s, I read Kohut and liked his view, which I saw as essentially an expansion of Rogers. Reading self psychology increased my understanding of both some of my own psychology and some of my clients' processes, especially those related to the regulation of self-esteem. In 1990 I entered a self psychologically oriented personal analysis, which was available through health insurance in Ontario, Canada. I stayed in the analysis for 3 years. Here I learned firsthand about psychoanalytic therapy. What I found most helpful was the therapist's empathic attunement. Interpretations related to the psychogenic roots of my experience were singularly unhelpful; what was helpful was a consistent focus on my daily experience, which was facilitated by the frequency of our sessions. This focus increased my awareness of links between daily events and my emotional experience and behavior. I found lying on a couch a useful experience because it freed me from dealing with the interpersonal interaction and allowed me to focus internally. I found, however, that my analyst was not systematically focused on promoting exploration of leading-edge experience but was more inclined to empathic summaries of what he heard and identification of links.

My immersion in the self psychological approach, both personally and theoretically, supported my already articulated views on the importance of emotion and empathic attunement to affect. I more and more saw emotion as being at the root of my experience—that the essence of trauma was unbearable affect and that affect and its regulation were the central organizing process of the self. This therapy experience both strengthened and revitalized my view on the importance of empathy, but I became even more focused on emotion and empathic attunement to it as the basis of personal meaning and development.

At this time I also began to work with a number of more borderline people in my practice. Although I was initially rather strongly opposed to diagnosis because it pathologized without leading to differential treatment, I came to see the usefulness of this and other diagnoses. The importance of diagnosis was brought home even more strongly when I ran a National Institute of Mental Health-funded project on the experiential treatment of depression, which had been funded only on the condition that the research was done on a diagnostic group. Here, I saw that similarities in the depressive processes of certain subgroups of people, such as self-critical or dependence, benefited from different interventions and that depressed clients who had Axis II diagnoses, such as avoidant or borderline personality (the latter were excluded from our study) were characteristically different from those who did not and required different treatment. The depression project changed me from being totally process oriented to recognizing that diagnostic grouping had functional significance. I also recognized the importance of forming a focus on the underlying determinants of the client's disorder as soon as possible in a brief treatment.

In the 1990s I also became involved in the development of an international society for constructivist psychotherapy; here again, supportive colleagues were important in broadening my view. I got to know Mike Mahoney, Vittorio Guidano, and Bob Neimeyer and their work, and they influenced me. I also became more involved in European and South American views of constructivist approaches to cognitive therapy, which led me to focus more in my practice on the creation of new meaning as an important goal of emotional processing. This fortified my views on the importance of constructivist metatheory.

I recently have been influenced by Marsha Linehan's work with people with borderline personality disorder and have come to see the importance of teaching affect-regulation skills to people with underregulated emotion, both in session and as homework, especially to those who regulate by self-medicating or self-harm. With the development of the new psychotropic medications and my ongoing experience with people who have taken prescription medication, I now also see a role for the use of medication in relieving suffering and see that psychosocial and psychopharmacological treatment can be profitably combined.

I have assimilated to my original client-centered and experiential views the following changes (in chronological sequence):

1. the value of therapist influence, which occurred slowly over time
2. intervening to change family contexts and, in particular, escalating cycles of interaction (my first major change)
3. using consciousness raising in relation to sex roles
4. adding practice and homework to my in-session here-and-now focus
5. working with transference at times, especially in more long-term therapies
6. suggesting the use of psychoactive medication in the treatment of the more functionally impaired
7. incorporating the formation of a collaborative focus on the underlying determinants of the presenting distress to guide treatment, especially brief treatment
8. breathing regulation and cognitive and behavioral skills training, both for affect regulation and as coping skills, for disorders in which emotional dysregulation is the problem.

In addition to a baseline of outstanding teachers and mentors, the factors that have influenced me to change, in probable order of importance, are

1. the demands of practice and reflection on them
2. empirical observation of what led to change
3. my wife and my experience as husband and father
4. contact with colleagues at professional associations
5. the opportunity to retrain on a sabbatical
6. changing cultural influences over the decades.

MY CURRENT APPROACH

I now believe that integration can take place at two different levels— at the level of practice or at the level of theory—but that it is far more difficult to integrate theories of functioning from the different perspectives than aspects of practice. One cannot, for example, easily integrate views of people as being unconsciously driven or fully determined with views of people as agents who are guided by conscious awareness and choice. At this point the notion of assimilative integration (Messer, 1992) at the level of practice appeals to me. I see myself as having assimilated interventions from other traditions into my emerging emotionally focused, constructivist– experiential theoretical views. At the level of theory I strive toward a high-level theory of functioning in general psychological terms that will subsume and explain school-based theory. I now envisage a psychotherapeutic theory that would understand function and dysfunction in terms of interacting systems of biology, temperament, emotion, motivation, cognition, behavior, interaction, and broader social context.

I try to work with an understanding of a variety of basic change processes at the different system levels. I apply different interventions, in local contexts, determining which intervention seems most appropriate for a given patient at the time. This approach involves developing a case formulation of the determinants of the client's problem along with the development of a focus as the treatment progresses. Even more important than an understanding of core issues and the development of a focus, how-ever, is the momentary identification of current experiential states that indicate current, in-session receptivity to specific forms of intervention. I still work to deepen experience, but I do it with a much greater appreciation of context, history, and individual differences in personality and in processing style. I now use many more interventions than empathic responding and gestalt experiments. At some opportune moment, I might use imaginal or in vivo exposure or, on occasion, use behavioral experiments as homework to promote new experience and examine assumptions. I identify beliefs and thoughts and, at times, highlight the irrationality of catastrophic fantasies. At other times I make pattern-linking interpretations or, in long-term therapies, offer here-and-now transference interpretations.

I might also use a reframe or paradoxical prescription or predict a relapse in individual or couple's therapy. In couple's therapy I identify negative interactional cycles on a regular basis. My practice with couples is still predominantly in accord with the emotionally focused couple's therapy approach. Having come to better understand the power of maladaptive emotional states, I now work more than I did before with helping partners deal with their maladaptive emotional states, which are at the basis of their negative interactional cycles. I do not work with families, but sometimes I adopt Bowenian strategies in individual therapy and have people do family-of-origin work. I ask them to draw family trees, interview their parents, or analyze with them the triangles and interactions in their families in which they are or were involved. Consistent throughout my current practice are efforts to provide an empathic relationship to promote deeper experiencing; to access, face, and reprocess avoided pain and other emotions; and to promote awareness of self and of interactional patterns. I consistently focus on symbolizing in words inchoate experience—both feelings and beliefs—and on accessing strengths and internal resources.

I see myself as having moved from a position of no influence to a position of being a collaborator and coconstructor of meaning. I work by both leading and following in a synthesis that when it works well, transcends the dichotomy of directive versus nondirective into a collaborative dance. In addition, I do a fair amount of experiential teaching. When clients are in particular experiential states, I teach them about what seems to be happening and what I see as a helpful change process for this problematic state. Thus I might talk concretely about such phenomena as resolving unfinished business; dealing with self-criticism and negative thoughts; the importance of attending to emotion; being more assertive; becoming aware of and disputing catastrophic expectations; regulating breathing; projecting the past onto the present; and a variety of other phenomena. I try to teach immediately after we have worked on the state, so that the teaching is "hot" teaching dealing with lived experience. I now see myself as an emotion coach—someone who empathically coaches people to deal in a new way with emotions, internal processes, and interactions. I am a type of mentor in the domain of emotional processes.

I believe that common factors, especially the relationship, awareness, and provision of new experience, are crucial to change. My current practice, however, is influenced most by my views on the role of emotion in human functioning. I increasingly see affect regulation as a primary concern in the development of psychological health because I believe disorder stems from problems in affect regulation. I thus view my therapy as helping people deal with emotion and its regulation. This leads me to attend to emotion above behavior, cognition, or pattern, although I deal with all three. I see emotion as a primary meaning system influencing cognition, behavior, and interaction and as being intimately involved in motivation. I thus work to be empathically attuned to feelings. This approach seems to work in three ways. First, it promotes the symbolization of previously unsymbolized feeling and mobilizes the needs and goals embedded in the feelings. Second, it helps clients experience and acknowledge disowned feelings, needs, and goals that have been avoided or interrupted because they are too painful or threatening. I believe that when a self-organizing system becomes clearly aware of a new effectively charged goal, it reorganizes to attempt to attain the goal. Third, this empathic attunement to emotion helps clients access maladaptive emotion structures in order to reorganize them. Those three effects change the basic organizing principles that govern the person's experience.

I see the primary unit of change when working with emotion as the *emotion scheme*, which I define as a structure formed by a complex synthesis of affect, cognition, motivation, and action. It provides the organizing principles that shape a person's experience and provides an integrated sense of self and world. Experience is created through the evocation of emotion schemes that produce a bodily felt sense as well and beliefs and action tendencies. I distinguish between primary adaptive emotions, which are people's most basic healthy emotions, and primary maladaptive emotions, which are the main source of dysfunction in the emotion system. I work to help clients access and attend to adaptive emotions in therapy that facilitate problem solving. Dysfunctional emotion schemes, however, which produce maladaptive emotions such as fear and shame, need to be accessed to make them amenable to change. I use active process–experiential interventions to evoke dysfunctional emotion schemes and have clients attend to, reprocess, and restructure those schemes. In addition to accessing adaptive emotions and restructuring maladaptive emotions, I work to move past the secondary feelings that obscure more primary feelings, such as accessing the hurt beneath anger. Finally, I help people become aware of when they are expressing instrumental feelings (i.e., feelings that are expressed to influence others, such as crying "crocodile" tears to get sympathy) and to find more direct ways of expressing their needs.

Paivio and I recently proposed a three-phase, eight-step framework (L. Greenberg & Paivio, 1997) that describes the kind of emotionally focused work I practice when it fits the person, the problem, and the moment. The first phase is the bonding phase, in which I attend to, empathize with, and validate the client's emotional experience. This type of bond is crucial for helping clients access their more vulnerable emotions. In this phase, I attempt to identify the underlying determinants of the client's present state and to develop a collaborative focus on those components (L. Greenberg

& Paivio, 1997). The second phase, evoking, involves arousing emotional experiences related to the core themes in the sessions. An important part of this phase involves an exploration and differentiation of emotional experience to access primary emotions and the thoughts and needs associated with them. Transformation, which takes place in the third restructuring phase, involves accessing both core maladaptive emotion schemes and primary adaptive emotional experience with which to restructure the maladaptive schemes. Restructuring of activated core maladaptive emotion schemes occurs through a self-challenging of the dysfunctional beliefs embedded in them, by means of newly accessed healthy emotions and needs. For example, the shame-based emotion scheme of worthlessness that results from abuse, once activated, is combated by tapping into currently accessible anger at violation or sadness at the loss associated with the abuse. This dialectical confrontation between the previously dominant maladaptive voice saying "I'm worthless" and the newly empowered adaptive voice in the personality saying "I'm worthwhile" provides the foundation for the development of a new self-organization. The therapist then supports and validates the client's new self-validating position and helps the client reflect on this new emotional experience. This process helps create a new narrative that symbolizes the new meanings developed in the dialectical synthesis of the dominant and subdominant voices. I see this practice as an integration of the different influences over many years from humanistic, dynamic, and cognitive therapy.

CONCLUSION

As I reflect on my change process, I see that I have both changed and stayed the same. This fits with my view of the human change process. We develop by differentiation and integration of new structures to increase our complexity and adaptive flexibility. At times of stress, we however may revert to more basic structures and ways of coping. Thus, although I have changed significantly by adding much to my practice from diverse influences, I have also remained the same, believing fundamentally in the power of choice, emotions, and relationships in the therapeutic enterprise. I still see individuals as active agents striving toward greater viability in the environments in which they find themselves, but I also recognize the myriad of ways that this tendency can be damaged and distorted.

REFERENCES

Barrett-Lennard, G. T. (1962). Dimensions of therapist response as causal factors in therapeutic change. *Psychological Monographs, 76*(43, Whole No. 562).

Carkhuff, R. (1969). *Helping and human relations* (Vols. 1 & 2). New York: Holt, Rinehart & Winston.

Eagle, M. (1984). *Recent developments in psychoanalysis*. New York: McGraw-Hill.

Fairburn, W. (1952). *Psychoanalytic studies of the personality*. London: Routledge & Kegan Paul.

Fisch, R., Weakland, J., & Segal, L. (1983). *The tactics of change: Doing therapy briefly*. San Francisco, CA: Jossey-Bass.

Goldman, A., & Greenberg, L. (1992). Comparison of an integrated systemic and emotionally focused approach to couples therapy. *Journal of Consulting and Clinical Psychology, 60*, 962–969.

Greenberg, J., & Mitchell, S. (1983). *Object relations in psychoanalytic theory*. Cambridge, MA: Harvard University Press.

Greenberg, L., & Johnson, S. (1988). *Emotionally focused couples therapy*. New York: Guilford Press.

Greenberg, L., & Paivio, S. (1997). *Working with emotions in psychotherapy*. New York: Guilford Press.

Greenberg, L., Rice, L., & Elliott, R. (1993). *Facilitating emotional change: The moment-by-moment process*. New York: Guilford Press.

Greenberg, L. S., & Safran, J. D. (1987). *Emotion in psychotherapy*. New York: Guilford Press.

Guntrip, H. (1969). *Schizoid phenomena, object relations and the self*. New York: International Universities Press.

Horvath, A., & Greenberg, L. (1989). Development and validation of the Working Alliance Inventory. *Journal of Counseling Psychology, 36*, 223–233.

Horvath, A., & Greenberg, L. (Eds.). (1994). *The working alliance: Theory, research and practice*. New York: Wiley.

Johnson, S., & Greenberg, L. (1985). Differential effects of experiential and problem-solving interventions in resolving marital conflict. *Journal of Consulting and Clinical Psychology, 53*, 175–184.

Messer, S. (1992). A critical examination of belief structures in integrative and eclectic psychotherapy. In J. Norcross & M. Goldfried (Eds.), *Handbook of psychotherapy integration* (pp. 130–164). New York: Basic Books.

Neisser, U. (1967). *Cognitive psychology*. New York: Appleton-Century-Crofts.

Pascual-Leone, J. (1987). Organismic processes for neo-Piagetian theories: A dialectical causal account of cognitive development. In A. Demetriou (Ed.), *The neo-Piagetian theories of cognitive development: Towards an integration* (pp. 531–569). Amsterdam, The Netherlands: North-Holland.

van Kessel, W., & Lietaer, G. (1998). Interpersonal process. In L. Greenberg, J. Watson, & G. Lietaer (Eds.), *Handbook of experiential psychotherapy* (pp. 155–177). New York: Guilford Press.

15

PATHWAYS TO A RELATIONAL WORLDVIEW

LYNNE JACOBS

What is a "gestalt psychoanalyst" anyway? It is how I would like to describe myself at this point in my life, except that no one seems to know what a gestalt analyst is! Aside from my academic training as a clinical psychologist, I have been trained and certified as a gestalt therapist, and I have been trained and certified as a psychoanalyst. The kind of psychoanalysis to which I subscribe, loosely called "contemporary psychoanalysis," bears a striking similarity to humanistic theories, so my marriage of gestalt therapy and psychoanalysis is not so strange as it might seem at first blush. I am currently active in both worlds as a teacher, writer, practitioner, and perpetual student of the theory and practice of psychotherapy. One of the interesting aspects of my current professional life is that my psychoanalytic teaching is an attempt to bring the clinical strengths of gestalt therapy into contemporary psychoanalytic practice, and much of my gestalt teaching and training is dominated by efforts to incorporate contemporary psychoanalytic wisdoms into gestalt therapy practice. I believe my teaching and my clinical practice reflect an amalgam of what I consider to be the best (i.e., the most usable aspects for me) of gestalt therapy with the best of contemporary psychoanalysis.

LESSONS ORIGINALLY LEARNED

I first read *Gestalt Therapy Verbatim* (Perls, 1971) when I was an undergraduate. I knew little about therapy at that time. What I found in the simple polemic by Perls was some hope for release from the prison of emotional isolation that I inhabited. I was most immediately drawn to Perls's emphasis on the person-to-person encounter and his emphasis on immediate, here-and-now emotional processes. Somehow I knew that I needed the lively emotional engagement Perls described, and I sensed that I needed a therapist who would not just stand back and assess me, diagnose me, and "treat" me from a distant, elevated perch.

Perls the therapist was creative, daring and, at times, loving and open. He also could be difficult—cruel even—when he felt manipulated by patients. He firmly believed that one thing that patients needed was authentic, person-to-person engagement between the patient and the therapist, an antidote to the depersonalization so rampant in modern culture. He also emphasized the value of emotional immediacy and vibrancy, hence his attention to what was transpiring in the therapeutic process in the "here and now." Frankly, although I am indebted to him for pointing me in a direction that was right for me, I am glad I never met him, for I think I might have been turned off to gestalt therapy by the harsher aspects of his personality. Laura Perls might have been a better match for me; she apparently was gentler and not inclined to "showboat."

Perls the theorist was a visionary former analyst who, along with his collaborators Laura Perls, Paul Goodman, and others, synthesized various cultural and intellectual trends into a new gestalt. As Smith (1976) pointed out, "Perls' genius was demonstrated not in his combining of elements from several traditions into a unique eclecticism but, rather, in his creation of a new system which in its essence goes far beyond the constituent elements" (p. 3). The constituent elements that Smith listed are psychoanalysis, Reichian character analysis, existential philosophy, gestalt psychology, and Eastern religion. Perls and his colleagues took those elements and the humanistic zeitgeist of the day and forged a radically alternative view of human personality and therapy from the psychoanalysts of their time.

Luckily for me, my first personal therapy experience, begun in the year preceding my discovery of Perls, was with a gentle, kind, and respectful (if somewhat reserved) psychiatric resident. His kind and respectful attitude, for which I am grateful to this day, helped me begin to believe that my experiences, perceptions, and world of meanings were worthy of attention and articulation.

A particular moment with him helped point me in the direction of the direct engagement proffered in gestalt therapy, although he himself was psychoanalytically oriented. We had been meeting for about a year, twice weekly. I was a "good patient": appreciative, eager to explore, but also painfully shy and skeptical of my own thoughts and feelings. He told me he would be leaving the current clinic a few months hence, and we were exploring the impact on me of his planned move to a different residency setting. When I first heard him say those words, my heart just plummeted because, although I rarely spoke of it, I was deeply attached to him and to the experience of being listened to with such kindness. He offered me the chance to move along with him and continue our work together.

As we talked, it emerged that his next residency was a family and child placement and that having me transfer along with him was not usual policy for either of the involved clinics. I was in a quandary. I very much wanted to continue seeing him and had become lethargic and depressed at the thought of ending prematurely but could not bear the prospect of creating difficulty for him or being a burden to him. I imagined that he felt trapped by my fragility, so that although he might rather be free to start with a clean slate at the new clinic, he saw me as too fragile to handle a transition to a new therapist. I also imagined that the authorities at the two clinics were annoyed and might create strain for my therapist. I tried haltingly to raise my concerns with my therapist, and I could barely speak. He said, "It sounds like you think our relationship is so tenuous it cannot bear any strain or difficulty." I was stunned. Actually, I had the sensation of a bomb going off suddenly under my chair. Did he say, *relationship?*

It had never occurred to me that he would consider us as being in a relationship together! Of course, I did move with him to his new setting, and we met for about 16 more months, until I moved away to attend graduate school. In one of our last meetings, as I was detailing my fears and insecurities about graduate school and said I was full of doubt regarding my ability to learn clinical psychology, he burst out with, "I have no doubt at all that you will be a fine psychologist!" Again, I was surprised that he had formed a personal opinion of me rather than just a clinical opinion. I carried his confidence with me like a talisman as I left on my new adventure. But that sensation of being stunned by the bomb under my chair because he said we had a relationship remains a touchstone for me. It always brings me back to the core themes of my personal and professional development.

I have found, over the years, that clinical theory is not useful to me unless it finds some emotional resonance in my own experience. I formed many of my ideas about good therapy from reading about, observing, and being a patient in gestalt therapy. Many of those ideas did resonate with my own inclinations, although some felt a bit foreign to me. Over time, I have come to cherish some of the first things I learned even more deeply, while others have faded in importance; I also have come to renounce a few ideas. My renunciation of some of my original learning has come about as I engage in a process of continual comparison and contrast among my original gestalt training, my more recent immersion in contemporary psychoanalytic ideas, and my personal development. But I get ahead of myself.

STRENGTHS OF ORIGINAL ORIENTATION

I became even more enamored of gestalt therapy as my understanding and opinions regarding various schools of psychotherapy developed. Gestalt therapy attends to process, to how something is being said or done, rather than merely attending to what is being said. This reflects the influence of Wilhelm Reich's breakthrough understanding of character styles and character armor. Reich's influence also shows in the gestalt therapy attention to posture, movement, and nonverbal expressiveness. Gestalt therapists are creative in their efforts to engage with patients by generating experiments in the sessions that may help the patient focus on, play with, and learn from his or her own body cues.

The influence of existentialism, humanism, and phenomenological currents of the day shows in the gestalt therapists' exquisite attention to patients' process of being aware of their own actuality: their goals, motivations, worldview, and wants and feelings, all on a moment-by-moment basis. Unlike the classical psychoanalysis of the day, which viewed the patients' conscious awareness as merely a defensive construction that could not be trusted as a guide, gestalt therapy viewed consciousness, or subjectivity, as a central guiding feature of human life.

In today's climate, where contemporary psychoanalytic theories also respect subjectivity as the key to understanding the patient, perhaps it is difficult to appreciate how much gestalt therapy was a breath of fresh air when it was first introduced. Along with other humanistic theories, it is full of spirit, immediacy, and play and is more respectful of the wholeness of people than one used to find in either behavioristic or psychoanalytic theories.

Gestalt therapy's respect for and curiosity about awareness (gestalt therapists say that expanding awareness comes through the process of merely attending to extant awareness) were freeing for me as a clinician in that I did not have to be a detective, looking for and figuring out what was missing in the patient's story or presentation, as psychoanalytic theorists espoused. I could merely attend to what was present in a patient's awareness, body cues, and so forth. I was not a good detective, and I tended to take patients' stories at face value, so gestalt therapy was a more natural fit for me than psychoanalysis.

One of the most important therapeutic gems in gestalt therapy is contained in an article titled "The Paradoxical Theory of Change" (Beisser, 1970). Beisser elaborated on a fundamental tenet, that change cannot be imposed but is a natural outcome of living. Aiming at changing oneself sets one in opposition to oneself, which impedes the natural growth and change that are inherent in living. A therapist need not be a "change agent"; rather, the therapist is there to establish a good quality of contact with the patient and to assist the patient in maintaining good quality contact with his or her own experiences as fully as possible. This particular notion is still less well developed in all other theories that I know of than it is in gestalt therapy. In training gestalt therapists, we focus specifically on helping the therapist recognize and suspend his or her efforts to change the patient. The result is the establishment of a more phenomenologically based exploratory process.

LIMITATIONS OF ORIGINAL ORIENTATION

As I have matured and the field of psychotherapy has matured and developed, I have come to think of gestalt therapy as having some internal contradictions. The Reichian influence has encouraged a confrontive ethos in the practice of gestalt therapy. Reich wrote about the need to confront the patient about repetitive character styles until the patient's habitual ways of being began to be experienced more as symptoms than as positive adaptations. Fritz Perls talked of the necessity to confront inauthenticity and avoidance. Yet our theory also emphasizes the paradoxical theory of change, a notion that implies a more accepting attitude, even toward so-called "avoidances." In general, I think confrontation is a poor modeling of that theory of change, and it is less in keeping with another important component of gestalt therapy—namely, the I–thou relationship.

A simple catchphrase of gestalt therapy used to be "I–thou, here and now." In an I–thou relationship, one has respect for the patient's world of meanings. One attempts not to change the patient but to meet the patient with as much heart and soul as the relationship and the task of therapy can support. One endeavors to understand the patient as he or she wishes to be known and to be present to the patient and open to how the patient experiences the therapist.

Although in the early days of my practice I confronted avoidance and inauthenticity frequently, I have become by now much less enamored of that approach and at times rueful about how my past toughness has injured people who entrusted themselves to me. There were times when I felt uneasy about my patients' discomfort, and I began to doubt that my toughness was helpful to my patients in the long run. My further reasons for the turnabout emerges as I detail my further development. I noticed, by the way, that the more confrontational edge of gestalt therapy has diminished greatly in much of the contemporary scene, so I am not the only gestalt therapist who has changed in that respect. Most of us have become more gentle and accepting as we have come to appreciate at a deeper level the simple power of meeting the patient with an attitude of respect, interest, I–thou, and the grounding in the paradoxical theory of change.

Although the I–thou relationship was posited as our ground for the nature of the therapeutic relationship, it had not been well elaborated. I was interested in it because I was trying to work out a particular clinical problem that remained unaddressed, as far as I was concerned. Gestalt therapy had long held that even in a relationship that might be shaped by 90% "transference," there always would be some element of newness, of contact, that was possible at any moment. I liked the vibrancy of attending to the contact between the therapist and patient in the here and now, but something was missing. I did not yet know how to think about it, but I thought we practitioners needed to understand better how the relationship itself developed over the course of therapy and how the relationship either facilitated or detracted from the patient's growth process. What we did not seem to have was an understanding of the meanings and therapeutic implications of the contacting process in the therapy process over time. We tended to treat each contact episode in therapy as though it stood alone, not meaningfully connected to what came before or to what was emerging next. This approach was a disservice to our patients, for whom a sense of the continuity of the relationship—one in which they were taken seriously, their stories were remembered and jointly elaborated, and the intimacy deepened over time—was profoundly meaningful.

I knew that I did not much care for the classical analytic notion of transference as a way to understand the ongoing relational themes that emerged in the course of therapy. I did not like it because it seemed to suggest that the patient's experience of the relationship was entirely determined by one's early relationships and that the current relationship had no life or character of its own. That view created two problems for me, both personally and professionally. First, it left me demoralized and alone again, as though the therapist were a mere shadow, whereas I believed I needed contact with a real human being as part of my therapeutic experience. Second, by suggesting that the therapist had no part to play in how the patient experienced the relationship, I was left to doubt my own sense of reality. Whatever problems I would encounter in the relationship would be viewed merely as signs of my pathology, not a reflection of something going on between me and the therapist. I had grown up in an alcoholic household where my sense of reality was constantly being denied, and my instincts told me there was something wrong with that attitude. I did not need it repeated in the therapeutic process, nor did I want to reduce my patients' experiences to being solely "within" them, as if I did not exist in their lives.

HOW CHANGE OCCURRED

Even with its shortcomings, transference as a concept conveyed some appreciation for the fact that a relationship existed in the therapy—that the moment-by-moment contact that gestalt therapy was so good at facilitating was happening within a broader context, namely the ongoing relationship. In my own gestalt therapy (which lasted several years and "brought me to life"), I had sensed deeply that something that was occurring in the relationship, something that I could not pick out in a particular moment of contact, was gradually helping me out of my imprisonment of isolation. I remember one particularly moving and poignant session about 4 years into the therapy: I "confessed" to my therapist, shyly and with great trepidation, that I was not really coming to therapy to *do* therapy. I was willing, of course, to look at myself, do experiments, notice my feelings, and so forth. But truth be told, I was really there just because I wanted to be in my therapist's presence. I just wanted—no, needed—to hang around him, to breathe the same air he was breathing. Luckily for me, my therapist, a man of wonderful open and steady presence, did not confront me on wanting to regress or merge or be confluent to avoid responsibility. Instead he merely smiled softly, with great warmth, and said, "yeah, yes."

In fact, my therapist seemed to have a natural bent toward being sensitive to my need to simply have the experience of establishing and expanding on "being-in-relation." His enormous skill at the technical side of therapy (e.g., method, knowledge of character style), coupled with his willingness to engage with me in a deeply personal way and to be affected by me, provided a strong model for my own practice of therapy.

While in graduate school I had begun to read the British object relations literature, especially Guntrip and Fairbairn. They were writing from a psychoanalytic perspective about the patient's need for a new relational experience! They provided me a beginning way to think of blending gestalt therapy's attention to contacting with more enduring relational themes because they did not posit that enduring relational themes were only a repetition of old relationships (i.e., transference) but that patients also were seeking a new relationship, which had to develop over time.

With the support of readings in object relations literature as a background, along with the readings of Martin Buber, my own experiences as both patient and therapist, and the collegial support of a few gestalt therapists who were struggling to articulate similar themes to my own (most notably, Erving and Miriam Polster, Gary Yontef, and Rich Hycner), I wrote my dissertation using Buber's I–thou relationship to try to bring attention to enduring relational themes into gestalt therapy. I tried to do this in a way that did not reduce these themes to transference and did not detract from the vivid immediacy that made gestalt therapy so compelling to me. It was the first step in what has been a continuing scholarly and clinical project for me. It has since been incorporated into a book, coauthored with Rich Hycner, which blended our interest in the I–thou relation, gestalt therapy, and modern psychoanalysis (Hycner & Jacobs, 1995).

Soon after completing my graduate work, I began teaching actively at the Gestalt Therapy Institute of Los Angeles (GTILA). I taught about the phenomenology of character styles, an area that required me to keep reading the psychoanalytic literature, but it was not a chore for me because I had discovered object relations writers. They did not write about mysterious drives that could never be directly known. They wrote about humanity's innate striving for relatedness, how experience in interaction shaped us, and how we sought interactions to shape and heal ourselves. They were writing about phenomena that I felt in my bones to be primary to my own life. After a few years, I joined the core faculty of GTILA and have remained to this day as a teacher and trainer in the gestalt therapy world.

I continued to be drawn to trying to understand and articulate the meaning of *relationship* and what the shape of the therapeutic relationship should be. I had been immersed in the gestalt community for about 8 years when I began to hear about a psychoanalyst named Heinz Kohut, who was revolutionizing psychoanalytic practice through his emphasis on "sustained empathic immersion," and his introduction to selfobject transferences. *Self-object transference* is his specific way of describing needed relational experiences, not just a transference of past psychological configurations into the current setting. Selfobject experiences are a particular dimension of relatedness that helps shore up and sustain healthy self-functioning, and they are needed throughout life. The particular way selfobject experiences occurs can change over a life; thus, they are always new experiences, not just a repetition of old experiences. I was reminded of my experience as a patient, where I just needed to hang around my therapist, not because he was like my mother or father but because being around him provided me with something new and nourishing, which sustained me as I navigated through my life.

Although I was excited by what I was hearing, I also was skeptical. I was suspicious of Kohut's emphasis on empathy. Although I had studied and written about a similar concept described by Buber (1967) and called *inclusion* ("the therapist must feel the other side, the patient's side of the relationship, as a bodily touch to know how the patient feels it"; p. 173), Kohut's version of sustained empathy seemed to require that the therapist recede entirely, keeping his or her own presence hidden. This disturbed me and did not square with my experience as a patient and clinician. It seemed to me that I and my patients longed for and benefited from the chance to be intimately engaged with the therapist as an authentic, particular, revealed, other. Also, Kohut seemed to be eschewing all confrontation, and I believed at that time that confrontations were necessary as an antidote to patient's wishes to avoid painful truths. I no longer assume that I know better than the patient what their "truth" is, but at the time, I saw patients as "avoiding"; their avoidance seemed to lock them into neurotic prisons of devitalized living. I thought that the energy and vitality of a confrontational approach at times held the possibility of liberation from the prison. I was to change my mind as circumstance brought me into closer contact with Kohut's ideas.

In late 1982 I met someone who has become my life partner. We met in a bookstore and began talking together about a book he was considering buying. He told me he was preparing to spend the next 4 years studying psychoanalysis at a local psychoanalytic institute. In 1984, he arranged to have me join him at an informal talk that psychoanalyst Robert Stolorow was giving to the candidates at his institute. I did not know much about Stolorow at the time, only that his work had been strongly influenced by Kohut's thinking.

I was enthralled at the talk. Stolorow's conceptualizations were remarkably similar to ideas extant in gestalt therapy! He was talking, for instance, about "experiencing" as an ongoing process of organization—not statically determined by the past, but continually shaped by forces present in the current field. Two major influences were the patient's patterns of organizing experience (what gestalt therapists call "fixed gestalten") and the therapist's capacity for empathic listening (i.e., what the therapist could not hear, the patient would not be able to articulate). He also described the line between what was conscious and unconscious as a flexible line that is in part determined by the patient's sense of safety with the therapist. This notion was radically different from the notion of a repression barrier and much closer to gestalt therapy's notions of awareness and unawareness as a shifting figure–ground process shaped by field conditions. In essence, he seemed to be bringing a more present-centered focus to psychoanalysis, with emphasis on experience instead of on drives and an emphasis on how the patient's experience of the therapeutic relationship was shaped in part by the analyst's subjectivity, rather than on the relationship being a product of mere transference.

I left the talk excited; I finally saw a way to bridge my two interests, gestalt therapy and psychoanalytic thought. Stolorow was developing a psychoanalytic vision that was part of a fundamental paradigm shift that brought psychoanalysis much closer to the humanistic theories than it did to classical psychoanalytic theories. This talk was my first exposure to the paradigm shift occurring in psychoanalysis, sometimes described as a shift from a one-person to a two-person model of human development.

Along with gestalt theory, contemporary analytic theories, such as Kohut's and Stolorow's, have developed in part as a reaction against the perceived limitations of classical psychoanalysis. Contemporary analytic theories eschew the reductionism and determinism of classic psychoanalysis and the psychoanalytic tendency to minimize patients' own perspectives on their life struggles, as weil as the psychological effects of their life experience. Whatever differences there may be among the contemporary theorists, some common threads comprise basic tenets of a contemporary perspective; and these tenets represent a fundamental humanistic, epistemological paradigm shift. The tenets are an emphasis on the whole person (and sense of self) rather than on mechanisms such as id, ego, and superego; an emphasis on subjectivity and affect; an appreciation of the impact of life events (e.g., childhood sexual abuse) on personality development; a belief that people are motivated toward growth and development rather than regression; a belief that infants are born with a basic motivation and capacity for personal interaction, attachment, and satisfaction; a belief that there is no "self" without an "other"; and a belief that the structure and contents of the mind are shaped by interactions with others rather than by instinctual urges. For the contemporary analyst, as for the gestalt therapist, it is meaningless to speak of a person in isolation from the person-in-relation.

As interpersonal analyst Stephen Mitchell wrote in 1988,

> the past several decades have witnessed a revolution in the history of psychoanalytic ideas. Recent psychoanalytic contributions have been informed by a different vision: we have been living in an essentially post-Freudian era. . . . We [people] are portrayed not as a conglomeration of physically based urges, but as being shaped by and inevitably embedded within a matrix of relationships with other people. . . . Mind is composed of relational configurations. The person is comprehensible only within this tapestry of relationships, past and present. (p. 3)

Gestalt therapy's original theorizing was an expression of this shift, to some extent, in the 1950s and 1960s, but current cultural trends have made it easier to see the radical implications of the paradigm shift. Gestalt therapy perhaps was at the beginning of a wave, and psychoanalysis is riding that wave at its crest now. This shift often is described as a post-Cartesian perspective. Breaking out of Cartesianism (e.g., the tendency to think of human beings as having intrinsically separate, isolated, encapsulated psyches) is not easy for either gestalt therapy or psychoanalysis because Cartesian thought thoroughly infiltrates commonsense notions of reality. The efforts being made from within both schools represent exciting, cutting-edge scholarship regarding theories of therapy and of consciousness.

Within a year or so, I began weekly supervision with Stolorow, which I used not only for case study but also to discuss his writings with him. At about this time, in collaboration with others, his distinct contemporary psychoanalytic perspective (now called "intersubjectivity theory") was beginning to coalesce. My supervision with him began a sea change for me. Through his writings I began to grasp the meanings of Kohut's selfobject transferences. My clinical work was profoundly altered by this. Instead of listening to patients from the perspective of "what is this patient trying to do to me (i.e., what defenses, manipulations, or avoidances is the patient engaged in)?" I began to listen from the perspective of "what does the patient need from me in order to heal and grow (i.e., what developmental striving is being expressed)?"

Both questions, or listening perspectives, have a long history in gestalt therapy. The first reflects Perls's teachings that neurotic process involves the wish to use the environment for support at times when self-support is needed for healthy self-regulation. The second question reflects the radical field theory notion common today, perhaps most eloquently described in Wheeler (1996), that all psychological phenomena are coshaped in interaction and that a patient may need a particular interactive climate to take the next step in his or her healing and development.

As I studied Stolorow's writings (see, especially, Stolorow, Brandchaft, & Atwood, 1987) and Kohut's ideas, however, I began to doubt the usefulness of the first listening stance, the one so heavily influenced by Reich. I began to appreciate Kohut's passion for listening to the patient in a sustained manner from within the patient's perspective. Instead of listening from a different frame of reference, one where I was judging the appropriateness of the patient's thoughts and feelings, I began to listen more systematically to how the patient's worldview could make perfect sense. Instead of how it might be a distortion of reality, especially when it did not match my own views, I listened for how it expressed a perspective that might actually expand my awareness. My own study and practice with Buber's notion of inclusion already had given me a head start in this direction. Certainly all good therapy involves some empathic grasp of the patient's perspective as he or she would want the therapist to know it, but Kohut emphasized listening systematically for sustained lengths of time from such a perspective. He also emphasized listening especially for how the therapist's interventions were affecting the patient. He argued that when a patient was thrown off, angered, or in some other way not receptive to the analyst's intervention, it did not mean that the patient was resistant to facing the truth. Rather it meant the analyst had lost touch with the patient's perspective and therefore had disrupted the needed selfobject tie to the analyst. Listening empathically seemed to encourage the development of a selfobject tie, and the establishment, elaboration, and development of sophisticated selfobject relatedness seemed to be curative for the patient.

From my gestalt therapy perspective, I saw that Kohut was describing therapeutic listening that appeared to facilitate the patient's chances for establishing nourishing contact with the therapist and, eventually, with others. As I watched my own work, I began to notice how my temptation to offer my patients some reality testing, to confront them with alternative perspectives, often came from my own frustration or from my feeling threatened and defensive. It seemed as though the listening stance that Kohut suggested was a good means for practicing the inclusion of what Buber had written, was an important ingredient for meeting the patient without an agenda of my own, and allowed me to be more faithful to the paradoxical theory of change. It was not an easy discipline to experiment with, but it was fruitful.

I am reminded of a telling experience with a patient. I had seen her for a number of years, once and twice weekly. She was easily hurt, especially by men, and quite afraid of them. She tended to interpret ambiguous interactions in ways that inevitably left her feeling hurt, betrayed, ashamed, angry, and once again let down by an insensitive man. I kept thinking that if only I could change her perspective just a little bit, she would suffer less. I thought she just needed to be able to "see around the corner," and a new perspective would open up. So I nudged her. I suggested alternative interpretations of the ambiguous interactions. I did this repeatedly, even though she kept telling me that I was hurting her, that I, like the others, did not understand her. I just could not restrain myself because I thought I could nudge her around that corner. Finally, with great exasperation, she told me the following story to illustrate her feelings about being with me:

> I was driving on the freeway, when a motorcyclist riding next to me hit some debris in the road. He lost control and went flying across the hood of my car and landed on the center divider. I stopped, and so did a highway patrolman who had seen the accident. We rushed to help the man. He was conscious but bleeding from a head wound. The police officer snapped at him, "Damn it, this is what you get when you don't wear a helmet!" Now, Lynne, this guy was shocky and bleeding! This was not the time to talk about wearing a helmet! He needed some care and comfort, not a lecture!

That story lingers with me as a powerful reminder of the importance of listening from the patient's point of view. She let me know graphically that I was failing her in that regard and that she could listen to my point of view only much later, after her pain had subsided and after she had repeated experiences of having her perspective affirmed as legitimate.

This is one of the most important lessons I have learned by studying Kohut and Stolorow and by being in my own therapies, and it has been reconfirmed in countless clinical experiences; one is more likely to be open to alternative perspectives when one feels securely affirmed in one's current perspective. Time and again, I have noticed that when I try to argue against, convince, or otherwise, however gently, move patients into a different perspective, they become more committed to their current perspective, more rigid and defensive. But if I can welcome their perspective, open myself to it even when it is full of anguish, then the forward-moving processes of life take over. The paradoxical nature of change is being carried by both patients and myself. Then the patients, who no longer feel under siege, disconfirmed, and unwelcome, can, over time, breathe and move, and their perspectives become more malleable and open to expansion, development, and change.

Meanwhile, the more I read in Stolorow's writings of archaic longings and yearnings to be understood, the more some longings to be deeply understood were being awakened in me. Stolorow not only was talking about listening from an empathic perspective but also was saying that attunement to the flow of the patient's emotions was particularly important. I decided to seek therapy from an intersubjective psychoanalytic therapist for myself. I was leery of seeking therapy with a psychoanalyst because I feared that an analyst would not be attuned to my emotional life, yet Stolorow's writings and teachings were stirring my longings enough that I wanted to give it a try.

When I first consulted with my analyst, I told her that I was seeking help in understanding a writing inhibition. I thought that I wanted to write articles based on ideas I had developed over the past several years, yet I was unable to commit my thoughts to paper. I also said that I was not sure whether my desire to write was a genuine expression of my interests and aspirations or was a compliant obeisance to an ideal that I and others had for me.

Then I confessed why I had truly sought her out. In my study with Stolorow of self psychology and what was later known as "intersubjectivity theory," I was experiencing the emergence both of hope and of painful longings and yearnings to be understood at a level that I had thought heretofore impossible. I described myself as living always behind a transparent wall between me and the "world out there." I thought that as a result of my prior therapy I had "thinned out the wall" and had frequently emerged from behind it, but only temporarily. In the past year or so, I seemed to be slipping further back into isolation. I sheepishly admitted to identifying myself as "schizoid," in the sense of being a person who is emotionally isolated, frightened, and ashamed of her needs for human engagement and who hovers on the fringes of social groups as a compromise between total isolation and terrifying intimacy. I expressed a wish to move beneath the level of "schizoid compromise," although I also had grave doubts as to whether such a radical restructuring of my self-experience was possible.

I told her that I had chosen to interview her after reading an article she had written in which it was clear that she had an intersubjective orientation and was particularly attuned to the patient's emotional experiences on a moment-by-moment basis. This was unusual for an analyst, but I thought if there was any hope for me at all, it rested in a therapeutic relationship wherein exploration of affect and the methodology of affect attunement were central. Although I was too embarrassed to tell her at the time, I had felt reassured of her potential to be tolerant of my depressive affects, particularly my prolonged bouts with despair, when I read the case example she used in her article.

I remember that I was struck in the first session by this therapist's warmth and responsiveness. I was not particularly compelled by her interpretations, but I was confident that she would listen with her feelings to hear and respond to my feelings, which was a great relief. She truly "pushed the envelope" on affect attunement as a mode of listening. Affect attunement incorporated listening from within the patient's frame of reference, especially listening and responding to the affective tone the patient was communicating. That mode of listening, coupled with her close attention to exploring the nuances of her impact on me, especially the negative impact on me when she was misattuned, was transformative for me. She strove to make contact with every emotional experience I had, however wispy or insubstantial and fleeting it might be. As a result, my emotional life became more robust, vivid, and, most surprising to me, my experience of myself in the world changed dramatically. I moved from a vision of myself as having certain experiences that were fundamentally impossible to share with others to a vision of myself that holds that all of my experiences are potentially shareable. I no longer live with a sense that at least some dimension of my experiential world is intractably isolated.

Now my work with my own patients began to reflect the experiences I was having in my analysis. I listened closely to their version of themselves, and I watched closely for signs that my listening failed to meet them, in even slight ways. The effect on my patients was dramatic. Almost to a one, over the course of the next several months, my patients spoke of how much safer they felt to bring their most vulnerable sense of themselves into the dialogue with me. They were speaking of things they had not been able to verbalize previously. They were braver and more forthright with their own anguish because they worried less about my judgments, and they were braver in pointing out both my positive and my deleterious effects on them. I had thought of myself as working deeply with my patients before, but our work deepened considerably as I listened in this more careful, systematically attuned way. I am humbled now as I think back on the difference such a change in my attitude, or my listening stance, has made in my patients' lives.

Another interesting parallel is that some of my patients began to increase the frequency of our sessions. The same thing had happened to me with my analyst. The exquisite experience of being with someone who listened so well, so deeply, and with such feeling, drew me like a magnet. In no time I was seeing her 5 times per week. Now that I was working in a similar vein, my patients also were drawn to come more frequently, and many have engaged in profoundly transformative therapeutic–analytic processes.

A few years later, I decided to seek psychoanalytic training at a contemporary analytic institute, in part because I was enthralled with the intelligent and thoughtful conversations I was having with analysts such as Bob Stolorow. I was not disappointed by the quality of the discourse at the Institute of Contemporary Psychoanalysis. I learned how to think critically about theories of therapy and about epistemological foundations, and I continued to synthesize contemporary psychoanalytic thought with gestalt theory and practice. I loved my years as a candidate, and now that I am a supervising and training analyst, I thoroughly enjoy mentoring other analysts.

MY CURRENT APPROACH

My analytic colleagues have asked me whether I consider myself an analyst first and a gestalt therapist second, or the reverse. I find that to be an interesting and complex question. In my bones I am a gestalt therapist, in the sense that I live and breathe here-and-now, affective immediacy, and person-to-person engagement. I sometimes think that I have learned how to think about and understand what I am doing by studying psychoanalysis, which is a thoughtful discipline. But I learned most of the praxis of therapy from my immersion in the experientially based training in gestalt therapy and from my personal therapy. The two major exceptions are that I learned about sustained listening from the empathic perspective from my supervision with Bob Stolorow and I learned not just the method but also the enormous transformative power of affect attunement from my analysis. Both the empathic listening perspective and affect attunement dominate my clinical approach, yet they are embedded within a gestalt therapy sensibility. Or is it better said that my gestalt-bred passion and skill with here-and-now, affectively engaged dialogue are now embedded within a contemporary analytic sensibility? I suppose it depends on with whom I am speaking at a given moment. Hence my identity is as a "gestalt psychoanalyst."

When I teach analysts about affect attunement, I often think they would benefit from a year of gestalt therapy training. Gestalt therapists, however, likewise would benefit greatly from a year of coursework in psychoanalysis and especially, perhaps, immersion in intersubjectivity theory. I firmly believe that what makes me a good analyst is my grounding as a gestalt therapist, yet culturally, at this point I may be more comfortable among analysts than gestalt therapists. Part of analytic training is an intense socialization into the identity of "analyst." Analysts develop an insider language and sensibility that alienate us just a bit from other therapists. Also analytic conversation is expansive, questioning, and full of ferment and excitement. I love being immersed among people with such exploratory mindsets. When it comes to teaching and the development of the praxis of therapy, I prefer teaching gestalt therapists rather than analysts, because their native understanding of therapy is much closer to my own. In fact, my latest excitement is a gestalt training program, developed with my gestalt therapy colleague Gary Yontef, called "relational gestalt training." In this program we have developed an approach in gestalt therapy that places greater emphasis on enduring relational themes as they evolve over the course of therapy. As I said at the beginning of the chapter, this approach combines my view of the best of gestalt therapy and the best of contemporary psychoanalysis, all revolving around my primary interest in how the relationship heals. I could not be happier, even if I do not exactly know where I best fit anymore.

I also do not know where I shall be in 5 years. When I started gestalt training, I never dreamed I would end up undergoing psychoanalytic training and two personal analyses (one of which has been transformative for me, the other of which has helped me radically change my sense of "place" in the world and helped me expand personally and professionally). As my analytic training took me deeper and deeper into the sanctum of psychoanalytic culture, I thought I might drift away from gestalt therapy. Instead I find myself with renewed excitement about and energy for expanding gestalt therapy praxis. So who knows what awaits tomorrow.

CONCLUSION

As I come to the end of my story, I am frustrated at how much I had to leave out, for instance, about my experiences as a patient in both cultures (I have been fortunate enough to have been profoundly positively affected by all of my therapies). I had to leave out much of the theoretical substrate of thought that has influenced me. My psychoanalytic years have been incredibly fertile and invigorating, and I think I have given those years short shrift. I realize only now, looking back over what I have written that along with my training, supervision, personal therapies, and clinical experiences, the written word has been a major influence on my professional direction. This is apparently true for my personal direction as well, since I met my life partner in a bookstore! I have to reign in my passion to explain to you, the reader, why I like this or that approach or concept. I wish I could just talk with you, a long and languorous conversation about how we each are developing as therapists. I also wonder how I would write my story differently if I were 10 years older. What an intriguing exercise!

REFERENCES

Beisser, A. (1970). The paradoxical theory of change. In J. Fagan & I. Shepherd (Eds.), *Gestalt therapy now* (pp. 77–80). New York: Harper.

Buber, M. (1967). The unconscious. In R. Anshen (Ed.), *A believing humanism: Gleanings by Martin Buber* (pp. 153–173). New York: Simon & Schuster.

Hycner, R., & Jacobs, L. (1995). *The healing relationship in gestalt therapy: A dialogic/self psychology approach.* Highland, NY: Gestalt Journal Press.

Mitchell, S. (1988). *Relational concepts in psychoanalysis.* Cambridge, MA: Harvard University Press.

Perls, F. (1971). *Gestalt therapy verbatim.* New York: Bantam.

Smith, E. (1976). The roots of gestalt therapy. In E. Smith (Ed.), *The growing edge of gestalt therapy* (pp. 3–36). New York: Brunner/Mazel.

Stolorow, R., Brandchaft, B., & Atwood, G. (1987). *Psychoanalytic treatment: An intersubjective approach.* Hillsdale, NJ: Analytic Press

Wheeler, G. (1996). Self and shame: A new paradigm for psychotherapy. In R. Lee & G. Wheeler(Eds.), *The voice of shame* (pp. 23–59). San Francisco, CA: Jossey-Bass.

16

THE INTEGRATIVE EXPERIENCE OF PSYCHOTHERAPY INTEGRATION

BARRY E. WOLFE

My journey toward psychotherapy integration began with a profound conviction that the symbolic, subjective experience of the individual is a necessary ingredient in any theory of psychotherapy. It was my conviction then—and now—that we therapists avoid this conclusion at the risk of retarding the usefulness of our theories and the effectiveness of our therapies. I came by this conviction as a solution to the profound epistemological doubt that I experienced in graduate school, and it was later confirmed through extensive experience as a practicing psychotherapist. A corollary insight that I acquired early and which continues to endure is that most psychopathology involves a person's struggle with his or her subjective experience: the pain of it and the shame of it. No theory of therapy can safely avoid this situation. No therapy can be effective without effecting changes in this realm.

This focus on the client's subjective experience may suggest that I am an experiential therapist rather than an integrative therapist. Although I acknowledge the humanistic–existential–experiential family of therapies as my home orientation, I have learned over time that by itself, the experiential therapy perspective is insufficient. A truly integrative therapy must embody the strengths of other existing therapeutic perspectives. Many ideas and therapeutic procedures from the other major therapy orientations are critically important in helping to bring about change in a person's relationship to his or her own experience. My current approach to psychotherapy integration could be described accurately as an assimilative form of integration. *Assimilative integration,* as Messer (1992) defined it, "favors a firm grounding in any one system of psychotherapy, but with a willingness to incorporate or assimilate, in a considered fashion, perspectives and practices from other schools" (p. 151). I am in the process of revising my theory to better accommodate the ideas of other therapy orientations and thus move closer to a more seamless integration at the level of both theory and practice. Currently, however, my integrative approach begins and ends with the subjective experience of the person and therefore still displays an allegiance to an experiential perspective.

LESSONS ORIGINALLY LEARNED

When I began my graduate training at the University of Illinois (UI) in the fall of 1963, I was deeply enamored of the scientific method. Before I fully understood the probabilistic nature of scientific truth, I believed that the scientific method would lead us to foundational truths about human behavior. Here was a methodology that through precise objective observation and experimentation, would nudge us incrementally toward sturdy truths. If psychology did not yet possess the major truths of human behavior and experience, the discipline at least (so I then thought) possessed a means by which to obtain them: the method of science.

Sometime during my graduate training at UI, I came to doubt the validity of the entire discipline of psychology. At this time, the psychology department at the university was increasingly influenced by behaviorism. Most classes possessed a behaviorist slant. Psychoanalytic ideas were—how shall I put it?—as scarce as its pundits were coming to be on the psychology department faculty. My response to this education (or, I should say, indoctrination) was interesting: Although I found the behaviorist critique of psychoanalysis to be persuasive, I also believed that behaviorism possessed little explanatory power. Too much in my experience and my observations led me to doubt the "truth" of the behavioral perspective. As for so many of us then with a humanistic bent, the behavioral language of control was, to say the least, off-putting. I remember, for example, reading Len Krasner's 1963 paper titled "The Therapist as a Social Reinforcer: Man or Machine" and wondering whatever happened to the venerable and ancient quest to understand and ameliorate the psychic pain of human beings. With psychoanalysis buried by the behaviorist critique and behaviorism crushed by my own experience, I was left in a profound state of doubt and intellectual confusion. I experienced both psychoanalysis and behaviorism as "gods that failed" (Crossman, 1965), and I desperately sought an alternative that was more human, if not more valid. Pain and doubt eventually drove me from UI in 1965. I then took a 2-year break from graduate school and purposely placed myself in intellectual and occupational limbo.

During my last year at UI, however, I had begun to discover the beginnings of a human alternative. I read Carl Rogers's (1961/1995) *On Becoming a Person* and was mightily impressed not only with his ideas but also with the process through which he came by them. I particularly was impressed with his willingness to rely on his own experience and observations. Rogers not only seemed to view experience and observation as critical tools in the development of scientific knowledge but also saw them as a methodology that a psychotherapy client could use to find his or her own way to psychological health. This was truly "balm" for a mind hurt with epistemological doubt. This approach not only had great intellectual appeal but also was ideal for a self-doubting therapist-to-be. The nondirective mandate of Rogerian therapy gives one the intoxicating promise of having an impact on a client's life without being too intrusive or responsible for the client's eventual life choices. The reader can be assured that I was not alone in my conflict over the desire to have a positive impact on a suffering client's life, on the one hand, and my fear of the responsibility of potentially making things worse, on the other.

By the time I entered the University of Florida in 1967, I was developing a fairly strong bias in favor of a Rogerian approach to psychotherapy. I felt I was in good company because many clinical students and practicing therapists during that time were becoming disenchanted with both psycho-analysis and behavior therapy. It was in reaction to the diminished view of human behavior and experience implied in both of those orientations that the humanistic psychology movement was born (Bugental, 1967).

When I began to work with a significant number of clients during my training at Florida, I set off on a naive quest: to inductively build an orientation to therapy based primarily on my personal experience as a therapist . . . and as a client. My personal therapy was enormously influential in extending my understanding of the client's struggle with his or her own experience. Yet at this point in time, the extent to which implicit theory guides observation and inference and, therefore, any developing therapeutic construct was not entirely clear to me. All therapists and theoreticians are unavoidably ensnared in the web of previously developed theoretical ideas.

I began my training as a therapist in earnest on a practicum rotation at the University of Florida Counseling Center. The guiding therapeutic orientation of the counseling center might be described as "talking psychody-namically but practicing Rogerian therapy." We conceptualized the client's problems from a psychodynamic standpoint, but our therapeutic practice emphasized the primary importance of the therapeutic relationship for client change. I conducted therapy primarily from a passive–reflective stance, albeit at times gently guiding patients to focus increasingly on their feelings. I would reflect the underlying affect as much as the content of the clients' communications. As trust developed, clients gradually allowed themselves to become aware of their feelings and to express them to me. The expression of disavowed feelings, I believed, led to a change of perspective; this was my early understanding of the process of therapeutic change.

In keeping with the zeitgeist, I gradually increased my identification with the evolving humanistic and existential points of view in psychother-apy. Consequently, my view of the purpose and meaning of psychotherapy subtly changed. Increasingly, the therapy situation struck me as a quintessen-tial context for human beings to engage in a process by which they could glean the meaning of their lives, the authenticity of their value commit-ments, and the congruency of their life goals (Bugental, 1965). Therapy at this time seemed to be more about values and meaning and less about psychopathology and its remediation; more about growth and secular salva-tion than about the resolution of conflict or the repair of psychological deficits. In fact, problems that in the past had been characterized as psycho-pathological were now construed as problems in living. I felt like I had entered the ranks of the "secular clergy" (London, 1986).

STRENGTHS OF ORIGINAL ORIENTATION

Initially, I was impressed with both my ability to "join the client" and the impact that the resulting therapeutic alliance had on the client's willingness and ability to experience and express his or her feelings. The evolving safety that my empathic attunement helped create often was suffi-cient for college students suffering a mixed profile of anxiety and depressive symptoms to obtain substantial clinical benefit from the therapy. The clients who I saw, first as an intern at the University of Florida counseling center and later as a full-fledged professional at the Michigan State University Counseling Center, often were steeped in shame over their symptoms and their real or imagined deficiencies. They feared—at times morbidly feared—that I would be judgmental. When they were met with empathy rather than criticism, they typically experienced such relief that they were willing—perhaps for the first time—to explore their deepest feelings about themselves, their significant others, and their futures (Beck, 1963).

Many of my clients, on the strength of my support and empathy, allowed themselves to accept, confront, and clarify painful feelings that they heretofore had denied to their awareness. This approach struck me then as respectful of the client's pain, individuality, and ability to solve his or her problems. I was amazed that by apparently "doing so little," my clients obtained such benefit. It was equally clear that the clients were not able to make this kind of progress without help.

These early lessons convinced me of the importance of the therapeutic relationship for achieving any kind of therapeutic progress. The therapist must not only build rapport and communicate understanding but also provide enough safety for the client to explore the most painful and shaming thoughts and feelings. I still view this as a necessary first step in any therapeutic endeavor. The importance of the therapy relationship for positive therapeutic change has become the quintessential integrative variable. Every therapeutic perspective now highlights the necessity of a solid therapeutic alliance for therapy to succeed.

LIMITATIONS OF ORIGINAL ORIENTATION

Those initial successes lulled me into a false sense of security—I actually was becoming a little full of myself. I appeared to be doing well as a therapist, and my chosen therapeutic approach not only was typically effective but also seemed to be generally applicable to the full range of emotional disorders and problems in living. My therapeutic successes were such a "high" that I could not see enough clients—I always wanted more. I was so enthralled by my therapeutic endeavors that all else paled by comparison. I remember a discussion I had during this time with two great friends and fellow graduate students in a local bar. We were speculating (in our cups, as graduate students are wont to do) what each one would do if we knew we had only 6 months to live. Both my friends would end their pursuit of the PhD immediately and travel to exotic climes or fill their lives with an accelerated rate of sensual gratification to partially compensate for the knowledge and dread of their foreshortened lives. I, however, could think of nothing that I would rather do than see as many clients as I possibly could in psychotherapy. Clearly, this was the calm before the storm.

I tasted failure for the first time when a series of students came into therapy wanting help with their specific phobias. My passive–reflective therapeutic style made these clients feel safe and allowed them to contact some previously disavowed feelings, but their phobias remained intact. Moreover, empathy alone did not seem to relieve the seriously depressed clients. My confidence as a therapist, however, received its biggest blow from students who would now be found to meet criteria for various types of personality disorder. In 1972, I did not recognize the extent of the personal and interpersonal pathology displayed by such student–clients. One patient demanded a hug from me at the end of each session; my refusal was construed as total rejection and abandonment. Another client would burst into tears any time I attempted to offer for her exploration an alternative construction of her situation, however gently I might tender it. These tears would be followed by an extended self-lamentation that would end with her pronouncement that she was hopelessly inadequate and unable to regulate various aspects of her life. I was unable to effectively interrupt this cyclical pattern of negative *self-focused attention*, which Ingram (1990) defined as "an awareness of self-referent, internally generated information that stands in contrast to an awareness of externally generated information derived through sensory receptors" (p. 156). I drew several conclusions from these dramatic and other, less dramatic instances of therapeutic failure.

- Providing Rogers's therapy conditions (i.e., empathy, genuineness, and prizing) was a necessary but often insufficient therapeutic strategy. Such a strategy represented an excellent means for building the therapeutic alliance and providing safety for the client to undertake arduous and tender therapeutic work, particularly the processing of painful emotions.
- My initial approach to therapy was not amenable to the quick resolution of manifest symptoms such as phobias and depression. It also was insufficient for the treatment of personality disorders or severe mental illness.
- The passive–reflective therapeutic stance, although useful for many patients and for most patients during the initial phases of therapy, is inadequate for many patients.

HOW CHANGE OCCURRED

The change in my therapeutic orientation was brought about by a mostly tacit but sometimes conscious processing of a variety of experiences occurring in three different contexts: my role at the National Institute of Mental Health (NIMH); my increasingly varied clinical experience, including the all-too-frequent acrid taste of failure; and my participation in a number of training experiences and immersion into a number of different psychotherapy manuals, from which I acquired knowledge and skill in the practice of a variety of psychotherapies.

Perhaps the process most responsible for moving me in the direction of psychotherapy integration was the cross-fertilization that developed between my work at the NIMH and my clinical work. I was exposed to treatment orientations and their specific techniques by means of my role as grant administrator at the NIMH. This exposure, in turn, would motivate me to obtain some training in an approach or, at least, study the treatment manuals that were included in research grant applications. I then would attempt to apply specific techniques or whole approaches clinically. My clinical work then would make me aware of the strengths and limitations of the therapeutic approach, which I then tried to articulate. It was my hope that the issues that emerged from my clinical work eventually would become the subject of NIMH-supported psychotherapy research studies. Of course, it did not always work out that way.

I obtained a position in the extramural program of the NIMH in 1972. The extramural program was charged with administering mostly investigator-initiated (and taxpayer-funded) research grants deemed worthy by a peer-review process. My 22-year tenure at NIMH was a rich experience, one that required me to stay on top of all the latest developments in the field of psychotherapy and psychotherapy research. Our responsibility was to remain open to but critical of any and all new developments. As Morris Parloff (personal communication, October 9, 1998) put it, "it often was like studying comparative religions."

One of my early responsibilities was to oversee the research grant portfolio on behavior therapy research. In this position, I became immersed in the latest developments and innovations in behavior therapy. One of my tasks was to organize workshops in target areas in which the NIMH wanted to stimulate research. The first workshop that I organized was held in 1980 on the topic of behavior therapy applied to the anxiety disorders. It was cosponsored by the State University of New York at Albany; thus, I worked closely with David Barlow in the planning, organization, and conduct of this workshop. We had invited the leading experts in behavior therapy research, particularly as it was applied to anxiety (Barlow & Wolfe, 1981). From this workshop, I obtained a number of strategies for working with phobic patients—extensions of techniques that I had learned throughout the 1970s at various workshops held at the annual meetings of the Association for the Advancement of Behavior Therapy. The techniques worked quite well for textbook cases of monosymptomatic phobic clients. Imaginal and in vivo exposure were particularly useful. It became clear that behavior therapy techniques were useful additions to my Rogerian therapeutic origins. Because the behavior therapy techniques worked, I took more seriously the behavioral conception of the acquisition, maintenance, and amelioration of phobias. I therefore had come to believe that anxiety somehow becomes conditioned to the phobic object and that imaginal exposure would allow the patient to experience the reduction of that anxiety by means of continual exposure.

Over time, I applied these behavioral techniques to more severe and complex cases of phobias. The results with those cases, however, were less promising. Moreover, I serendipitously noticed that with imaginal exposure in particular, patients began to be aware of morbidly catastrophic imagery directly involving the phobic stimulus. Typically, this imagery was experienced in conjunction with intensely painful emotions, such as humiliation, rage, and despair. The imaginal scenes that spontaneously arose would find the patient in a powerless position, about to be humiliated or badly harmed by the phobic object. As my patients and I explored their catastrophic imagery, we would find that they either were recapturing long-forgotten traumatic events in their own history or that the images had been automatically created by them as constructed prototypical experiences, which symbolize the helplessness, powerlessness, and doom originally experienced much earlier in life.

As catastrophic imagery became a routine product of imaginal exposure therapy with phobias, I was increasingly struck by the irony that unconscious conflicts were being elicited by a therapeutic approach that denied their existence. Of course, this situation was not new. Feather and Rhoads (1972a, 1972b) demonstrated a similar phenomenon when they used systematic desensitization to previously elicited unconscious fears. Even before that, Stampfl and Levis (1967) highlighted the importance of psychodynamic issues in the development, maintenance, and treatment of phobias.

As my experience with treating phobias grew, I observed that phobias were characterized by multiple etiologies that responded differentially to exposure therapy. With this realization came another: The classification of a phobia tells a therapist little about what he or she needs to know to effectively treat it.

Take, for example, the cases of three clients who met criteria for a specific phobia, all of which involving a severe fear of driving. The first client was an 18-year-old woman who was involved in a serious auto accident and refused to get behind the wheel of a car. Six sessions of therapist-guided but self-initiated in vivo exposure therapy were sufficient to render her phobia free. She drove again without restriction. This was a textbook case.

The second client was a 30-year-old married woman who presented with a driving phobia of several years' duration. Imaginal exposure of her driving away from her house produced such anxiety that she could hardly engage in the therapy. A second effort at imaginal exposure produced the following catastrophic image: She saw herself driving to another city and never returning to her husband and child. She felt a great sense of liberation and relief during this image, but this relief was quickly followed by terror as she realized she would be all alone. She believed that she was incapable of living on her own, and the mere thought of such an eventuality was terrifying. The thought, however, of remaining in what was for her a loveless marriage plummeted her into despair. In vivo exposure was minimally helpful to her. Exploratory individual therapy followed by marital therapy eventually resolved her previously unconscious conflict.

The third client was a 35-year-old graduate student who presented with a severe driving phobia that left him entirely dependent on others for transportation. Unlike the above two cases, this patient's driving phobia began after a major panic attack. The panic attack occurred when he was driving with his wife and she informed him that their marriage was over. Since that time, he had been unable to drive at all. (Incidentally, this situation was in ironic contrast to an earlier period in his life when, as an adolescent, he would drive 25 miles every day to visit his girlfriend, who lived in a neighboring town.)

A clinical history revealed that this was not his first panic attack. The first attack occurred in childhood (at age 8) when his parents left him alone and completely responsible for two younger siblings. His mother had accompanied his alcoholic father during one of his drinking binges at a local bar. The attack came when my patient called his parents at the bar, and his urgent pleas for their return went unheeded. This was one of many traumatic family events that impeded the development of his sense of self-agency. Consequently, my patient had a lifelong difficulty in assuming responsibility for his life, always searching for someone to take care of him. This pattern had indelibly marked his relationships with women.

Treatment began with imaginal exposure involving his driving alone as far from home as possible. This scene quickly revealed tacit, catastrophic imagery involving the conflict that so many agoraphobic patients experience—between freedom and isolation, on the one hand, and between security and being controlled, on the other. It is interesting to note that although he experienced great fear as he imagined himself driving miles away from home, he also became aware of great anger, particularly at his mother for her previous neglect. At one point, he had an insight that his phobia might be related to an effort to make her responsible for his well-being in adulthood because she had neglected that responsibility in his childhood. Given his family history, this was not an unreasonable hypothesis on his part. In any case, in vivo exposure therapy produced significant progress in his ability to drive short distances (no more than 8 miles) by himself, without, however, completely resolving his phobia (Wolfe, 1992b).

These three cases illustrate that the *Diagnostic and Statistical Manual of Mental Disorders'* (4th ed. [*DSM-IV*]; American Psychiatric Association, 1994) classification of specific phobia, situational type, neither tells us much about phobias nor sheds much light on treatment planning. To rely only on a *DSM*-based classification of phobias is to retreat to a position of vacuous nominalism. Although exposure therapy and breathing retraining may be the place to start, it is clear that for many—if not most—phobias, a treatment plan based only on these procedures will leave much to be desired. At NIMH, I would encourage researchers to study the underlying determinants of simple phobias—with little success in encouraging, I must sadly add.

Without question, my therapeutic efforts with phobias and other anxiety disorders were significantly enhanced by incorporating behavior therapies. I was forced by my clinical experience to overcome my biases against behavior therapy that originally had developed during the attempted force-feeding of behavioral ideas in my graduate work at UI. Working behaviorally also convinced me that therapists sometimes need to be active, even proactive, in structuring and guiding the therapeutic process, an idea that contravened my earlier Rogerian tilt toward a passive–reflective therapeutic stance. By the same token, it also was clear that what used to be called "simple phobias" were not so simple. A careful analysis of the actual determinants of a phobia had to be carried out before an effective treatment plan could be developed. In my clinical experience, such analyses indicate that more than just exposure therapy was often necessary to resolve a specific phobia. What was true for phobias turned out to be true for other anxiety disorders as well. Those experiences convinced me that although behavior therapies were important additions to the therapeutic armamentarium, they clearly represented no panacea.

By the late 1970s and early 1980s, NIMH was beginning to support research on the cognitive and cognitive–behavior therapies. My initial reaction to the cognitive therapies was one of skepticism, particularly regarding the efficacy of focusing only on conscious cognitions and of directly challenging long-held beliefs rooted in fear. At the level of theory, however, the addition of cognitive ideas was a welcome advance over the purely behavioral conceptualization of psychopathology. The following ideas had become increasingly clear:

- Non-cognitive–behavioral conceptions of psychopathology were inherently limited, and it therefore was necessary to include some type of mediating variables in order to achieve more accurate and complete etiological formulations and more effective treatment strategies.
- With the addition of cognitive variables, behavior therapies necessarily must enter the world of depth-oriented therapies and become concerned with the inner world of patients.
- The key insight of all cognitive therapies, which basically is that our ideas have a major influence on our thoughts, feelings, and behavior, was fundamentally sound.

Ever since I first encountered George Kelly's (1955) theory of personal constructs, I have been impressed with the power of one's construals in determining how one behaves and feels. But it also was clear that cognitive and cognitive–behavioral approaches were limited by their exclusion of emotional and unconscious factors in the acquisition, maintenance, and amelioration of specific forms of psychopathology.

By the early 1980s, then, I was beginning to see that the four major therapeutic orientations—psychoanalytic, Rogerian, behavioral, and cognitive—all had important ideas and procedures to contribute to our understanding of psychopathology and to the enhanced practice of psychotherapy, but I also saw that no orientation was by itself sufficient.

During the same time period, part of my role in the nascent Psychotherapy Research Branch at NIMH was to identify psychotherapies that were commonly practiced but rarely researched. The vast majority of our research grant portfolio at this time (1980–1985) included outcome studies involving behavior therapy and cognitive–behavior therapy. I organized a workshop on psychoanalytic and psychodynamic therapies in 1982 and a workshop on experiential forms of psychotherapy the next year. The workshops and my more routine work at the NIMH kept me abreast of all research developments in the area of psychotherapy. I was impressed with the excellent therapeutic ideas coming out of these rarely researched therapies, and I tried to use them in my clinical work.

Another push toward integration came from the research literature. Empirical support was growing for the contention that no therapeutic approach was consistently superior to any other therapeutic approach (Smith, Glass, & Miller, 1980). Data suggest that behavior therapies might be superior to non-behavior therapies for specific delimited problems (e.g., phobias) but that few other instances existed in which a given therapeutic approach was superior across the board. Although this conclusion has been challenged by proponents of behavioral and cognitive–behavior therapies, from the vantage point of the NIMH, there were too many questions about the data from behavior therapy studies and too little data from other forms of psychotherapy commonly practiced for any of us to rest comfortably with the notion that behavior therapy should be generally viewed as the treatment of choice for most mental disorders. Both my clinical work and my oversight role as a research grant administrator at the NIMH had taught me that no single therapeutic orientation was consistently superior to all others: "All had won and all should get prizes," as Lester Luborsky had suggested (Luborsky, Singer, & Luborsky, 1975). At the same time, we were cognizant that for too many problems and disorders, psychotherapy of any stripe was not consistently effective.

By this time, a number of therapists and clinician–researchers were beginning to speak out about their dismay regarding the sectarian hostilities expressed by pundits of one psychotherapeutic orientation against another (e.g., Goldfried, 1980; Wachtel, 1977). The research increasingly suggested that if we therapists could systematize our typically eclectic efforts in therapy, we might be able to develop a better therapy, one that could consistently effect more comprehensive and more durable changes in our patients. It seemed to be an idea worth exploring.

Both my review of the research literature and my clinical work had primed me for an exploration of psychotherapy integration, but one experience tilted me completely toward integration. In 1981, Mardi Horowitz hosted a meeting in which a number of therapist–researchers who represented several different therapy orientations traveled to Langley Porter Neuropsychiatric Institute to view some psychotherapy tapes and compare how we each would conceptualize the presented case and develop a treatment plan. The ostensible goal of the 2-day conference was to see whether therapists of different orientations could actually communicate regarding psychotherapy cases (Goldfried & Newman, 1992). The invitees included Sol Garfield, Marv Goldfried, Stanley Imber, Phil Kendall, Hans Strupp, Paul Wachtel, and myself. After watching a tape of a young woman who was suffering from what Mardi had labeled a "pathological grief reaction," we each expressed our view of the case and how we would go about treating it. I believe we were all struck by the similarities as well as the contrasts in our approach to this problem. I thought the idea of borrowing techniques from different orientations seemed to be not only useful but also mandated by the details of this case. It also seemed that each participant's theoretical conceptualization was both useful in some respects and limited in many others. The need for an integrative theory as well as an integrative treatment model seemed clear.

A network of professionals interested in the prospect of integrating the psychotherapies, or at least in bringing about a rapprochement among the major schools of psychotherapy, was growing. In 1982, Wachtel and Goldfried sent a questionnaire to this informal network of professionals to assess their views regarding the future directions of the developing interest in this area. The consensus of the 162 responses they received was that the field needed a newsletter and an organization that would consider the prospects for rapprochement and psychotherapy integration. In the summer of 1983, six of us formed an organizing committee for the establishment of a new society, which came to be known as the Society for the Exploration of Psychotherapy Integration (SEPI). The committee included Lee Birk, Marvin Goldfried, Jeanne Phillips, George Stricker, Paul Wachtel, and myself.

SEPI held its first meeting in 1985 in Annapolis, Maryland. I served as the local arrangements chairperson, and it was truly a labor of love. As so many participants told me at the meeting, I felt that I had found a home, a reference group that truly expressed my stance toward psychotherapy. I have continued on the SEPI steering committee ever since and have found the experience of facilitating the growth of the organization to be synergistic with my personal quest to contribute to the development of a model of theoretical integration for psychotherapy.

One other training experience has had a significant impact on both the way I practice psychotherapy and the way in which I conceptualize its process. In 1983, I began a 2-year seminar in gestalt therapy at the Washington Gestalt Therapy Center, led by Rudy Bauer. This experience again confirmed for me the importance of the experiencing process in human functioning. Rudy's approach to gestalt therapy involves a kind of integration: He attempts to combine gestalt therapy, object relations theory, and Zen Buddhism. This made for interesting discussions. At times, I had the urge to chant at the self-object sitting in the empty chair.

This training experience taught me how I could be an active facilitator of a client's experiencing process both through assuming a particular stance toward a client's experiencing and by applying a number of specific gestalt therapy techniques. This seminar clarified the myriad ways in which human beings interrupt their immediate experience of the self, world, and others. In addition, it clarified two issues for me: First, the usual trigger of self-interruption was the fear of painful feelings, and second, feelings did not get adequately expressed and processed because of these interruptions. Much of problematic human behavior and thinking seem to relate to the pain and shame that people may feel about their subjective experience and to the problematic ways in which they act to avoid, deflect, or cope with those painful feelings.

Moreover, I learned a number of ways to interrupt the interruptions. One of the most useful was a specialized application of a focusing technique. The assumptions underlying this technique is that painful feelings often are somaticized and that those feelings can come clearly into view and be experienced if one maintains a constant focus on the bodily location of one's tension or anxiety. Preceding the actual focusing is a brief induction technique that begins with the client breathing normally when focusing on the sensations of his or her breathing or on some other constant stimulus. This procedure seems to be particularly useful with patients suffering from an anxiety disorder (e.g., panic disorder). In fact, the actual details of this form of focusing are quite similar to the behavioral technique of *interoceptive exposure*, which involves exposure to frightening bodily sensations. The difference, however, is that I am interested not only in desensitizing a patient to his or her fear of bodily sensations but also in helping him or her experience the feelings that typically underlie the specific bodily sensation. Once the feeling and its associated imagery emerge, one can engage in a guided imagery technique to explore the various meanings associated with the emergent feelings. The practical and theoretical implications of the learning that I obtained in gestalt therapy are vast. What I took away from this seminar has had an enormous effect on the way in which I now think about anxiety disorders and their treatment.

MY CURRENT APPROACH

I think it is clear by now to therapists from any perspective that the first task of therapy must be the solidifying of the therapeutic alliance. Many reasons exist for doing this, but I believe that the core reason is that clients have difficulty accepting the fact that they need therapy. For many clients, being in therapy is a shaming experience, a personal defeat. This is not a function of being a client and needing psychotherapy but rather an existential given, a grounding reality (at least in Western culture, which puts such a premium on self-reliance and autonomy).

Clients therefore come into therapy already feeling "one down" to the therapist. They recognize the need to speak about matters that will shame them even more, but they are loathe to do so for that very reason. The client's ambivalence toward the therapist is the necessary starting point of most psychotherapy. That ambivalence must be dissolved in the therapist's communication of nonjudgmental understanding of the client. Empathy and acceptance are therefore critical formative elements in the glue of therapeutic relationships (Rogers, 1957).

The therapeutic alliance is crucial for another reason, also with existential implications. This reason involves the pandemic problem of human trust and trustworthiness. Violations of trust are such a frequent experience in every life that by the time we reach adulthood, most of us recognize the necessarily slow evolution of trust in relationships. For those who have been the repeated victims of interpersonal betrayal, they may entirely lose the ability to discriminate the trustworthy from the untrustworthy. This awareness is compounded by another fact that characterizes many clients in therapy: Trusting others is intricately connected to trusting oneself. Because most clients enter therapy with impairments in their self–self relationships, including the willingness to trust themselves, they have great difficulty trusting the therapist. If the actions and communications of others toward us suggest that we are not trustworthy, or if our general experience with others is that they are not trustworthy, then the task of coming to trust ourselves and others is made all the more difficult. In like fashion, difficulties in trusting oneself will impair one's ability to trust others, regardless of how one is in fact being treated by others. Thus, the personal and interpersonal dynamics of trusting have their source in the close and reciprocal relationship between how one is treated by others and how one sees oneself. It follows that repairing clients' ability to trust other people contributes to their ability to trust themselves and vice versa. Trust, therefore, is usually the first issue that is negotiated in therapy, either explicitly or tacitly. Unless the therapist can pass the explicit or implicit tests that clients set before them, clients are unable to benefit from any specific therapeutic technique (e.g., exposure therapy).

I do not want to give the impression that the therapeutic alliance, once established, needs no further concern. On the contrary, the therapeutic alliance requires constant monitoring and management and is subject to the oscillations that characterize any relationship. One must be vigilantly alert to possible ruptures in the alliance (Safran, 1993), particularly when the client does not communicate the fact that a rupture has occurred. Monitoring the alliance is crucial because the specific work that the client undertakes obtains its support from the therapy relationship. Even when it seems like the therapist is doing little more than witnessing the client's exploration of his or her own vulnerability, the safety that the therapist provides allows the client to explore such tender material without feeling shamed, panicked, or rejected.

A second step in my current approach to psychotherapy involves choosing an access point for specific therapeutic work. Depending on the nature of the problem and the characteristics of the client, I will begin the specific therapeutic intervention in the behavioral, cognitive, or affective realm. Mostly, the characteristics of the client determine the access point. Typically, the affective area presents the greatest difficulty for most of my clients and is therefore likely to be the final point of access in psychotherapy. The interpersonal dimension cuts across all three realms, and many client problems occur, or play out, in an interpersonal context. Although it is my belief that the core locus of most psychopathology resides in the processing (or lack thereof) of painful emotions about the self, the choice of initial access point must be determined by what is acceptable to the client. The importance of choosing an access point that is acceptable to the client is illustrated by an encounter I once had with a depressed attorney. When I attempted to do some imagery work designed to access and explore his emotional reactions, he interrupted me by stating, "I am not comfortable with the language of feelings."

Because I work with many anxious patients, I have found that behavioral and cognitive interventions—what I would call action-oriented and construction-oriented tasks—usually precede emotional processing tasks. I learned this the hard way—by first trying to access catastrophic emotional imagery through various focusing procedures. Often clients felt they were losing control and therefore found the task difficult. It became clear that most anxious patients need a sense of control over their anxiety symptoms before they can engage in any depth work. In other words, clients need to be taught ways to turn off the "alarm switch" (Barlow, 1988) and to cope with their anxiety when they encounter the phobic object or, in the case of panic patients, when they experience frightening body sensations. Diaphragmatic breathing is usually the first technique that I teach anxiety patients. They are taught this slow, deep-breathing procedure for use during imaginal and in vivo exposure therapy. Generally, it has been successful in bringing about an immediate decrease in the level of anxiety.

A second procedure attempts to deal with the catastrophic thinking that usually accompanies the experience of frightening body sensations. Didactic prompts are used to reassure patients that the anxiety they are experiencing, although unpleasant, will not lead to any life-threatening cardiovascular dysfunction or make them crazy and will eventually decrease. Patients are told to reflect on recent experiences of anxiety or panic attacks to verify that these catastrophes did not take place.

A third procedure involves an effort to undercut the reflexive awareness of anxiety (e.g., the fear-of-fear response). I first have the client experience the difference between focusing attention on the anxiety and focusing attention on one's anxiety about one's anxiety. Experientially, they come to see the difference in intensity associated with each of the two layers of anxiety. Then I ask the person to allow him or herself to experience the anxiety, stay with the anxiety, and use diaphragmatic breathing to reduce the anxiety rather than shifting his or her attention to a fearful awareness of his or her fear. These techniques can be used in conjunction with imaginal and in vivo exposure to fearful situations as well as exposure to the internal sensations of anxiety (interoceptive exposure).

After patients feel that they have some control over the anxiety symptoms, they are asked whether they would like to explore the underlying determinants of the anxiety. If not, the therapy is terminated. If they do wish to continue, we proceed to the next phase of therapy. We begin with a modified version of imaginal or interoceptive exposure, but with a different purpose in mind. After an initial breathing induction procedure to help the patient better tune out competing stimuli from the external environment, I ask him or her to focus intensively on an image of the phobic object or situation (in the case of phobia patients) or on the bodily sites of fearful sensations (in the case of panic patients). The patient is then invited to be receptive to his or her internal productions (i.e., to any thoughts, feelings, images, or ideas that arise automatically). In the case of phobias, the patient is asked to imagine the feared object or situation and, while intensively focusing attention on the phobic scene, to notice any automatically arising feelings or thoughts. In the case of panic disorder, the patient is asked to identify the most prominent bodily sites of anxiety or fearful body sensations and to maintain a strict attentional focus on these sites. This often results in the appearance of several thematically related and emotionally laden images. The imagery is imbued with themes of conflict and catastrophe that the patient is helpless to prevent or terminate. As mentioned above, the goals of this version of imaginal exposure depart somewhat from the behavioral version. The experience of anxiety is not only for the purpose of learning that the feared disaster will not take place or that the anxiety will habituate (it does not always) but also for the patient to uncover the felt catastrophe and to experience the associated feelings.

This procedure typically uncovers the underlying catastrophic fear that has become connected to the specific phobic object or to specific bodily sensations. The catastrophic imagery may reveal an intrapsychic conflict; an automatic, negative schema; or disavowed feelings, all of which point to a "self" experienced in great jeopardy. Elsewhere, I have labeled this experience self-endangerment (Wolfe, 1992a, 1995). *Self-endangerment* experiences appear to be mostly confined to the psychological realm; to fears associated with interpersonal rejection and loss; to experiences of loss of self; and to the processing of extremely painful, self-diminishing emotions, particularly shame, humiliation, or despair. In fact, these self-endangerment experiences are close to those originally mentioned by Freud (1926/1959): He proposed that anxiety is the experience of helplessness or a signal of impending helplessness. The actual content varies with developmental level. He referred to this phenomenon as the *epigenetic unfolding of danger situations*, which includes, in developmental progression,

- fear of being overwhelmed by traumatic excitation, from without and from within
- fear of loss of object of primary care and attachment
- fear of the loss of the object's love
- fear of castration or other bodily punishment or hurt
- fear of superego, conscience, or social condemnation
- fear of abandonment by the powers of fate.

Self-endangerment experiences reflect various forms of self pathology (Wolfe, 1995). Self pathology involves the experience of a core threat to one's subjective experiencing that derives from a variety of contents and processes of self-experience, including the following:

- negative self-beliefs, such as believing oneself to be unworthy, unlovable, incapable, or unable to cope
- the fear of any immediate experience of self that would activate a negative self-belief, such as the experience of self-diminishing emotional appraisals, (e.g., humiliation, shame)
- the fear of any immediate emotion-laden experience of self that would bring retaliation if expressed (e.g., anger)
- conflict between two or more aspects of self-experience, such as discrepancies between self-beliefs and self-standards, discrep-

ancies between standards and immediate self-experience, and discrepancies between self-beliefs and immediate self-experience

- actions motivated by a desire to escape a hated, shamed, or disapproved-of self
- inconstant sense and concept of self (identity diffusion).

In addition, a person may use an entire catalogue of psychological defensive maneuvers to avoid, deflect, or disavow painful or diminishing self-relevant emotional information. The techniques include such well-known psychoanalytic defenses as repression, emotional numbing, projection, denial, reaction formation, and intellectualization and such gestalt therapy defenses as confluence, clouding of awareness, and deflection. In addition, people use a number of strategies to prevent themselves from owning their actual, immediate self-experience. All of these defenses protect the person from pain and shame in the short run, but they also preserve the various forms of self-pathology in the long run. Thus, in the broadest sense, what needs to change are the negative core self-beliefs, including their organization and the various processes involved in their construction.

A Case of Panic Disorder With Agoraphobia

A fairly prototypical case of an anxiety disorder and its treatment illustrates the current status of this integrative model and how it is applied. Joan S. was a 30-year-old housewife with two young children; she developed the symptoms of panic disorder with agoraphobia 3 years before coming to see me. She had an unexpected panic attack while driving her children to an afterschool activity and became so frightened that she had to pull the car off the road. Her husband had to come pick them up. As a result of this panic attack, Joan was unable to drive her car. Several interconnected fears inhibited her ability to get back into the car: fear of having another panic attack, fear of losing control and wrecking the car, and fear of seriously injuring herself or the children. She began to be fearful of having additional panic attacks and began to restrict her activities in an effort to control the venues in which she might have a panic attack. After some time, it became difficult for her to go into public restaurants that were too great a distance from home.

Joan had been married for almost 10 years to an attorney who was just beginning to become successful. They had recently moved into my area from another Washington area suburb. In her old neighborhood, she had made many friends and was active in the neighborhood, performing a variety of community services and volunteer activities. In her new neighborhood, she was having difficulty making friends and had not yet become active. The move represented a tangible sign of her husband's success: The new house was much larger and much more expensive than their previous one. For her, the rise in socioeconomic level, represented by the move, meant a change in the kind of people whom she would now encounter—people with whom she felt much less comfortable and to whom she felt inferior. Joan would clearly meet *DSM-IV* criteria for panic disorder with agoraphobia.

Joan was weighted down by a number of negative self-beliefs that revolved around her diminished sense of self-efficacy and sense of inferiority. In addition, she was frightened by her emotional experiences, often not allowing herself to experience or "own" painful or rage-based emotions, and her behavior patterns frequently revealed a split between the "self" that she wished to present to the world and her actual self-beliefs. Often this involved wanting to present herself to the world as a nice, sweet person who did not harbor angry or spiteful thoughts.

Joan began therapy quite reticent and not eager to share any information that might lead me to reject her or think her inferior. In fact, it took the first two sessions of therapy, characterized primarily by little else than empathic attunement responses from me, before she was ready to begin any kind of structured, symptom-focused program of anxiety management. I learned a great deal about the processes and content of her self-experiencing, however. She was in a constant state of self-monitoring and self-evaluation, what I have referred to as "reflexive self-experiencing." She was trying hard to manage the impression that I should have of her.

Joan appeared to have a number of grievances against her husband but would not allow herself to experience or express her apparent rage at him. She often would refer to how she saw herself as a nice person and said that the few times she did get angry, she would immediately say to herself that she "was not herself." In other words, there was a clear split between her "ought self and her actual self," to use Higgins and Strauman's terminology (Higgins, 1987; Strauman, 1994). She also referred several times to how she thought she was basically okay but was afraid that she would not be good enough for the people in her new neighborhood.

By the third session, she was ready to undertake the symptom-focused treatment. The rationale for beginning with the symptom-focused treatment involved two considerations: First, she came into therapy to be freed of the panic attacks and fear of them, so to begin here was responsive to what the patient wanted; second, before she could undertake some of the other treatments designed to address her self-pathology, she needed a sense of control over the symptoms. The cognitive–behavior therapy consisted of diaphragmatic breathing, interoceptive exposure, and cognitive restructuring, and it did, in fact, help her gain some control over her anxiety.

We next endeavored to discover the underlying meaning of her panic attacks. By focusing intensively on the sensation of lightheadedness, which she particularly feared, she contacted a significant amount of rage toward her husband for moving her from a comfortable house and prior existence, for not being attentive enough to her needs, and for leaving her with virtually the complete responsibility for raising their children. Joan had great difficulty accepting the fact that she was that angry. Her rage violated the concept that she held of herself as mild mannered and pleasant. We began work to help her accept and own her emotional experiences. Eventually we moved to some empty-chair work to help her express her rage and her other authentic feelings to her husband. Expressing rage at her husband in the empty chair revealed a split between viewing herself as a nice person and her legitimate grievances. This was a signal or *marker* (Greenberg, Rice, & Elliott, 1993), for use of a two-chair dialogue between her actual self and her ought self. During the course of therapy, Joan also engaged in reparative guided imagery to enhance her sense of self-efficacy. This involved imagining a series of scenes in which she is taking charge, taking the initiative, engaging in difficult tasks, and accepting whatever feelings emerged during the guided imagery. Finally, cognitive and experiential techniques were used to work on her self-representations as inferior to the people in her new neighborhood. Joan made significant progress during the therapy in being able to accept a broader range and intensity of her feelings and in accessing how she really felt about situations in her life and using this information to help her make decisions.

How I Currently View the Process of Change

Behavior change typically precedes change in cognitive and affective function. One's core beliefs and attitudes about the self constitute the most difficult layer to change (Howard, Kopta, Krause, & Orlinsky, 1986). In my model, change in the short run is brought about by the restoration of immediate or sentient self-experiencing, during which the client begins to have in-the-moment change experiences (i.e., doing, thinking, or feeling things differently). As one acts, feels, and thinks differently in the short run, over time it is presumed that those changes will modify one's underlying images and beliefs about oneself and one's capabilities. Thus, unencumbered direct experience should lead to changes in conceptions about one's self, others, and the world, which then should influence one's subsequent experience. But the immediate experience of self typically is not unencumbered. Such experience is often unpredictable, and if it is painful, the information is usually defended against (i.e., is prevented from either awareness or from having a modifying effect on one's core beliefs).

For self-beliefs to change, one first must be able to allow oneself to experience in-the-moment, or immediate, experience. To become more willing to permit such experience, one must surmount, circumvent, or break through one's defenses against becoming aware of painful emotional experience about the self. The common metaphor of emotional processing implies all of these concepts, including

- working through the defenses against painful (and sometimes positive) information about the self
- allowing and getting used to a new kind of emotional experience
- understanding the self-relevant meanings of the emotional experience
- allowing the new emotional experience to alter old beliefs
- taking new actions to validate the changed self-concept.

This, of course, does not occur overnight; it is not one-trial learning. How quickly changes in core self-beliefs take place depends on many factors, including the duration and intensity of the emotional self-belief, the strength and automaticity of one's defenses, one's willingness to be proactive in the quest for change, and one's tolerance for painful affects.

Once the pathway is cleared, new experiences can begin to build new "self structures" on top of the old; that is, new conceptualizations of the self begin to take shape. These new structures supersede but never replace the old. This explains why, in times of stress and self-endangerment, people switch from the new ways of functioning and self-perception back to the old ways. This view, of course, is nothing more than a cognitive–experiential conception of regression.

The process of therapeutic change rarely runs as smoothly as may be implied by the above description. The dynamics of change appear to be characterized by oscillations between old and new patterns of belief and functioning and between expansions and contractions in self-experiencing (Mahoney, 1991). From the point of view of the subjective experience of the patient, any change will be experienced initially as dissonance relative to the person's current level of self-organization. Accordingly, change tends to be resisted, not just because change is painful or because of pathology, but rather because of, as Mahoney (1991) put it, "individuals' healthy caution about embarking upon or embracing experiences that challenge their integrity, coherence, or (felt) viability as a living system" (p. 329). Resistance to change, therefore, is viewed as a precondition to change. The therapist attempts to work toward identifying the sources of resistance and endeavors to help patients understand its necessary functions. Patients need to accept that they can resist change as much as they need to but accept other aspects of their current functioning (i.e., feelings and appraisals). The acceptance of "who they are" at the moment is an enabling condition of change. For patients with panic or phobias, for example, resistance to change is manifested by avoidance of situations and feelings that appear to threaten the viability of self-experience. Whenever patients try to enter a particular context of fear, they experience the growing presentiment of self-annihilation. Therapist empathy and patient acceptance of this experience are necessary prerequisites of change.

Everyone resists change and does so in many different ways. But all of these patterns of resistance serve the same function: to protect the person's current understanding of self-in-the-world. No matter how painful the current organizations of experience may be, patients resist change because the disruption of the meaningful order of experience is feared to be even more painful or frightening.

CONCLUSION

In summary, the evolution of my own thinking about—and practice of—psychotherapy began with a frame of reference that combined Rogerian therapeutic practice with psychodynamic conceptions of psychopathology. For a while, I conceived of therapy and practiced it in more existential and humanistic terms. Later, I added behavioral techniques and flirted with behavioral conceptions. Still later, I saw the potential and limitations of cognitive and cognitive–behavioral approaches and included what I found useful from that perspective. I eventually became more active and experiential as a therapist, as the significance of the emotional processing of painful feelings came more clearly into focus. All of these perspectives contributed insights and practical intervention approaches, but their limitations highlighted the need for an integrative framework.

I am working on a theoretical integration that highlights the layered process of change and the increasingly penetrating influence of psychotherapy. The theory describes a process that begins with surface behavior change and moves—if one is fortunate—toward a fundamental change in one's perspective on the core self that one constructs. This more fundamental change involves how one not only thinks about oneself but experiences oneself in the moment. Although my theoretical integration emphasizes the development and alteration of what I have labeled "self-pathology," a view that I believe takes in many of the insights from all of the extant perspectives, my current practice of psychotherapy still is characterized by a technique-based eclecticism. It is my hope that I will be able to approach a more seamless integration at the level of both theory and practice.

REFERENCES

American Psychiatric Association. (1994). *Diagnostic and statistical manual of mental disorders* (4th ed.). Washington, DC: Author.

Barlow, D. H. (1988). *Anxiety and its disorders*. New York: Guilford Press.

Barlow, D. H., & Wolfe, B. E. (1981). Behavioral approaches to anxiety disorders: A report on the NIMH–SUNY Albany research conference. *Journal of Consulting and Clinical Psychology, 49,* 448–454.

Beck, A. T. (1963). Thinking and depression. *Archives of General Psychiatry, 9,* 324–333.

Bugental, J. F. T. (Ed.). (1965). *The search for authenticity.* New York: Holt, Rinehart & Winston.

Bugental, J. F. T. (Ed.). (1967). *Challenges of humanistic psychology.* New York: McGraw-Hill.

Crossman, R. (1965). *The god that failed.* New York: Bantam Books.

Feather, B. W., & Rhoads, J. M. (1972a). Psychodynamic behavior therapy: 1. Theory and rationale. In J. Marmor & S. M. Woods (Eds.), *The interface between the psychodynamic and behavioral therapies* (pp. 293–309). New York: Plenum Press.

Feather, B. W., & Rhoads, J. M. (1972b). Psychodynamic behavior therapy: 2. Clinical aspects. In J. Marmor & S. M. Woods (Eds.), *The interface between the psychodynamic and behavioral therapies* (pp. 313–330). New York: Plenum Press.

Freud, S. (1959). Inhibitions, symptoms, and anxiety. In J. Strachey (Ed. & Trans.), *The standard edition of the complete psychological works of Sigmund Freud* (Vol. 20, pp. 87–172). London: Hogarth Press. (Original work published 1926)

Goldfried, M. R. (1980). Toward the delineation of therapeutic change principles. *American Psychologist, 35,* 991–995.

Goldfried, M. R., & Newman, C. F. (1992). A history of psychotherapy integration. In J. C. Norcross & M. R. Goldfried (Eds.), *Handbook of psychotherapy integration* (pp. 46–93). New York: Basic Books.

Greenberg, L. S., Rice, L. N., & Elliott, R. (1993). *Facilitating emotion change: The moment-by-moment process.* New York: Guilford Press.

Higgins, E. T. (1987). Self-discrepancy: A theory relating self and affect. *Psychological Review, 94,* 319–340.

Howard, K. I., Kopta, S. M., Krause, M. S., & Orlinsky, D. E. (1986). The dose–effect relationship in psychotherapy. *American Psychologist, 41,* 159–164.

Ingram, R. F. (1990). Self-focused attention in clinical disorders: Review and a conceptual model. *Psychological Bulletin, 107,* 156–176.

Kelly, G. A. (1955). *A theory of personality: The psychology of personal constructs.* New York: Norton.

Krasner, L. (1963, August–September). *The therapist as a social reinforcer: Man or machine?* Paper presented at the 71st Annual Convention of the American Psychological Association, Philadelphia, PA.

London, P. (1986). *The modes and morals of psychotherapy* (2nd ed.). Washington, DC: Hemisphere.

Luborsky, L., Singer, B., & Luborsky, L. (1975). Comparative studies of psychotherapy. *Archives of General Psychiatry, 32,* 995–1008.

Mahoney, M. J. (1991). *Human change processes: The scientific foundations of psychotherapy*. New York: Basic Books.

Messer, S. B. (1992). A critical examination of belief structures in integrative and eclectic psychotherapy. In J. C. Norcross & M. R. Goldfried (Eds.). *Handbook of psychotherapy integration* (pp. 130–165). New York: Basic Books.

Rogers, C. R. (1957). The necessary and sufficient conditions of psychotherapeutic personality change. *Journal of Consulting Psychology, 21*, 95–103.

Rogers, C. R. (1995). *On becoming a person*. New York: Houghton Mifflin. (Original work published 1961)

Safran, J. D. (1993) The therapeutic alliance rupture as a transtheoretical phenomenon: Definitional and conceptual issues. *Journal of Psychotherapy Integration, 3*, 33–49.

Smith, M. L., Glass, G. V., & Miller, T. I. (1980). *The benefits of psychotherapy*. Baltimore: Johns Hopkins University Press.

Stampfl, T. G., & Levis, D. J. (1967). Essentials of implosive therapy. *Journal of Abnormal Psychology, 72*, 496–503.

Strauman, T. J. (1994). Self-representations and the nature of cognitive change in psychotherapy. *Journal of Psychotherapy Integration, 4*, 29–316.

Wachtel, P. L. (1977). *Psychoanalysis and behavior therapy: Toward an integration*. New York: Basic Books.

Wolfe, B. E. (1992a). Self-experiencing and the integrative treatment of the anxiety disorders. *Journal of Psychotherapy Integration, 2*, 29–43.

Wolfe, B. E. (1992b). Integrative psychotherapy of the anxiety disorders. In J. C. Norcross & M. R. Goldfried (Eds.), *Handbook of psychotherapy integration* (pp. 373–401). New York: Basic Books.

Wolfe, B. E. (1995). Self-pathology and psychotherapy integration. *Journal of Psychotherapy Integration, 5*, 293–312.

V

THERAPISTS ARE SIMPLY MORE HUMAN THAN OTHERWISE

17

CONCLUSION: A PERSPECTIVE ON HOW THERAPISTS CHANGE

MARVIN R. GOLDFRIED

Some years ago, I was fortunate enough to view a most unusual film, in which Marc Chagall was engaged in the process of painting a picture. The film had been made over the course of several weeks, and it vividly illustrated the difficulties and frustrations associated with creating a painting that ultimately turned out to be a marvelous work of art. In much the same way, I feel fortunate to have had the opportunity to witness this evolutionary process in the professional lives of my colleagues.

In preparing this volume, I read each contributor's reflections several times. At each reading, I felt myself deeply immersed in their lives. I have known most of the contributors for many years and have enormous respect for their professional competence and knowledge. Indeed, I consider them to be at the top of their form as therapists. Although I thought I knew them fairly well, their reflections provided me with a deeper insight into their professional and personal evolution over the years. In particular, their narratives dramatically brought home the point that competence as a therapist does not come easily, and I was readily able to empathize with their confessions of early doubts, fears, and lack of confidence. In the narratives, the contributors provide realistic role models for what is involved in mastering the role of therapist. Beginning therapists typically have contact with mentors who are already seasoned clinicians, thereby coming into contact with the "outcome"; the reflections in this book present the "process."

As revealed in the accounts of many of the contributors, therapists do not always begin with a theoretically "pure" orientation. Most clinicians trained prior to the 1970s typically had a background in psychoanalytic and client-centered therapies. Consequently, some contributors have been able to provide insights into the strengths and limitations of their later predominant orientations as well as earlier lessons that were learned. What follows is my attempt to present the thematic issues that characterize the reflections of psychoanalytic, experiential, and behavioral contributors.

Psychoanalytic Therapy

Strengths

Even with their evolution and growth, psychoanalytic therapists point to certain enduring characteristics of this orientation. One is the assumption that all human behavior is motivated, even if the motives are not always readily apparent. For example, Wachtel emphasizes that behavior should not be taken at face value and that more subtle aspects of what one sees need to be explored more carefully. Even what appears on the surface to be primarily an interpersonal issue, notes Eagle, may actually reflect an intrapersonal conflict. In a related vein, even such therapists as Fensterheim and Lazarus, who went on to work within a behavioral orientation, note that their earlier exposure to psychoanalytic therapy helped them become keen observers of human behavior.

Another enduring strength of the psychoanalytic orientation that the contributors note is its emphasis on the importance of understanding the meaning that a person attributes to various life encounters. Moreover, an invaluable way to learn about a patient's motivational system is through his or her developmental history and its impact on the patient's adult functioning. The psychoanalytic orientation has underscored the importance of understanding how the issues of the past are reflected in one's current thinking, feeling, and behavior patterns. Often, those patterns play themselves out within the therapeutic relationship; how patients resist the change process also can provide an understanding of their more general personality style.

Another strength noted about the psychoanalytic orientation is that it has provided a compelling theory for understanding human behavior. Although this also may be seen as a limitation, Stricker nonetheless suggests that believing that the model and the theory were correct provided him with an important source of comfort as a beginning therapist.

Limitations

Although psychoanalytic theory can at times be compelling, Benjamin suggests (as does Goldstein, whose primary orientation later became behavioral) that the therapeutic guidelines that followed from theory left much to be desired. In many instances, note Eagle and Jacobs, psychoanalytic theory can take the form of authoritarian pronouncements and may be used for the purpose of impressing one's colleagues. Fodor's earlier psychoanalytic training taught her that is was more important to understand the dynamics of the case than to be concerned with change. Fensterheim's early psychoanalytic experiences led him to conclude that although case formulations were "awe inspiring and beautiful" (p. 108), they rarely provided any insights on how to make a therapeutic impact, particularly on more disturbed patients.

Several of the contributors report having been put off or constrained by the orthodoxy of theory and clinical methods. Rhoads feels that theory typically did not lend itself to short-term interventions, which clinical reality often requires. Goldstein is struck by the assumption that the theory was always right. Stricker notes that theoretical guidelines often did not work in bringing about change, a realization that came at the cost of the uncomfortable feeling that he did not always know what he was doing. This was particularly the case when patients' goals did not match what the theory suggested they should be. Stricker's experiences bring to mind an encounter I once had as a dental patient. Upon finding a cavity that needed to be filled, the dentist treating me recommended that the tooth be filled with a gold inlay. When I asked if it would be more durable, he indicated no; however, given the strong and healthy quality of my teeth, he felt it would only be fitting to have gold in my fillings. Clearly, our goals were different.

Several contributors complain that it was the nature of psychoanalytic theory to pathologize people and everything they did, a comment made by those who retain their original analytic orientation (Eagle, Wachtel) and those who moved on to a behavioral (Fodor, Goldstein) or experiential (Bohart) approach.

Wachtel reports having felt clinically limited by the emphasis placed on the use of only classical psychoanalytic methods. Similarly, both Benjamin and Eagle recall feeling constrained by the prescribed psychoanalytic role of the therapist, where the clinically aloof, "blank screen" stance placed a limit on therapeutic empathy and honesty. Moreover, because of this passive role of the psychoanalytic therapist, Benjamin reports that "therapy felt like treading water" (p. 26), especially in working with personality disorders. Wachtel adds that another limitation was the lack of emphasis placed on the importance of emotional experiencing and the lack of attention paid to the role of sociocultural and economic factors.

Behavior Therapy

Strengths

Not surprisingly, the strengths noted by behavior therapists are quite different from those reported by therapists involved in psychoanalytic therapy. To begin with, the causes of human behavior are viewed as being more than just a function of the individual. External, situational influences can play an important role, as Fensterheim notes. In learning about the behavioral approach, Fodor is struck by its focus on the reality of the client's current life dilemmas, not just his or her earlier experiences. Goldstein suggests that because the behavioral approach did not carry with it certain assumptions of pathology, there was an accompanying respect for the client. With this respect, adds Mahoney, is a perception of people as active agents participating in their growth and development. In contrast to a disease model, behavior therapy is based on an educational model, whereby therapists help people learn skills for coping with their current life problems.

Another strength noted about the behavioral orientation is its emphasis on outcome. An important question that is frequently asked is, "Is the patient changing?" Fensterheim reports having been particularly receptive to this emphasis within behavior therapy, especially having worked with neurologically and physically disabled patients earlier in his career, where the goal was tightly focused on behavior change. When behavior therapy was introduced to the clinical scene, he reports that it was like "coming home." Having demonstrated its ability to deal with patients' fears and anxieties, behavior therapy demonstrates itself as an approach to symptom reduction, the success of which, Goldstein and Mahoney note, is reflected both in clinical observation and controlled research.

In contrast to other therapeutic orientations, Lazarus underscores the more active nature of the intervention associated with behavior therapy, which provides clear therapeutic guidelines that differ according to the nature of the clinical problem at hand. An individualized case formulation, called a *functional analysis,* addresses itself to the questions of who, what, when, where, and how. In providing answers to those questions, the behavior therapist is better able to construct a formulation that has clear implications for treatment.

A final strength of behavior therapy relates to Mahoney's observation that this orientation provides an important contribution by emphasizing that small steps can be taken in reaching a clinical goal. With its roots in experimental psychology, behavior therapy can approach complex human problems by thinking of them as "variables." That is, behavioral interventions involve dimensionalizing a client's problems, so that easier difficulties are dealt with before more complicated ones. Thus, rather than concluding that "the client was not ready for change," behavior therapy is able to specify hierarchies of increasingly more anxiety-producing situations with which the client can learn to cope. Fensterheim, Lazarus, and Wachtel all suggest that many clinical problems (e.g., problems with intimacy) can be thought of as being anxiety-related hypersensitivities to which patients can become gradually desensitized.

Limitations

In specifying the limitations of behavior therapy, Mahoney correctly points out that in its early days, the attempt was made to explain all human functioning by means of conditioning, neglecting the role of cognitive constructs. In its youthful—if not somewhat immature—period, behavior therapy operated on the assumption that everything was a habit and that everything could be changed. With the maturity that comes with clinical experience, there is now a greater recognition that it is a disservice to both the patient and the therapist to assume this overly optimistic stance (Goldfried & Davison, 1994). As Eagle similarly observed is the case with psychoanalytic therapy, setting unrealistic standards for change only results in the feeling that one has failed as a patient or therapist.

Although behavior therapy has been shown to be successful in treating certain anxiety disorders, the fact of the matter is that it does not always work, as Fensterheim observes. Fodor, who went on to become involved in experiential therapy, suggests that simply changing behavior and cognitions was not always sufficient. Lazarus conducted follow-up evaluations of clients he had "successfully treated," only to learn that a number of them had relapsed. He also observed the limitations of behavior therapy when he departed from the carefully delineated systematic desensitization procedures that were designed to decondition patients to their fears. Even though there were no "therapy manuals" at the time, behavioral procedures were nonetheless carefully specified. By being less structured in the implementation of systematic desensitization and in following the client's lead, Lazarus discovers that more was occurring during desensitization than had been believed. Contrary to the theoretical underpinnings of behavior therapy at the time, through his studies he found that clients had thoughts, beliefs, and attitudes that were relevant to the problem at hand. This realization became even more evident when he began to work with couples.

Although Fensterheim firmly believes that behavior therapy was a major advance over his earlier training in psychoanalytic therapy, he nonetheless at times felt that he was treating problems rather than people. With its emphasis on techniques, behavior therapy held the danger of ignoring individual differences, a problem that could certainly contribute to its inconsistent results. Goldstein observed that behavior therapy lacked a focus on the humanistic and personal relationships that were present with experientially oriented therapists. In my own clinical work and observation of other behavior therapists, it also became apparent that the coping-skills model underlying many of the procedures at times caused therapists to lapse into an overly directive and didactic mode.

Fodor, making the same criticism that Wachtel does of psychoanalytic therapy, feels that behavior therapy fell short in not acknowledging the cultural contributions to people's problems. Drawing on her own personal and professional experience, Fodor says it became evident to her that behavior therapy failed to recognize how gender constraints affected women's lives. Although a strength of behavior therapy is that it acknowledges the importance of environmental influences, its fine-grained analysis of problems can obscure the bigger picture at times; examining problems under high-magnification narrows the field of vision (Goldfried & Castonguay, 1993).

Experiential Therapy

Strengths

The experiential therapists contributing to this volume share a consensus that the therapist–patient relationship is at the core of the change process. Lazarus, who was exposed to client-centered therapy at the outset of his training, feels that the experience sensitized him to the importance of therapeutic listening skills. For experiential therapists, however, the clinical importance of the therapeutic relationship goes beyond this sensitivity. As noted by Beutler and Jacobs, therapeutic empathy, acceptance, and attunement to the phenomenological perspective of the client contribute to a relationship that is healing in and of itself. In elaborating on this idea, Bohart notes that the therapist sets the stage and provides the context that can enable clients to become better aware of the felt meanings—cognitive-affective associations—that are relevant to understanding the key issues in their lives. In addition to observing this phenomenon professionally, both Jacobs and Wolfe report having personally experienced this situation first-hand when they were in therapy. Indeed, Jacobs states that she believes that the nature of the therapeutic relationship was at the heart of her personal change, even when being seen by a psychoanalytic therapist.

The experiential therapists concur that the therapeutic relationship facilitates the client's own ability to grow and change, especially when there is a focus on the in-session, here-and-now process. As suggested by

Greenberg, the therapist's empathic understanding—"being with the client"—is accompanied by an attitude of acceptance. When clients disclose and explore their emotional experiences, thoughts, desires, and actions and are met with empathy and not criticism, they not only experience relief but also engage in the therapeutic process and learn to be more accepting of themselves. Greenberg observes that clients' awareness of their emotional experience may unfold by simply having the therapist provide the empathic and accepting facilitative conditions. Other times, as in the use of gestalt experiments, the therapist may "lead" as well as "follow" in helping the client become more aware of those experiences.

Limitations

Several of the contributors report that excessive reliance on the passivity of client-centered therapy is a limitation of that approach. As important as the therapeutic relationship might be in bringing about change, Beutler notes that "caring is not enough" (p. 206). Bohart similarly observes that the experiential approach was limited when something had to be done, such as a course of action that needed to be taken by the client. In addition, although the passive–reflective style seemed to work well with clients who needed to sort out issues in their lives, Wolfe observes that it did little to reduce phobias or make a therapeutic impact with personality disorders.

In making specific comments about gestalt therapy, Bohart indicates that despite its generally open and permissive philosophy, a message was nonetheless conveyed that it was the therapist, not the client, who "owned the truth." Jacobs was put off by the confrontational approach, particularly as advocated by Perls, when the client was avoiding or not being open and honest. Even with more recent attempts made by gestalt therapists to maintain a therapeutic alliance and be less confrontational, Jacobs and Greenberg note that the gestalt approach provides no clear understanding of the therapeutic relationship, such as how it develops over time and how it leads to change. Moreover, Greenberg notes that the "one-size-fits-all" assumption inherent in the approach, of necessity, failed to work well with some clients.

HOW CHANGE OCCURRED

The dissatisfaction with their psychoanalytic, experiential, or behavioral orientations provided the contributors with opportunities to consider the possibility of changing how they functioned clinically. I turn now to the factors that made them open to change and the actual sources of influence.

Readiness to Change

Even before there was actually a shift in their original orientation, several therapists—representing all three schools of thought—indicate that certain conditions and personal characteristics made them more susceptible to change. For example, many of the contributors note that their grounding in a scientific approach to human behavior allowed them to be more likely to change how they worked clinically. This background worked well for Eagle, who generally views himself as more of a critic than a true believer. Wachtel's grounding in learning theory made him more open to developments in the behavioral approach. He cites Dollard and Miller's (1950) *Personality and Psychotherapy* as an important influence in his early training because it provided a bridge for interacting with his behavioral colleagues. (It is interesting to note that the same book had an important impact on me during my graduate training and provided me with the same bridge on which to cross but from the behavioral side.)

Benjamin and Fodor, both of whom had their training experiences in the prefeminist 1950s, provide an account of what it was like for a woman being trained at the time. With few role models available to them, they offer an outsider's account of how to pursue one's goals in the absence of external support. Being married to a feminist also had a significant impact on Greenberg's perspective, as it did with me. Fodor, describing the personal and professional upheavals she experienced as she was drawn to the feminist movement, indicates how she turned a crisis into an opportunity. Even though behavior therapy had little to say about gender, it nonetheless provided techniques for dealing with issues about which many women were concerned, such as ways of facilitating assertiveness and reducing anxiety. Consequently, she was readily able to integrate a feminist perspective into the practice of behavior therapy.

There was another interesting factor that contributed to the readiness to change across the theoretical orientations, as described by Stricker and Mahoney. Reflecting his psychoanalytic roots, Stricker reports an early memory he had of wandering away from home but feeling confident that everything would be all right. Indeed, he enjoyed his explorations, and he suggests that this experience contributed to the foundation that allowed him to move from his psychoanalytic home base to greater involvement in exploring psychotherapy integration. Mahoney reports a similar characteristic when he states, "I enjoy getting lost. I enjoy creating and re-creating. I episodically rearrange my physical life space, usually for no conscious motive other than the change and novelty that it affords" (p. 184).

No doubt, numerous other factors enabled the contributors to move beyond their original orientation. Whether they simply were not reported or were not in their awareness, one may safely assume that various other conditions and characteristics contributed to a greater openness to external sources of influence. One characteristic of all contributors that is evident, however, is that they are far more comfortable with unanswered questions than they are with unquestioned answers.

Sources of Influence

As reported by Skovholt and Rønnestad (1995), a key influence in the evolution of the professional careers of therapists was their interaction with other people, especially clients and colleagues. For example, Rhoads began to question the psychoanalytic model when circumstances placed him in the position of having to use it to conduct time-limited interventions with clients. Stricker similarly learned to deviate from what he originally learned once he realized that it was unfair to blame clients for not being "good psychodynamic patients." Bohart called into question his experiential model when he observed that some clients failed to change, even though experience levels were high, whereas others did even under conditions of low experiencing.

Another important influence from clinical practice occurred when therapists noted change resulting from their use of methods from orientations other than their own. For example, in my own clinical experience, I have found the use of the gestalt two-chair technique to be fruitful, especially in uncovering implicit meaning structures that behavior therapists have referred to as the "internal dialogue" between the realistic and unrealistic parts of oneself.

Some years ago, my colleagues and I (Friedling, Goldfried, & Stricker, 1984) studied the impact of clinical experience on therapists' tendency to broaden their theoretical outlook. We surveyed two groups of psychologists, one trained at a school having a behavioral orientation (Stony Brook) and the other from a program with a psychodynamic orientation (Adelphi). The participants responded to a questionnaire on therapeutic practices, comprising procedures that were traditionally associated with each of the two orientations. For example, an item generated from the psychoanalytic approach involved the therapeutic use of one's own reactions to understand the patient's problems. An example of an item from the behavioral approach consisted of discussing the patient's day-to-day, between-session activities. Participants indicated whether each item characterized what they did in practice. We found that approximately 78% of the dynamically derived items were used by both orientations, as were 55% of the behavioral practices. Surprisingly enough, we found no relationship between the number of years of experience and the tendency to use clinical practices from the other orientation. However, we did find that behavior therapists who worked with children—typically using reinforcement methods—were more likely to remain within their orientation than were those who worked primarily with adults. For psychodynamic therapists, there was a positive relationship between the tendency to use behavioral techniques and the percentage of lower socioeconomic patients they saw in their clinical work. Inasmuch as approximately half of the Stony Brook graduates went on to academic and research careers, it was possible for us to compare their responses to those who primarily were practicing clinicians. Not surprisingly, practicing clinicians were more likely to use psychodynamic methods.

Although the study reveals that experience per se was not a factor associated with questioning of one's therapeutic orientation, it did find that the specific nature of the experience had an effect. As Dollard and Miller (1950) suggested, people are not likely to change unless they are confronted with a "learning dilemma" in which their usual ways of responding to a situation no longer seem to work for them. This was very much the case for clinicians whose personal reflections have been presented throughout this volume.

Virtually all the contributors indicated that their interactions with colleagues of a different orientation had an important effect on their clinical work. Through discussions, direct observations, or workshops, respected colleagues of a different orientation served as significant role models. At times, the influence was reciprocal in nature; for example, Wachtel reports an increased appreciation for behavior therapy from interacting with Goldstein, and Goldstein indicates that his respect for psychoanalytic therapy came from his interactions with Wachtel. In addition to serving as role models, colleagues also offered personal and professional support—either individually or collectively, in the home base provided by the Society for the Exploration of Psychotherapy Integration (SEPI)—for altering one's approach to therapy in a guilt-free context.

Interpersonal experiences that occurred outside of one's role as a therapist also had an important effect. One's partner, children, and grandchildren provided the life experiences that added to the texture and complexity of the contributors' lives, affording a more comprehensive perspective on what it takes to be both effective and human. Support from colleagues during times of personal crises similarly had an important influence, as did experiencing therapeutic change oneself. For example, Fodor indicates that the emotion she experienced during gestalt therapy had an effect that was more significant than what had occurred during her personal analysis. Similarly, being in personal therapy with an experiential therapist similarly was a profound personal and professional experience for me. One particularly important event occurred when I arrived at a session feeling stressed, and my therapist suggested that I lie on the floor and relax. Although relaxation certainly was not novel for me as a behavior therapist, the fact that she cradled my head in her hands as I did so made a major impact. My immediate reaction was, "Is this allowed?!?" It was directed not so much toward what she was doing but rather to my own (unusual and positive) experience of passivity while being cared for.

Although Greenberg originally operated therapeutically on the assumption that change occurred through the therapist's acceptance of and positive regard for the client, his own personal experience in couple's therapy provided him with a greater appreciation for more active attempts at changing behavior. Another relevant personal corrective experience is reported by Stricker: Even though he had been involved in the psychotherapy integration movement, he expressed doubts about the use of behavior therapy to alleviate his fear of heights when several of us paid a postconference visit to Iguazu Falls in Argentina. His exact words were "if you want me to believe in that behavioral crap, do something about *this*" (Stricker, 1995, p. 266, emphasis in original). As Stricker notes in his reflections, much to his surprise and delight, the brief behavioral intervention by a team of therapeutic colleagues proved to be quite successful.

Teaching and supervising beginning psychotherapists provided several of the contributors with an impetus to broaden their theoretical perspectives. Lazarus points to the opportunity for ongoing self-questioning that those experiences provided, and Benjamin similarly notes how her own professional and personal introspection was stimulated by students asking "Why did you do that during the session?" Rhoads reports that the use of works of literature to train counselors helped him move beyond the orthodox psychoanalytic perspective he had been taught.

Many of the contributors indicate that reading the works of others expanded their therapeutic horizons. Wolfe notes that 22 years as a grant administrator at NIMH provided him with the opportunity to learn about different therapeutic approaches that were being evaluated. A good deal of the research involved behavior therapy for anxiety disorders, which he applied in his own clinical practice, finding it to be far more effective than his client-centered approach. He did recognize, however, that even phobic clients can be complex and that behavior therapy alone may not always be sufficient. This realization led to his active involvement in the psychotherapy integration movement, which further encouraged him to move in the direction toward which he already was heading.

Beutler's nondirective approach was influenced by the basic research findings on persuasion, which indicated that some people need more active interventions than others. A source of influence in Greenberg's movement beyond experiential therapy came from his own research into the process of change, which sensitized him to the different ways therapists typically intervened under different circumstances. Perhaps reflecting his earlier engineering background, he became more aware of the implicit rules that therapists use under different circumstances.

Other influential experiences reported by some of the contributors occurred well out of the realm of psychotherapy. For example, Benjamin notes that studying music (and trying to keep up with her brother athletically) taught her how persistence and patience are needed to learn complex skills. She also indicated that her early experience with an untamed horse provided her with insights about the change process. From this experience, she learned "to take things slowly and with great patience" (p. 29). She notes, "I also learned about the impossibility of controlling another creature. The most one can do is persuade and negotiate for mutual interests as one moves with the other. Only under the most desperate conditions would one move against another" (p. 29). As a remarkable coincidence, Beutler also notes that one of the major lessons he learned about therapeutic change came from observing a horse trainer. In this experience, Beutler learned much the same lesson: "Patience is part of this key. Let things happen that happen. Let people find their own comfort. Allow them to learn through struggle. Don't rescue, just support" (p. 215). From this experience, Beutler witnessed firsthand the importance of blending a respectful and sensitive attitude with an appropriate and creative use of technique. These observations, made by two practicing therapist–researchers, reflect a true blending of art and science.

It has not been my intent to offer any firm conclusions about how all therapists change. After all, this book presents anecdotes and reflections from a small group of highly experienced therapists. Still, it appears that the change process among this small and unique sample of therapists closely parallels the ways in which clients change during the course of therapy: Within a supportive interpersonal context, the person becomes aware of things in one's life that are remnants of the past and do not necessarily work in the current situation. With the encouragement and support of others, he or she is exposed to new learning situations that provide the kind of corrective experiences that alter how one emotionally, cognitively, and behaviorally approaches various events. This is how our clients change and how many of us as therapists change. As Sullivan once suggested, people are more human than otherwise.

THE MANY FACES OF PSYCHOTHERAPY INTEGRATION

Just as diverse paths led each of the contributors to expand his or her therapeutic approaches, so do different approaches fall under the general rubric of psychotherapy integration. Although they vary as a function of their theoretical starting point, specific experiences, and other factors, what is common to all the contributors to this volume is that they make every attempt to intervene on the basis of the case at hand without feeling unduly constrained by a given orientation. For some contributors, the learnings from other orientations create dominant themes in their practice, but for others, they create more of a leitmotiv. The unique combination in any given therapist is clearly a function of his or her personal preferences and abilities, what has been found to work clinically, and the empirical evidence at hand.

In reviewing the reported strengths and limitations of the three major orientations, it becomes evident that a strength of one orientation can synergistically complement a limitation of another. As noted earlier, psychoanalytic therapy can sensitize us as therapists to the possibility that there is sometimes more there than meets the eye and that a patient's developmental history may help shed light on those issues. It also alerts us to the possibility that a patient's problematic patterns of functioning may be played out within the context of the therapeutic relationship. The behavioral approach offers the prospect of having specific techniques that allow the therapist to intervene more actively, especially in helping to bring about symptom reduction. The underlying philosophy that change can be gradual and that methods exist for encouraging such change can be useful to therapists of other orientations. The experiential approach to clinical work can provide the therapist with an empathic view of the client as a human being struggling to overcome the limitations of his or her past rather than someone whose behavior is based on certain pathological forces. That approach also brings with it a keen sensitivity to the subtleties of what is occurring within the therapeutic situation and the methods for enhancing emotional experiencing.

A theme that characterizes all the therapeutic approaches described in this volume is the need to provide clients with learning opportunities—corrective experiences—that may help them become happier and more effective in their current life situations. Moreover, a lesson that many of the therapists report having learned is the importance of "patience" in providing clients with such experiences.

The more one examines the notion of patience, the more complete an understanding one can obtain about what is essential to a therapeutic relationship. A clearer understanding of the importance of patience is revealed by considering its opposite—impatience. To the extent that a therapist is impatient with where clients are or with their progress, he or she sends the message that the clients are not doing what they are supposed to do. That impatience provides a subtle criticism that clients are not good enough—a message about which they already may have great sensitivity. At times, this therapeutic impatience can take a subtle form, such as a tone of voice or facial expression when a client does not accept a particular interpretation, has not done his or her homework, or is being superficial in the expression of an emotional reaction. Research shows that when therapists react negatively to patients' failure to act in ways in which they are "supposed to," it results in the absence of clinical change or actual deterioration (Henry, Schacht, & Strupp, 1986).

When therapists show patience with their clients, they essentially are accepting them for where they are at the time. In essence, there is respect for the fact that clients are able to do only what they are able to do, and it is not their fault for not being different. They are good citizens of human nature: They obey all its laws. Jacobs clearly reflects this attitude when she described the following:

> Time and again I have noticed that when I try to argue against, convince, or otherwise, however gently, move patients into a different perspective, they become more committed to their current perspective, more rigid and defensive. But if I can welcome their perspective, open myself to it even when it is full of anguish, then the forward-moving processes of life take over. The paradoxical nature of change is being carried by both patients and myself. Then the patients, who no longer feel under siege, disconfirmed, and unwelcome, can breathe and move over time, and their perspectives become more malleable and open to expansion, development, and change. (pp. 282–283)

The essential role of acceptance and its relationship to change have been clearly spelled out by Linehan (1993) in her description of what is needed when working with borderline personality disorders—typically characterized as being highly sensitive to criticism. In attempting to use behavioral procedures to actively intervene in the lives of borderline patients, Linehan found that because of their ultrasensitivity to not being accepted by others, the suggested behavioral interventions communicated an invalidation of the patient's current status. To bring about change with such patients, suggested Linehan, the therapist must walk a careful line between accepting them just as they are and being willing and able to help them change when they feel ready. The need for a dialectical balance between "following" versus "leading" the patient is a theme that indeed runs through many of the contributions to this volume, and it is an issue that is relevant in working with most patients. As my colleague Jerry Davison put it, the truly effective therapist is one having a firm hand in a velvet glove.

CONCLUDING COMMENT

We have the unusual opportunity to gain some insight into the professional lives of 15 experienced therapists whose clinical practice has been uniquely seasoned by professional and personal life experiences. Having seen others travel the road, and having traveled it themselves, the contributors to this volume provide us with a rare and candid perspective. As therapists, we have long known that clinical experience can soften the sharp theoretical differences often seen in less experienced therapists (Fiedler, 1950). This effect occurs in professions other than psychotherapy as well; master professionals (e.g., musicians, athletes) do not always "follow the book" (Schön, 1983). Experience creates more of a sense of flow in what therapists do clinically, and it generates an integration of who they are as people within their role as therapists. With such experiences, therapists learn to intervene both by—and with—heart.

As is the case with our clients, we therapists originally learn what we are taught, both through our role models and our direct experiences. Moreover, we learn as best as we can to do what works at the time, perhaps at the expense of not being fully prepared to deal with the new and difficult challenges we encounter at a later point in time. As suggested earlier, for us to change, we often need a supportive and understanding interpersonal context, either in the form of colleagues who are willing to support our professional explorations or therapists to help us in our personal lives. This interpersonal context is important in that it helps us become better aware of our methods of functioning that may not longer work, allowing us to realize how we may inadvertently be limiting ourselves. As we become aware of such limitations and potential alternatives, we are in a better position to consider the possibility of attempting new ways of functioning. In making such attempts, corrective experiences are essential in helping us become more effective in our functioning—both as people and as therapists.

REFERENCES

Dollard, J. & Miller, N. E. (1950). *Personality and psychotherapy.* New York: McGraw-Hill.

Fiedler, F. E. (1950). A comparison of therapeutic relationships in psychoanalytic, nondirective, and Adlerian therapy. *Journal of Consulting and Clinical Psychology, 14,* 436–445.

Friedling, C., Goldfried, M. R., & Stricker, G. (1984). *Convergences in psychodynamic and behavior therapy.* Paper presented at the meeting of the Eastern Psychological Association, Baltimore, MD.

Goldfried, M .R., & Castonguay, L. G. (1993). Behavior therapy: Redefining strengths and limitations. *Behavior Therapy, 24,* 505–526.

Goldfried, M. R., & Davison, G. C. (1994). *Clinical behavior therapy* (rev. ed.). New York: Wiley Interscience.

Henry, W. P., Schacht, T. E., & Strupp, H. H. (1986). Structural analysis of social behavior: Application to a study of interpersonal processes in differential psychotherapeutic outcome. *Journal of Consulting and Clinical Psychology, 54,* 27–31.

Linehan, M. M. (1993). *Cognitive–behavioral treatment of borderline personality disorder.* New York: Guilford Press.

Schön, D. A. (1983). *The reflective practitioner: How professionals think in action.* New York: Basic Books.

Skovholt, T. M., & Rønnestad, M. H. (1995). *The evolving professional self: Stages and themes in therapist and counselor development.* Chichester, England: Wiley.

Stricker, G. (1995). Comment: Confessions of a reformed psychodynamicist. *Journal of Psychotherapy Integration/SEPI Newsletter, 5,* 266–267.

INDEX

Benjamin, L. S., 28–30
Fodor, I. E., 137
Personal realities, 197
Personality and Assessment (Mischel), 90
Personality disorders, EMDR treatments, 120
Personality theory, 128–129
Phobias
  behavior therapy, 295–298
  descriptive classification, 153
  desensitization, 165–166
  exposure to cues, 96
  treating adults, 127
  treating children, 129–131
Physical rehabilitation, 110
Pinsof, B., family therapy, 256
Play therapy, therapist–patient relationship, 126, 204
Positivism, 193
Posttraumatic stress disorders, 55
Posttreatment assessments, 131
Prejudices, 134
Process–experiential therapy, 241
Professionally coached self help, 238
Psychoanalysis, 327
  authenticity of therapist, 49–51
  behavior therapy uses, 94
  Benjamin, L. S., 20–21
  blank screen, 21, 40–41
  cognitive–behavioral integration, 4–5
  complexity of mental life, 39
  deep interpretations, 44
  dehumanizing nature, 222–223
  diagnoses, 108
  distortion, 21
  Eagle, M. N., 40
  Fensterheim, 115
  Fodor, I. E., 126, 132
  free association, 106
  genuineness of therapist, 49–51
  Goldstein, A. J., 147–148
  inner conflicts, 39
  lack of emphasis on research, 41
  limitations. See limitations of psychoanalysis
  observation, 114
  one-upmanship, 42–44
  patient dynamics, 107
  Pavlovian conditioning, 6
  self-reflection, 39

strengths, 316
structural changes, 86
therapist as person, 115
transference, 47–48
unexplored issues in treatment, 44–45
Wachtel, P. L., 89
working through, 22
Psychoanalytic ego psychology, 84–85
Psychoanalytic psychotherapy, 86
Psychodynamic therapy
  developmental histories, 19
  Feather, B. W., 60
  individual attributes, 114
  inner conflicts, 39
  memoirs, 19–35, 37–39
  Stricker, G., 70–73, 78
Psychoses, drug treatments, 60
Psychotherapy by Reciprocal Inhibition (Wolpe), 60, 149
Psychotherapy integration, 5–8
  approaches to integration, 326
  areas of focus, 10–12
  common factors, 11–12
  Eagle, M. N., 52–53
  Rhoads, J. M., 63–64
  technical eclecticism, 10–11
  theoretical integration, 11
  Wolfe, B. E., 290, 299–300

Rapaport, D., passive ego, 121
Rational–emotive therapy, 136
Readiness to change, 322
Rebirth in treatment, Guntrip, H., 52
Reciprocal inhibition, 166, 170
Reflection, 26
Reich, W.
  character styles, 274
  confrontation, 275
Relaxation, 129, 165
Research
  lack of emphasis in psychoanalysis, 41
  treatment outcomes, 153
Resistance, 134, 138, 309
  desensitization therapy, 62
  psychodynamic therapy, 70
Response, learning theory, 84
Response couplets, 167
Response networks, 158–160

Revised Marital Satisfaction Questionnaire, 176
Rhoads, J. M.
behavior therapy, 65
drug treatments, 64
healthcare issues, 65
literature to illustrate psychological
concepts, 58
psychoanalysis, 55–58
psychotherapy, 57, 63–64
Rogerian therapy, 234
Rogers, C.
baseline traits of good therapist, 21
client-centered therapy, 149, 205
free will, 205
warm reflection, 26
Role models for women, 125
Ryle, A., cognitive–analytic therapy, 78

SASB. *See* Structural analysis of social be-
havior model
Scaffolding self healing, 237
Schema theory, 128, 140
Schematic patterning of anxiety, 142
Scientific method and therapy, 152
*Scientist as Subject: The Psychological Imper-
ative*, 190
Schizophrenia
as attempt to break through to
health, 224
as biological disorder, 225
drug treatments, 60
psychoanalytic approaches, 108
Schneirla, T., 106
The Second Sex (de Beauvoir), 135
Self, ought and actual, 307
SEPI. *See* Society for the Exploration of
Psychotherapy Integration
Self-change, 184
Self-deception, 83–84
fear as motivation, 96
misreading human needs, 99
transparency, 99
Self-endangerment experiences, 305, 307
Self-esteem issues in women, 136–137
Selfobject, 278, 281
Self-reflection, psychoanalysis, 39
Self-regulated thought control, 189
Self-restricting avoidances, 97
Self-understanding, 71, 144
Self-healing, 236

Sensations modality, BASIC I.D., 174
Severely disturbed patients, 26
Sex role socialization messages, 136
Shaping, 192
Shapiro, F., EMDR, 120
Short-term psychotherapy
interventions, combining clinical
procedures, 7
Rhoads, J. M., 57–59, 60, 64
Situational cues to phobias, 96
SICSCA. *See* Sensation, imagery, cogni-
tion, sensation, cognition, affect
Skovholt, T.
internal professional influences for
change, 14
supportive professional context for
change, 13
Social learning theory, 93, 129
Societal prejudices, 134
Society for the Exploration of Psychother-
apy Integration (SEPI), 7
Fensterheim, H., 119
formation, 8–9
mission statement, 62
psychotherapy integration, 75
Sources of influence for change, 323–326
Specificity of behavior, 93
Spiegel, J. P., posttraumatic stress disorders, 55
spirituality as catalyst of change, 29
Stereotypes, female socialization, 136
Stimulus, learning theory, 84
Stimulus–response analysis, 166
Stolorow, R., intersubjectivity theory,
280
Strachey, J., transference interpretations
and emotional immediacy, 47
Strategic therapy, 232
Stricker, G.
behavior motivation, 71
central role of unconscious, 71
cognitions, 71
historical determinism, 72
limitations of psychodynamic therapy, 72
local clinical scientist model, 80
motives, 71
psychodynamic therapy, 67–69, 78
resistance, 70
self-understanding, 71
therapeutic relationships, 72

ABOUT THE EDITOR

Marvin R. Goldfried, PhD, is a professor of psychology and psychiatry at the State University of New York at Stony Brook. In addition to his teaching, clinical supervision, and research, he maintains a limited practice of psychotherapy in New York City. He is a diplomate in clinical psychology, recipient of the Distinguished Psychologist Award from the American Psychological Association's Divisions of Clinical Psychology and of Psychotherapy, past president of the Society for Psychotherapy Research, founder of the journal *In Session: Psychotherapy in Practice*, editorial board member of numerous professional journals, and author of several books. Dr. Goldfried is cofounder of the Society for the Exploration of Psychotherapy Integration.